Double Century

DOUBLE CENTURY

CRICKET IN THE TIMES

VOLUME TWO 1935–1990

Edited by Marcus Williams

THE PAVILION LIBRARY

First published in Great Britain by Wm Collins Sons & Co. Ltd 1985

Copyright © Times Newspapers Ltd 1985/1990
Introduction, notes and selection copyright © Marcus Williams 1985/1990

First published in the Pavilion Library in 1990 by
PAVILION BOOKS LIMITED
196 Shaftesbury Avenue
London WC2H 8JL

Series Editor: Steve Dobell

A CIP catalogue record for this book
is available from the British Library

ISBN 1 85145 476 4 Hbk
ISBN 1 85145 481 0 Pbk

Printed and bound in Great Britain by
Biddles Ltd, Guildford

DOUBLE CENTURY

200 Years of Cricket in
THE TIMES

Edited by
MARCUS WILLIAMS

ACKNOWLEDGEMENTS

I cannot overstate my indebtedness to Gordon Phillips, a close and valued friend, who has a remarkable knowledge of the workings and history of *The Times*. His contribution towards this book has been prodigious – without him it *might* have been ready for the 205th anniversary – his resourcefulness at times of seemingly insurmountable crisis inspiring, and his service beyond the bounds of normal duty, such as highly competitive games of cricket with my small sons, utterly devoted.

Thanks are due to many others, notably: Tim Jollands, for his initial confidence and constant enthusiasm for the project, and a kindly editorial hand; to Humphrey Stone, who maintained a family link with *The Times* by designing the book; and to many colleagues at *The Times*, especially Michael Roffey, Picture Librarian, and his staff; Colin Wilson, Head Librarian, and his staff; Anne Piggott, Archivist and Records Manager, and her assistants; Norman Fox, Sports Editor and head of my department, and John Woodcock, Cricket Correspondent; to Stephen Green, Curator of M.C.C.; to another Stephen Green, Head of the British Newspaper Library, John Westmancoat, Information Officer, and other members of staff at Colindale; to Philip Spink, Librarian of The Advertising Association; to my wife, Wendy, for her patience, encouragement and practical assistance; and, of course, to all the writers and sub-editors whose work appears in *Double Century* and to Times Newspapers for readily giving permission to reproduce it.

The main works of reference consulted were: *The History of The Times* (vols. I–V); James D. Coldham's series of articles, *Some Early Cricket Reporters*, published in The Journal of the Cricket Society (vol. X no. 2– vol. XI no. 4); *Wisden Cricketers' Almanack*; and, not least, *The Times* itself.

INTRODUCTION

A daily newspaper is by strict definition ephemeral, but as recorder, commentator and interpreter of contemporary events it undoubtedly has a more enduring value. When a newspaper has managed to perform that function over a period of years – and has, moreover, come to be regarded as a national institution – it must contain a good deal that is worthy of study and preservation. When that institution, *The Times*, reaches its 200th birthday, it is also a cause for celebration – and how better to celebrate the occasion than to collect some of the best of its contents on a subject dear to an Englishman's heart throughout that period: cricket.

The story starts with the gentlemen of the White Conduit Club, the forerunner of M.C.C., and ends with a pair of England batsmen who had the presence of mind to mark *The Times*'s bicentenary year by becoming the first from their country to score double centuries in the same Test match innings. (To forestall inquiries the title of this book had already been settled before that happy coincidence.) The period embraces the whole panoply of cricketing giants: Beldham, Mynn, Pilch, Grace, Ranjitsinhji, Hobbs, Bradman, Sobers, Botham; but there is a fair slice of human life here too, from assault, divorce, fashion, libel, murder, the occult, politics, racial discrimination, riot and suicide to a cricketing dog, physically handicapped players and a pathetic paragraph about a Nottingham club forced to sell its pavilion to meet a rates demand of £36 but falling £11 short.

It is an awesome task to compress two centuries' writings, even on one topic, into a few hundred pages, not to mention the feelings of regret – and guilt – at not having the time to examine, while perusing miles of microfilm and sheaves of cuttings, what "The Thunderer" was saying about the French Revolution, or Waterloo, or World Wars, or the dozens of other cataclysmic events of the past 200 years. For the early decades, at least, selection was governed by the limited amount of cricket material that appeared in the paper, but this period will nevertheless be found rich in variety and entertainment.

The advent of an occasional feature article on cricket in 1875 broadened the field beyond the mainly factual and unvarnished reporting of matches, and the introduction, at the behest of the proprietor, Lord Northcliffe, in January 1914, of a light leading article (later known, and now fondly remembered by older readers, as the "fourth leader" and by older members of staff as "the funny") introduced a dimension of wit and humour which may surprise those who thought of *The Times* as dry and humourless. So felicitous, indeed, were the light leaders on cricket from the 1920s to the 1960s – notably those charming essays written by Bernard Darwin, Dudley Carew, Patrick Ryan and Peter Fleming (brother of the novelist, Ian) in the 1940s and 1950s – that although they are well represented in this book, there was a temptation to use all of them.

The light leaders apart, and because a newspaper's primary task is to provide information about current events, selection of the material has been dictated by its content and, occasionally, by the significance of its author: the quality of much of the writing is a considerable bonus and a tribute to the practitioners of the journalistic art. Although not every major cricketing event is covered, I trust that not many have been overlooked. In addition, room has been found for the minor: thus, while you will find the first big match at Lord's, the All England XI v. United England XI, the first Test matches played in Australia and England, Hobbs equalling Grace's record of first-class centuries, Holmes and Sutcliffe's first-wicket partnership of 555, Laker's 19 wickets in a single Test match, the unique tied Test match, the first World Cup final, and Bodyline (remember that *The Times* like almost all its British counterparts did not send its own man to cover the tour and seems, with hindsight, rather out of touch), you will also discover 19th century country-house cricket in Scotland, Grace playing table cricket, Hobbs visiting under-privileged children, a British author injured on the Hill at Sydney and, one to evoke memories in many cricket watchers, a lad consuming his sandwiches before the start of the lunch interval.

The publishers have been generous in allowing the book to stretch far beyond its original bounds, but even then limits have had to be imposed. The most convenient space-saving device, once I had recovered from heartache, was to condense all but a few of the scoreboards. However, the main individual performances (40 runs and four wickets upwards) have been included, together with the result of the match and, where relevant, the intermediate score for the day's play to which the report relates. In order to give period flavour the distinction between amateurs (with Mr., till 1921, and initials) and professionals (surname only), as indicated in *The Times* before being abolished at the end of 1962, has been retained. The initials themselves are those given by *The Times*, except where they were typographically or factually incorrect. Scoreboards from some of the early matches have been published in full for the sake of historical comparison and as a guiding principle thereafter, though there are exceptions, everything covered since its foundation in 1864 by *Wisden*, the most readily accessible cricketing reference work, has been abbreviated.

Profiles of leading players are presented either directly or through their obituaries (the latter not, as my wife avers, for reasons of morbidity but because there were few formal profiles of players of earlier days) and cricket also raises its head in leading articles – light and thunderous – law reports, arts and broadcast reviews, verse, the diary and personal columns, indeed just about everywhere in the paper at some time. Alas, much digging has failed to unearth the classic, though perhaps leg-pulling, advertisement in the personal column, from the period when it still appeared on the front page, which read: "Curate wanted for country parish, slow left-arm bowler preferred." Only one, very brief, letter – which was published in 1867 and is directly relevant to another item – has been included; cricketing letters to *The Times* were covered in *The Way to Lord's* (Collins Willow 1983; Fontana Paperbacks 1984).

To give an accurate picture of how *The Times* has covered cricket, in almost every case the text reproduced here is faithful to the original as published in the edition of the date indicated – this despite an urge to abbreviate or re-organize some of the pre-1914 match reports into more modern form (cf., for instance, the accounts of Cobden's match (June 1870) or Jessop's historic hundred against Australia (August 1902) with John Woodcock on the nail-biting finish to the Lord's Test match of June 1963). This adherence to the original may admit an occasional error of fact, but typographical blunders, it is hoped, have been remedied. In a few cases the text or headlines have been cut or amended in a minor way to suit the production of the book and all crossheadings have been omitted. There has been no attempt to impose a uniform textual style to cover two centuries; spellings and forms adopted by *The Times* at different stages of its history have thus been retained.

Cricket, as a rule, has had a healthy share of the space allocated in *The Times* to what used to be called Sporting Intelligence (only horse racing has had more), although until the 1980s sport was given but passing recognition by the editorial hierarchy. A most extreme example of this attitude was an extraordinary letter from the Editor, G. E. Buckle, to the Manager, C. F. Moberly Bell, in 1908 when he stated that it was "very clear that many of the sporting correspondents, and some of the best known ones, are people we should studiously keep clear of"; so it is not surprising that the first four volumes of the paper's official history, amounting to more than 3000 pages and published in the 1930s, ignored sport.

However, two of the chief proprietors in the 19th century, John Walter III and his son, Arthur Fraser Walter, were accomplished cricketers, both playing for Eton and the latter also winning his Blue at Oxford. Furthermore, A. F. Walter married into a cricketing – and light blue – family, his wife being a daughter of T. A. Anson, whom *Wisden* described as a "famous Cambridge wicketkeeper". By contrast with the Walters, Lord Northcliffe, who owned *The Times* from 1908 to 1922, had no love for cricket. In 1918 he wrote to the Editor:

> The article on baseball is quite good. There is just a touch of English hypocrisy in avoiding any reference to the fact that before the war cricket was dying, largely because of the canker of pro-

fessionalism and gate money. Baseball is an honest professional game, as is Association football. I do not imagine that the Victorian cricket will ever return. Cricket as described in "The Times" one hundred years ago – the quick, single-wicket game – must have been good sport, though nearly always played for large sums of money.

In 1919, the year of the abortive post-war experiment with two-day county matches, he fulminated:

> I suppose we are right in giving so much space to cricket, though I am told by those who have been to see them that most of the county matches are very poorly attended, and chiefly by old men. I sent some Americans to see a cricket match the other day, and there was practically nobody there.

It is a relief to know that the proprietorial balance towards cricket was restored by Northcliffe's successor, the Hon. J. J. Astor, who played for Eton and Buckinghamshire. It was more than coincidence that during his presidency of M.C.C. *The Times* published its supplement, on 25 May 1937, to mark the club's sesquicentenary.

The Times has been fortunate in having some outstanding writers on the game, but, with a few exceptions, their identities were concealed until 1967 behind the mask of "Correspondent" – be it "Cricket", "Special" or simply "A" – or "Staff Reporter" or no signature at all. The names of members of staff were never disclosed on their reports for *The Times* until "Our Cricket Correspondent" was transmogrified into "John Woodcock, Our Cricket Correspondent" on 20 January 1967 (vid. introduction to chapter 4). However, the anonymity rule was less strict when well-known figures from outside the portals of Printing House Square contributed the so-called "turn-over" articles, which began on the right of the right-hand centre page and turned over on to the next page. Thus, Lord Harris's name appeared on an article about Amateurs and Professionals (1909), Sir Arthur Conan Doyle's on a tribute to the recently deceased W. G. Grace (1915) and that of the Australian Test player, J. W. Trumble, on a tribute to the "Demon" Spofforth (1928), while the Hon. G. W. Lyttelton had his name on a piece commemorating the hundredth Eton and Harrow match (1929) and Sir Donald Bradman on one in 1953 about the Australian touring party, with a protective "World Copyright" label.

Thanks to the Contributors' Marked Copies (bound or microfilmed volumes of *The Times* for almost every day since 1890 which indicate the source of each editorial item) it has been possible, almost certainly for the first time, to unmask the authors of many of the anonymous contributions. They are given belated recognition in the pages that follow, their names appearing between square brackets. In keeping with *The Times*'s persisting practice, leading articles and obituaries have been left unsigned.

Some familiar names who wrote for *The Times* sometimes went to great lengths – or were they having a joke at the paper's expense? – to conceal their identities. For instance, Pelham Warner, in his long series of Cricket Reminiscences published in *The Times* in 1919 and signed "From A Correspondent", used the first person "I" throughout but also referred in the third person to "Mr. Warner" and made so immodest at one point as to write: "In that match, 20 years ago, Mr. P. F. Warner played a faultless innings of 150". We also find Warner, before the First World War, reporting for *The Times* matches in which he was playing and sending a summary of the 1911–12 tour of Australia, from which illness prevented his taking an active part as the selected captain.

Similarly, Henry Leveson Gower sent dispatches from two tours of South Africa in which he was participating, in the latter as captain, and he continued to report matches for *The Times* after the First World War. G. J. V. Weigall, a great character of cricket in the early part of the century, is also to be found writing about matches in which he played and later about matches involving Kent, whom he served as coach. The constraints of *The Times*'s anonymity rule prevented these men from referring in print, and doubtless general conversation, to working for the paper, and the tradition died hard: even in 1980 members of A. C. M. Croome's family were unaware that he had been Cricket Correspondent of *The Times*, although they knew that he had, simultaneously, been Golf Correspondent of the *Morning Post*. Other Times . . .

INTRODUCTION TO THE 1990 EDITION

The original edition of the original *Double Century* – the title was subsequently also adopted by those concerned with M.C.C.'s bicentenary story – ran to well over 600 pages and was thus too large to be accommodated as a single volume in this Pavilion Library series. The work has therefore been divided into two parts: the first, covering the initial 150 years of *The Times*'s life, was published last year; this, the second, takes the story forward to the paper's bicentenary in 1985 and beyond. A few minor corrections and amendments have been made in this volume, but all the original material has been included, together with a fresh selection covering a further five years.

M.W.
January 1990

THE FOURTH HALF-CENTURY
from 1935

In the wake of Bodyline the first part of this era (half-century is now used in its cricketing sense of a total of 50 or more, but less than 100) was comparatively tranquil, but, once the flush of post-war enthusiasm evaporated, the game in England was in financial distress by the late 1950s. The succeeding decades have been marked by revolution and controversy, which have often dragged cricket off the sports pages on to the main news and opinion pages: the ending of the amateur-professional distinction; one-day and Sunday county and international matches; the problems of links with South Africa and the consequent cancellation of tours and banning of players who have gone there; intimidatory bowling; the Packer invasion; internecine strife in Yorkshire and Somerset; the confrontation between an England captain and a Pakistani umpire which provoked cricket's fiercest international contretemps since the Bodyline episode. The way the game has changed was aptly summed up in a Letter to the Editor published in 1968. "We used to turn from the depressing political news to the cricket page for relief; now the cricket page is depressing and as political as any other."

"Beau" Vincent continued as The Times *Cricket Correspondent during the early years, which are typified by the gaiety of the fourth leaders. Neville Cardus told a nice story involving Vincent, which gives some more flavour of those pre-war days; it concerns the England v. Australia match at Lord's in 1938, "the beginning of the typewriter efficiency epoch in cricket reporting". Vincent, sitting next to Cardus in the press box, searched his pockets (where he was also alleged to keep his dentures) in vain and asked his neighbour: "Got a pencil?" Cardus produced the stub of one and gave it to him. Cardus then conducted his own search, turned to his colleague and said: "Forgot to bring any copy paper. Got some?" Vincent tore several sheets from his pad and handed them over. Next morning the typewriters had produced numerous small paragraphs, but Vincent and Cardus had a column and a half each.*

During MCC's tour of Australia in 1946–47 The Times *shared Cardus's Test match reports with* The Manchester Guardian*; for the next visit, in 1950–51,* The Times *decided to send its own man for the first time. Alas, Vincent, uncomfortable at travelling outside London to cover a Test match,* *broke down completely when he reached Australia and retired soon afterwards from his post. Raymond Robertson-Glasgow, known affectionately as "Crusoe" after an opponent had returned to the dressing room to tell the next man in that he was out "first ball from a chap named Robinson Crusoe", stood in as Special Correspondent for that tour and the following summer Geoffrey Green, already achieving distinction as* The Times's *Association Football Correspondent (not to mention a stint as Lawn Tennis Correspondent), doubled as Cricket Correspondent. When Green became Sports Editor, briefly, in 1954, a new Cricket Correspondent was recruited in John Woodcock, whose journalistic career had begun in 1950 as E. W. Swanton's assistant and film cameraman in Australia [vid. report 22 August 1951] and had continued with Test match coverage for* The Manchester Guardian. *Woodcock was appointed on 26 April 1954, at 27 the youngest of all* The Times *Cricket Correspondents, and by the time he moved down the batting order at the end of 1987 his tenure was, by more than a dozen years, greater than that of any of his predecessors. Widely respected in the world of cricket, he followed in the footsteps of George H. West and Sydney H. Pardon by combining his post on* The Times *with the editorship of* Wisden *for six years from 1981 and was elected to the MCC committee in 1988.*

Woodcock – the Sage of Longparish (his Hampshire home) as he was dubbed by a fellow Times *cricket writer, Alan Gibson – holds a particular distinction in the history of the paper: apart from contributing probably more than four million words to its columns he was the first specialist staff correspondent to be named above one of his articles. He had been sent at short notice to South Africa to cover a Test series against Australia and was to work for both* The Times *and its new bedfellow,* The Sunday Times. *The editor of the Sunday paper sought permission to use Woodcock's byline with his first dispatch for them, to be published on 22 January 1967.* The Times, *having kept the identity of its Cricket Correspondent secret – in its own columns at least – for so long, but having taken the momentous decision to name all Correspondents from 23 January, felt that it could not be "scooped". So, when Woodcock previewed the third Test match on 20 January, his mask of anonymity was duly removed.*

He was succeeded by Alan Lee who, although only 33, had already covered 12 overseas tours and had a reputation for news-gathering which kept his rivals in all echelons of the press constantly on their toes.

New Player's Great Achievement

20 *May* 1935. A hitherto completely unknown cricketer, 20 years of age and making his first appearance in a first-class match, stole all the honours at Frome on Saturday. Somerset, after having six men out for 107 runs, finished with a total of 337 and followed up their advantage so well that they dis-

missed five Essex batsmen for 87 runs. Harold Gimblett, the young player in question had the unique distinction of scoring a century on his first appearance in a county match, which has been done only once before for Somerset, by B. L. Bisgood at Worcester in 1907.

Not only did Gimblett, who is an all-rounder from Watchet, in Somerset, score a 100, but he did it in the remarkable time of 63 minutes, and so is in the running for the Lawrence trophy awarded for the fastest 100. Against the well-varied and accurate Essex attack Somerset found themselves engaged in an uphill struggle, but Gimblett completely altered the aspect of the game. Showing what was, in the circumstances, amazing skill and resource, he made 50 in 28 minutes, reached three figures in 63 minutes, and altogether hit up 123 in 80 minutes. Gimblett did not give the slightest chance and hit three 6's and 17 4's. Judged upon this performance, Gimblett is a born cricketer and, as he bowls fast medium extremely well and is a smart fieldsman, it seems as if Somerset have made a real discovery. Andrews followed Gimblett's example and trounced the Essex bowlers. His 71, including three 6's and five 4's, in 50 minutes was a brilliant effort.

When Essex, with two hours left for play, went in to bat Wellard, keeping a fine length, caused a collapse. Only Rist, who plays football for Charlton Athletic, faced him with any confidence. He stayed for rather more than an hour and a half and his 41 included six 4's. Wellard, who got plenty of pace from the pitch, claimed five wickets for 36 runs and was helped by two fine slip catches by J. W. Lee.

SOMERSET 337 (Gimblett 123, Andrews 71, Lee, F. S. 41; Nichols 6 for 87)
ESSEX 141 (Rist 41; Wellard 5 for 66, Lee, J. W. 4 for 26) and 147 (Lee, J. W. 5 for 67)
Score after first day: Somerset 337, Essex 87 for 5
Somerset won by an innings and 49 runs

Lord's and Leather-Jackets

11 *July* 1935, *Leading Article*. In the second Test Match South Africa won the toss and the game. In the University Match Cambridge won the toss and the game. The conclusion is too obvious to be disputed. To win the toss at Lord's this summer is to win the game. The reason is not so easy to see as the fact. Creeping, materialistic minds will seek for physical causes; and some will hasten to an explanation which has been a blessed refuge to every side beaten at Lord's this summer. It is all the fault of the leather-jackets. Whereon other minds of the same order will reply that to talk of the larva of the daddy-longlegs or any other sort of long legs is a silly point; and that the dusting of Oxford's jacket had nothing to do with the leather-jackets, which had done the pitch little harm. While both sides are flatly contradicting each other, higher minds will tell them that, like the disputants in the old nursery poem

about the chameleon, they both are right and both are wrong. The toss and the leather-jackets won the match for Cambridge; but not by the dull, matter-of-fact method of making the bowling difficult. No! there are such things as *imponderabilia* – causes hidden from the materialist, but perceptible by the psychologist. Oxford men – even Brasenose men and cricketers – are notoriously sensitive, imaginative, psychic. The idea means more to them than the fact, the spirit than the matter. Legions of leather-jackets, a pitch of soft mud irregularly set with pointed flints, could not have put the very feeblest of the Oxford batsmen off his game, but that the dread of something underground puzzled the will. The idea of leather-jackets, the awful spectre of leather-jackets, the mental picture of their foul and hidden orgies, the ineluctable fate of having to bat twice after Cambridge on a wicket beneath which leather-jackets might still be teeming after their creepy-crawly kind – that was the doom that turned the Oxford hearts to ice, the Oxford knees to water, the Oxford bats to walking-sticks for graceful use between pavilion and wicket and back again.

Imagination, it is rumoured, is not hotly cultivated at Cambridge; but there is no knowing what PROFESSOR SIR ARTHUR QUILLER-COUCH may not have been up to, nor what effect the science of SIR JAMES JEANS and of PROFESSOR SIR ARTHUR EDDINGTON may not insidiously have worked upon the strict Cambridge ethos. And, unless the terror that now haunts the wicket at Lord's can be exorcised before next season, the University match may be reduced to the wearing of clean flannels and blues, and tossing up, and luncheon, and nothing more. The fear of the leather-jackets may not be real; but, like the young person of Deal, sensitive players hate the fear that they fancy they feel; and, as the complaint is one of suggestion, so must the remedy be. When leather-jackets, having ruined a lot of golf greens, were under discussion in this journal in 1932, it was recorded that leather-jackets were a favourite food of starlings. Lord's has leather-jackets; Trafalgar Square has starlings. If the leather-jackets will not go to Trafalgar Square (which is unlikely), the starlings must be taken to Lord's. They might be taken by aeroplane, as the winter-bound swallows were once taken South from Austria. Small boys might be forbidden to ask for autographs until they could prove that they had brought one or more starlings to Lord's. Some grandiose political scheme might include the organization of the unemployed into corps of beaters, to drive starlings up Regent Street and Portland Place (with the B.B.C. making records of the starlings' chatter and of the appropriate speech of a leading politician) into the Regent's Park, and so to Lord's; and flocks of starlings, collected overnight in cages, might be released each morning at the beginning of play. The thought of the presence of the avenging hosts would set at rest the imaginative terrors of sensitive cricketers; and the starling might be to Lord's what the goose was to the Capitol.

A Chat with Ranji

The Great Cricketer Remembers

BY J. B. BOOTH

26 *August* 1935. Test matches, whatever may be their virtues or their vices, have, besides a trick of making history, the effect of rousing Laudator Temporis Acti from his slumbers; and in present-day conditions the gentleman is too often more than a little peevish.

When he comes in with his old music, the note is sadly apt to be harsh. Perhaps it was always so, and from now and then having right on his side he has grown to consider himself infallible, and to hug himself joyfully at the thought that he has outlived the best of everything. In such a case, an occasional antidote has its merits. There is nothing new in this; 20 odd years ago the cricketing Laudator was much the same as he is to-day, and was all the better for the occasional antidote expertly administered.

Thoughts such as these sent me to an old diary, in which were scrawled notes of a talk with Prince Ranjitsinhji in 1912, when, one evening during the Scarborough festival, he chatted freely of the sportsmen of the past, and of changes in the cricket world. It was a cold, wet summer, and, fresh from India, the Jam Sahib shivered and dug his hands deep in his trouser pockets. Those same hands had not, however, lost their cunning, and more than once brought off the lightning catch that made their owner famous in the field. Age had told a little; the Prince was slower between wickets, but the great batsman was still there, and the panther-like spring at any fielding chance seemed as lithe as of old. Some of the Pavilionites, whose own chests had "slipped," professed to regret that the Jam was "putting it on," but most of the girth was amassed in the dressing-room. Feeling the cold intensely, each day he bought something fresh at the hosier's – an extra vest, another cholera belt, a woollen waistcoat – and had the cold lasted he certainly would not have been able to pass out of the dressing-room door.

Shrewd, modest, good-humoured, the Jam had strong views on the game he loved, and in that old diary I find some hastily written notes of his views and opinions as he expressed them one evening that week to a few friends. He didn't believe in "Test temperament"; in fact, jeered at it. "There's no such thing," he said contemptuously, "except amongst Pavilion cricketers." Then someone asked the obvious question. "Charles Fry is the best bat in the world at the moment," he declared roundly, "because he's the soundest. He can play on any wicket. That's the test. Some fellows are better on slow wickets, some on fast; they're all the same to Fry."

Then came the other obvious question. "On the whole, I'd call W. G. the greatest cricketer of all time. Not that he was a greater bat than half a dozen, at least, but because he was a pioneer. W. G. was the first of the great all-rounders. Look at the history of the game, from the old top-hat days, the days of Mynn, Carpenter, Pilch, and the rest. One, you read, was a back player; another depended on a forward game; another was a stonewaller; another a hitter. Each had a speciality he relied on. Grace could do anything, and, in spite of his weight, was a magnificent field, to say nothing of his bowling. If it hadn't been for the old man there would have been no Steel, Ulyett, Lohmann, Barnes, Hirst, Jackson and the others."

"How would you compare W. G. with Trumper?" someone asked.

"You can't compare the incomparable. Each at his best was incomparable. Trumper too, was a pioneer. Twenty years ago at Eton he'd never have got his colours, simply because his strokes were unorthodox. All reformers start as heretics. Look at what they had to say about Jessop."

As to the greatest bowler, he would not commit himself. In make and action, I remember, he seemed to think Tom Richardson the ideal fast bowling machine. "In spite of his pace, the naturalness and ease of his action took so little out of him that he could – and did – bowl unchanged for hours, with no diminution in pace, length and sting." The modern fast bowler – "modern" being the year 1912 – with a tendency to lose length and become exhausted after a dozen overs, the Jam Sahib seemed to regard a trifle contemptuously, as a sort of hothouse plant.

Taking things as a whole, the Prince roundly asserted that the general average of cricket had vastly improved in his own time. "When I began," he said, "there were only about a hundred really first-class players in the game. Now there are at least four times as many."

The Jam Sahib had one surprise for most of his little audience. "Of course, W. G. didn't have modern wickets to bat on," observed someone. "Grounds have improved enormously." And to our vast astonishment Ranji would not have it for a moment. "Don't you believe it!" he retorted. "Forty years ago there were some wickets every bit as good as the best we have to-day. W. G. told me that himself. Lord's, the Oval, the St. Lawrence ground at Canterbury and about half a dozen others were as good then as now."

Out of the recent past come these haphazard reflections of one who was, perhaps, the greatest batting reformer in the history of the game, the player of whom Andrew Lang wrote: "I cannot write an account of Ranji's batting, because I am not a really great poet."

A Few Words from Dr. Grace

Obiter Dicta of 1884

BY M. H. SPIELMANN

2 *September* 1935. While the memory of great cricketers of the past is being revived the record of a conversation which I had in 1884 with Dr. W. G. Grace may be welcome.

That was the year in which he was held to have surpassed his achievements for a long while before, and in which his performances against the Australian team in particular were so brilliant as completely to dispel the previous year's growing impression that "the Doctor was growing old and stale."

During the rather absurd match, as we thought it, of "Smokers v. Non-Smokers" (September 16, 1884) I was his guest in the pavilion at Lord's. Grace was a non-smoker, but he scoffed at the idea that anything was to be proved by the result of the match. "The rules of health for a cricketer," he said, "are merely the ordinary common-sense ones; moderation in all things, and above all plenty of rest. Tobacco moderately used certainly does no harm." At that moment Gunn, "far out in the country," made the catch which dismissed Stanley Christopherson. "It's the most wonderful catch I've ever seen in my life," commented Grace – and he was once more the elated and enthusiastic schoolboy who at the age of 18 had played for England v. Surrey and had carried his bat for 224.

"Are you as good now, do you consider, as you were then?" I asked. "My defence is as good," he replied, "but I can't punish the bowling as I used to do. Besides, as you get older you lose your activity and can't field so well. I shall play only for the county next season; and I shall take only three weeks' holiday. Cricket interferes with my practice; patients don't like an assistant, however good he is. I have a good practice which increases every winter when I am at home, and decreases every summer when I am in the cricket field. And it makes me wonder if I shall ever get to Harley Street." Cricket was in his blood, thanks to both his parents, as he explained: "My father was a very keen cricketer, and my mother, as you know, had a passion for the game and took great pride in her youngsters' play."

With a wonderful memory he began to detail some of his past performances and I put in a remark about his self-confidence. "Self-confidence?" he questioned. "I have never gone in to bat without my knees knocking together from nervousness throughout the first over!" (What an encouragement and consolation for the rest of us poor humble outsiders.)

"Spofforth says that you are far and away the best cricketer in England; and after you A. G. Steel. Do you agree?" "So I read," he replied, smiling. "A. G. is a grand all-round cricketer, and I would rather have him on my side than any other cricketer I know. You will always find," he went on, "plenty of good cricketers cropping up from time to time, and some years will bring more than others. . . . You will find that all counties have a run of success and then of bad luck. Look at Lancashire, which was at the top of the tree and is now worse than Gloucestershire. But we've got Painter, a new man." (Poor Painter. The Doctor could be very hectoring in the heat of the game, and as the professional let it be known "It's Painter here" and "Painter there" until he "sometimes wondered if he loved his Chief as much as he thought he really did." But as to his veneration he never had the slightest doubt.)

Grace maintained that the rules of cricket were good and sufficient, but needed to be made plainer for the umpires, who evidently did not always understand them! In support of this view he cited the case which at the time was being widely discussed. The middle stump had been bowled so as nearly to fall out of the ground, but owing to the outside stumps pinching the bails failed to fall. "If the stumps and bails had been properly made and pitched," said W. G., "the thing could not occur. But as it happened the umpire had to give his verdict, and tying himself to the word and not to the spirit of the rule he gave it not out. I should certainly have given it out."

For a moment he was silent. "Smokers v. Non-Smokers," he muttered and shrugged his shoulders. "What next, I wonder? What does it matter? – it's always cricket." "Remember," he added as a farewell, "the first essential in a good innings is to get safely through the first over. By then you ought to have played yourself in; it's the first over that settles you. Remember my knees: but that's between ourselves."

'Willow the King'

30 *April* 1936. To anyone who loves cricket with that strange, mystical love which makes a man regard the winter months as though they were so many traitors to a glorious and lovely cause, the closing days of April bring the indescribable thrill of the knowledge that summer and cricket are coming into their own again. Last night there was broadcast *Willow the King*, "a cricket miscellany with actors from the village green, the county ground, and even from Elysian Fields." The broadcast was written and arranged by Mr. Herbert Farjeon, and in verse, song, and prose does its best – and a very good best it is – to put into words the atmosphere of the game wherever it is played, whether in back gardens, in villages among club cricketers, or on the solemn, protected pitch of a Test Match.

The broadcast begins with the welcome note of the cuckoo and the sound of a roller, and then goes on to explore all those delightful avenues which lead into the heart of cricket. There is the pavilion gossip – "Do you remember C. S. T. Dash, good fast bowler?" and the erudite reply: "That wasn't C. S. T., that was C. S. D." – there are the stumbling exchanges of courtesies after the battle of the village green has been lost and won, and there is an impassioned appeal for the revision of the law that the juvenile player in the garden shall be out should he hit the ball over the wall. How, it was rightly demanded, can a small boy indulge his natural instincts and hit a full pitch on the leg-side for six and glory when the penalty is the surrender of his bat to the bowler? And why does not the M.C.C. get up a fund to pay all glaziers' bills incurred in the playing of good, spirited, and honest cricket? There follows a reading of Mr. Neville Cardus's record of that never-to-be-forgotten Test Match at Old Trafford in 1902, when the unfortunate Tate at square-leg dropped Darling at a critical moment and was himself bowled when England needed only four runs for victory. This broadcast miscellany was a fitting prelude to the start of the first-class season this week.

Cheap Wickets at Lord's

FROM OUR CRICKET CORRESPONDENT [R. B. VINCENT]

29 *June* 1936. The bowling of Amar Singh, the batting of Leyland, and the wicketkeeping of both Duckworth and D. D. Hindlekar between them prevented the play during the first day of the Test Match at Lord's on Saturday from being anything but amiably futile. All-India, who were told to bat first on a wicket which might have been difficult if the sun had shone more strongly after Friday's rain, started well enough, but after the first wicket had fallen there was no reason or sense in their batting, and when England went in to answer a score of 147 with a total of 132 for seven wickets there was little to suggest that we were watching a game glorified by the name of Test Match.

The crowd thoroughly appreciated the quick fall of wickets, sickened as they have been on previous occasions by a glut of runs, but they must have known that they were wickets rather shabbily taken. G. O. Allen, captaining England for the first time, had a look on his face which declared that if he won the toss he would send All-India in to bat, the dropping of the unlucky Gover was a further indication of the purpose of the selectors, and even those who insist that W. G. Grace preferred emphatically to bat first whenever he had the chance had to admit that Allen was right.

It must be borne in mind, however, that this is not a single-innings match and that the value of Gover on the second day might be more valuable than that of Langridge on Saturday. The wicket actually was never difficult, and the strongest telescope in the world could not have discovered any exaggerated turn of the ball once it had touched ground. The telescope was not much wanted except when Amar Singh and Mohamed Nissar were bowling, for a more riotous display of full pitches and long hops can never before have been seen in a Test Match. Poor in quality the cricket may have been, but exciting also it was, for one never had an idea that swells such as these could get themselves out in such an amazing manner. . . .

INDIA 147 (G. O. Allen 5 for 35) and 93 (G. O. Allen 5 for 43, Verity 4 for 17)
ENGLAND 134 (Leyland 60; Amar Singh 6 for 35) and 108 for 1 (Gimblett 67 not out)
Score after first day: India 147; England 132 for 7.
England won by 9 wickets

Queen Willow

9 *September* 1936, *Leading Article.* There is "sweet English music" in the words men have used to praise the cricket-bat, the pliant, springy, glossy, sweet-sounding blade. With no inkling of its real nature they have honoured it as King Willow. With what now seems masculine cocksureness the poet sang :–

> "Willow the King is a monarch grand,
> Three in a row his courtiers stand."

For a century there has been no suspicion that King Willow could be a fraud, or that sex might enter into the matter. But presumption must now yield to truth and the world know that the true willow is a "she," that she is the bat's mother and no other. King Willow has been caught out; his offspring are suspect; they are not chips of the old block. For the experts say that the male willow is too often a hybrid and degenerate, who will wilt and warp in the battle with the ball. Now and then a male will pass the test of true willowhood; then he is a king among bats, a he-bat. But the traditions of cricket, it seems, have descended on the distaff side. Tardy honours must be paid to many scarred and bandaged and anointed "shes," Amazons of the game, who have stood up to fast balls, lashed at low ones, and stared the googly undaunted in the face. No longer, then, is "it" or "he" the bat's pronoun. No ill-advised personification this, as FOWLER might call it. "She" is the one and only word for a thing that has been found to be feminine.

Habit of course dies hard in a summer game, and the revelation has come late in the season, too late to affect the players and the counties whose exploits our Cricket Correspondent sums up this morning. But in Australia there will be cricket and a whole summer for controversy. Would it be too much to ask of a Test team that they should establish "Queen Willow" in the language before they reach Australia? Otherwise it must be left to the first match-winner who pats his bat lovingly and calls "her" a beauty. Or to the first batsman who comes runless from the wicket cursing the fickleness of feminine nature. After all, "she" will be no intruder; every cricketer with a fancy felt long ago that the manliness of cricket had been exaggerated. The ball, it is true, fierce, red, and glossy, is a masculine thing. But the soft soothing whites and greens of cricket have always shown a feminine touch.

Now that we know the truth about the willow, questions will be asked about the ash, the pine, and the yew. Have the oar and the cue, the racquet and the golf club a similar secret of sex? They too are often blamed for fickleness of form, and, what is more, women have used them as effectively as men. No one can say that of the cricket bat, which is sullen and timid in a woman's hand. The batmakers assert with some scorn that the racquet and the club have felt the cold hand of steel, that even though they might be female in origin they are no longer pure wood. For such hybrids, as for the late King Willow, the only word is "it." But the case of the cricket willow is beyond argument. Could there be a clearer claim on the well-known chivalry of cricketers than the cause of one who has served them gracefully, manfully, and anonymously? Let the Gentlemen of England close the season with a toast and the cry: "King Willow is dead. Long live the Queen!"

"Little" Cricket
The Stonyhurst Game

FROM A CORRESPONDENT [REV. HERBERT THORNTON]

12 *September* 1936. There cannot be more than a score or two of people now living who have taken part in a game of "Stonyhurst cricket" as it flourished under primitive conditions at the college rather more than 60 years ago. If I am not mistaken it went out of favour in 1873, and though spasmodic attempts to revive it occurred from time to time, it was never reinstated in its original glory, and for quite half a century has been extinct. But before all memory of it perishes it may be worth while to call attention to the way in which the peculiar features of that game seem to throw light upon the earlier stages of cricket proper. In many respects they show points of agreement with eighteenth-century records, and in particular with the pictures of that date, including those in Sir Jeremiah Colman's collection, which was not long since exhibited in the Tate Gallery.

At Stonyhurst the new form of cricket with the Marylebone laws was at first called "London cricket" to distinguish it from the indigenous variety. The Stonyhurst game was played upon the earthen surface of the playground the pitch being carefully rolled, whereas, of course, for the other a field was necessary. Consequently the older sport was not at once given up. Football ended with Shrovetide, and in my time Stonyhurst cricket came in very handy to fill the gap during March and April until the weather was dry and warm enough to pitch orthodox wickets on the turf.

There cannot be much doubt that in the course of the seventeenth century the English lads of good family who for the sake of religion were sent to be educated abroad at the Jesuit college of St. Omers took with them the games of football and cricket as they were accustomed to see them played at home. Cricket is likely to have become crystallized under conditions which, while allowing the essential features to be retained, inevitably introduced certain modifications. The game soon acquired definite rules, and when after a series of migrations the school, at the height of the French Revolution, was transferred in 1794 from the Netherlands to Stonyhurst, in Lancashire, the boys brought their old traditions with them. At St. Omers the English college lay within a walled city. It covered a good deal of ground, but the space for recreation must have been relatively cramped. Double-wicket cricket could not be thought of there, but by arranging a number of pitches side by side and all facing one way, as is often done at practice nets, several single-wicket games could be played simultaneously without much mutual interference. A grass surface was also out of the question, and, without turf, wickets which were destined to be continually knocked over could not be kept upright. Unfortunately we have no records concerning cricket at St. Omers, so that all this is conjectural, but we do know the conditions and rules which governed the game at Stonyhurst from 1794 down to 1873.

A wicket, of course, is a little gate or door, and anyone who studies the two uprights surmounted with a bail, as they are represented in some of the pictures of the Colman collection, will at once recognize that the term is not inappropriate. In 1744 the London rules determine the height of the uprights, still only two in number, as 22in. and the bail as 6in. in length. At Stonyhurst on a playground surface wickets could not be used, and they were replaced by stones hewn for the purpose. These had an iron ring let into the top to facilitate removal to a new position. The stones were 17in. high, 13in. wide, and 8in. thick at the bottom, though they were somewhat thinner at the upper end. This, I fancy, corresponded roughly with the objective which the bowlers in England had to aim at before the end of the seventeenth century. At Stonyhurst the batsman was out when the ball hit the stone. In the southern English game, down to 1744 and later, a bowler who sent a perfectly straight ball between the wickets without touching either them or the bail apparently gained nothing. The batsman, it seems, was not out unless the bail was disturbed; in fact the 1744 rules ordain expressly: "The Bail hanging on one Stump, though the Ball hit the Wicket, it's Not Out." It cannot have been very long, however, before the absurdity of penalizing the ball which went between the two stumps without hitting either attracted attention, and the matter was remedied by placing a third stump in the middle.

As for the bats, the Stonyhurst implement which we used in 1872 had many points of resemblance with those depicted in the earlier Colman pictures. There can be no doubt that the original weapon had no proper blade with square shoulders, though the lower end was thick and heavy. On the other hand, it was longer than those in present use and had a slight but very perceptible curve. The lower end of the Stonyhurst bat was a block of wood (alder?), roughly oval in shape, about 4½in. wide and 2in. thick, slightly curved, with the concavity on the striking side. This was spliced with strong twine to a round ash handle, the length of the whole being about 3ft. As will be readily understood, the whole driving power of the implement was near the bottom, and it was held, almost as one would hold a golf club, close to its upper end. The very make of the bat was sufficient to suggest the manner in which it was meant to be employed. All the bowling was underarm and along the ground; in fact, the bowling of sneaks was compulsory. A batsman could not be bowled out by a full pitch or even by a first bounce, unless he offered at it, and similarly a ball jerked or thrown was accounted an unfair ball. It was at the option of the striker to offer or not at any such delivery. But he was obliged to slog; he was not allowed to block or merely play the ball, and if he flagrantly offended against this rule he was out.

All these features of the Stonyhurst game seem quite in accord with the practice of the early eighteenth century, at any rate in single-wicket matches. The attitude of many of the bowlers in the pictures of that date suggests a very low ball. Moreover, the wickets were so low that not one modern length ball in 50 would hit them, however straight it might be. Meanwhile the batsman crouches watching intently to see if it will give a little hop, for then he rises to his full height and, certain of his stroke, with all the force of tense muscles sends it whizzing into the far distance. My clearest recollection of Stonyhurst cricket is of the satisfaction with which the batsman realized as the ball came hurtling along the ground that some little inequality in the surface had converted it into a long hop and that he had it for certain in his power to strike with all his force and send it where he liked.

The balls used for Stonyhurst cricket were of domestic manufacture. The inside was made by the boys themselves out of cork and worsted, wound very tightly into a sphere, and then immersed in boiling glue. For days while this was going on certain parts of the house reeked with the odour. The carcasses thus prepared, after being allowed to dry, were sent to the college shoemaker who enclosed them in two hemispheres of leather and stitched these together. This rough-and-ready method left a raised seam right round the ball, more or less like the rings of the planet Saturn. It was one of the rules of the game that the bowler should "bowl with the seam," and I think that the excrescence added a certain liveliness to the ball's movements. It travelled along the ground but not in continual contact with it, thus big hits became more possible, and that, after all, was the great interest. Speaking of cricket in the early eighteenth century Mr. Neville Cardus says with fine insight:–

> The batsman, therefore, concentrated on offence. He gave himself over entirely to a primitive appetite for honest clouting. Think of it – O ye Woodfulls and Watsons – in these pristine days of the summer game, no batsman gave much thought to defence. But this kind of cricket, happy-hearted though it probably was, can scarcely have been cricket at all. It seems to me to have mingled the crudest principles of skittles and golf. Cricket proper began with the length ball.

All this is fully in accord with the spirit which animated Stonyhurst cricket and "London cricket" respectively in the days when they were played, so to speak, side by side.

Making County Teams

BY P. G. H. FENDER

25 *May* 1937, *M.C.C. Number*. County cricket, in England, has always been a thing apart, by comparison with the cricket of any other country. To many players it has been the height of ambition, though a few, a very select few, have regarded it merely as a stepping-stone to the highest honour in the game, a place in England's Test side.

There is no doubt about the position of county cricket as a forcing house in the English game, for it offers to the individual player an opportunity for intensive practice of the game in competitive conditions, if he chooses so to regard his place in his county XI, and at the same time it offers him an almost day-to-day indulgence in one of the greatest pleasures possible to a cricketer, that of playing the game in good-class company to his heart's content.

County cricket is an end in itself to most players, and a most delightful one at that, and not one of those among us who have partaken of that joy in the game which it provides have failed to appreciate it on that basis, whether or not we have aspired to the greater heights.

It has been suggested that the big difference between a good club player and a good county player is nothing more than experience, and this, very probably, is as good a definition of that difference as it is possible to give. County cricket offers to those who have the time to devote to it an opportunity for playing the great game in such company, and with sufficient continuity, for it to be thought of as the "make and break" of the man as a cricketer.

A player who graduates from any other cricket into the county side meets something which he can seldom have encountered before, for even the intensity of a 'Varsity match only provides him with an opportunity of appreciating "atmosphere," while county cricket frequently, if not always, forces him to play in an atmosphere which is similar, while, in addition, he has to meet a greater degree of ability in the individual player, as well as in the matter of team work, than anything to be met in a University match.

County cricket takes the outstanding player from any other grade of the game, if he has the time to spare, and "produces" him, and he either keeps his place against other competitors for that place, or fails to do so. If he fails to do so it may be for one of two reasons, either that he has not the ability for the higher class in the game, or that he is slow to acclimatize himself to the new conditions as compared with those from which he came. If he makes good and holds his place in his county side he may either progress or merely join the main body of those who are of a certain standard of ability and can get no further, or he may be one of those who are slow to improve but well capable of holding their own. These latter seldom rise to the Test side.

For this reason county cricket is a most healthy and wholesome thing in the game, and something of great value no matter from which point of view it is regarded. It represents the high standard of the game in this country and maintains that standard, so far as it is possible to do so, by assiduous practice and the provision of opportunity for continuous practice and the gaining of experience. In England this latter is of paramount importance to the game because, in the conditions under which we play cricket, as opposed, for instance, to the Australian, the very first essential in a cricketer's make-up is versatility. The Australian makes his way along the high road of assiduous practice to perfection of stroke play on account of the constant nature of the wickets upon which he learns the rudiments of the game, whether in batting or bowling. He can always rely upon the ball doing the same thing, day in and day out, if it is delivered from the same height, and at the same speed, and pitched in the same place with the same spin. An Englishman cannot so rely, because, on account of the difference of climate and weather under which he has to study, he is likely to have to play upon several different wickets in the course of any one week.

The high road to greatness for an Australian is assiduous practice, for by that means he may achieve perfect stoke play, and after that the learning of versatility is easy by comparison with the reverse process. An Englishman has to learn versatility first, for otherwise he will not have sufficient opportunities to achieve perfection in his stroke play or in his technique. County cricket provides him with the chances to be assiduous in his practice and, providing that he can hold his place in his county side, the player can, if the ability is there, learn and progress.

There is another side, however, to county cricket, and that is what it does, through its nurseries, to improve the standard of play in the districts, and to train young men who otherwise might never be able to afford the luxury for the carrying on of the standard of cricket in the county.

Most, if not all, counties do what they can afford to train young men, especially those who are ultimately to become professionals, and it is only such organizations which provide the necessary influx of new blood into the game. The universities, in their especial categories, and the clubs in theirs, do a tremendous lot of the necessary pioneer work, but it is the counties which are the test and which, once the initial trials are justified and satisfactorily answered, take up the "higher education" of the embryo first-class cricketer.

It is true that some counties do more than others in this respect, but that is only natural, because such efforts are very largely governed by the financial position of the particular county. National cricket depends almost exclusively on the counties, while it is almost entirely through the county clubs that a club player may progress, so that the counties are really the mainspring of the game in the manner in which they provide the training ground for the advanced player on his way to the highest honours, and at the same time the facilities for cultivation of the club player.

In writing this it must not be thought that I in any way minimize the great value to the game which club cricket represents. Without club cricket there would be little, if any, cricket at all, but I do feel that without county cricket there would be a complete loss of standing among cricketing countries of the world, and that such a position would very soon lead to such a lowering of the standard of the game in this country as to be virtually the end of cricket as we know it. Some might say: "So much the better," and insinuate that the game would be the better for a return to those conditions under which the game first raised its head, but that is another point.

The game as it now is cannot get on without that which county cricket means to it – an enormous hive of intensive cultivation – the sudden withdrawal of which would mean the loss of the mainspring of the present-day game.

It is curious to note, however, that, in different parts of the country the method of preparing the material for the intensive cultivation of the counties varies quite a lot. In the South it is club cricket which provides and gives the initial training to the raw material, while in the North it is the leagues.

More often than not the clubs provide amateurs, and the league the professionals, but the very nature of the games played under the auspices of the one and the other also varies.

Club cricket, while as keen as one could wish, does not offer the same competitive opportunities to its players, and, mainly as a result, the player who comes from the league to county cricket is usually the more experienced of the two and more ready for the fiercer atmosphere of the higher grade. This is probably one of the main reasons why the North have, in the past, played such a very big part in the County Championship. The material which comes to Yorkshire and Lancashire, for example, is more "ready," and, as a result, learns more quickly and finds its new surroundings less strange.

Derbyshire, last year's champions, and Notts have a lot for which to be thankful to their local leagues, and I cannot help the feeling that the difference between the atmosphere of the clubs and the leagues is responsible for the greater consistency of the Northern sides by comparison with the Southern. Southern counties are frequently brilliant and rise to great heights, but it cannot be denied that the general form of the Northern counties is, on the whole, more consistent.

No matter how one may view the game of cricket in this country, however, one thing is certain, and that is that the game as a whole, in the eyes of the world, is viewed from the standpoint of the counties, and without the work which they do we should never be able to place a Test side in the field at all with any real hope of taking and keeping a high place in the world game.

On the Village Green

BY HUGH DE SELINCOURT

25 *May* 1937, *M.C.C. Number.* It is pleasant to notice the quickening effect of a great national occasion upon activities, however humble, throughout the country. A general rejoicing, unenforced, tips the scale naturally to the doing of what has been hitherto cautiously postponed or warily rejected.

The meeting of our cricket club in the library of the village hall bore ample witness to this spirit of derring-do. In Coronation Year – not to have a new coat of paint on the Pavilion! Absurd. Not to have water laid on – preposterous, in Coronation Year! And a small pipe extended to the square (at such trifling cost) so that in the event of a drought (we heard the perpetual rain falling outside and stamped in furious applause) – in the event of a drought (I repeat the word as the dauntless speaker repeated it) the pitch might be watered, the grass kept green, the turf in smiling, proper condition. There never was such a meeting. When enthusiasm simmered down a little from boiling point to more normal procedure the flame was turned up, relit as from fresh jets, by astute reference to his late Majesty's Playing Fields Fund, and to the 150th anniversay celebration of the great home of all cricket – "our own ground, gentlemen, being hardly less ancient; famed in story, though not named in Wisden."

There never was such a meeting. It was almost funny. It was almost frightening. The staider members were thankful that the whole meeting did not emerge *en bloc* to the ground, collecting cans of petrol on their jubilant way, apply a match to the tumbledown wooden shack that disgraced the name of pavilion, and, while they watched the glad blaze in the dark, damp Spring night, vote vociferously that a new pavilion should arise in stone glory like a Phoenix from the smouldering ashes of the old.

Much the same sort of thing, from what I hear, must surely have been happening all over the countryside. True, to our meeting came a new member, kept by years from playing cricket but whose devotion to cricket was fanned by years and made wise by years to bestir his energy for the best interests of the game. And what cards these great national celebrations put into his hand! The recalcitrant could not for once plume themselves on their policy of caution: could not fail, indeed, to appear something worse than foolish, something little better than unpatriotic. After conscientious attendance at a series of lectures in the village hall on the proper use of the gas mask – similar lectures in various languages to those being given at present all over the civilized world – it was so refreshing to be aware of our common humanity in terms that were not repulsive, that we may be excused, perhaps, for allowing enthusiasm to run high, almost to riot, in our midst. For love of country was at length being used, nor for enmity and destruction, but to spread happiness and to create.

With the glow of this meeting still warm, it seemed odd to remember how many sage heads have been sadly wagging, in bar parlours, in august club-rooms, in members' enclosures, and elsewhere, over the decline of cricket, which has been, I am told on good authority, at times even mentioned in the Press. Perhaps the fantastic changes that have overtaken all the conditions and circumstances of life in town and country – transforming the appearance of the countryside often beyond recognition, sweeping away like a high flood old barriers, old ways, old habits of mind – have induced this pessimistic outlook and forced from many a disturbed onlooker the lament that even cricket is not nowadays what it was. Last year's deplorable summer, with its cutting effect upon county finances, did not favour a rosy view. Allowance, too, must be made for the deep, concealed, yet aching sadness of men doomed by age to be lookers on merely at the game, when everything in them but their bodies – *hinc illae lacrimae*! – longs to be playing themselves.

But a man can only speak from his own experience. My own experience of village cricket ranges – with one big gap in it – over a period of 45 years, round and about the same stretch of country. I played as a boy for a village on the other side of the Downs to the village for which I have played for the last 17 seasons, and hope to play again this summer. And jolly as those early games were – driving to away matches all together in an old large two-horse brake, over crunchy roads that were roads – there can be no shadow of doubt that the whole standard of play, grounds, kit, and apparel has quite vastly improved. The correct public schoolboy – myself – who turned out, rather shy and stiff, possibly, became, as shy stiffness melted, the object of much witty good-humoured comment, 'im and 'is cricketin' fallals.

Bill Awker, a wiry old chap who opened the bowling for a neighbouring village, found him especially amusing. Bill scorned to be dressed up in pretties. He lurched out in huge hobnailed boots and corduroys to the wicket, took off his collar and tie, put them in the pocket of his jacket, which he removed, and handed to the umpire. Then he rolled up his sleeves, fitted his cutty behind his buckled belt, spat on his hands, took the ball from his trouser pocket, stepped two paces back, and crying out "Look out for this one, then," proceeded to deal the swiftest lob that skimmed like a frantic little wood gone crazy over the grassy pitch at a petrifying pace, a real authentic daisy-cutter, dead on the wicket. Bill gave his hands an extra rub when he observed my exquisitely accoutred approach to the wicket, and greeted my immediate discomfiture with a horrid shout of laughter. Out came his cutty, out came exuberant puffs. I could never play him then. I am sure I could not play him now. Well, old Bill has gone – rest his soul! – and many like him. I have not seen such bowling of late years (fortunately for my self-respect), and it is the man or boy not in full cricketing kit who is apt to rouse good-humoured comment now.

Gone, too, are those old stinging wooden weapons, known as bats, perfect for the slow safety of the dead bat game; we wield our lively Bradmans to some purpose, and our Surridges with Flexo handles, more anxious to test the bat's quality with drives hard and true than content to remain there, stopping ball after ball, a lifeless bit of wood in lifeless, though perhaps orthodox, hands. There is no time to wear the bowler down; he must be knocked irreverently off his length, if any game is to be won. A too slow side declared, leaving us an hour and a half in which to make the runs they had themselves taken three good hours to compile. We won comfortably with three minutes to spare. Their bowling was watched, mastered, and hit.

Grounds, like kit and apparel, have not only improved but have become more numerous. It is difficult to say what is and what is not a real village team. We are a village side, I suppose; yet I see on our fixture list for this season – not, it is true, without trepidation – matches arranged on county grounds (Hove, Horsham, and Worthing); with touring sides from London (a famous publishing house runs a team and is playing us – may we crush them!) as well as with Priory Park, Chichester, Littlehampton, and Steyning – not to mention East Preston, the village I played for as a boy. On every side, Thakeham, Ashington, Washington, Findon, Amberley, Watersfield, Pulborough, villages have their grounds and know the sides with whom they will get good games. Cricket is without any doubt whatsoever flourishing as it surely has never flourished before.

Changed conditions, with ease of transport and the growth in number and improvement of public grounds, may have adversely affected the delectable sociability of country-house cricket. There are certainly fewer private grounds; but they exist, though the games played on them may have changed their character a little. A new private ground for instance, has lately been made in this neighbourhood, where a club, known as The Triflers, composed largely of men from Cambridge, play their home games during vacation. I have unfortunately been prevented from visiting the ground, but I have played against them on other grounds, and I have never seen a keener fielding side. Really, to a man, they gave an example, a delight to watch, of how men in the field should conduct themselves, showing, indeed, an alert keenness which the usual amenities of country-house cricket, both at table and buffet, have been known to dull and damp, if not totally to extinguish.

Their keenness is not exceptional. This very April, inclement as it has mostly been, I have seen a mat placed on a lawn before a stump and bowlers doing that spade work of practice – finding their length, changing their pace with no change in delivery – for which no batsman is necessary; for which, in fact, a batsman is most definitely in the light.

The new zest for physical training which is spreading throughout the land is partly responsible for this willingness to undergo the spadework of practice. Men are beginning to learn into what good servants their bodies may be trained. Yet still the standard of bodily control among bowlers is deplorably low, as compared with the standard of bodily control common among executant musicians, though a bowler needs a twentieth part merely of the scale work to which a musician must submit.

"On his day, when he has found his length, So-and-so is without doubt a very fine bowler, whom it is a genuine pleasure to watch." Words to this effect I have seen written of a bowler in the very highest class of cricket. "On his day, when he hits the right note, there is no doubt that So-and-so is a very fine pianist, whom it is a pleasure to hear." It is merely the standard of bodily skill due to the spadework of practice among musicians and the complete lack of it among bowlers which makes the one sentence read like perfect sense and the other like arrant nonsense. A keen kid or two will come to realize the immense untapped possibilities waiting in intelligent bowling practice – the lithe conditions of body and power of control that may be developed by intelligent training – and soon will come an outcry for stumps to be lowered again.

All through April all over the countryside we have been oiling our bats, have been knocking ball on bat to hear the music, and eyeing still sodden grounds rather resentfully, trying not to think with too much envy of those lucky schoolboys already practising away at Lord's, and hoping that this Coronation year may be blessed all through the summer with Coronation weather, that our prowess with bat and ball throughout the season may be as memorable as the gallant meeting with which the season opened.

And now the season has opened: the first games have been played. Have high hopes been justified, or were they possibly set too high? The great question is being answered one way or another everywhere now; nor does the question mainly matter. What matters is that the games, win or lose, should be good games, well worth playing and having been played, well worthy of remembrance.

"How's That?"

The Umpire's Point of View

BY FRANK CHESTER

25 *May* 1937, *M.C.C. Number*. "I thought I knew all about cricket until I started umpiring," said a former England player to me once. "Then I found that I was only half an international."

The umpire sees quite a different side of the game from the player, though no man can make a good umpire unless he has had experience as a player in first-class cricket. Theory alone is not enough. Other necessary qualifications are sound health – for the physical and mental strain is greater than is commonly realized – and good eyesight and hearing. Special attention is given to these last points at the medical examination which the selected umpires have to undergo every year. They are chosen annually at a meeting of county cricket captains held in December. Reports signed by both captains at every match at which they have officiated during the past year are then brought forward and considered. Three adverse reports, provided both captains agree, involve dismissal, and there is always a waiting list of younger men ready to fill the vacant place.

About a month before the beginning of the season each of the selected umpires receives from the secretary of the M.C.C. his list of fixtures for the year, together with the M.C.C. Instructions to Umpires brought up to date. The compilation of the fixture list is an intricate business, for a man may not be appointed to umpire in a match if he was formerly qualified to play for one of the counties concerned. Distance has also to be taken into account, for no travelling expenses are allowed.

On the average we officiate in about twenty-two matches a year. In each of those matches the umpires always "lose the toss" except when it rains. They are the first to arrive on the field and the last to leave it. They get no rest except during the intervals – unlike the players, who may spend a whole day in the pavilion. They are standing, perhaps under a hot sun, and they are concentrating on cricket all the time. The strain is greatest in a Test Match. The atmosphere then is electric and the fate of the Ashes may rest on an umpire's decision.

One often hears it said that quick decision is among the qualifications of a good umpire; but I consider it unwise to make decisions too quickly, especially under the new l.-b.-w. rule. It is far better to take a second or two to think than to be rushed into a hasty decision by a smart appeal. An umpire cannot afford to make many mistakes. If a batsman makes a mistake it may be called "bad luck." When an umpire makes a mistake it is a "bad decision," and as such it is marked up against him. The most difficult decision to make, in my opinion, is on an appeal for a catch on the leg side when the ball is near the batsman's body and his bat, pads, and gloves are all tucked up together. Next to that comes a close "run out." The new l.-b.-w. rule has increased the umpire's difficulties considerably. Personally, I treat it in the same way as I did the snick rule. I give the batsman out only when he plays back. I do not consider that the new rule has improved off-side play. It has undoubtedly helped the bowler. Last summer many decisions were called for on the ground of bad light. This is always one of the most trying questions with which an umpire is faced – even worse than a wet wicket. We can do something to dry a wet wicket, but we cannot yet control the light, even to oblige the spectators.

I am sometimes asked how I count the balls in an over. I have used the same six pebbles for the purpose ever since I started umpiring sixteen years ago. I hold them in my hand and drop one into my pocket as each ball is delivered. Those pebbles have done duty now in thirty Test Matches.

I was young when I began as an umpire – so young that when I arrived at the ground for my first match at Northampton the gatekeeper asked if I was a player. When I said, "No, I am an umpire," he replied, "You've come to the wrong ground. This is a first-class match." He is still on duty there, and we enjoy a laugh over it whenever we meet again.

From the Scoring Box

BY H. STRUDWICK

25 *May* 1937, *M.C.C. Number*. Scoring in first-class matches is by no means the dull occupation that some people imagine; at times there is even plenty of excitement.

Each county has its own scorer, who goes round with the team. But although the two scorers at each county match are generally old county players the scoring box is neutral. Even a visitor to the box, if he begins to take sides, is politely told to keep quiet.

Some scorers give more details than others. There are score-books which have the spaces not only for the batting order but for times of going in and out for each batsman, and for the bowling analysis; others, besides all this, have places for the scorer to record the direction of the wind at the beginning of each day's play, the state of the weather, the chances missed, stating by which fielder and where he was fielding, and the state of the wicket. Although "weather dull" is usually a fairly safe description – at least, it was all last summer – it is not always easy to say what is the state of the wicket, and one sometimes wonders who will want to know that in 20 years' time. Again, when a player misses a very hard chance the scorer is often in doubt whether it was a possible catch or not.

The scorers see more of the game than any spectator, and should become good judges of a player, for we have to watch every ball bowled and to know every fieldsman and where he is fielding. Above all, we have to keep our eyes on the umpire, for he is dictator of every run that is recorded, and indicates how the runs shall be put down by a series of signs. . .

When the score-board goes wrong when a batsman has scored nearly 50 or 100 it always seems so much worse. If he is credited wrongly with runs and gets out before increasing his score the wrong total may be telegraphed all over England before it can be rectified. If a batsman comes in out of his turn, or a bowler is changed, and the wrong number is put up on the board even for a few seconds I get a ring from some impatient member through the office to ask if the board is right, though nearly every time I have rung up the score-board to call their attention to the mistake.

At the fall of each wicket we total up the score and the analysis to see if they balance. Then we send down the scores to the printers and answer any questions the representatives of the Press wish to ask. If it is a new man they want to know his life story. By this time the next batsman has taken his first ball.

Two examples will show the vital need for concentration. I was scoring in the Surrey trial match by myself last year. Someone opened the door behind me to ask a question. I turned round to answer him, and on looking back to the field of play I saw one of the batsmen leaving and Alan Peach pitching the ball in the air. I did not know how he was out, and though there were two men on the score-board they could not tell me. I had taken a chance and put down "caught Peach" before I received a 'phone message to say that the last man was out l.-b.-w. Again, in one of our Surrey trial games Geary was batting and Brooks keeping wicket. A ball was sent down and the wicket-keeper took it. I put down a dot in the book, and on looking up saw Geary walking away from his wicket. There had been no appeal either from the bowler or the wicket-keeper. I sent out to know what had happened. It appears that Geary had been lifting his back foot just as Brooks was returning the ball to the bowler. One of the fieldsmen had pointed this out to Brooks, so next time he did it Brooks went through the action of throwing the ball back, but did not loose the ball, and nipped off the bails. Geary was stumped, and I had missed Brooks's action by dropping my head to put down the dot.

I had an exciting time at the Oval in 1934 when Oxford University were playing Surrey. For some reason Oxford never have a scorer, and it is very difficult to score by oneself in those matches because members of the University team have so many pretty caps. A man you have noted in the morning as So-and-so, wearing such-and-such a cap, may be wearing a different one after lunch, and perhaps another after tea. I remember one scorer saying that he put down "a dirty pair of trousers" against one man; but he had changed them at lunch time.

In the Oxford v. Surrey match of 1934 Oxford declared, leaving Surrey 103 to win in less than an hour. Surrey got the runs for the loss of five wickets. They made a slow start, but the finish was very exciting. It was a severe test for the single-handed scorer, for as fast as one man was out there was another at the crease. There were four catches, and while I was trying to find out who took the catch, enter the fall of the wicket, and send it down to the printer, besides keeping the scores of the batsmen and the analysis and keeping my eye on the board, the next man was in.

The most difficult decision for the scorers to see is when a batsman plays at a ball which is very near his pads and the wicket-keeper takes the ball. It might be either l.-b.-w. or caught at the wicket. Both bowler and wicket-keeper appeal, and the appeal covers both a catch or l.-b.-w. The umpire gives the man out and leaves us to guess how he was out. When a wicket-keeper catches a man out and puts down the wicket with the batsman out of his ground both umpires may be giving the batsman out, but the catch stands. If a ball touches a batsman's leg and the wicket-keeper takes the ball and puts the wicket down and the man is out of his ground the right decision is "run out." I never agree with this decision.

Of all the good, bad, and indifferent score boxes I have worked in, I like my own at the Oval best. But the box at Lord's, I suppose, is best of all.

There the man who works the board sits at the end of the scorers' table. With a turn of a wheel rather like the steering-wheel of a motor-car he puts up the numbers almost before the run is completed. There is no worry for scorers at Lord's.

The most remarkable figures I have put down against a bowler were a hat trick and nine balls to one over to Parker, of Gloucestershire. I have recorded six 4's in one over to Peach against Warwickshire. Two successive overs off Iddon in the Rest of England v. The Champion County in 1928 were 0 6 2 4 4 6, 4 6 1 6 6 2.

The Times M.C.C. Number was a 24-page tabloid supplement to the issue of 25 May 1937, commemorating the 150th anniversary of the club. It was re-published as a book, price 1s. (5p), and subsequently reprinted because of an error in a picture caption (opposite page 48, where Storer had been incorrectly identified as Mr. G. R. Langdale in the Derbyshire championship-winning team of 1936).

Ye Batte and Balle

26 *May* 1937, *Leading Article.* By a melancholy coincidence, on the very day when *The Times* M.C.C. Number showed Broadhalfpenny Down through the genial eyes of SIR JOHN SQUIRE, news came of the threat to alter the Bat and Ball Inn, once the clubhouse of the Hambledon Club. Our Special Correspondent's account this morning may cause SIR JOHN to regret that, in shortening his quotation from JOHN NYREN, he left out one regular sixer of a phrase – "the immeasurable villainy of our vintners." In NYREN's day their offence (which he ascribes, in the Peacockian mode, to "the march of intellect") was trying to water the beer. Clearly JOHN NYREN and his amanuensis or collaborator, COWDEN CLARKE, were not afraid of the law of libel; but certain moderns are surely chafing at not being able to open their shoulders and hit out equally hard at the present successors of those im-measurably villainous ones. Every age has its tender spot. In the eighteenth century it was victuals and drink. If the twentieth century should but sip at the punch and the barleycorn gulped down by NYREN's "fine brawn-faced fellows" of Hampshire farmers it would soon be very sorry for itself and grateful for any immeasurably villainous reduction of the alcoholic content. The twentieth century's own tender spot is historical association. And that is what the proposal to alter the Bat and Ball inn has touched. The eighteenth century would have welcomed any alteration or destruction which allowed room for more people to drink more punch and barleycorn. The twentieth century drinks, by comparison, little barleycorn and less punch, and both much weaker than the Nyrenian brews; but touch the historic inn, and it is up in arms. And the protests have come not only from the "stage army," as

thwarted Vandals like to call it, the recurrent procession of National Trust, S.P.A.B., and C.P.R.E. The M.C.C. itself – no highbrow pack of aesthetes and sentimentalists – objects to the proposal; and so does the Petersfield Rural District Council.

The brewers wish to enlarge the Bat and Ball. That must mean either that they have, or that they hope to have, more custom than the inn can now conveniently satisfy. SIR JOHN SQUIRE writes of "an occasional slumbrous carter" as its only patron nowadays. But has acutest memories of Broad-halfpenny are of mid-winter; and another account, inspired at the season "when primroses are out at Hambledon," gives an impression of more activity:–

> Hither, as of old
> Come players for the game: moon follows moon,
> Still the same happy echoes fill the wold,
> Still from the down's deep wood the pigeons croon,
> About the old inn parlour village shoon
> (Ale-fragrant still the air) go clattering,
> And gardeners bowl and blacksmiths catches fling,
> And bat from ball cracks music.

If MR. ERIC PARKER is right, the brewers' need for more space may be a present need. If SIR JOHN SQUIRE is right, it may be a need that will be created by the provision of the supply. If, that is, the motorist and the cyclist and the hiker learn that at the Bat and Ball – a historic inn in a spot of singular beauty, alongside the cradle of (modern) cricket and rich in associations and relics – there is what the roadside notices ambiguously call "accommodation" (whether it includes a swimming-pool and a ballroom or only means comfortable chairs and a cocktail bar), then those pilgrims in search of natural beauty and historic interest, of the quaint, the old-world and the truly rural, will make their way thither and reward the brewers' expenditure. In either case, be the demand a fact or a prophecy, it would surely be wise to leave unaltered the parlour, the one public room, which was the Hambledon men's clubroom.

Ladies at the Oval

Lessons for Men Players

FROM OUR CRICKET CORRESPONDENT [R. B. VINCENT]

12 *July* 1937. The third and deciding Test Match between the ladies of England and Australia was begun at the Oval on Saturday, and at the close of play Australia had scored 201 runs for the loss of eight wickets.

Those who had not before been privileged to watch a cricket match between two teams of ladies of the highest class – and I admit that I had never attended such a ceremony – must have left the ground amazed at what they had seen. The normal spectator no doubt approached the ground with the impression that he would be granted no more than a curious experience of ladies attempting to achieve something beyond their physical power. What he did see was a game played with technical efficiency, liveliness, and enthusiasm, which made the thought of a county match seem humdrum. In every respect, in bowling, batting, and fielding alike, there was a lesson to be learned by men who relatively potter about at their game. Strokes were made, gallant and fluent strokes, which gathered pace as they reached the farthest end of the Oval; the bowling remained tidy until the last over of the day; and the fielding was brilliant. I had been falsely told that ladies could not throw. I hope those who had formed that idea were present on Saturday to see a lady fling the ball back from Sandham's particular corner near the gasometer, bang, full pitch into the wicket-keeper's hands.

If one may for one moment criticize what in other respects was a wonderful display it would be to say that the backing-up was a little haphazard with just too much leaping about to save overthrows. As to the placing of the field only those who thoroughly understand ladies' cricket are entitled to speak, but it did seem that at times it was a little widespread, although there was some great work done close in on both sides of the wicket, and, joy of joys, there was a lady standing at the good old-fashioned position which used to be called "point."

Australia began their innings with Miss P. Holmes and Mrs. M. Peden, both of New South Wales, to the bowling of Miss Belton and Miss Maclagan. Miss Belton, who managed to bring the ball back from the Vauxhall end, bowled at a pace sufficiently fast for the wicket-keeper, Miss Snowball, to stand back. And here a word of praise for Miss Snowball, who throughout the day took the ball cleanly and with ease, even when it had to be done with one hand on the leg-side. Miss Belton all but bowled Mrs. Peden with the first ball of the match, and Mrs. Peden having survived that discomfort went on to play an innings which consisted mainly of short-armed prods. She was clearly the Woodfull of the side. Miss Maclagan tossed the ball well up, with some variation of flight which was certainly deceiving. Miss Holmes, who has a noble stance at the wicket, with her left shoulder pointing down the pitch, played beautiful strokes from the moment that she was in. They were strokes made with a free uplift of the bat and a beautiful follow-through. She drove one ball to the off from Miss Belton which counted 3, all run, and then swept Miss Maclagan away to the square-leg boundary.

Miss Whelan came on at Miss Belton's end when 19 runs had been scored, followed by a quarter of an hour's hiatus while rain was falling. When they came out again Mrs. Davis bowled from the Pavilion end, and nothing in the day was better worth the watching. She bowls left-handed with the body arched and that free swing of the arm which reminds one of Rhodes or Blythe. High praise it may sound, but it is true, for hers is indeed a perfect action. She just had time to get Mrs. Peden out with a ball of exact length before a deluge of rain fell. In a quarter of an hour there were vast pools of water lying on the ground, and there were grave fears that never a ball would be bowled again all day.

Ladies, however, have their own ideas about the conditions in which cricket can be played. So soon as the rain stopped, and it had been falling then for two hours, the captains and umpires dragged out the groundsman and told him, no doubt quite plainly, that they wanted to get on with the match. So out they went again soon after 3 o'clock with every chance of the ladies who were fielding in the deep slipping up and being drowned.

The pitch was then playing dead easy. Mrs. Davis continued to bowl from the Pavilion end, steadily enough, but she could not make sufficient haste off the pitch to beat either Miss Holmes or Miss Pritchard. The batting of these two ladies was entirely delightful. Miss Holmes made her strokes with the left leg flung down the pitch; Miss Pritchard, who is a busy batswoman, was more inclined to jump down the pitch. Together they took the score to 84 before Miss Pritchard, who had made some grand drives to the off, was bowled by England's captain. Miss Antonio is another batswoman who looks for runs; on this occasion she was, maybe, a little greedy, for she had some narrow squeaks when nibbling at the ball just outside the off stump. In the end she fell that way.

Miss Holmes having done most of the scoring during their partnership reached her 50 with a sweep to leg which sent the ball with a crash against the boundary boarding. There followed a period of shockingly bad light, but if it had been pitch dark these ladies would have insisted on playing. Miss George clouted the ball on the off-side, while Miss Holmes both in attack and defence played with an absolutely straight bat. If a treatise on ladies' cricket is written, it well might include illustrations of the methods of Miss Holmes. The score was mounting hopefully for Australia when Miss George was out to a well-judged catch at deep-square leg and then England came in to their own, thanks to the bowling of Mrs. Davis. She bowled Miss Smith, had Miss Holmes leg-before-wicket to a twiddler, and then held a miraculous catch off her own bowling, high and wide to the left, to send back Miss McLarty.

By way of variation Miss Taylor came on to bowl round the wicket from the Vauxhall end, well enough to get Miss Walsh out. But Miss Hudson and Miss Flaherty refused to give Mrs. Davis, who in her second spell had taken four wickets very cheaply, any more encouragement. Australia certainly had shown some signs of wobbling in the middle of the innings, but theirs is a fine score which will want some passing.

AUSTRALIA 207 for 9 dec (P. Holmes 70; J. Davis 5 for 31) and 224
(H. Pritchard 66, K. Smith 45)
ENGLAND 308 for 9 dec (E. Snowball 99, M. Hide 64) and 9 for 3
Score after first day: Australia 201 for 8
Match drawn

E. A. McDonald

FROM OUR CRICKET CORRESPONDENT [R. B. VINCENT]

23 *July* 1937. The death of E. A. McDonald, who was killed in a motor accident near Bolton yesterday morning, will be mourned all the world over where cricket is played. His career was short – all too short – in first-class cricket, but during that time he had established himself as one of the greatest fast bowlers of all time. No man in so brief a period can have achieved such great things or have granted such pleasure as he did.

The great men of this, or even of a previous, generation who bowled habitually and successfully at more than a fast-medium pace are few in number, McDonald was one of them. The horrors which England suffered in the summer of 1921, when Armstrong's team conquered the best that an after-War England could offer, was attributed to a great extent to the combination of Gregory and McDonald, and of the two, with all due respect, I believe McDonald to have been the greater match-winner. Gregory was fiercely, ferociously fast; McDonald was the more restrained, the more accurate, and the more dependable. He had above all the ability, such as Lockwood had, to bowl at his full pace when the wicket was slow, and sawdust was poured into the foot-holes. He was a bowler – and a man – of moods.

It was said by the ungenerous cricketer that he bowled short to intimidate the batsman. That I am sure he would never have done. He said to me once on the Aigburth ground that if the batsman walked away from his wicket the ball had a habit of following the batsman. A fairer comment could not be made, for above all he was a fast bowler. Whatever his record may be, of his technique there can be no question.

Once there was shown in a cinematograph exhibition a slow-motion picture of McDonald which well might have been distributed to every club and every school. The slow, almost lazy, arrival from the take-off of his run, like an animal which peeps its head from rushes; the gradual acceleration of pace; and then, with the left shoulder full to the bowler's bat, an action which was perfect and joyous to watch.

McDonald was born in Tasmania in 1892, and having gone to Melbourne worked his way through various forms of cricket until he came to be recognized as a fast bowler. Before he came to England he had played in three Test Matches against J. W. H. T. Douglas's team in the winter of 1920. During that season of Test Matches he took six English wickets at a cost of 65 runs. He then came to England with Armstrong's side, and in those Test Matches took 27 wickets with an analysis of 24. .

Then came his association with Lancashire in 1924. In the season of 1925 he took 205 wickets in all matches, and later relapsed to League cricket. His record, whether it be for Australia, for Lancashire, or in League cricket can never explain the bowler that he was. Those that saw him bowl will never forget.

Underhand Bowling
A Lost Art

FROM A CORRESPONDENT

28 *August* 1937. So far as I can ascertain not a single over of underhand bowling has been seen in county cricket this season. Two county captains of my acquaintance say they would willingly make use of it in an emergency – *e.g.*, when two stodgy batsmen have dug themselves in – but they have nobody in their sides with any practical knowledge of it. If an expert were available one of them admitted, the attitude of the crowd would have to be considered. His appearance as a bowler would be greeted with derisive laughter – for the average spectator thinks the "lob" is as absurd as its name, and a childish device for giving easy runs to the enemy. For this and other reasons underhand bowling seems to be extinct in first-class cricket just as in first-class baseball the underhand pitcher has been finally extinguished, though he could jerk very nearly as his modern successors can throw and had a command of the curves.

In club cricket also the "lobster" (apt fishy facetiousness!) is despised, and some years have elapsed since I saw him plying his craft for a suburban eleven of good standing. He then took four wickets at a reasonable cost. Afterwards he told me that he had been equally successful on a Sussex green, and that his captain had privately apologized to each of his victims for subjecting him to an ordeal suspected to be unsportsmanlike. As you descend through the lower circles of cricket you find the schoolboy's aversion from "sneaks" reappearing as a grown-up obsession.

The writer's qualifications for advocating a revival of this lost art must be briefly stated. He has studied it ever since he was at his "Prep.," and in the course of an obscure career has taken over 1,500 wickets. He never bowled in a county match, but has beguiled a number of county batsmen into getting themselves out. In his young days, he enjoyed much country-house cricket, and Alfred Lyttelton would introduce him as "a rare monster, a *left-hand* lob-bowler." And his friend in later years, Arthur Croome, Master of Games, thought he could at times produce some nasty stuff.

Despite the brilliant example of G. Simpson-Hayward, who went on first for "Fostershire" and would take his 100 wickets in county matches season after season, he is not so foolish as to believe that underhand bowling can ever again be made the main part of an attack. The batsman gets a much quicker sight of it than of the deliveries of a bowler whose "hand brushes his ear," as the saying is. The underhand bowler cannot flight the ball as could

Rhodes, who made it wander in the air like a lost soul. Though fast-medium pace can be secured (as it was by D. L. A. Jephson), only a jerk is able to make it really fast – and that is illegal, being an underhand throw. [Such bowlers have been known to profit in this matter by the forgetfulness of umpires.] But accuracy and varied spin are more easily attained than by the overhand bowler.

The higher the action, the more effective the delivery must be. Nyren says of the majestical David Harris: "He would bring the ball from under the arm by a twist, and nearly as high as his armpit, and with this action *push*, as it were, from him. How it was that the balls acquired the velocity they did by this mode of delivery I could never comprehend." The writer once saw a village bowler who had this Harrisian knack; though slow through the air, he was fast off the pitch, and had to be carefully watched.

But it is the psychological factor – *unusualness* – which would make underhand bowling dangerous in these days. Meeting it perhaps for the first time even a first-rate batsman might become too cautious or too ready to take risks. More often than not he would expect, and be expected by the crowd, to set the figures flickering on the score-board. That is why bad lobs can be strangely effective. The classic instance is of course Alfred Lyttelton's four wickets for 19 against Australia. W. G., the English captain, said his lobs were very bad, when he ordered him back into his wicket-keeping gloves and pads, and an eye-witness told me some were "like a snail," and one bounced three times. . . . Perhaps enough has now been said to justify this plea for the revival of a venerable, if unvenerated, art of cricket.

Maurice Tate

FROM OUR CRICKET CORRESPONDENT [R. B. VINCENT]

21 *October* 1937. Cricket this last season saw the passing of two great players in Hendren and Sandham, and now comes the news that Tate will no longer be the pride of Sussex. Pride he has been, an honour richly deserved, not only on the Hove ground but also away in the North of England; greeted and recognized as one of the greatest cricketers of his generation.

The son of an illustrious father, who bowled his heart out when Sussex claimed the greatest batsmen of the time but had small answer when the other side went in, Maurice, too, had to work uncommon hard for his county, and also for his country. England in slender years sorely lacked the length bowler; Geary there was – Larwood was not allowed because he bowled too fast and too straight – and in these years since a new cricket was born after the War Tate was the model bowler, the successor to J. T. Hearne. He had not quite the fire, the versatility of Barnes, but he was on all occasions a "bowler." Some say he was inclined to bowl just a shade short of a length;

those who kept wicket to him could tell how fast the ball came into their hands. His technique was perhaps surpassed by the cheerful complexion he gave to the game. His was essentially a jolly game of cricket. He first played for Sussex in 1912, when he was only 17 years old.

The War followed, and he was not the great man we knew him until 1924, when he and his captain, A. E. R. Gilligan, bowled South Africa out at Birmingham for 30 runs – the smallest total ever recorded in a Test Match in this country. He then went to Australia to establish a record which still stands, taking 38 wickets during the series of Test Matches. From this time onward he established a record unsurpassed in this country. In eight successive seasons he made 1,000 runs and took 100 wickets, and on three occasions, in 1923-24-25, he took more than 200 wickets in a season. He has taken more wickets than ever any Sussex bowler has done before, and will be remembered wherever cricket is played long after his retirement.

The Game's the Thing

28 *May* 1938, *Leading Article*. DON BRADMAN became once more the hero of the piece – or should we say of the play? – when he established a double record yesterday by scoring a thousand runs before the end of May for the second time in his career, and scoring the thousandth on an earlier date than anybody before him. To be sure he was almost beaten in this respect by EDRICH, of Middlesex, who got to within nineteen of it some days ago; and WALTER HAMMOND has still a few days in which to equal the feat of making his May thousand for the second time in his career. The Gloucestershire batsman did it before in 1927, and the Australian captain did it on his first appearance in this country in 1930. Curiously enough, BRADMAN then completed the thousand at Southampton in the match against Hampshire, just as he did yesterday.

He is a truly great batsman, and a great captain, in spite of that pardonable lapse at the Oval the other day, about which scores of letters continue to reach this office. Hardly any of them, it must be admitted, have so far been in MR. BRADMAN's favour – except indeed our own Cricket Correspondent's, who thinks that the Oval crowd treated him scurvily. The Australian side had scored 528 (the captain's own innings, not for the first or the last time, having been the highest of the innings), and Surrey replied with a mere 271, which left them 257 behind. Now, if the Australian captain wanted to win the match, he ought obviously to have tried to get Surrey out a second time as quickly as possible. But not a bit of it. He sent in a couple of his middle-of-the-side batsmen to pile up the runs. His reason was intelligible. The team have had bad luck in the way of accidents and minor ailments – E. S. WHITE had, unfortunately, to be added to the list of casualties yesterday – and, with his eye fixed on the first Test Match about fifteen days ahead, he did not want to put a heavy strain on the best of the regular bowlers who were left to him. And he did not like the idea of doing what he could with the talent that remained. So the match dragged on without any possibility of a result; and, when DON BRADMAN eventually declared and led his men out of the pavilion to field and bowl, he had the strange experience of being booed by a section of the crowd all the way out to the middle of the ground.

It was a sad moment. But, after all, the spectators had come to see a match, not an uncompetitive exhibition of batting; and they had paid their two shillings, and they did not think it was cricket. And MR. BRADMAN himself would be the first to agree that cricket would be ruined if his example were followed. Moreover first-class cricket, when all is said and done, can only flourish on the grist which the spectators bring to its mill; so they feel entitled to have a voice in the matter – even if the Oval voice was a bit raucous, and perhaps rather hostile in its tone to a great cricketer and a great gentleman, whose whole soul is set, not on personal records, but on winning those Test Matches. Therefore he wants, as our Cricket Correspondent says, to conserve the energies of his team. The point is intelligible, but cricket will lose all its flavour if such considerations are allowed to count more than playing the game to win it.

Test Match Televised

25 *June* 1938. The televisor brought yesterday's Test Match at Lord's into the homes of thousands. The television cameras were swung smoothly about the field so that every detail of the play could be followed from the moment the ball left the bowler's hand till it reached the fielder or the boundary. The transmission was a striking example of the advance in television and the great improvement in receiving apparatus. So successful was the television of the match that a further transmission was given from 6.15 p.m. till the close of play to enable City workers to see the match in their homes. To-day the match will be televised from 11.30 to 12.30, 2.30 to 3.30, at 3.50, and again, it is hoped, for a quarter of an hour before the close of play.

27 *June* 1938. Test cricket was the delight of television viewers on Friday and Saturday, and long periods of play were visible, morning, noon, and evening. It is a happy thing to be one with the Test crowd in your own home, and to see the batsman sending the ball to the boundary and to hear the roar of the crowd. The transmissions were indeed excellent, and at times the viewer must have felt himself almost on the pitch.

Last week was the right time to televise R. C. Sherriff's delightful comedy *Badger's Green*, for it centres in a game of village cricket which changed the course of events and saved the village from the depredations of a company promoter who wanted to ruin it. It was produced by Mr. Eric Crozier, with a film of village cricket on a real village green inserted in the middle of the play to make it more actual, which was most successful.

England Declare at 903 for 7

Hutton Breaks All Records

FROM OUR CRICKET CORRESPONDENT [R. B. VINCENT]

24 *August* 1938. The Test Match at the Oval made considerable progress yesterday, for after England's innings had been declared closed with their score standing at 903 for seven wickets the Australians lost three good wickets for 117 runs. For Australia it was indeed an unlucky day, as D. Bradman when running up to the wicket to bowl fell down and sustained a fracture of the tibia, the larger of the two bones in the leg. He was carried from the field and soon after the close of play he was conveyed to his hotel. It was stated officially that he will take no further part in the match.

As there are doubts as to whether J. H. Fingleton will be able to take any further part in the match Australia are in a poor way to answer so huge a score.

As befits a time-limitless Test Match still more records were broken yesterday. In the first place Hutton by passing Bradman's score of 334 at Leeds in 1930 played the highest individual innings in the history of matches between England and Australia. It was also much the longest that has been played in these games. England's total also easily surpassed that which either country had previously amassed, the Australians having made 729 for six wickets before their innings was declared closed at Lord's in 1930. The other new record of note which was established was the partnership for the sixth wicket between Hutton and Hardstaff, which produced 215 runs, so beating the 186 by Hammond and Ames at Lord's earlier this season.

For Hutton himself the match has been a triumphant one, and when once the reason of a time-limitless match is recognized it must be said that no one could have played his part more adequately. Throughout his innings, while making it his main object to remain as long as possible at the wicket, he took every opportunity which he considered safe to score runs. Whether this is a desirable form of cricket is a matter of opinion, but the majority of a crowd of 31,000 who were at the Oval yesterday seemed thoroughly to enjoy it.

The Australians with their limited supply of bowling never wilted. W. J. O'Reilly and L. O'B. Fleetwood-Smith, both of whom were called upon to do an enormous amount of work, continued throughout to keep a remarkably good length, and keener fielding could not possibly have been demanded.

England's score when play was begun in the morning stood at 634 for five wickets. Hutton then being 300 and Hardstaff 40. O'Reilly and Fleetwood-

Smith began the bowling on a wicket which as yet was not likely to offer them much encouragement, and the large crowd sat in the sunshine waiting for the moment when Hutton assuredly must achieve his record score. Actually he had to work very hard for his runs, anxious as any man well might be in such circumstances, and those who were prepared to watch stroke play rather than revel in statistics had most to admire in the batting of Hardstaff. Fleetwood-Smith was bowling exceedingly well, and when he bowled on the leg stump to a fine short-leg and a forward short-leg, with no one in the slips, he wanted a deal of watching. Hardstaff once glided a ball away to fine-leg, but he was once drawn out to pop a ball up in the middle of the pitch before he reached his 50 with a lovely cut off O'Reilly's bowling. Bradman was again to the fore with some glorious fielding on the off side, and it was hereabouts remarked how splendid in fact the fielding of the whole Australian team had been throughout their ordeal.

Fleetwood-Smith took as many men away from the off side as he could afford when bowling to Hutton, but he had to move one back when Hardstaff was taking the strike. Hutton once was beaten by a leg-break from Fleetwood-Smith which whizzed across past the off stump, an error he covered by hitting the next ball away to deep square-leg. The score had been taken to 670, with Hardstaff taking every opportunity he could find of exhibiting his lovely off drive, when Waite and McCabe came on with the fourth new ball of the innings. That phase of attack did not last long before O'Reilly, once more starting off with a no-ball, came on again. Hutton was certainly taking his time in compiling his record-shattering runs, for he scored 21 runs only during the first hour of play, but he sent the 700 up with a late cut off Waite which flew away down to the pavilion railings. He wanted only four more runs when O'Reilly provided him with a no-ball, but he missed it, and he had to wait some considerable time before he received a ball which he considered safe to cut and to pass Bradman's 334.

This was the occasion for a great demonstration of praise, combined with relief; the entire crowd rose to its collective feet, the cheering was prolonged, and the Australian team, led by Bradman, who for some time had been lurking close to Hutton's bat, shook hands with him. The opportunity was taken for a waiter to bring out some refreshments, and thereafter the business of the time-limitless Test Match was continued. Record after record was broken, while Hardstaff, still continuing to bat elegantly and easily, approached closer to his individual century. It was noticed that McCabe was occasionally making the ball turn, but Barnes when he was given a trial provided little difficulty, and with O'Reilly given a rest in the deep field the luncheon interval arrived with the score 759.

Hardstaff reached his 100 with an off-drive off Fleetwood-Smith in the first over after luncheon. A few more runs and a miracle occurred; Hutton hit a ball from O'Reilly not only in the air but straight into the hands of cover-point, and an innings which it had seem would last so long as he was provided with a partner came to an end. He had scored his 364 runs in 13 hours and a quarter, during which time he had hit thirty-five 4's and had given an exhibition of self-control which it would be hard to surpass. Quite apart from the raids which have been made upon Test Match records Hutton's was the highest innings which has ever been played on the Oval ground, the previous highest being the 357 not out of the illustrious Bobby Abel for Surrey against Somerset in 1899.

Australia having rid themselves of an obstacle which looked likely to become permanent, there arrived the cheerful Wood to cause them more trouble. Wood, no doubt considering that the state of the game permitted some freedom, disclosed some of the strokes which he employs when Yorkshire have gained a reasonable lead over Lancashire. He was especially partial to the sweep to leg, caring little whether the bowler was O'Reilly, Fleetwood-Smith, or anybody else. Bradman considered the occasion to be appropriate to try out Hassett as a bowler, and he even treated himself to a short spell. Hardstaff had by then become thoroughly infected with the Test Match bacillus, and the crowd must be excused if they found his batting a little lethargic. The strokes were beautifully constructed, but their scoring value was at one time scarcely noticeable. He made a drive past cover-point off Fleetwood-Smith and another straight drive off O'Reilly which remain in the memory, but for the rest he relied mainly on deflections or pushes.

Wood when he had made 47 might have been caught at square-leg off Waite, and the partnership had produced 106 runs before Barnes held a catch off his own bowling to dismiss Wood and to allow another Yorkshireman to have a look at the bowling. Verity had not been in long when the accident occurred to Bradman, but Hardstaff found time to make some more strokes on the off side before the tea interval arrived and with it the surprising news that England's innings had been declared closed, news which could scarcely be believed until the groundsmen appeared on the scene with their light roller and paint-pot.

Australia began their innings at 5 o'clock, and five minutes later they had lost their first wicket. K. Farnes, who started the bowling from the Pavilion end to three slips and a gully, made the ball come off the pitch at a great pace, but it was Bowes in his first over from the other end who had C. L. Badcock caught at short mid-wicket before a run had been scored. S. McCabe made three good forcing strokes to the direction of long-on off Farnes, Leyland having to toddle a long way to retrieve the ball, before he mistimed his stroke and was caught at square-leg. That was two wickets down for 19, a dismal enough start even without Bradman and Fingleton on the injured list. Hassett came to the rescue with an innings which, while it lasted, was a joy to watch. Twice in one over he turned balls from Farnes away to the leg boundary, and when Edrich came on he at once banged him away past square-leg.

Hassett was lucky to see one ball fly off his bat over the head of second slip, but in the same over he made a grand square cut. That, alas! was the end of an innings which was worthy of a proper cricket match, for in hooking a short ball from Edrich he hit the ball into the hands of long-leg. S. Barnes as soon as he was in crashed the ball square on the off side to the boundary. He was not particularly impressed when Verity came on, nor was he worried by a silly mid-off, and for all the anxiety that he and Brown showed Australia might well have been already piling up a big score. Brown made one exquisite leg glide off Verity, and if he was fortunate with one stroke which sent a ball from Edrich streaking under the hand of second slip, he was helping the runs along so well that the 100 went up when the innings was only 70 minutes old. First Farnes and then Bowes was tried again in an attempt to take one more wicket, and in one last endeavour Leyland, who bowled to three short-legs, was put on, but the day ended without any further incident.

> ENGLAND 903 for 7 dec (Hutton 364, Leyland 187, Hardstaff 169 not out, Hammond 59, Wood 53)
> AUSTRALIA 201 (W. A. Brown 69, A. L. Hassett 42, S. Barnes 41; Bowes 5 for 49) and 123 (B. A. Barnett 46; K. Farnes 4 for 63)
> Score after third day: England 903 for 7 dec; Australia 117 for 3
> *England won by an innings and 579 runs*

More Fame Comes to Pudsey

Day of Acute Tension

24 *August* 1938. Fame has come once more to Pudsey. This very plain little industrial town midway between Bradford and Leeds, with a name (pronounced Poodsa) that has been a blessing to many a comedian, like Wigan or Nether Wallop, was aglow yesterday. Round about midday the inhabitants of Pudsey were holding breath. In the homes, in the local inns, in the mills, and in the post-office the tension was acute. For once more a son of Pudsey was on the verge of a great achievement on the cricket field.

Years ago Tunnicliffe, known affectionately as Long John, had retrieved the name of Pudsey from humour. With Brown at the other wicket, he took part in many huge first-wicket partnerships for Yorkshire, and his agility in the slips has become a legend in those parts. Then came Sutcliffe, who, with Hobbs, has given the Australian bowlers gruelling hours in the heat of an Australian summer, and who, at the moment, is striving manfully to keep the Yorkshire flag flying while five of the county team are playing for England. And yesterday, one of those five, the *protégé* of Sutcliffe [*Hutton*], broke all records in Test Match cricket. He has become a fixture among the great men in *Wisden*, and the men of Pudsey are all wearing county caps.

Timeless Test Matches
Some Observations

FROM OUR CRICKET CORRESPONDENT [R. B. VINCENT]

15 *March* 1939. The welcome decision by those in authority at Durban yesterday that the exhausted players should be allowed to pack their bags and go home was an admission that there can be a limit to time-limitless Test Matches. Whether the M.C.C. team could have been transported in time to catch their boat or not, it seems to have been agreed that honours could rest easy, and that 10 days of such cricket was enough. Whatever may be said about this form of amusement, which bears as much resemblance to cricket as marathon dancing or pole squatting does to athletics, there is every respect to be paid to the players, and especially the English team.

It was a match in which no restriction was to be made as to the time taken in scoring runs, and South Africa, quite naturally, having won the toss, settled down to make the fullest use of a new wicket. It seemed after several days that they had achieved their object, and England, set the gigantic task of scoring 696 runs in order to win in the fourth innings, seemed to be in an impossible position. It appeared unlikely that the wicket, however carefully it had been manufactured, could endure for ever, but one day of rain and another day of rest on the Sunday gave England renewed hope, for when rolled the pitch became bound together, and the players were given a rest of which physically and mentally they were in greater need than their opponents.

When the game was continued on Monday it was the South African side that had to bear the strain of toiling all day and watching the match gradually slip out of their grasp. England, for their part, adapted themselves entirely to the circumstances, and the play of Edrich in particular, who has gallantly belied the unkind things that have been said of him, and of P. A. Gibb, W. R. Hammond, and Paynter as well, deserves the approval of even the most censorious Australian critic. It was without question a great feat, but one cannot help feeling that it should never have been demanded of them, and that such misapplied courage will never again be required either in this country or in South Africa, where opinion, quite clearly, is against this form of the game.

It is, and always has been, an admitted fact that time is an essential factor in a game of true cricket, and it is impossible to understand why, because the game happens to be between two countries, the time limit should be discarded. Once any regard for time is ignored, the essence of the cricket departs and the game resolves itself into a spurious run-making competition, in which little matters but the establishment of so-called "records." Those who were at the Oval last August remember the grotesque situation which culminated in tragic comedy, and this last pitiful example at Durban can only have strengthened their opinion. Certainly it is absurd to expect a team to go halfway round the world to watch rain falling, as it fell at Old Trafford last year, but there must be some middle line between no play and endless play.

The suggestion put forward by M.C.C. to the Australian Board of Control that the duration of a Test Match should be limited by the hours actually available for play and not by days, during which there might be rain, must surely be the sensible solution. Nothing can be done to make cricketers complete a match during days of rain, but something can be done to insist that they should arrive at some conclusion at the end of a specified number of playing hours. If they cannot do so then the game is drawn, and there is no harm in that, provided that each has had a fair chance of winning. But to ask lovers of cricket to accept a state of affairs which entails 10 days without providing a result is beyond reason, and one can only hope that this is, indeed, the end.

The Hon. Robert Lyttelton

9 *November* 1939. Princess Antoine Bibesco writes:–

Certain families possess defined flavours – Cecils, Churchills, Cavendishes, Lytteltons. The aroma pleases or prejudices – Bob Lyttelton belonged to his family, but even in an age of individualists he would have stood out as an individual. When you say of him "a great gentleman" it is the gentleman who benefits by the phrase.

He was a natural writer. Told that an extract from a cricket report he had written [*his account of Cobden's match-winning over in the 1870 University match, published in The Badminton Library* Cricket] was included in "Q's" anthology of English prose he could hardly believe it. Not that he was modest – he did not need to be, he was himself. His family sagas, rich with his own humour, were untainted either by admiration or censure. Figure after figure emerged intact without the misrepresentation of presentation. He had the supreme gift of the raconteur. The strong flavour of his personality never impeded the view. To those who knew him – in other words to those who loved him (it was the same thing) – his combination of dryness and warmth will remain a memory unforgettable and without possibility of counterfeit.

If cricket did not exist Bob Lyttelton would have created it. If sportsmen still exist his ghost will give them substance.

11 *November* 1939. Mr. A. A. Milne writes:–

I should like to add one story to the many which will be told of this enthusiastic lover of cricket, although, for reasons which will be seen, I feel a little diffident about telling it. I was introduced to him at a Test Match by a woman whose enthusiasms were more literary than sporting; and, to my great embarrassment, she could think of no better way of explaining me than by saying brightly, "This is Christopher Robin's father." Robert Lyttelton got the introduction back to its proper footing. Showing an interest which surprised me for a moment, he said, "Ah! Any relation to the Middlesex Robins?"

The Centenary Match at Rugby

FROM OUR SPECIAL CORRESPONDENT [U. A. TITLEY]

18 *June* 1941. There could hardly have been a more perfect day than yesterday at Rugby for the centenary celebration of Tom Brown's cricket match against M.C.C. On this occasion the school did rather worse than they did 100 years ago and were beaten by 118 runs, M.C.C. having declared at 149 for nine wickets. The school could only muster a modest 31, but considering what they were up against they might have fared even worse. J. Smith took six for eight. Luncheon, as on that other famous occasion, was taken in Old Big School, and two of those present formed a direct link with Tom Brown's team.

Both the headmaster and Sir Pelham Warner, who said that he was very happy to have lived to see this day, spoke of Mr. R. B. V. Currie and Mr. P. A. Landon. The former, a youthful 81, is a nephew of Currie Esq. major and Currie Esq. minor, while Mr. Landon, better known as vice-president of Trinity College, Oxford, is a great-great-grandson of Mr. Aislabie. Had M. M. Walford been able to accept an invitation to play, there would have been one more link. The presence of Sir Pelham Warner was extremely apt and his influence on cricket in general is too well known to need comment here. A more modern note was struck by the presence of a young gentleman who was alleged less than 12 hours earlier to have been throwing things much more dangerous than cricket balls at Germans.

The school won the toss and put M.C.C. in. This argued a certain distrust of their batting, which has been very variable on this season's wet wicket, but in the circumstances their policy was prudent, especially from the point of view of the large number of spectators – and they began well, too. R. H. Twining gave a chance at the beginning of the opening over and departed at the end of it. They had to wait some time for further success while R. I. Scorer and R. E. S. Wyatt had a long look at the bowling. Wyatt was at length out to a good catch and H. C. Munro followed before luncheon, when the score was 73 for three.

Afterwards E. R. T. Holmes got frolicsome, but Smith, to the school's regret, failed to disturb the rooks in the tops of the elms. The Boddington family had a private tussle and at 4 o'clock the M.C.C. declared. Wyatt bowled down Rugby's first two wickets before tea. The school's tale of woe continued afterwards and Smith bestirred himself to the extent of doing the hat-trick. R. E. S. Wyatt bowled very steadily and was rather too much of a handful for the boys. It was all over by a quarter to 6. Rugby may not have shone at batting, but at any rate most of their fielding was well up to scratch.

MCC 149 for 9 dec
RUGBY 31 (J. Smith 6 for 8, R. E. S. Wyatt 4 for 14)
M.C.C. won by 118 *runs*

A Festival Transplanted

12 *July* 1941, *Leading Article*. When the Derby is run at Newmarket there can be no complaint that the Eton and Harrow match becomes a movable feast, and to-day it will be played at Eton. In Tom Brown's match, recently celebrated, the venue seems to have been changed almost at the last moment "to the sorrow of those aspiring young cricketers who have been reckoning for the last three months on showing off at Lord's ground." Here is no such sudden disappointment, but sympathy is none the less due to those robbed by inexorable events of something of their birth-right. They are in better case than their elder brothers at the Universities who gain but makeshift blues; they will have the right caps, and these uncoupon'd, but Lord's is Lord's and there are moments that can never be recaptured. Among elder persons there will be many who find the change far from disagreeable; rejoicing not merely in green and open spaces but in the absence of tail coats and stiff collars. Nothing can ever again be so apoplectic as were such garments in a crowded carriage in the neighbourhood of Baker Street station in the dear, dead, smoky days of the old Underground. Since then, however, we have grown more in love with casual ways and demand "wentilation gossamer" almost as of right. If only the sun shines, as we are allowed to know it did in June, there will not to-day be many pleasanter spots than Agar's Plough.

With this change of battlefield comes a certain change of heart, and perhaps battlefield is no longer the right word.

> A gentleman's a-bowling
> And down the wickets go.

Their downfall will be duly acclaimed, but to a sensitive ear there may be something lacking, not merely in the volume of the shouts but in the raucous venom of them. Whatever happens, however tense the crisis, it is unlikely that elderly gentlemen will bury their faces in their hands, unable to endure the horrid spectacle, or leave the ground and wait palpitating to hear the issue outside. These amiable follies belong only to Lord's. On the face of it there has hardly ever been a more exciting match than last year's at Harrow, when, with comfortable victory in sight, the Eton wickets fell like corn before the sickle, and the last man had to go in to make, after an interval of delicious agony, the winning hit. Yet in fact the genuine agony was, by a consensus of opinion, never quite reached. Here and there a partisan may have been seen, like SIR HORACE MANN of old, "cutting about with his stick among the daisies"; but in the end both sides united in thinking that here was a good game with a capital finish, and went home neither overmuch elated nor depressed.

"There was too much levity about our game to-day," said old MR. SUTHERLAND many years ago at St. Andrews. Whether in brighter days the new spirit of vanity, almost bordering upon levity, will survive in our games no one can now tell. Doubtless we ought to hope so, but doubtless also the perfect admixture of emotion is not easy to attain. It would be a little sad to think that never again would there be that exquisite torture produced by a last over or a place-kick at goal on which the fate of empires appears, however fallaciously, to hang. As in far graver matters it is wisest not to prophesy, but simply to be glad that to-day at least we can watch a game of cricket with pleasure and without too much solemnity, likewise that we have become, if it may be so expressed, more one-day-minded. We no longer say that this is "only a one-day match." We have adjusted our point of view to the cricket that was good enough for the heroes of Hambledon; they not merely finished their match in a day but, in the words of WILLIAM BELDHAM, who lived twenty-seven miles off, "used to ride both ways the same day early and late." The players too have adapted themselves to this new order. To their cricket as to their more serious employments old NYREN might to-day transfer his famous description of the punch drunk at Broad Halfpenny and call it "good, unsophisticated, John Bull stuff."

Kenneth Farnes

24 *October* 1941. Pilot Officer Kenneth Farnes, R.A.F.V.R., whose death on active service at the age of 30 was announced in our later editions yesterday, was a fast bowler in the true sense in which the adjective is applied to Kortright, Lockwood, and Richardson, and to no other Englishman of his generation except Larwood. He was, perhaps, a bowler of moods – either destructively hostile or complacently amicable – but in his full fighting feathers he was a danger to any batsman in the world.

An easy and economical run up to the wicket was the prelude to a controlled delivery from a great height, and he had the pace to make the ball rise sharply and to excuse what in the case of others might have been regarded as a shortness of length. E. A. McDonald, that prince of modern fast bowlers, once remarked that when batsmen edged away from the wicket the ball was liable to follow them. Woe betide those, too, who ran away from Kenneth Farnes.

Son of Mr. Sidney H. Farnes and the late Mrs. Farnes, he was educated at the Royal Liberty School, Romford, and went to Pembroke College, Cambridge, in 1931 to gain his place in the University XI as a Freshman, having already had some experience of County cricket in the Essex XI. He again played in the University match in the following two years, and by then he had established himself as an outstanding bowler. In 1934 he played in two Test Matches against Australia in this country, and in 1938 was a regular member of England's team. He went out to Australia with G. O. Allen's side in the season 1936-37, and he took part in each of the Test Matches in South Africa under W. R. Hammond's captaincy in 1938-39. One of his most notable successes was in the Gentlemen and Players match of 1936, when he spread havoc among the professional batsmen. It would have required a George Gunn on that day to have tamed him. His progress on the cricket field was interrupted when he became a schoolmaster at Worksop College, but he has left a memory of a young man of a charming modesty and a gentleness of manner, who did much to lend distinction to amateur cricket at a time when talent was not easy to find.

28 *October* 1941. The Headmaster of Worksop College writes:–

The news of the death of Kenneth Farnes has come as a great shock to all who knew him at Worksop. To the majority of his countrymen the news has come of the loss of one of the greatest of fast bowlers; to masters and boys at this school it means the loss of a valued friend and counsellor. Farnes was an energetic and untiring teacher of History and Geography, and an able and much-loved Housemaster. To this latter position he was appointed at an unusually young age, and his success therein was largely due to the quite natural modesty of the man, which made him as willing to learn from boys as they were to learn from him. A giant in stature, he had that gentleness of voice and manner which so often accompanies great size and strength, and, though on the cricket-field he would rouse himself to devastating action, he never let his strength run away with him in his dealings with boys.

Sacred Turf

9 *May* 1942, *Leading Article*. Everything must give way to the winning of the war. So much being granted, many people whose patriotism is above suspicion must have been pleased to learn that, whereas parts of college gardens at Cambridge have been surrendered to vegetables, the turf of Fenner's remains untouched. That turf is primarily sacred in the eyes of cricketers as the track surrounding it is sacred in those of runners. To it belong the names of STUDDS and STEELS and LYTTELTONS, of MACAULAY and TINDALL and FITZHERBERT. Thousands of obscure mortals have drowsed pleasantly here in the sunshine or stood well wrapped up in the chilly Lent term watching the immortals at play. It has, moreover, its enduring place in literature. There

are many who do not care overmuch for blues but love their C.S.C., and, if
the tap of memory be turned on, can recite on the instant :–

> I have stood serene on Fenner's
> Ground indifferent to blisters,
> While the Buttress of the period
> Bowled me his peculiar twisters.

They may not be exactly aware who Buttress was any more than Mr. Micawber was aware what gowans might be, but they are moved by the thoughts of
their youth even as Mr. Micawber was when he joined fervently in Auld
Lang Syne.

Some there may be who having another background to their lives believe
that Fenner's has been spared its cabbages through some undue partiality,
but this is not so. We are expressly told that the grass which is daily mown
there has proved of exceptional value for cattle food. Fenner's like Todgers's
can do it when it chooses and it is doing its bit now. It is obviously too early
to assert that the cattle imbibe all unknowing some of the qualities of its
great men. It would be pleasant to think that a cow would come nearer to
jumping over the moon by dint of the grass on which some mighty high-
jumper has lightly laid his foot. But without indulging in such fantastic
speculations we know that, through Fenner's, the cow will be a more acceptable sacrifice in the cause of the nation's food.

That turf has for many of us a unique and venerable quality is beyond
doubt. Each blade of grass at Lord's and the Parks, Newmarket and Epsom,
Wimbledon, Twickenham and St. Andrews can give a peculiar thrill to
somebody, according to his tastes and his memories. Everything changes;
groundsmen and green-keepers are not the hide-bound slaves of tradition;
and even the most historic of turf is relaid. The young cricketer in his first
innings at Lord's is not playing on the same pitch whereon W. G. remembered
having in his youth picked up a handfull of small pieces of gravel. The pilgrim
holing out under critical eyes at St. Andrews is not in fact doing so on the
green where ALLAN ROBERTSON holed his last putt in his famous 79
against MR. BETHUNE of Blebo. But what matter if they hold fast to their
faith and think that they are? The principle is the same. On all these spots
there may be heard by ears properly attuned the sounds of heroes,

> sounds
> Of undistinguishable motion, steps
> Almost as silent as the turf they trod.

If to-day, with cricket once more upon us, they are mingled with the mooings
and bleatings of happily replete cattle, so much the better.

The Last Survivor

1 *August* 1943, *Leading Article*. When there dies the last survivor of some famous band of men it "leaves a gap in society." Even in these days when serious cricket seems dim enough, the death of T. W. GARRETT, the last of the Australians who played in the first Test Match, must send the mind roaming for an instant over battlefields that were once grim enough, but appear to-day wholly green and friendly. He was not the oldest of all such survivors, since there remains one illustrious player from COBDEN's year, 1870; but 1877 is sufficiently long ago and the Test Match marked the beginning of an epoch. How much the name of GARRETT means to the modern cricketer it is hard to say, but to those at least who have read their history it may still bring a sensation akin to terror, for he was an actor in two events which in their time seemed terrible indeed, the obliteration of landmarks and the opening of flood-gates. One was the defeat of the M.C.C. in a single day's play on the 27th of May, 1878; the other, on a second day of rain and puddles and ominous cloud, four years later, the first loss of the Ashes on the 28th of August. On that day GARRETT was one of the historic conference between innings at which SPOFFORTH declared that "This thing can be done" and done it was. A name always sounds the more stirring when it is indissolubly linked with others of equal fame so that they go with a swing. "Harry the King, Bedford and Exeter" are not more exciting in a cricketer's ears than those in PROWSE's often quoted line

> Felix, Wenman, Hillyer, Fuller Pilch and Alfred Mynn

and GARRETT's name, though commemorated in no verse, is one of a company that haunt the memory. To 1878 belong four tremendous Australian bowlers – SPOFFORTH, BOYLE, GARRETT, and ALLAN. ALLAN, "the bowler of a century," dropped out and in 1882 come the four with an even more alarming ring – SPOFFORTH, BOYLE, PALMER, and GARRETT.

The student who murmurs to himself those four names may feel a cold thrill up the spine; he may "crawl with invidious apprehension" but, even as the small boy, pale green over a first cigar, he "likes the feeling." If it be not too close to us there is nothing like the formidable and that is surely the epithet for those early Australians, as indeed for their successors. They look formidable as we scan their photograph of 1882. Each flank is held by a black-bearded hero; on the left GARRETT himself, on the right BLACKHAM. Next to GARRETT towers the giant BONNOR with a beard of lighter hue and in the middle, bearded again, is BOYLE, with his hands casually and defiantly in his pockets. Close behind him in a rustic garden sits a stone lion, the animal destined to be so signally humiliated. In those days England itself possessed the most formidable of all men with a black beard, and perhaps beards were then less charged with meaning, but to-day they strike an awe upon the sight, and their wearers look, as MR. CARDUS wrote of SPOFFORTH, "Stark men," full of hostility and resolution. That bearded old gentleman of eighty-five who has just passed away must have had many great memories to go back and back to in his last years.

Captain H. Verity

FROM OUR CRICKET CORRESPONDENT [R. B. VINCENT]

2 *September* 1943. Captain Hedley Verity, of the Green Howards, whose death in hospital as a prisoner of war in Italy on July 31 was officially announced yesterday, had already in his 10 years of first-class cricket established his position as a worthy successor to Peel and Rhodes as Yorkshire's slow left-handed bowler, and he had played in 40 Test matches.

Always a bowler of extreme accuracy and patience, even on the truest of wickets and against the most formidable batsmen, he developed as his career advanced a greater ability to flight the ball, and on a sticky wicket he was unsurpassed. He was born at Headingley in May of 1905, and when quite young played as an amateur for Rawdon in Yorkshire Council matches, later appearing as a professional for Accrington in the Lancashire League. He played first for Yorkshire in 1930, in which season, although he did not obtain a regular place in the side, he took 52 wickets for 11 runs apiece. In 1931 he came fully into his own, making full use of many rain-damaged pitches and taking 138 wickets in the season, including all 10 in an innings against Warwickshire at Leeds for 36 runs. In the next season he took all 10 Nottinghamshire wickets for only 10 runs, and in 1933 at Leyton he took 17 wickets in a day. In 1934 when England beat Australia in an innings at Lord's he took 14 wickets for 80 runs during the course of one day, taking 15 wickets in all in the match, a feat which no one else has ever achieved in a Test Match except Rhodes at Melbourne in 1904. These were exceptional performances, but frequently Verity took seven or eight wickets in an innings at an absurdly low cost.

His career in matches on tour, during which he played in Australia, New Zealand, South Africa, the West Indies, and India, was equally remarkable, his accuracy even on the hard Australian pitches being of inestimable value to his captain, who could rely on him to keep runs down at one end. His ability to keep the batsman playing was demonstrated by the fact that even to Bradman he could place a silly point. In these tours in various parts of the world he took 224 wickets at a cost of 19 runs each, and as a batsman he at one time showed signs of following the example of Rhodes by transforming himself from a Number 11 into an opening batsman.

A keen student of the game, there never was a cricketer of a more becoming and gentle modesty than Hedley Verity, who on all grounds was regarded with the utmost respect. Before this war he had made a keen study also of soldiering, was one of the first cricketers to join the forces, and had served three years in the Middle East before he received his severe wound in Sicily.

An All-American Match

22 *September* 1943. Two teams composed of officers of the United States Army Air Force, representing Stations 103 and 112, recently met in a cricket match in this country. This is believed to be the first cricket match played by all-American teams in England, at least during this war. The batting and bowling were much above the standard expected by the English spectators.

> STATION *112* 92 (Capt. Mitchell 60; Capt. Barry 7 for 56)
> STATION *103* 35 (Capt. Podwajsky 5 for 13)
> *Station 112 won by 57 runs*

Judgment against Hotel
Constantine v. Imperial London Hotels Limited

BEFORE MR. JUSTICE BIRKETT
HIGH COURT OF JUSTICE : KINGS BENCH DIVISION

29 *June* 1944. His LORDSHIP gave judgment for the plaintiff in the action in which Mr. Learie Nicholas Constantine, of Meredith Street, Nelson, Lancashire, claimed damages from Imperial London Hotels, Limited, on the ground that the defendants refused to receive and lodge him in the Imperial Hotel, Russell Square, London, in July, 1943.

The defendants denied that they refused to receive and lodge Mr. Constantine, and pleaded that, after he had been received in their hotel on July 30, 1943, he voluntarily left that evening and was provided with accommodation at their Bedford Hotel.

Sir Patrick Hastings, K.C., and Miss Rose Heilbron appeared for the plaintiff; Mr. G. O. Slade, K.C., and Mr. Aiken Watson for the defendants.

His LORDSHIP, in giving judgment, said that there was no claim for damages for breach of contract, it being conceded that Mr. Constantine had a contract with the defendants and that on breach of that contract he would be entitled to nominal damages. The plaintiff's claim was simply that the defendants were innkeepers; that the Imperial Hotel was a common inn kept by them for the accommodation of travellers; that they were under a duty receive and lodge him; that they refused to do so; and that he was compelled to go elsewhere and was put to much inconvenience.

It was conceded, for the purpose of the case, that the defendants were innkeepers; that the Imperial Hotel was an inn; that the plaintiff went there on

July 30, 1943, and requested the defendants' servants to receive and lodge him; that they had sufficient room for the purpose; and that the plaintiff was ready and willing to pay the proper charges and had paid a deposit of £2. It was further conceded that Mr. Constantine was a man of high character and attainments, a British subject from the West Indies, and that although he was a man of colour no ground existed on which the defendants were entitled to refuse to receive and lodge him.

The issue of fact was a narrow one. Did the defendants by their servants refuse to receive and lodge Mr. Constantine, or did he, as the defendants asserted, leave voluntarily after having been received into the Imperial Hotel? He (his Lordship) would first deal shortly with the question of fact. Mr. Constantine was perhaps best known as a cricketer of great renown who had won the admiration and, indeed, the affection of the cricketing public in many parts of the world. He was also employed by the Ministry of Labour as the local welfare officer on Merseyside.

There was to be an international cricket match at Lord's on August 2, 1943, and Mr. Constantine was given special leave to play in it. When rooms were booked at the defendants' hotel for Mr. Constantine and his wife and daughter, the question was asked: "Have you any objection to coloured people?" and the answer received was "No." On July 30 Mr. Constantine went to the hotel accompanied by Mr. A. R. Watson, his superior officer in the Ministry of Labour, and Mr. W. C. Leatherbarrow, the manager of the match which was to be played.

His LORDSHIP reviewed the evidence given on both sides regarding what took place at the hotel, and said that he accepted without hesitation the evidence of the plaintiff and his witnesses and rejected that given on behalf of the defendants. He was satisfied that the manageress of the hotel was grossly insulting in her references to Mr. Constantine. It was enough to say that from the outset the manageress made it clear to Mr. Leatherbarrow that Mr. Constantine could not stay in the hotel; that she used the word "nigger" and was very offensive; and that she declined to receive the party and refused to listen to reason. He (his Lordship) also accepted the evidence that Mr. Constantine removed to the Bedford Hotel, on the advice of Mr. Watson and not of his own free will, because of what the manageress and manager said.

In the witness-box Mr. Constantine bore himself with modesty and dignity, dealt with all questions with intelligence and truth, was not concerned to be vindictive or malicious, but was obviously affected by the indignity and humiliation which had been put on him and had occasioned him so much distress and inconvenience, which he most naturally resented.

He (his Lordship) found on the facts that the defendants did refuse to receive and lodge the plaintiff in their hotel without any just cause or excuse, and that Mr. Constantine did not leave voluntarily.

His LORDSHIP then proceeded to deal with the question of law raised by the defendants – namely, that the present action was an action on the case, that the gist of such an action was the damage actually suffered and proved, and that in the present case no damage was suffered and no special damage was alleged and proved. He reviewed the authorities at length, and said that there was no express authority to guide him. He held that the action was maintainable without proof of special damage, since the plaintiff's right, founded in the common law, had been violated and denied, and in those circumstances the law afforded him a remedy. He (his Lordship) had been urged to award exemplary damages because of the circumstances in which the denial of the plaintiff's right took place. He did not feel on the authorities that he could do that, having regard to the exact nature of the action, and he therefore gave judgment for Mr. Constantine for nominal damages only, which he assessed at five guineas.

A stay of execution was refused.

Solicitors. – Messrs. Isadore Goldman and Son, for Mr. Sydney W. Price, Liverpool; Messrs. Durrant Cooper and Hambling.

Ball and Beard

8 *August* 1944, *Leading Article.* There are some articles of faith which an Englishman will surrender only with his life, and of these one of the most dearly cherished is that ERNEST JONES bowled through W. G.'s beard. He would as soon discredit the story that PRINCE JOHN pulled the long beards of the Irish chieftains who came to do homage. On this sacrosanct belief doubt has lately been cast and, of all people, by SIR STANLEY JACKSON. *Et tu, Brute* will exclaim all true believers in awe-stricken chorus. This statement, akin to blasphemy, occurs in the new Wisden in a very interesting record of a talk with the greatest of all Yorkshiremen. SIR STANLEY places the incident, for he admits an incident, at Sheffield Park, not at Lord's, and here, unless indeed the thing happened twice, he will find the bulk of historians against him; but that is a small matter. In all the details but one he cannot affront the most bigoted. That W. G. came menacing down the pitch, that HARRY TROTT said "Steady, Jonah," that JONES proffered the famous apology, "Sorry, Doctor, she slipped" – on all these points he is orthodoxy itself; but then come these dreadful words, "I do not think the ball actually touched W. G.'s beard." Your true fundamentalist is impervious even to such shocks as this, but those of weaker faith will have found their spirits much refreshed by a letter from a correspondent published on August 4. He was at Lord's watching a Test Match; he was sitting square with the wicket, and on the evidence of his own eyes and those of all his neighbours, as well as on that of the Doctor's "reactions," he believed and still believes that the ball did go through the beard. England will stand behind him to the last man.

That memories of great events grow hazy, even in cricket is undeniable. Anyone who has studied in W. J. FORD's history of Cambridge cricket the accounts of COBDEN's over, given by those who played in the match, will find surprising variations. Who fielded the first ball of the over, and whether BELCHER was bowled off his legs – an insinuation which the bowler bitterly resented – are but two points in doubt. The great YARDLEY went so far under some strange hallucination as to put COBDEN bowling at the wrong end. But COBDEN's over is "another story," and as to the Doctor's beard argument is barely allowable. Once upon a time he was not the only bearded hero; the early Australian teams bristled with them: BONNOR's, BLACK-HAM's and GARRETT's beards were familiar and illustrious. To-day they have all grown dim save to those who pore reverently over faded groups. Only W. G. remains for ever *senex promissa barba.* as clear and vivid a picture to those who never saw him as to those who played with him. Even SIR STAN-LEY JACKSON admits that the Doctor came up the pitch stroking his beard. There is yet time for him to recant on the major issue. Will he not do so and so ease the hurt of many worthy souls?

> There was an old man with a beard
> Who said, "It is just as I feared,"

but he can never have imagined so fearful a heresy as this.

The evidence of the reports in The Times, *though favouring Sheffield Park, is inconclusive. On Sheffield Park (13 May 1896): Mr. Jones (very fast) and Mr. M'Kibbin were the bowlers. "W.G.", after being twice badly hit in the first over from Mr. Jones, began to force the game at a great pace, and the last two balls of the over he drove and cut to the boundary. On Lord's (23 June 1896): Jones started the bowling from the pavilion end, and from a short and fast ball Grace got a two through the slips. In the same over there was a bye and a four and a two by Stoddart through the slips.*

Mr. A. C. MacLaren

25 *November* 1944. Mr. R. H. Spooner writes:–

It was with deep sorrow that many, and particularly those in cricket circles, heard of the passing of Archie MacLaren. In my opinion he was not only the greatest captain ever, but was always a valued friend and adviser to the youthful cricketer during early appearances for his county. When captain he was always ready to give up his usual place in the batting order should he feel that that would benefit his side. He never thought of himself, and there was no one stricter in seeing that cricket was always played as it should be. Ever a delightful companion to cricketers in the British Isles, Archie Mac-Laren was a universal favourite and, rightly so, oversea, and nowhere more so than in Australia.

Australia's Good Start against England

FROM OUR CRICKET CORRESPONDENT [R. B. VINCENT]

7 *August* 1945. Lord's ground had never before held so many people as were there yesterday to see the first day of the fourth "Victory" match, during which Australia, having first use of the most perfect of wickets, had placed themselves almost invulnerable to the uncertainties of cricket by scoring 273 runs for the loss of five wickets.

The limitations of England's attack, well directed as it was by their captain and nobly supported in the field, were obvious, their medium-paced bowlers – for they had no really fast bowlers – relying over-much on the ball pitching on, but missing, the leg stump. The Australian batsmen are adepts at forcing the ball off their legs, whereas the best of them can offer a catch in the slips to the ball which goes away. W. R. Hammond for a long time was a solitary figure in the slips, while three men close in on the on-side could expect to do little else than pick up the ball or watch it pass by on the ground.

England had a most encouraging start when J. A. Workman, a useful man to be rid of, was out leg-before-wicket with only 15 runs on the board, and Australia to good fielding and accurate bowling had a severe hour's play in front of them. R. S. Whitington and S. G. Sismey maybe were unadventurous in their strokes, but it was obvious that in a side not over-strong in batting it was essential that a batsman should be well dug in to partner K. R. Miller when that potentially match-winning batsman came in later. In fact, Whitington did most of the scoring, but as events proved later it was Sismey who was the support Miller had looked for.

A short break before luncheon during a thunderstorm left Australia at the interval with 65 runs scored and only one wicket down, Whitington then having made 43. It can be truthfully said that after luncheon England's bowlers were unlucky in that D. V. P. Wright beat Sismey's bat times beyond count and Pope twice beat bat, pads, and wicket-keeper. The score had advanced slowly, but with purpose, to 70 before Whitington was caught at forward short-leg, but there well might have been another wicket if a second slip had been moved in a little sooner to Wright's bowling. Sismey when he had made 21 was all but out to a great attempt at a one-handed catch by J. D. Robertson at backward short-leg, and England had to wait until 108 before the dangerous A. L. Hassett was caught at fine-leg.

This brought forward Miller, who having survived a "yorker" to his first ball from Pope, and with a rather uncomfortable stretch, or lean, forward to Wright, settled down to take what runs were offered him, more especially from the allowance which was granted to him on the leg side. W. Roberts was tried at both ends, but he passed the bat only with those balls which could be ignored, and with Miller hastening, but never reckless, and Sismey obdurate Australia's batting policy was amply explained.

Sismey's valuable innings was interrupted when a rising ball caused him to go in for temporary treatment, and while he was away R. M. Stanford's wicket was lost, but Miller had seen to it that enough had been done by ten minutes past six, when a poor light, but nothing comparable in gloom to that in which England had at one time batted during the previous match at Lord's, ended the day's play, a curtailment which many may have thought unnecessary. More than 30,000 people paid for admission, and it is estimated that in all over 33,000 saw the game.

AUSTRALIA 388 (K. R. Miller 118, S. G. Sismey 59, C. G. Pepper 57, R. S. Whitington 46; G. H. Pope 4 for 83, R. Pollard 4 for 145) and 140 for 4
ENGLAND 468 for 7 dec (C. Washbrook 112, W. R. Hammond 83, W. J. Edrich 73 not out, L. B. Fishlock 69)
Score after first day: Australia 273 for 5
Match drawn

The First Day of Summer

1 *May* 1946, *Leading Article*. Almanacs and dictionaries may say what they please but for thousands of people the first day of summer is that on which there first appear in modest type and as the tail end of a column the magic words "To-day's Cricket Fixtures." Therefore it is incontestable that in 1946 the 27th of April was the day. It might have come before, but where alas! are the Notts Colts of yester year? Time was when they regularly opened the ball on Easter Monday, but either they are less hardy than the Shrewsburys and Gunns and Attewells who burst on the world on that inclement date or else owing to the scarcity of paper their deeds have been buried in oblivion. Failing them there could be none so appropriate as the "unassuming" freshmen who took the field at Cambridge. There was a Surrey trial match and an Oxford one as well, but there is a bloom of youth, a coltishness about freshmen which supremely fits them for this ceremony of initiation. The earliest practice of cricketers, the first stinging of bat and of hands, is occult from observation, though there are agreeable and historic facts to tell us that they indulge in it. The pitch at The Chestnuts at Downend was always ready in March, and cricket began, subject to the immemorial rule of a quarter of an hour's innings for adult Graces and five minutes for the boys. Still earlier we know how the "Little Farmer" bowled for hours at a hurdle while tending his father's sheep and how "many a Hampshire barn resounded with bat and ball as well as threshing." But as far as our own observation goes the freshmen stepped straight on to Fenner's, straight out of spring into summer and into the glory of restricted print.

The sound of the ball on the bat is as unique and characteristic as the cuckoo's call. The one we have been hearing now for some time; for the other we may yet have to wait a little while, but at least we can read the scores, and for many people that almost suffices. Cricket is a religion on which they have been brought up and to which they adhere even though they seldom attend its celebrations. "I can remember," wrote that charming essayist The Londoner, "the varnishy smell of a new bat that I held in my hands when I was a very little boy, an innocent child that never dared doubt cricket to be part of the whole duty of man." For a while he became a heretic, but it is pleasant to know that he came back or nearly back into the fold at last, for "now that no one has schoolmasterly authority over me in the matter of cricket or the irregular Greek verbs, I can more easily sympathize with those who have kept the faith." So it is with many others; after a time of doubt they return once and for all and of their own free will to a mild but unwavering orthodoxy. On this particular first day of summer cricket had serious and superficially more important rivals, for Derby County were at length defying the gypsy's warning and winning the Cup at Wembley, while HENRY COTTON was doing some incredible number under an average of fours at Wentworth. But those were just two more matches; the freshmen at Fenner's were taking part in a solemn and a sacred rite.

Old England at the Oval

FROM OUR CRICKET CORRESPONDENT [R. B. VINCENT]

24 *May* 1946. The King was present at the Oval yesterday when the ground was *en fête*, with an immense crowd and the Union Jack flying perkily from the top of a gasometer.

The occasion was a one-day match in aid of Surrey's appeal for funds, in this the centenary year of the club, between a team styled Old England and the present Surrey side. Indeed the spectator could be excused an excess of nostalgic memories, for, with Surrey batting first, there in the fielding side was a gathering of cricketers who between them, with the two umpires, Hobbs and Strudwick, could boast of 370 Test matches.

Maurice Tate, one of England's greatest bowlers of all time, started from the Pavilion end; there was Woolley at short slip, and giants of equal eminence scattered liberally over the ground. The old men had done well enough to be rid of Fishlock with only 46 runs scored against them, but they had a toilsome time while Gregory and Squires were together. The fielding stood well up to the test, even if there was once a slight difference of opinion between two most distinguished men as to who should run away to the far distance to retrieve the ball.

Fender it was, insinuating as ever, who took Gregory's wicket and at luncheon five men were out for 190. Appropriately enough during the interval the band of the East Surrey Regiment, among other stirring airs, struck up with "Boys of the old Brigade." Another 58 runs and the innings was declared closed.

The start of Old England's innings was tragic, the great Sutcliffe, saviour of England in many a hard-fought match, being leg-before-wicket and Sandham caught high up in the slips with but two runs on the board. And so, after all these years, Woolley, greeted as ever he was all over the world, and Hendren batting together in the sunshine at the Oval. Could the heart of a cricket lover ask for more? Woolley with his elegant ease lofting the ball over the bowler's head or placing it with exquisite timing to the on; and Hendren, still nimble of foot, advancing out to tame the bowling. Together they had added 102 runs in a partnership glorious to watch before Woolley was out to a hero's death, caught in the deep. Hendren carried on the good work, and Jardine, of the immaculately straight bat, made some noble strokes, but 79 runs to be made in the last three quarters of an hour to win was a little too much to ask for even on so joyful an occasion as this.

SURREY 248 for 6 dec (H. S. Squires 68, R. J. Gregory 62)
OLD ENGLAND 232 for 5 (E. Hendren 94, F. E. Woolley 62, D. R. Jardine 54)
Match drawn

Regency Style Cricket

Top Hats and Hard Hitting

FROM OUR SPECIAL CORRESPONDENT [PHILIP URE]

8 *August* 1946; *Brighton, 7 August.* The Regency cricket match played this afternoon on the Brunswick Lawns at Hove has been a remarkably successful event in the Regency Festival. It provided a picturesque scene and was an excellent sporting event. Indeed, the finish quite put in the shade any thoughts – friendly or otherwise – one had earlier entertained about this atmosphere. In the end, the Regency Club of Brighton beat Hambledon by nine runs.

At the beginning, the match was definitely a dress parade. The Hambledon men had it on colour, for their jackets, knee-breeches, and stockings included all those within the rainbow, and each player had an assortment of three colours all to himself. The Regency Club men were all in white, but their top hats of the Regency style varied from silver to gold, and russet and green. The one outstanding example was a black topper of exceptional width and brilliant lustre.

The bats had been made as exact copies of the famous old bat at Winchester, and so had a peculiar air of antiquity. The umpires and scorers were somewhat more elaborately dressed than the players; or was it the length of their coloured frock coats that made it seem so? Of the two scorers, one "notched" an ash stick and the other used book and pencil.

There was one other preliminary with a Regency flavour, for the captains made a formal challenge for a stake of an 18-gallon barrel of punch, which is believed in fact to have turned into beer – a solemn thought for Regency enthusiasts.

In general, the match was remarkable for the little damage it caused in proportion to the peril in which it placed modern traffic on the highway beside Brunswick Lawns. A dozen or more times a good hit sent the ball right into Brunswick Terrace, and sometimes to the beach, but not quite into the sea.

The match was played under the "new articles of the game of cricket as settled and revised at the Star and Garter, Pall Mall, February 25, 1774, by a committee of noblemen and gentlemen of Kent." That meant, among other things, that the Regency Club went in first. The bowling was all under arm, and it was obvious that neither Regency nor Hambledon have any lob-bowlers to-day. The rules allowed only four balls to the over. Another unexpected detail of Regency cricket as applied to modern times was the number of players who suddenly discovered that their breeches had split in a rather vital spot, but this became so common an experience that players ceased to worry.

The Regency Club scored 183 for 10 wickets and then declared as there was apparently a time limit to the match. Hambledon made 174 all out and only just failed to win the game during its closing stages.

The Autograph Hunters

11 *October* 1946, *Leading Article*. The great mass of mankind is exempt from one of the most prostrating penalties of fame. No small boy lies in wait for them with his autograph book. They may not therefore fully appreciate the protection extended to our cricketers who have lately landed in Australia. It has been decided that neither on the ground nor in the dressing room shall there be any signing of books or score-cards or bats. This will not ensure complete immunity since the players may possibly be besieged in their hotel and will certainly be waylaid in the street, but it is a respite to be grateful for. Small boys to be sure do not constitute the only menace, for the English captain is said to have signed his name two thousand times on the voyage out, when his pursuers were presumably old enough to know better and he, poor man, short of throwing himself overboard, was entirely at their mercy. But it is the boys who are at once the most formidable and the most appealing. It must be hard to refuse that eager petition, but the celebrity who hesitates is lost. While he pauses for an instant to scrawl his signature the rest of the pack will be upon him and pull him down like so many wolves. It may well be that our cricketers will have to take their walks abroad in couples, as do

policemen in dangerous neighbourhoods, or travesty themselves by the disguise of red side-whiskers and window-glass spectacles.

It would be interesting to know when this ruthless hunting of great men first began. When Lavengro saw the bruisers of England walking on the bowling green, "the men of renown, amidst hundreds of people with no renown at all, who gaze upon them with timid wonder," no one asked TOM CRIBB for his signature and the champion might have been hard put to it to oblige. Perhaps the mania for autographs is one of the less praiseworthy results of the spread of education, but that is but one question out of many. Is there any definite table by which relative values in the market can be estimated? Do two Huttons equal one Hammond, or does it all depend on the taste of individual fans? Does the possessor of an enviable collection, being suddenly in want of something more material and less romantic, realize part of his capital and sell a second-best wicketkeeper in order to buy an ice cream? Again we should like to know the value of a test match cricketer in some alien currency, such as the names and numbers of railway engines, which are to-day, as once were alley tors and commonies, "much prized by the youth of this town." These things are hidden from such of us as do not even pass our menus round at a dinner for the signatures of our fellows, being perfectly sure first that we do not want them, and secondly that we should lose them even if we did. Without incurring too grave a suspicion of sour grapes, we can thank heaven for our own obscurity, as we pass unmolested through the wildest herd of small boys that ever tore a cricketer in pieces.

England Save the Game

FROM OUR SPECIAL CORRESPONDENT [NEVILLE CARDUS]

8 *January* 1947; *Melbourne, 7 January.* After an exciting finish England to-day just saved the third Test match, but they scarcely deserved to escape punishment for a rather unconvincing rearguard action. The innings would have been invertebrate except for Washbrook, whose first century against Australia restored among those who have known him for years faith in his stroke-play and technique generally.

Everything was a collaborator this morning to England's effort to save themselves; the wicket was easier, perhaps, than ever before for some unfathomable reason, probably geological. The ball seldom, if ever, turned and then only gently; and all the time heavy clouds overhead promised to appear as an ally for Hammond at any hour. But the army of clouds, not far distant for long, seemed to wander and vacillate and never find real contact with the main forces, like Napoleon's meandering army at Waterloo. A shower actually stopped play for a quarter of an hour after luncheon and imparted a momentary liveliness to the pitch, and it was now that Ikin got out to a hopeless stroke, caught at silly mid-on. But the mainstays of the English innings largely contributed to their own ends, apart from Washbrook and Hammond, both well and truly bowled.

For an hour after the sixth day opened Washbrook and Hutton suffered no hardship at all; Hutton was satisfied to defend, and when Hutton does not wish to score on a somnolent turf there seems to the spectator no legal means of getting him out. Washbrook played a grand innings, for though he kept a resolute watch and ward he allowed no atrophy to visit him. He was usually making strokes with ease; some of his square drives and square pulls were of the authentic Test match style and dignity. If circumstances for more then three hours compelled his bat to perform the service of a stout oak door, there was some fine carving on it.

Hutton, also a sentinel for three hours, chose at last to essay a drive from a ball of short length from Toshack, only to loft his stroke to the off near the bowler, where Bradman made an easy, but triumphant, catch, throwing up the ball as though to say, "When he's out, they're all out." Edrich, after one splendid off-drive, fumbled here and there against spin that was potential rather than actual, and succumbed leg-before to McCool, who was brought back to the attack by Bradman with only a few minutes to go before luncheon. Throughout the match Bradman has been not only a vigilant captain but quick to make deductions from evidence, psychological as well as technical.

The sad mishap or folly of the day occurred just after half past 2. Compton drove exquisitely to the off, was nearly stumped off McCool, and then he hit again with grace and speed to the offside near cover point and dashed for a run, even though the ball went quickly near to Miller, a superb fieldsman whose pick-up and return to Tallon left poor, misguided Compton swinging his heart, soul, and body round in an agonized attempt to retrieve his impetuosity. Not for worlds would the present writer chide Compton for impulsiveness in the right place and moment; to-day it was his duty to absent himself from felicity awhile. England's position here was one in which runs were a vanity, and boundaries mere baubles. Washbrook proceeded on his way, and with Hammond next as his companion there was, of course, much strength left yet in reserve for England.

Bradman asked Dooland to bowl again, and with a ball of alluring length (and Dooland had bowled much short stuff so far) he entirely broke through Washbrook's forward defensive push with possibly a googly. So a match that at 1 o'clock had seemed to have no more problems for England to solve became alive and extremely quizzical. All the time the weather was intimidatory to Australia; the sky lowered and cleared tantalizingly. After tea, to end an innings so strong and calm that it was as a classic pillar or column, Hammond was bowled by Lindwall with a ball that kept low.

The time of day was 20 minutes past four; another 10 minutes of interference by rain only stimulated the occasion, and the sight of Bedser coming out to join Yardley provoked resignation in an Englishman's breast, not unmixed with humour. Especially when Bedser put a bat to the ball of such certainty and nonchalance that it might well have been performing the great ceremony of opening an England innings with Hobbs at the other end. As Yardley, as usual, was apparently a batsman without sense of error or difficulty, 10 minutes past five arrived to find Australia after all assuming an air of impatience and frustration, while the sky glowered again as though indicating that six days of hard labour had been lavished on a cricket match.

But the combatants were back and at it again at 25 minutes past five in a gloom so encircling that only good sportsmanship prevented an appeal. Compared with this visibility, the light appealed against the other day by Barnes was as the light of the garish universe. To sustain to the end a capriciousness that has enlivened us since the New Year another cloudburst emptied the field from half-past five to 20 minutes to the close of play.

In an improved light Bedser succumbed and palpitation afflicted us in earnest; three wickets to go, opportunity for hat tricks and catches terribly missed or as terribly held. Evans faced the music with the calm and composure of Toscanini, while Yardley continued with that imperturbability which a man presumably acquires while playing in the more searching atmosphere of Lancashire and Yorkshire matches. Appropriately he was undefeated to the end.

AUSTRALIA 365 (C. McCool 104 not out, D. G. Bradman 79, S. Barnes 45) and 536 (A. Morris 155, R. Lindwall 100, D. Tallon 92, D. G. Bradman 49, C. McCool 43)
ENGLAND 351 (W. J. Edrich 89, C. Washbrook 62, N. W. D. Yardley 61, J. T. Ikin 48; B. Dooland 4 for 69) and 310 for 7 (C. Washbrook 112, N. W. D. Yardley 53 not out, L. Hutton 40)
Match drawn

Sir Stanley Jackson

20 *March* 1947. Sir Pelham Warner writes:–

I had known Sir Stanley Jackson since 1889 when Harrow met Rugby at Althorp Park. On that evening began a friendship which grew with the years and which I prized greatly. "He was my friend, faithful and just to me," and though we all have to face the Pale Horseman there is no need to be afraid of him, and I am certain Sir Stanley faced with the same calm courage as he showed in the great matches of his day. He was a splendid all-round cricketer – one of the finest in the history of cricket – and never was he finer than in a crisis; and it was a stirring sight to see him come down the pavilion steps to set right any early failures there may have been; immaculate in his flannels and his beautifully cleaned pads and boots, with his neat trim figure every inch a cricketer. Others will deal fully with his figures, but it may be said here that no English cricketer, not even Hobbs, Hammond, or Sutcliffe, had a finer record in England against the Australians. And then, when he gave up, he sat on the Woolsack of Cricket, as president of the M.C.C., and at the time of his death he was a trustee of Lord's, chairman of the Cricket Committee, and president of the Yorkshire C.C.C. To the end he took the greatest possible interest in M.C.C. Never a week passed, even during the winter, that he was not at Lord's, and in the summer he was the best known of all the men who delight in the charm and atmosphere of the famous ground. He was busy with every avenue and aspect of the game and his enthusiasm never flagged. That he had been seriously ill for some time was obvious, but only a few days before he died he telephoned asking me to come to see him. I found him in good spirits, saying that he felt so much better that he had good hopes of coming to Lord's for a committee meeting.

I will try to describe the sort of batsman he was. First of all he was soundness itself with all the strokes – what I call a "complete" batsman. His style was easy and natural and he inspired confidence. As a bowler, medium pace, he had a beautifully easy action, and kept a length. In 1905 he not only headed the England batting averages with an aggregate of 492 runs and an average of 70.28, but was also at the top of the bowling figures. As a fieldsman at cover point, his invariable position, he was not a Hobbs, or a Jessop, but he was a good cover point, active and quick, who missed few chances. In a gallery of great players it is impossible to have a fixed order of merit, but he was in the first class of an honours school of cricket both as a batsman and an all rounder.

When you have known and been very fond of a man for nearly 60 years it is not easy to write exactly what you feel about him, but this I will say, that he had charm of manner, was always easy and pleasant, and in the cricket world, by young and old alike, he was welcomed, appreciated and respected. He meant much to me in my cricket life and though it was in the natural order of things that he should pass on, his absence leaves a big void.

Luncheon Interval

29 *April* 1947, *Leading Article*. There are some changes in the established order which even to the least bigoted appear as the opening of floodgates and the obliteration of landmarks. Of such is an experiment which is being considered by the Leicestershire County Cricket Club. There is to be – the shocked pen almost refuses its office – no luncheon interval. Play will begin at 1 o'clock, tea will be from 4.15 to 4.45 and stumps will be drawn at 8. In itself the proposal, which only applies to the first two days, seems sensible and practical enough. Advantage will be taken of the light afforded by double summer time and spectators can do a morning's work and yet get a full day's cricket for a half-day's idleness. The players will doubtless not go hungry, and in any

case the modern rush for food has brought lunch time nearer and nearer to breakfast time. The spectators will nibble their sandwiches in their seats as of old. But no luncheon interval! It is the sheer iconoclasm of the thing that takes the breath away. Those whose memories are of a far less exalted class of cricket, perhaps in school or village matches, look back to the lunch as one of the features of the day. "Lots of beer – hogsheads; rounds of beef – bullocks; mustard – cartloads" as Mr. Jingle observed of the repast at Muggleton. And what, purely from the spectator's point of view, of lunch at Lord's, haply on a coach with the pleasant popping of corks, and the promenade afterwards on historic turf, while casting a knowing eye at the wicket? Must all these delights go?

It is the interval quite as much as the lunch, with its break in the tension and its friendly meetings, which is so essentially sacred an institution, and nothing could quite make up for it. He who occasionally goes to watch cricket, having of course a perfect excuse for a day's pleasuring after weeks of application, never ceases to be surprised at the large number of other people who are apparently in a similar situation. He wonders how the world's work is getting on without them, and supposes enviously that they are all gentlemen of independent means who can live a life of cultured ease. However that may be, there they always are, from the first ball bowled and before it. Now they will have to fill their ample leisure in some other way. Very long and blank and dreary will their mornings appear. It is impossible not to sympathize with them. And to think that this proposal should come from a proud city of which it was once written

> And Leicester beans and bacon, food of kings!

What must be must, but there are things . . . It is surely a rash and impious hand that touches the cricketer's lunch. "There was high feasting on Broad Halfpenny during the solemnity of one of our grand matches." So wrote JOHN NYREN, and he could never have been stirred to such immortal gusto by tea consumed between 4.15 and 4.45.

The Wearing of the Blue

19 *July* 1947, *Leading Article*. A famous Cambridge cricketer has lately expressed in a letter what a number of obscure persons must have been thinking. Their eyes almost popped out of their heads when they read that in the University match the opening pair of Cambridge batsmen did not wear light blue caps; one was arrayed as a Quidnunc and the other as a Crusader. This is a free country in which the tyranny of colours, like other tyrannies, is to be resisted, but to most people the wearing of the blue on this one occasion appears a usage established from time immemorial and not lightly to be disregarded. So far only one side has been heard; the other has reserved its defence, if it may so be termed. It may be that the two batsmen believed their

respective headgears to be lucky, even as VICTOR TRUMPER had a run-getting shirt which he had washed nightly till it resolved into its elements, or as one great Oxford batsman remained covered for years in his Harlequin cap. If so, the belief was justified, and the Cambridge captain may appear for ever in blue striped with yellow, in gratitude for a true captain's innings. It may be again that those detestable clothing ration books were at the bottom of it, and no one will sneer at an honest poverty in coupons. Yet, as MR. ROCKLEY WILSON says, the right caps might have been borrowed. Many a venerable blue would have been only too glad that his treasured cap should bloom again in the good cause.

There was a time, if memory serves, before Test match caps were invented, when the England eleven took the field with each man in his own club or county cap. This added a pleasant touch of colour to the scene and enabled the less instructed to know

> By post and vest, by horse and crest
> Each warlike Lucumo

though to be sure no bars of red and yellow were needed to identify the noblest Lucumo of them all. Some may regret those variegated days, but even then blues were blues and the University match a thing apart. MR. WILSON adduces a historical parallel from forty years ago, when a distinguished Cambridge batsman wore a Crusader cap, because it had a larger peak to protect his spectacles from a drizzle. That reason will never serve again, for all caps to-day have almost monstrous peaks. How much they have grown the elderly warrior will scarcely realize, unless he unearths from a drawer some coloured cap of his boyhood "with the little round button at top." He will find it hard to believe that his head has not swelled owing to subsequent if necessarily lesser distinctions. It seems indeed an absurd little garment and if he wears it at some family frolic of dressing-up, perhaps at Christmas-time, he may rely on peals of irreverent laughter. Yet the line must be drawn somewhere; blue caps are hardly a subject for merriment, and the more solemn at any rate will hope that University elevens will never again disturb their "fearful symmetry."

He Clean Bowled Grace

20 *August* 1947. Mr. H. W. Shepherd, chief rating and valuation officer for the Penge district of S.E. London, who retired yesterday, remembers when, in his early twenties, he clean bowled W. G. Grace in a match at the Crystal Palace between a Sydenham and district side and London County, which Grace captained. Grace, he said, came straight over to him, slapped him on the back and said, "My boy, if you live to be 100 you'll never send down another ball like that one."

Rolling On

5 *November* 1947, *Leading Article*. It may be that the souvenir hunter is, taken by and large, weak in intellect and feeble in memory. It should not need some monstrous vase with "A Present from ——" enscrolled among the twining roses to bring back the scent and smell of the crowded beach under the August sun and the faint, pleasant, irritant of sand between the toes, and no fragment of bomb or German helmet is necessary to recreate in the mind the horrors of air raids and war. Nevertheless every now and again it is easy to understand and sympathize with the impulse which would preserve some relic from the past, and not only the sentimental will rejoice that W. G. GRACE's old lawn-roller is not to be permitted to rust away in idleness and oblivion. It has been bought for £21 and will be handed over to a cricket club which will both use and appreciate the gift.

There is little danger of a man falling into a mania for collecting garden-rollers as others collect hats and walking-sticks which once belonged to the illustrious dead, but a roller, for all that, is not without its charm and its romantic appeal. To be sure, there is little lovable in the impersonal monsters that do duty on our Test match grounds, and the days when Dobbin, that faithful and intelligent animal, would put himself between the shafts at the fall of the ninth wicket seem remote indeed. Not all cricket grounds are first class, however, and the humbler lawn-roller, with its personal squeals and habits, has still an important part to play. Besides, did not the great Doctor learn his cricket on a lawn by a Gloucestershire orchard, an orchard not far in time or spirit from that in which Shallow and Silence nodded their heads and spoke of old Double who was dead, and perhaps the fortunate club will receive the self-same roller as that which trundled down that homely pitch and so helped the career of the man who turned the game of cricket into a many-chorded lyre destined to make its enchanting music heard the world over. The wheelbarrow and the broom are now more useful about the garden than the roller, but its day will come again, sooner than now seems possible, and once more its pleasant services will be in demand on lawns and village greens. One club at least will have reason to savour the ritual of the first rolling of the spring, and its oldest member, with the memory of a black beard and a red and yellow cap still fresh in his mind, may well murmur

> Oh! scenes in strong remembrance set!
> Scenes never, never to return!

as the veteran squeaks and rumbles its way over the lumps.

Conflict of Emotions

24 *May* 1948, *Leading Article*. The time of the first Test Match draws ever nearer and, with the first appearance of the Australians at Lord's, interest is steadily mounting. Enthusiasm for cricket takes many forms, but it has been left to the LORD MAYOR of ADELAIDE to think of a new one, at once most generous and ingenious, whereby Australians shall celebrate the feats of their players by contributing gifts of food for British war widows. The scheme appears assured of success, since already 500 country towns have agreed to take part. A tariff has been suggested of a shilling for the fall of an England wicket or for an Australian century, with proportionate amounts for boundary hits and a bonus of particular liberality "when a sixer climbs the sky." It is pleasant to picture thousands of listeners sitting up into uncharted hours of the night and, as the commentator announces a hundred by BRADMAN – or BARNES or BROWN or MILLER or MORRIS – exclaiming with tears of joy and pride "Bang goes another leg of mutton." Here indeed is a plan to be received with nothing but gratitude; and yet we may spare a moment of not too serious pity for our own enthusiasts at home. It seems that they must inevitably be torn by two conflicting emotions, one of wishing all possible good to the war widows of their own country and the other of wishing all possible ill, in a friendly way, to its formidable invaders.

Even in normal circumstances this painful alternative confronts the spectator at a Test Match. In the most unlikely event of BRADMAN being dismissed for a duck he will doubtless rend the sky with shouts of triumph, but he will also be a little disappointed since he is robbed of the sight of that terrific run-getting machine in full blast. It would not have been so in his school days, when he was a purer and a better hater, and would have hailed the opposing captain's downfall with savage glee. Now, however, he is not all partisan but has in him something of the artist, and so patriotism and selfish enjoyment of consummate art tug at his heart-strings in opposite directions. There is a story of FULLER PILCH standing umpire in a match in Kent, in which E. M. GRACE, then an infant phenomenon, was taking part. He refused an appeal, which he ought to have answered in the bowler's favour, on the ground that he "wanted to see the young gentleman bat." It is human and natural to want to see BRADMAN bat, if only he does not bat too long. Now the LORD MAYOR of ADELAIDE has intensified the struggle that must go on in many a respectable bosom. Luckily, watching cricket has much the same effect as, according to DR. JOHNSON, a man's knowledge that he is to be hanged in a fortnight; "It concentrates his mind wonderfully." Only perhaps when the day's play is over will our onlooker remember once again those kindly parcels of food.

"Greatest Cricketer That Ever Lived or Ever Will Live"

FROM A CORRESPONDENT [BERNARD DARWIN]

14 *July* 1948. On July 18, 1848, after an interlude of inconsiderable daughters, a fourth son was born to Dr. Henry Mills Grace and his wife (*née* Martha Pocock), of Downend, in Gloucestershire. It was an event destined to change the face if not of England at least of the great English game of cricket; if John Small the elder, of Hambledon, had been the "man who found out cricket," it was William Gilbert Grace who raised it to heights, alike of skill and popularity, undreamed of before his day. At the time it seemed doubtless an event of purely domestic importance and we do not know if Dr. Grace, when he came riding home from his long round, praetermitted for once his cricket practice in the evening. It is pleasant to fancy that he did not and that Mrs. Grace, who according to Richard Daft knew ten times as much about cricket as any lady he had ever met, was soothed, as she lay in bed, by the familiar sound of bat and ball amid the Downend apple trees.

Since it is primarily the birth of a hero that is being celebrated we may look back to those early years in which the small Gilbert (how impossible it is to fancy him as ever being small!) was first able to take part in the family ritual, with his father and elder brothers and perhaps a cousin or two of the clans of Rees and Gilbert. At intervals there ring out the excited barks of Don, Ponto, and Noble, that immortal trinity, as they pursue the ball into the outfield or oppose to it their dauntless breasts. Mrs. Grace is there to look on with serious, appraising eyes and the girls throw up the ball if it comes their way or perhaps bowl one in a little game of their own to the still toddling Fred. And of course there is Uncle Pocock. If anyone watches the centenary matches with exultation from Elysian wickets it should be he. He made Gilbert his peculiar care, insisting that he should not, like his brother E. M., be corrupted into the heresy of the cross bat by being given too early a bat beyond his strength; preaching to him the virtues in life that really matter, the straight bat, the left shoulder forward, defence before hitting, and, above all, patience, that endless patience that was never to desert him and caused the appetite for runs to grow only more insatiable in the making. Uncle Pocock must never be forgotten.

Comparisons between the champions of different generations are nearly always as futile as ungracious. If they are to be made at all it must be by someone with claims to which the present writer has no pretensions whatever. This is a moment when hero-worship may be given free play, and unlearned worshippers at least will accept Mr. C. E. Green's fine, defiant eulogy, "The greatest cricketer that ever lived or ever will live." But perhaps one exception to this wise self-denial is permissible. No one can ever have attained to greatness at so tender an age. The true Infant Phenomenon was not Miss Ninetta Crummles but Master Gilbert Grace. Let those who spill too fervent ink over a promising colt or a schoolboy given a trial for his county eleven, ponder over a line or two of statistics. At ten W. G. played in his first match for the West Gloucestershire Club and at 12 made 51 against Clifton. At 14 he played against the All-England Eleven and faced two famous fast bowlers, Tarrant and Jackson, whom all his life he regarded as among the very best. The bowling had to be changed and Tinley brought on with his crafty lobs before the boy was bowled – for two and thirty runs. At 15 he himself played for the All-England Eleven and not much more than a year later for the Gentlemen against the Players and for England against Surrey. The day of the Australians had not yet come and so, as far as representative honours were concerned, the boy of a little over 17 had become a youthful Alexander with no more worlds to conquer.

He had not yet reached his ultimate pinnacle, but it was not far off. In 1867, which he deemed his best bowling year, only one professional, Wootton, took more wickets than he did. We think now of a venerable bearded giant beguiling youth with slows of innocent aspect, such as old William Beldham would have called (as he did Tom Walker's) "such baby bowling." So it is worth recalling the thin, lanky boy, with an incipient black scrub on his chin, bowling fast medium round arm, straight at the stumps, with no great guile but trusting to the wicket to do the rest. And, apropos, how bad were the wickets on which W. G. was soon to gather so monstrous a harvest of runs? It is a subject on which it is for ever interesting to speculate and perhaps easy to exaggerate. We have his own word for it that in the sixties many of them, and Lord's in particular, were very rough indeed. There is further Tom Emmett's testimony to his own and George Freeman's "expresses flying about his ribs, shoulders and head." But no doubt there came an improvement and W. G., never anxious to take undue credit, told at least one distinguished batsman of a later era that many of the wickets on which he played in his prime were very good. Good or bad he soon became, according to all previous standards of scoring, thoroughly outrageous upon them, and it was in 1870, when he was still but 22, that Emmett crystallized the general feeling in a memorable sentence: "I call him a non-such; he ought to be made to play with a littler bat."

A non-such he remained from then till that far distant year of 1895 with its crowning glory of 1,000 runs in May and the hundredth 100. And all that time the vast W. G. legend was growing and growing. It is a tribute to his surpassing fame that many fine cricketers of his prime are now only known, save to the more assiduous students of Wisden, because they played with him. Emmett was a great bowler and a great character, but men remember not what he did but what he said of W. G. The first thing recalled about J. C. Shaw is that twice he got W. G. out for a duck in the first innings of a benefit match and paid dearly for such presumption in the second. Their places in the averages are long since lost; their places in the legend make their names secure.

Popular fame is not necessarily evidence of real, enduring greatness, and the immensity of the legend is not cited with any intention of making back-handed comparisons, but it does show the extraordinary position which one player of a game attained almost as a boy and never lost. As long as he lived he remained the best known man in England, at whom the inescapable finger would always point, a figure to be instantly picked out even in a Derby Day crowd, unique, not to be mistaken. To be sure this could not have been so had W. G. been merely a supreme cricketer. There were contributory causes. His huge and, as the years passed, almost lumbering frame, his mighty beard growing gradually a "sable silvered," marked him as a colossus. Furthermore he was essentially a man of character. His simplicity and his guile; his words often spoken in deadly earnest but giving delighted if concealed amusement; his boyish jollity and his occasionally boyish pettishness; his intense keen-ness, which sometimes led him too far but had in it nothing of rancour or malice; finally his obvious lovableness – these things were all blent in a pic-ture which was a public possession, a picture of one who in some obscure, indefiable way was a great man.

To meet him casually, and there could be no one more friendly, was instantly to be impressed by several things – his kindliness, his true modesty which took himself for granted, his complete simplicity of demeanour and perhaps above all his great natural dignity. He was easily approachable but to take a liberty with him seemed unthinkable. If that casual acquaintance, desiring to probe further, asked questions of those who really knew W. G. and had played with him, there was but one answer. If ever he had a weakness it was an amiable one and no fault was to be hinted, no word heard against him; he was a dear old man. To be thus held in memory is surely something for which any man might be grateful on his birthday.

W. G. Grace Centenary

20 *July* 1948. SIR W. SMITHERS (Orpington, C.), on a point of order, said he had asked permission to put down a motion on the Order Paper to commemorate the centenary of W. G. Grace, but the Speaker had not allowed him to do so. He bowed to that ruling, but he could not let the centenary of the greatest cricketer of all time pass without his name being mentioned in the House. (Cheers.)

The SPEAKER. – The hon. member certainly wrote to me and asked me if he might put a motion on the Order Paper to that effect, but I declined to give my leave. It seems to me that if we put such motions on the Order Paper we might start with W. G. Grace, and we might go on to Bradman, and I do not know where we would end. (Laughter and cheers.) We put motions on the Order Paper to deal with Parliamentary matters. However much we might admire the cricket record of W. G. Grace, I do not think it would be in order to put it on the Order Paper.

SIR W. SMITHERS, pointing to the Government front bench: At least he knew how to play the game! (Laughter.)

Mr. CRAWLEY (Buckingham, Lab.). – Lest it be thought that the commemoration of W. G. Grace is a party matter, I arise to say that, had the motion been allowed, I should have been pleased to second it.

Farewell to Bradman

24 *September* 1948, *Leading Article*. If statistics were the last word in cricket, then it would be easy to prove that DONALD GEORGE BRADMAN is the greatest cricketer who has ever lived. Happily they are not and memory, warm with summer days stretching back for nearly a generation, rather than pedantry brooding over decimals, prompts the good-bye and come back if only as a visitor that speeds the Australian captain on his homeward voyage. He sailed yesterday with an unbeaten team after making a century in his last match in England as he did long ago in his first. His own summing up of all that happened between was to express a mild hope that he had made "some contribution to international cricket." A fairer way of putting it is to say that no player, since history was made in the Hambledon era on Windmill Down, has contributed more to the game.

Comparisons are odious, and when they arise in the minds of cricket lovers, who as a class take fond delight in remembering the old giants, they are apt to mislead. Who can say with real confidence what GRACE would have done against modern bowling or how BRADMAN would have adapted himself to Victorian wickets? Who, indeed, really cares? An early champion in retirement asked, as he watched a new fast bowler at Lord's, whether he himself had been faster in his youth, and on being tactfully reassured on this point went back to the country content. Lucky elders who saw GRACE and RANJITSINHJI, the middle aged who are still true to TRUMPER, and the middle ageing for whom HOBBS will always be the hero may match those great figures against the little man who has just left, but the rivalry leads nowhere except to a pleasant airing of good stories.

To have seen BRADMAN at the wicket is to have enjoyed the precision of the art of batting. LARWOOD's fierce attack and the cunning of VERITY's spin – and, in the last chapters, BEDSER's patient industry – tested his almost inhuman quickness and certainty of reaction, but only to remind spectators that he was a miracle of flesh and blood and not a little robot under a long-peaked green cap. ARTHUR SHREWSBURY used to say, when he went out to bat after lunch, "Bring me a cup of tea at half-past four." BRADMAN, but for the dusk that causes stumps to be drawn at the end of even the longest afternoon, could with equal confidence have ordered his dinner in advance to be sent out on to the field. At the top of his form there was no getting him out. Some baby now toddling after a soft ball in New South Wales may grow up to be the scourge of English Test teams in the sixties. Old stagers who then watch him piling up a century will be able, however finely he plays, to murmur: "Ah, but you should have seen Bradman."

England Win from Last Ball

FROM OUR SPECIAL CORRESPONDENT [T. D. NELSON]

21 *December* 1948; *Durban*, 20 *December*. There will never be a more stirring or breath-taking finish to a Test match than that which ended here this evening with the very last ball of the match and England winning in bad light by two wickets.

Appeals against the light, or negative tactics by the South Africans, could have closed up the game, but it was fought out to the bitter end, and the result hung in the balance throughout a long, dramatic afternoon with South Africa, who at one time had appeared to be doomed to defeat, coming within an ace of snatching a most sensational victory. The thousands of people who saw this match will never forget it, nor regret the result. It was cricket played by both teams in the highest traditions and has set the seal on the success of the M.C.C. tour. F. G. Mann must be greatly satisfied with his *début* as a Test captain, but had defeat been England's lot he would have emerged with just as much credit.

When the match was resumed this morning England were in a strong position to force a win since the South Africans, with four wickets down, still required two runs to equalize the scores. It was generally expected that unless the overnight rain had caused an improvement in the pitch South Africa would be out before lunch, leaving the road clear for a comfortable English victory. Mann relied on Wright and Bedser to take early wickets, but Wade and Begbie, batting splendidly in unfavourable conditions, gave a much better complexion to the innings than the most optimistic South African supporter could have expected.

As the morning wore on, with the batsmen beaten by the occasional lifting ball and Begbie offering a difficult chance to Simpson at deep point with his score at 13, South Africa's chances of saving the game improved. Mann, frequently consulting with Hutton, made frequent bowling changes without effect, and when he requisitioned the new ball Begbie promptly hit Bedser for a six, a most rare occurrence in Test match cricket. Bedser eventually broke this threatening match-saving partnership at 174 when he dismissed Begbie, but Wade went on to reach 63 before Jenkins bowled him round his legs. After this there was valuable time-saving batting by A. Rowan and Tuckett, but the innings closed soon after half past three.

England were set 128 runs to win and left 135 minutes to do it in. Hutton and Washbrook left no doubts about their intention of going all out for victory. Hutton cut the first ball from McCarthy fiercely down the gully where Nourse took it on the knee, causing the game to be held up for five minutes while he received medical attention. Then Washbrook should have been out in the next over. He swung at his first ball from Tuckett, giving Wynne an easy catch on the boundary, but the ball was dropped.

Then rain curtailed England's batting time by another 10 minutes. A big setback was in store for England on the resumption. Hutton had scored only five when he lifted a ball to silly mid-on. One down for 25. F. G. Mann ran out to the wicket, still intent on racing the clock, and helped Washbrook to add 24 quick runs before N. Mann got a leg before decision against Washbrook. Two down for 49.

Mann, still determined on victory and hitting out strongly, was dropped in the deep, but was almost immediately afterwards brilliantly caught in the slips by Mitchell. Three down for 52. Then, for the first time in the whole match, the South Africans came within sight of victory as McCarthy crashed through the defences of Watkins, Simpson, and Evans, and, with an hour to go, England still wanted 56 runs and South Africa wanted only four more wickets.

The match had taken a complete somersault, and now England's fate was in the hands of the imperturbable Compton and the stout-hearted Jenkins. The crowd was in a fever of excitement as they followed the tense struggle ball by ball, run by run and minute by minute. But the light was deteriorating, threatening an anti-climax to the great events of the day. With half an hour to go England required 33 runs to win. The match, however, did race to a climax, with victory in the hands of either team during the last half-hour of breath-taking cricket.

Excitement rose to a high pitch when McCarthy bowled Compton, and then, with only one run added, got Jenkins caught behind the wicket. Eight wickets were now down for 116 runs, and 12 runs wanted in the last 10 minutes, with Bedser and Gladwin left to do or die. The bad light justified an appeal, but both teams were determined to fight it out to the last. Gladwin was dropped at mid-on before he had scored, but the margin was reduced by four runs as Tuckett took the last over with eight more runs wanted. A leg bye and a four to Gladwin as he galloped up the pitch waving his bat joyously, two more leg byes as the batsmen swung desperately, and then the last ball of the match with one run wanted to win. Gladwin jumped up the pitch and swung his bat wildly as the ball went off his leg. There was a desperate scramble for the creases with a near run out, and England had won.

SOUTH AFRICA 161 (A. V. Bedser 4 for 39) and 219 (W. Wade 63, D. Begbie 48; D. V. P. Wright 4 for 72)
ENGLAND 253 (L. Hutton 83, D. Compton 72; N. Mann 6 for 59, A. Rowan 4 for 108) and 128 for 8 (C. McCarthy 6 for 43)
England won by 2 wickets

Vendetta

8 June 1949, *Leading Article.* It can hardly be expected that to-day's cricket match between a team of authors and a team of publishers will exhibit the normal relations between these two classes of person in any very realistic light. If they had challenged each other at (say) the Wall Game there might have been scope for their mutual antipathies to express themselves in overt or covert acts of violence, and there is little doubt that in such a case the casualties among the publishers, even if they had won the game, would have been heavier and more serious than on the other side. For no publisher could ever bring himself to kill or even to disable an author. It would not, or at least it very easily might not, pay. Even if the author's works are published by some rival house, the publisher is well acquainted with the fickleness of the species. Who knows but what the gifted creature may one day, in a tantrum, take his deathless or anyhow profitable manuscripts elsewhere? The publisher may be unable, in the heat of the struggle, to restrain himself from giving the author a little, irritable push; but he will not stamp upon his face.

No such quality of mercy resides in the author's savage breast. Incapable of gratitude, he regards every publisher as his natural enemy. Bloated middlemen, parasites who draw their over-abundant sustenance from the life-blood of his Muse, publishers arouse in him the same sort of tacit antipathy which infantry entertain for the staff. He knows, moreover, that there are plenty of them. His genius is irreplaceable; of their meagre administrative and commercial talents there is, if anything, a glut. Place one of these bloodsuckers at his mercy and he will not hesitate to wreak upon him an exemplary vengeance.

In a cricket match, however – even in a cricket match between literary gentlemen – the opportunities for inflicting serious injuries on one's opponents are limited. A fast bowler might, it is true, stimulate a demand for stretcher-bearers; but authors, haled from their desks to blink like owls upon the unaccustomed turf, are not the sort of team to throw up a fast bowler, or not at any rate a fast bowler who will bowl fast for very long. Publishers, moreover, have acquired by virtue of their calling considerable evasive agility. They may not be able to return the deliveries of some insensate poet quite as smoothly and dexterously as they are accustomed to return his manuscripts; and they cannot avoid a rising ball, as they can a writer who seems unlikely to rise, by pretending to be in conference; but they are sharp-witted fellows, full of cunning, and though they may not come off scathless the authors will be lucky if the venom which inspires their attack is matched by the damage which it inflicts on their exploiters. When stumps are drawn old scores will still remain to be paid off; and whether, in the interim, any scores worth mentioning of another kind will have accrued to either side remains to be seen.

Border-line Cricket

24 *August* 1949, *Leading Article*. There are more ways of getting a man out than are known to the Laws of Cricket. A well-chosen umpire with the right ideas on local patriotism is a help and so is one who reacts easily to suggestion and can be bluffed by a loud, self-confident appeal. He is especially useful in doubtful cases of L.B.W. because nine umpires out of ten (beyond the narrow circle of professionals) are a bit hazy about the exact wording of the rule and are, in any case, seldom quick enough to see just where the ball pitched or where, if unobstructed, it would go. The wicket-keeper (who used to be called the "Aunt Sally" and has to put up with all the knocks) is sometimes accused of crouching, with outspread gloves and protruding pads, over the stumps, intent on flipping off a bail, morally dislodged by a ball that beat the batsman. Jocular remarks between overs may serve (but not with Australians) to induce a momentary care-free mood that is good for a dolly catch. Queer stories in this *genre* are told of W. G. himself.

Such artful aids to a bowling analysis are strengthened by freaks within the law. Hitherto, the record in this class has, perhaps, been held by the entry, still surviving, in an old County score-book, "C. G. Taylor, hat knocked on wicket, b. Hillyer, 89." That white beaver, skittled down from the head of its wearer by a fast, rising ball, must have gone long since to the moths and, now, its claim to fame is surpassed. It cannot compete with "Townsend, j R.A.F. Pilots, c. Eagar, b. Carty." This unlucky Warwickshire batsman, who fell to an attack consisting of two Hampshire men and three diving aircraft, may console himself with the thought that he has been "jetted" into cricket history. At the cost of no more than the loss of his wicket, he joins the sparrow which shares with the ball it fatally obstructed a glass case in the pavilion at Lord's. Destruction from the air is evidently a two-way traffic and it remains for some Jessop to land one in the cockpit, thus starting a new variant of the schoolboy question about what happens in a match – without boundaries – if the ball is hit into a passing train. The proviso of no boundaries seems unnecessary with a stroke into an aircraft, for, however high it went, it could hardly be ruled to have crossed the line. A long-winded pair of batsmen might run it out until the ball was returned from the airfield; but, if they did so, they might find themselves cut down to a beggarly six. They might be tripped up by the rule about a ball that "cannot be recovered" or even – although this seems a far-fetched definition of jet-propelled flight – by the one about being "finally settled."

Projection of the hazards of cricket into another dimension will be poorly viewed by players for whom the turf and the fauna upon and around it already get too effectively in the way of their centuries. Spectators prowling behind the bowler's arm, flies and wasps dancing above the pitch, and sunlight catching on glass have all taken wickets – or at least batsmen, as they took off their pads, have been heard to say so. Providence kindly tempers the wind of these misfortunes for the weaker brethren. The worse a batsman is the more stoutly he often triumphs over distraction. Let the sight-screen be wrongly placed and the light fade and the band blare away at the neighbouring flower show and he is just as likely as not to get runs – or to get out. He rises above the pettiness of fate just as he scorns the bowler's skill. Googlies are wasted on him, for he could not, if his life depended on it, tell by the delivery which way the thing was coming at him and, if he could, how would the foreknowledge help him? Against such a man – and he is the salt of cricket – dive-bombing is a farce. All he needs is a straight ball; he is not particular about its length.

Oh, What a Beautiful Season!

10 *May* 1950, *Leading Article*. Once more the court of King Willow resounds with the gladsome music of bat meeting ball. . . . Perhaps nobody writes quite like that in these days, but it is one of the standing duties of occasional literature to salute the opening of the cricket season, and this duty is now being faithfully discharged on all sides. Though their language may be rather less lyrical than of yore, though it is comparatively rare to find a closing paragraph which begins "But ere long the lengthening shadows will caress the verdant green-sward," the writers still contrive to strike that note of seemly jubilation which has always been *de rigueur* on this occasion. What they are saying is, in effect, that it is now once more possible for Englishmen to play cricket; and, though they cannot exactly be accused of mafficking, they say it in accents vibrant with a deep and holy joy.

It cannot be said that, this year, they have quite succeeded in capturing the atmosphere in which many of us played the first game of the season. Not insensible though we were of the privilege of being allowed to play cricket again, it was the idea of desisting from this sacred pastime and getting into a nice hot bath that was uppermost in our minds during the actual game itself. Far above our heads the rooks clung precariously to the thrashing elms or, becoming air-borne, were whirled instantly into the next parish. The tins on the telegraph rattled like a Bren-gun carrier. Underfoot the ground was sodden, and in (among other things) its colour and consistency the bowler's pile of sawdust resembled sausage meat. The ball which occasionally, and so far as the batsman was concerned unintentionally, came our way was a raw, pink, slightly swollen object; it did not skim along the turf, but progressed in a series of long, low, venomous, squelching bounds until after punishing our frozen finger-tips it struck us upon the knee-cap with fearful force. The sleet which fell from time to time was never quite enough to stop play.

Upon the football field there would have been violent exercise, at the point-to-point there would have been cherry brandy; but at the court of King Willow there was only cricket, an odd enough game at the best of times; in the rough winds of this May a rigorous ordeal. Shivering, grumbling, dropping catches, falling over and getting run out, we played the summer game in winter weather. And, so strange is the British character, so oddly formed by this and similar pursuits, that when the match was over and we trooped off the desolate field in our damp, discoloured flannels, some of us had actually enjoyed it and the rest of us believed that we had.

Lord's Calypso

30 *June* 1950, *Leading Article*. Playing on their own sunny ground West Indian cricketers have beaten English teams before. Once, at Sydney nineteen years ago, they beat Australia, with BRADMAN playing. But yesterday was their finest hour. They have handsomely laid an All England XI low at Lord's. JOHN GODDARD and his men have made a new mark in cricket history. To win by 326 runs at the headquarters of cricket, in spite of the brave English recovery led by WASHBROOK on Wednesday, puts these West Indians for good among the great ones. There have been giants before in West Indian cricket – GEORGE CHALLENOR, LEARIE CONSTANTINE and GEORGE HEADLEY, each of them among Wisden's best through the ages. This is the first West Indian team to bring the promise of so many fine cricketers to full fruition.

These West Indians play cricket – as their fellow countrymen watch it – in their own gay way. Even if this game had gone against GODDARD's team these men would have stayed in the memory: RAE's solid hundred dotted with hard hits to the ring, STOLLMEYER's elegance, the flowing eagerness of WORRELL, the forceful skill of WEEKES, the happy mastery of WALCOTT behind the stumps and his massive batting – above all the spinning duet of RAMADHIN and left-arm VALENTINE, striplings both with more experience gained in this one match than in all their brief career before. The proper Test cricketer mixes the right alloy of patience, precision in technique and attacking spirit. Only patience and the dourer experience of more sober cricketers have been lacking before. This time the West Indians mixed the elements right. Under GODDARD's long-headed leadership West Indian cricket has come of age. There will no doubt be a calypso about it all. Perhaps it has been already composed by the knot of gleeful islanders on the stand behind the sight-screen, with their cries and calls, their songs and music sounding pleasantly strange in the Lord's hush. It will be sung as a battle-honour wherever West Indians bat and bowl.

Australia Well Beaten

FROM OUR SPECIAL CORRESPONDENT [R. C. ROBERTSON-GLASGOW]

1 *March* 1951; *Melbourne,* 28 *February.* Shortly before 5 o'clock this afternoon Hutton turned a ball from Hassett to leg for a single and England had won the fifth Test match againt Australia by eight wickets. So victory came after 13 years. It was a resounding victory won against chivalrous, but tough, opponents by a team of cricketers who, if late in the series, answered both the leadership of a true captain and their own latent powers.

Luck did not unduly help either side. The pitch remained good to the end. To the end, too, if we allow for the pleasing comedy of the last six balls from Hassett, the Australians strained spirit and sinew in defence of their invincibility. Their fielding was superb and when Washbrook was out at the total of 32 and only 65 runs were needed still, we were half ready to believe that Iverson would suddenly reveal some further freak of spin, or that Lindwall and Miller would rise to demoniac strength and unearthly brilliance and snatch victory from England at the last. But whatever fantasies may have clouded or illumined the minds of the spectators, there was one man out in the middle, Hutton, who stood no nonsense from sceptic or bowler.

As is the way of greatness, he controlled and commanded without fuss. Early in the innings he hit Lindwall for a sizzling 4 past cover. Then, when Iverson came on, he knew and showed himself to be the master. Praise, too, to Simpson. Late, but not quite too late, he found his own high artistry of stroke-play, put away the pedestrian accuracy of the mere workman, and turned a position of doubt to one of lively hope.

So much for the batting. In the bowling Bedser once more showed that he is the best of his kind in the world to-day. Throughout the match, indeed throughout the series, no Australian batsman wholly mastered his late swerve either way, his accuracy of direction, and his stinging pace from the pitch. His was a double task to quell runs and to take wickets, and he achieved it. Wright also, that variable genius, had his share in the victory. He ended both Harvey and Hassett when each was set and happy. As an old Yorkshire player once remarked: "Any fool can bowl batsman when he's made nowt."

In the morning when Hassett and Hole continued from a total of 129 for 4, Brown was faced with a tactical problem, mild perhaps in retrospect, but real enough when every Australian run was a drag on hope. Should he or Bedser bowl during seven overs before the new ball was due? Bedser has no dislike of work or of a ball of moderate age, but this part-rended ball had apparently grown senile early. So Brown took it and in the first two overs by him and Wright singles came with an ease that was alarming or reassuring according to party.

Hole did once glide Wright in the air not far from Bailey's outstretched hand, and Hassett did have some trouble with Wright's googly. But the googly on the middle-and-leg is ever the spinner's second best, and it was a beautifully pitched leg-break which, at 142, beat Hassett's back-stroke and hit his middle and off stumps. Wright, a man of quiet temper, jumped in triumph. That was the second ball of an over. The seventh Johnson ballooned to very deep mid-on, and Brown never looked as if he would not catch it.

So Lindwall joined Hole and Bedser came on at the Richmond end for Brown. He harassed Lindwall, who was almost caught by Sheppard diving to the right at short-leg. Suddenly Wright lost accuracy, and Hole, who now carried the Australian innings and hopes with debonair courage, cracked him thrice in one over to the boundary – two hooks, then a late cut off the faster ball. Forty minutes before luncheon Bedser took the new ball and Bailey succeeded Wright. Drinks, irrelevant to most, were brought out. Then Bedser had a duel with Hole. Evans missed a chance of stumping on the leg side, and Hole made an uppish stroke wide of the slips, then a beautiful drive for 4 past mid-off. Soon after Hole reached his 50. Lindwall, never so convincing in his more sedentary mood, edged Bedser for 4 between the slips, who rearranged themselves with postdated care.

At the pavilion end Bailey lapsed into eccentricity with two overhead full tosses, then he cooled himself down to a more methodical attack at the leg-stump with three close leg fielders. Hole was quietened and when he did try a drive Bailey almost caught and bowled him with a goalkeeper's fling to the right. Then Bedser, as if tired of other people's oddities and luck, bowled Lindwall, who was framing vaguely for a cut. That was 192 for seven and Tallon walked in very slowly with head cocked a little to the side as one who hears the deadly approach of the tumbril. He scored one run to leg. And so to lunch – 193 for seven and Australia only 90 ahead. Hole had then scored 61.

After lunch the air was heavily humid and a slight mist as of autumn come too soon hung over the scene. Bailey tried no more ballistic experiments and bowled Hole with a fast and well-pitched-up ball. Hole will surely be seen with the next Australian team in England. He batted for two hours and 40 minutes. And now Bedser who had taken the first two wickets, took the last two also. He pierced Johnston's airy defence and caused an outswinger to whizz from the edge of Iverson's antique bat into Compton's hands at second slip. No nonsense about it. He had taken 30 wickets in the five Tests.

After use of the light roller Hutton and Washbrook went out to face Lindwall (pavilion end) and Miller just before a quarter to three. Lindwall went through more unlimbering exercises than usual and some prophesied an attack of much height as well as speed. But it was speed only, and in the very first over Hutton drove a 4 off Lindwall like the crack of a pistol. Miller once passed Hutton with a beauty, but Hutton did not mean to play any game with time and 17 runs were on the board, 16 to Hutton, when after two overs each, Lindwall and Miller were succeeded by Iverson and Johnston, the latter using his slower method. Washbrook, never happy to Iverson, swatted away in a whole over without effecting anything except complicated fusion of himself with Tallon, who kept wicket in quite his old style. Hutton, by contrast, interpreted Iverson as flowingly as a scholar translates a once puzzling passage. At the other end Washbrook hit Johnston square to the off boundary. Then he cocked up the easiest of catches to short-leg. Sixty-three to win when Simpson came in and rain now threatening.

Simpson began with a few deflections, then attacked, hooking Johnston violently for 4 past short-leg's head. Twenty minutes before tea Johnson bowled an over of convenience to let Iverson and Johnston change ends. Harvey's fielding at cover-point was a sight to see. Still Hutton batted with a free certainty, and the issue must now be sure. But at 62 Simpson drove Iverson to Harvey's right and ran. Harvey, who had once already thrown down the bowler's wicket, did so again and Simpson was far run out. Now the spectators began to cheer nearly everything, and Compton came in. He turned Iverson to leg for 1, and so to tea with 31 needed for victory. Hutton had scored 40 out of 64.

Afterwards some thought that Hassett might bring on Lindwall and Miller again for a last fling. But he kept on Iverson and Johnston. A light rain now fell. In 2's and singles the runs came and Hutton reached his 50 – 16 to win. When 8 were needed Hole came on for Iverson; with 4 to win Hassett took the ball from Johnston. With humorous care he called long-leg in closer. A run to Compton, a run to Hutton, another to Compton. Then Hutton, with ironical precision, pushed a single to leg and all was over. And soon the two captains, Hassett and Brown, were making speeches on demand to the cheering throng.

AUSTRALIA 217 (A. L. Hassett 92, A. R. Morris 50; Bedser 5 for 46,
F. R. Brown 5 for 49) and 197 (G. Hole 63, R. N. Harvey 52, A. L. Hassett
48; Bedser 5 for 59)
ENGLAND 320 (R. T. Simpson 156 not out, Hutton 79; K. R. Miller 4 for
76) and 95 for 2 (Hutton 60 not out)
England won by 8 wickets

Only Four Bats

24 *March* 1951, *Leading Article*. "Washbrook broke his bat." What a tragedy might have lain behind that bald statement of our Special Correspondent in New Zealand if the player had not gone on to make a creditable fifty-eight in the Christchurch Test and if the rest of the team had not raised the score to the nowadays un-English total of more than 500. Every sportsman or player of games knows how a particular bat, club, gun or fishing rod can bring to its wielder just that touch of added confidence which may make the difference between success and failure. In this instance the accident might have had even graver results. Our Correspondent adds that "owing to restric-

tions on luggage carried by air, M.C.C. have only five bats in New Zealand between them. These are now reduced to four, so M.C.C. are now no better equipped than Much Grabham on tour." This is indeed reducing cricket to a game, and brings visions of the Much Grabham team on its way to Snatchem Parva in a horse-drawn brake, which lurches through flower-scented lanes. Some of the side wear bowler hats and high collars, and the bars are as gnarled, mahogany-faced and wrinkled as any veterans should be. In fact, our apparent lack of cricket impedimenta in New Zealand seems to have narrowed the gap between our Test team and those real enthusiasts who pass the one bat to friend or foe indiscriminately, and whose wicket is a pile of boys' caps or a chalk mark on a wall.

No doubt, if a real crisis arises during to-day's Test at Wellington, New Zealand will come to the rescue with some loans. If so, M.C.C. will be able to congratulate themselves that they are not engaged in a golfing encounter. Though the golfer has the seemingly generous limit of fourteen clubs in which to carry out his task, the Royal and Ancient demand that "the addition or replacement of a club or clubs must not be made by borrowing from a partner, opponent, or fellow-competitor." But it is the well-worn favourite that counts, and it is to be hoped for the sake of M.C.C. to-day that the weather (in spite of all forebodings) is such as our Correspondent described in the Otago match at Dunedin, when "it was cool like an English October morning," and a hit to long-leg "scattered the parliament of seagulls." We cannot afford a risk of heat of the West Indian intensity which blistered Jingle's bat in his memorable encounter with Sir Thomas Blazo and Quanko Samba. Without reflection on England's tail, which has often wagged so effectively, it may be wished that the four remaining bats belong to the four best performers. Some particular virtue attaches itself to the bat of the great. Even the stamped signature on a blade may deceive the indifferent club player or schoolboy into thinking that one day he will be a Compton or a Hobbs. How much greater confidence can be gained by handling the master's very own. If before flying to New Zealand the team had been reduced to such scarcity, and HUTTON could have been prevailed upon to lend his bat, or, when he carried it through the innings, even his second favourite, to some of his colleagues, there is no knowing what might have happened, even in Australia.

The Occasional Cricketer

30 *July* 1951, *Leading Article.* The occasional cricketer is in some ways a rather pathetic figure. He is not to be confused with the man who has not touched a bat for fifteen years, who has a different outlook and different coloured trousers and very often makes fifty. Roped in to fill a gap at the last moment, this carefree fellow starts with all the advantages of the licensed

jester. He may not actually wear braces, but as he advances to the wicket his costume makes it clear that this was not the way in which he had planned to spend the afternoon. As the ironic applause and the facetious exhortations die down the fieldsmen close in like a wolf-pack waiting for the kill. Laughter greets the batsman's ungainly flourish at his first ball, the convulsive undulation with which he avoids the impact of the second; but at the third there is a sudden, mellow crack and the cheers take on a different timbre as mid-on jogs back to retrieve the ball from the winter oats beyond the boundary. After that all is plain though often hazardous sailing, and in no time at all the buffoon has become a hero with a strong claim to local immortality.

To the occasional cricketer this sort of thing never happens, even during his day dreams at long leg. For one thing, he would be miscast in this particular role. He cannot claim not to have touched a bat for fifteen years. The whole point about him – if there is any point about him at all – is that three or four times in every season he does touch a bat, though it seldom amounts to very much more than that. By a diminishing number of people he is still thought of, if not exactly as a cricketer, at least as a cricket-playing person. There is in practice almost no limit to the number of feats which he will never accomplish upon the cricket field; but to make an unorthodox invasion of the game from outside it is the only triumph of which he has not – in imagination – been the protagonist.

Since he cannot bowl, or anyhow is not asked to, and since his innings, even if the time spent in walking to and from the wicket be included in it, is never a very long one, the occasional cricketer has plenty of opportunity for exercising his imagination. As he stands out there on the greensward he does not look a very formidable figure; his white trousers are too short and the moth pastures show like snowdrifts upon the summit of his faded cap. He himself realizes, now, that it is not much good dreaming, as he used to years ago, of centuries, and no good at all – unless two or three of his fellow-players sprain an ankle – even thinking about the hat-trick; but he still sees himself achieving some minor, unexpected distinction – a faultless late cut to the boundary, an almost impossible catch taken and held with the left hand, low down. The truth is that he needs these dreams. Were it not for them he might read the writing on the wall in the unhesitating regularity with which the batsmen cry "Come one!" every time they hit the ball in his direction. Were it not for them he might divine too easily the thoughts of his opponents when – batting rather earlier than usual, owing to somebody's car having broken down – he comes in at No. 8. A slogger? They soon see he is not that. A spin-bowler? Before the match is over they realize that he was not being played for his bowling. He is only – as the more astute of them will have divined from the moment he took guard – an occasional cricketer; the bowler's friend when he is at the wicket, the batsman's accomplice when he is in the field. Every summer his trousers, and his breath, get shorter; every summer it gets harder to decide why he is asked to play. But he is a likeable chap, he lives near at hand, and in another year or two no doubt he will do the Big Thing. "No, I won't play," he will say, "but I'll come and umpire if you like." And as he stands out there, year after year, in his white coat the players will no longer be faintly puzzled by his presence.

Cricket on the Screen

22 *August* 1951. For all those lovers of cricket who devoured the daily dispatches of the M.C.C. tour in Australia last winter and later completed their education, in a detached way, by reading of the tour again in concentrated book form, there has now come a film on the same subject, one hour in length. It is called *Elusive Victory*, photographed and assembled by Mr. John Woodcock, with Mr. E. W. Swanton as the chief narrator, and supporting commentaries by Mr. R. C. Robertson-Glasgow, Mr. Rex Alston, and Mr. S. C. Griffith.

As a tranposition of the printed word into terms of vision and sound it has an unquestioned educative and entertainment value. More than a mere pictorial impression – the first of its kind on this subject – it brings one closer to the heart of an undertaking across the breadth of a continent. Here one can see and feel the game in Australia; the huge crowds, vast enclosures, and sense of urgency surrounding the Test matches. One can sense, too, the strain of such a tour with its exhausting travel, and its heat, brought into relief when the players are caught in their moments of relaxation.

Clearly the film faced certain problems and limitations. Every ball bowled, for instance, could not be recorded. Yet in spite of that the camera has effectively caught many vital moments of the struggle. It shows, above all, the full implications of an Australian "sticky" wicket at Brisbane, where batsmen fell like ninepins.

Application for hire of the film, in either 16mm. or 35mm size, by clubs, firms, and other organizations should be made to Mr. John Woodcock, Bodley House, Vigo Street, London, W.1. Schools – the enthusiasm of the young cricketer is perhaps the main target – should apply to Mr. John Green at the same address. The film is an hour well spent of a winter's evening.

Averages and Asterisks

12 *September* 1951, *Leading Article*. To-day the final table of averages announces all too clearly that cricket and summer are done. Already the appearance one by one of the county averages had warned us of the impending doom, but still, on its very brink, many of the players continued to indulge in the feverish gaiety of festivals. It was but a putting off and now the neat patterns with their columns spotted with the little asterisks that signify

"not out" make the temporary epitaphs of those who have cheered us during the past months. They are tucked up in their dark wintry beds till "spring shall blow her clarion" to waken them once more, when we shall have ungratefully forgotten the less illustrious of their names.

The list as a whole makes necessarily sad reading, but it is in the details of the county averages that individual pathos is to be found. Look, for instance, at the names of those who find no place in the tables, but figure only in the postscript as "Also batted." Here is one whose entire contribution to his county's score was 0 not out. For all we know he never made contact with a single ball, since as soon as he had taken his place at the wicket his colleague incontinently allowed himself to be bowled. What sad stories we can invent for ourselves about him. With what joy he received the invitation to play, believing his fortune made. What a send-off he received from his village; how he lay awake half the night wondering and hoping, and all for 0 not out. He may not have had it in him to make a hundred, but double figures – those he might have achieved and they with an asterisk would have been at least a cheering memory, but he never had a chance. Yet he will always be able to muse on what he might have done, a pleasure scarcely to be enjoyed by the man who in four completed innings achieved an average of 1.75.

Apart from such palpably heart-rending cases fate seems strangely capricious in this matter of asterisks. As we know they are of great value in swelling an average, since the total of runs is increased, but not the number of innings by which it must ultimately be divided. He who goes in last is likely with ordinary luck to accumulate a little treasure of asterisks, but the tables show that among the eminent persons who go in high on the list some are much more richly dowered than others. In one county are two batsmen who have each gone to the wicket five and forty times; each has a highly respected average and to neither has fate awarded a single one of her mathematical favours. Another and possibly rather more distinguished batsman on the same side has a positively miserly store of seven. There seems here some malignity of fortune at work. Again some tables are entirely honest and produce precisely the expected results. Here is Yorkshire with HUTTON easily head in the batting and that new and romantic figure, APPLEYARD, in the bowling. The proper gods are in their respective heavens and all's right with the world. Now and again, however, we find one who has toiled and sweated and carried his county on his back relegated to second place by some little over-asterisked being of whom we have barely heard. Then our only comfort must be that figures can prove anything.

Nawab of Patuadi

4 *January* 1952. The Nawab of Patuadi, who died at New Delhi suddenly on Saturday, from a heart attack while playing in a polo match, will be long

remembered for the pleasure he gave to countless spectators in various parts of the British Commonwealth by his cricketing prowess.

Nawab Muhammad Iftikar Ali Khan Bahadur was born in March, 1910, and at the age of 19 succeeded to the rulership of Pataudi, a small State in the Gurgoan district of what is now East Punjab. He came to this country in 1926 to go up to Oxford. He was coached by Frank Woolley, the Kent and England batsman, who forecast a brilliant cricket future for him and gained his Blue in 1929 scoring 106 and 84 against Cambridge. Two years later he established a new record by making the highest individual score in these University matches in remarkable circumstances. In the Cambridge first innings A. Ratcliffe scored 201, so breaking the record which had been held for 27 years. Ratcliffe's honour lasted only a few hours, however, because Pataudi obtained 238 not out for Oxford. It is said that before going in to bat Pataudi declared his intention of trying to pass Ratcliffe's score.

Pataudi went to Australia as a member of D. R. Jardine's team in the 1932-33 tour. He scored a century in his first Test but, after one more game for England, was left out of the side. He reappeared for England when Australia came here in 1934, by which time he was playing for Worcestershire, but his next Test appearances came in 1946, when he led the Indian Test team to England and played in all three Tests. On that tour Pataudi did not enjoy the best of health and he disappeared from first-class cricket after his return home, but last autumn he returned to England for a visit after finding a school in Switzerland for his 11-year-old son. When he was in England Pataudi made contact with his former county and Worcestershire successfully applied to the Advisory County Cricket Committee for him to be regarded as still qualified to play for them. He hoped to turn out for them occasionally next season when visiting his son at school.

After a long engagement arising from tardy consent by her father, the Nawab of Bhopal, one of the most important Muslim-ruled States in India, he married the second daughter of that prince in 1936, and he leaves a son and three daughters.

C. B. Fry

25 *April* 1952, *Leading Article.* If MR. CHARLES BURGESS FRY had never been born, as, fortunately, he was, eighty years ago to-day and in Surrey of all Home Counties, it would have been necessary to invent him. The authors of serial stories in a boy's own paper – say in *C. B. Fry's Magazine* – had to learn that life is not a bed of roses. They, feebly letting truth set the pace for fiction, had for long allowed their heroes a blue or two, a goal here, a try there, a decent show in school sports, and just enough book-learning to avoid rustication. More than that, they feared, was over the odds of probability, and then a Reptonian was elected Senior Scholar of Wadham, with

the future Lord Birkenhead coming in fourth. After that, fiction gave up the race and sat gasping in amazement while truth sprinted off down the straight. The facts about MR. FRY's record as an undergraduate are so famous and so familiar that any writer must blush to recite them in detail. Captain of Oxford against Cambridge at cricket and at Association football was not enough – a century had to be made at Lord's (not out, of course), and a blue for Rugby football only missed through a last-minute accident. A performance for the O.U.D.S. as the Prince of Morocco in *The Merchant of Venice* crowded a second night house to enjoy an athletic rendering of the line "Oh, Hell, what have we here?" A meeting with MR. MAX BEERBOHM of Merton led to the coining of the phrase "Golf is glorified croquet." A taste for taking exercise against Cambridge, without the distractions of a ball, caused the setting up of a world's record for the long jump.

Those were salad days triumphs. The best was yet to come. Among the many good reasons for having been alive and taking notice in the earliest years of this century must have been that K. S. RANJITSINHJI and C. B. FRY were Sussex batsmen together. This partnership, it has been said, turned MR. FRY from a good to a great player. He needed little turning. Upright at the wicket, with bat lifted back over the middle stump, he made the Hove ground seem too small to contain a cricket-ball. His straight drives and his on strokes were a delight and, when deluded fielders suspected him of being weaker to the off, he taught them better. Statistics embalm the thousands of runs in a season and the row upon row of centuries. They cannot recapture the grace of the artist at the wicket.

Sport, even at this high Olympian level, had to take its place in the queue of MR. FRY's accomplishments. He has written well in prose and verse. He has stood as a Liberal for Parliament. His long service in the Mercury rightly earned him at the age of seventy-four the honorary rank of Captain, R.N.R. A horseman and an angler, a marksman and a motorist, he has preserved through all his strenuous versatility as an out-of-doors man an unquenchable zest for good talk. Those who have been privileged to hear him agree that there is no subject, from Greek music to the gold standard, in which he will drop a catch. The great sportsman is a good companion and his memories are rich. He recalls MEREDITH asking him if the whip stroke was better than the long swing, and BARRIE – that ardent amateur of cricket – "not minding a bit" when his Scottish terrier nipped her fellow-countryman in the Achilles tendon. With so much gaiety and such well-earned fame behind him, MR. FRY should go forward confidently to complete his century.

A Caravan of Bats

12 *May* 1952, *Leading Article*. Neither the Foreign Office nor the M.C.C. has seen fit to comment on a report from Kalimpong that a large consignment

of cricket bats, transported on the backs of mules, is on its way to Lhasa at the behest of the education authorities in Tibet. Accustomed as we are to being baffled by International affairs, it is difficult to recall any recent development in that sphere of which the significance was harder to evaluate. There is, of course, nothing odd in the Tibetans wanting to play cricket; the natural and salutary aspiration does them credit. The mountain torrents of their native land and her frequently frozen lakes severely limit the opportunities open to wet-bobs, and it was perhaps inevitable that a passion for our national sport, repressed for centuries, should break out sooner or later.

It is, all the same, a little surprising that King Willow should come into his own at a time when Tibet is under Communist control. It may, of course, be that the new régime in Lhasa sees in cricket an opiate or anodyne which will confer upon the people partial oblivion of their sufferings; and it is certainly true that the history of the game is unsullied by any connexions with counter-revolutionary activity. But there are, after all, other sports less closely associated with the Imperialist tradition; and, however much one reveres cricket and however little one knows about Tibet, it is difficult to believe that this incomparable game is ideally suited to the conditions obtaining on the Roof of the World.

There may – indeed there must – be more in this business than meets the eye. It looks like some sort of a move in the Cold War. Readers with romantic minds will toy with the idea that the whole thing has been organized for subversive purposes, by the British Secret Service – that at the head of the caravan (humming the Eton boating song to put people off the scent) strides, heavily disguised, some agent of the calibre of Colonel Egham or Big White Carstairs. Alas, it is more likely to be the other way round. World Communism, though it has many conquests to its credit, has as yet made little impression on cricket; but its outward indifference to the sport (the Russians have not even bothered to claim that they invented it) may well mask a respect for its civilizing influence and a determination to adapt it to conform with the exigencies of Marxist doctrine. It is true that Tibet does not seem a particularly sensible place in which to initiate this project; but it is remote and secluded, and the inhabitants have no preconceived bourgeois ideas on the subject which need to be eradicated. It seems all too probable that the report from Kalimpong may foreshadow the launching of a vast conspiracy throughout the New Democracies to undermine the influence of cricket by evolving a similar but ideologically sounder game. How fast or how far this threat to one of our dearest institutions may develop it is impossible to say. It depends to a certain extent on whether the people in Lhasa remembered to order any balls.

Hutton Captains England

Break with Tradition

26 *May* 1952. L. Hutton, the Yorkshire professional opening batsman and first choice for England for many seasons, is to captain England in the first Test match against India at Leeds on June 5. N. W. D. Yardley, Hutton's county captain, who is chairman of the England selectors, announced this after a meeting at Nottingham yesterday. He added that the side for the first Test would be selected next Thursday.

All four selectors were at the meeting. Besides Yardley, they are F. R. Brown, who had stated that he would like to give up the England captaincy for a younger man, R. E. S. Wyatt, and L. E. G. Ames, who was the first professional to be appointed a member of the selection committee.

Our Cricket Correspondent [Geoffrey Green] writes:–

For the first time a professional player has been chosen to captain England. Though there are many who will look back with anxious eyes and with sorrow at the passing of an age, there are yet those who will welcome the ending of an anachronism. The amateur, in the older meaning of the word, no longer truly exists. He has largely been destroyed by the economic circumstance of mid-twentieth century. Further, to find such a man, both with the character to lead and also the quality indisputably to hold a place in an England team, has progressively become more difficult. When F. R. Brown was called on by the selectors two years ago the writing was on the wall. Brown's unqualified success, heartening though it was, solved nothing. It merely postponed the hour that has now come.

The selectors, who for some time have been struggling to balance the requirements of tradition with the needs of the moment, are to be congratulated on the action they have taken. They have shown a boldness that one had not expected of them yet. But sooner or later this last step seemed to be due. It was presaged by the reinstatements of W. R. Hammond, who led England after the war against Australia, and W. J. Edrich, joint-captain of Middlesex; by the responsible parts played in the counties by Compton, Dollery, and John Langridge.

In this age of so-called equal opportunity for all the professional player has at last attained his fullest stature, and it is now up to Hutton to prove not only himself but also his colleagues worthy of the new principle which has been established. Certainly tradition has died hard and to Hutton now goes the new honour.

Actually there have been instances in the past of England being led on the cricket field by a professional in the absence through illness or injury of the amateur captain. Hobbs, of Surrey, once captained the side against Australia in the fourth Test match at Manchester in 1926 after A. W. Carr had been struck down by tonsillitis; Compton took over from F. R. Brown in the fourth Test match in Australia during the 1950-51 tour after Brown had been hurt in a car accident; Hutton himself was at the helm for an hour or two at the Oval last season against South Africa while Brown was having a strained leg attended to.

Whether this new title will become a burden that will affect Hutton's full efficiency as a great batsman remains to be seen, but the eyes of the country will be upon him as he accepts the accolade before his own Yorkshire people at Headingley.

Art for Sport's Sake?

20 *October* 1952, *Leading Article*. There are many signs that the great gulf which once separated the Hearty from the Highbrow is gradually being narrowed. The contemptuous hostility with which each used to regard the other has been modified to a quizzical tolerance, and a sort of demilitarized zone has been created where both are apt to find themselves on common ground in their liking for detective fiction, village cricket, and the drawings of MR. OSBERT LANCASTER. One symptom of this *rapprochement* is the tendency for people who write about sport to write about it in a prose liberally incrusted with cultural allusions. The dexterity of a late cut is compared with the virtuosity of an epigram by OSCAR WILDE, the names of leading ballerinas are invoked to convey to the reader the peculiar prowess of a stand-off half, and a rally on the Centre Court is described in terms of contrapuntal orchestration. Nobody quite knows whether the Hearty actually likes this sort of thing; but it undoubtedly makes it easier for the Highbrow to follow his activities.

It has been very noticeable, however, that in the partial reconciliation between these two factions the concessions have all been made by one side. Accounts of cricket and golf, of football and steeplechasing, have – often at the cost of baffling the sportsmen themselves – steadily increased their potential appeal to persons of culture and refinement; but from the other side, from the Highbrow camp, has come no gesture of response. One does not know for certain whether or not MR. ALEC BEDSER has ever been compared, in print, to MR. T. S. ELIOT, but one would not be particularly surprised if he had. One does on the other hand, know – absolutely for certain – that MR. T. S. ELIOT has never been compared to MR. ALEC BEDSER. This unforthcoming attitude on the part of the Highbrows may be due to arrogance, to a sort of constitutional inability to mix a few acorns with the pearls they cast before the swine; or it may be simply that they do not know where to go for acorns.

Whatever the cause, it is reassuring to be able to report an indication, even if it is only an isolated one, that they are prepared to repay the Hearties in their own coin. A review recently published in a Bloomsbury periodical of an exhibition of abstract paintings (just the sort of homework a Hearty most needs help with) concluded as follows:–

His most successful paintings, such as the large yellow canvas with the black bicycle-framed grid and the lopsided blue carboard planet, are only successful within their own absurdly limited terms; terms which make it impossible for the spectator to be involved in their success. One is reminded of a good shot only shooting duck which he himself has released.

The intention here is excellent. Partially successful abstract painting, if it has got to be interpreted, must be interpreted in terms of something; and to select for the purpose a Philistine pursuit like wildfowling shows a laudable desire to reach out to a wider and more oafish audience. It would be hyper-critical to suggest that a one-man *tir aux canards* is not a spectacle of which many of us can claim to be reminded, even by a lop-sided blue cardboard planet. The main thing is that the ice has been broken, and if all goes merrily forward in the right direction, we may soon hope to hear KAFKA being discussed in terms of beagling, and to be told that M. ANOUILH is the P. B. H. MAY of the Paris theatre.

Giants in those Days

13 *December* 1952, *Leading Article.* "Ah! but you should have seen Kortright." Those words, heard so often as LARWOOD or LINDWALL or FARNES was bowling, echo to-day in the December half light from the news that, ripe in years, the fastest bowler of all time has died. Great sportsmen share with great actors a fate from which authors and other artists in lasting media escape. They depend for their fame on action and once they quit field or stage they become ghosts, doomed to flit to and fro in the memory of a dwindling few. But here and there a GARRICK or a GRAY projects so vivid a shadow into the future that he stirs curiosity in younger generations as to what exactly he was like in his prime. KORTRIGHT stands out in this way among those he himself called "the old-times men of pace."

There is a thrill about fast bowling especially when it is watched from the safety of the stands. KOTZE, GREGORY, MCDONALD, KNOX, FIELDER, CONSTANTINE – the roll-call could go on to make a full eleven – return easily to the mind's eye of anyone who saw them and bring back vanished days of hot summer sunshine to dispel mid-winter gloom. Purists may say that the subtle beauty of the game does not lie in speed, and nobody will contradict them. But the thrill remains. KORTRIGHT once recalled how one of his yorkers rebounded from the bottom of the stumps and went back past him almost to the boundary. Some of us would rather have seen that than have sat through a whole scientific century by A. N. Other. A batsman for whom fast bowling has no terrors is deservedly a hero. That was one side of the splendour of GRACE, who reached three figures against KORTRIGHT when his partners were making no secret of their discomfort.

Recollection, aroused by thoughts of KORTRIGHT, turns to an even farther away giant whose prowess earned ever greater praise. If the tales are true SPOFFORTH was the demon king of bowlers. Speed served him but it is his legendary cunning that looms larger in retrospect. He would lie awake at night turning over the best ways of attacking the mighty opponents who were to face him in the morning. When he was at his most deadly he brought London swarming up to Lord's for an afternoon in which he mowed down the flower of English cricket. That was an occasion as famous as an Irving first night. But SPOFFORTH never, as KORTRIGHT did, bowled a ball which rose almost straight and went out of the small ground without a second bounce, thus giving away a unique six in byes. Such was this Victorian out of Essex and he found a wicketkeeper in MACGREGOR to stand up to him in spite of his "muzzle velocity" which SIR PELHAM WARNER has reckoned probably to have been a hundred miles an hour down the pitch. Giants there indeed were in those days.

Jack Hobbs at 70 not out
Birthday Memories of Great Games and Players

BY OUR SPECIAL CORRESPONDENT [JOHN HARTLEY]

16 *December* 1952. John Berry Hobbs is 70 to-day. This astonishing fact has come as a surprise to many lovers of cricket for whom the memory of this legendary figure is still as green as the Oval table in the days, not so long ago, when he stood slim and erect in the middle and the runs flowed in an effortless stream from his bat.

To Hobbs himself the achievement of threescore years and 10 has come as no less of a surprise. But for the publicity it has aroused and the requests for interviews – such as the one he gave to your Correspondent – the date might have passed unnoticed. For at 70 he is still slim, still alert and nimble; there is scarcely a line of his face and his hair is not, as he claims, "picked up eleven-a-side."

As a batsman Jack Hobbs was always a delight to watch. He attacked the bowling, scored freely and fast, except when occasion demanded he should just stay there, and he delighted in short runs. He had a zest and passionate enjoyment for cricket as a game which was transmitted to the crowd. He has always been modest, but, having decided to delve into the past as a form of birthday celebration, he has brought up memories and comments all reflecting a love of the game.

From his early days he was a natural batsman. His father was groundsman at Jesus College, Cambridge, and in Jesus Close he used to practise hitting the ball. He would set up a stump as a wicket, and with a stump as a bat would get a friend to bowl to him with a tennis ball – "and stumps were thin in those days, too."

His trial and acceptance for Surrey came on Tom Hayward's recommendation after an unofficial trial on Parker's Piece, where a wicket was set up and Hayward and Reeves (of Essex) bowled to him. In his first game for Surrey, against the Gentlemen, Hobbs came up against Dr. W. G. Grace. "I had never seen him before, except at a distance. It was a very proud moment for me when I faced up to him. He bowled those donkey drops of his. I cannot say I found him difficult; but I did not take any liberties with him, I must admit."

In his next match – against Essex – he made a century. "I thought I knew it all then. Later I found I did not. Opening with Tom Hayward, I learned what balls to leave alone and what to go for. I learned the scoring strokes to improve and those to drop." Later he came to prefer other partners. "Poor old Tom, he did not like the short run, he was too heavy. It was lovely with Wilfred Rhodes when we started the short run business. Sutcliffe and Sandham liked cheeky runs, too. I think a lot of short runs are missed these days."

Jack Hobbs looks on the period 1910-14 as his most brilliant. He could attack the bowling with zest when he felt like it. "You could play cheeky shots and make 50 or 60 and feel life was worth living. Then came the exasperation when they started counting your hundreds, publishing averages, and it was all figures. They think too much of figures these days." This from the man who made more runs than anyone else has ever done – 61,221 – and whose 197 first-class centuries is also a record. [*61,221 was the figure given in the 1952* Wisden. *The following year it was amended to 61,237, which is now generally, though not universally, accepted.*]

Batsmen to-day have all Hobbs's sympathy. Bowling has become defensive and wickets are slower. In-swingers across the wicket from outside the leg-stump do not give batsmen a chance. "If you try to glide them now you get caught, and all the beautiful shots on the off-side that one used to see have been shut up. An off-drive by Hutton or Compton is something to admire, but you no longer get much wristy cutting. It is much easier to stay in now, but not so easy to score runs. Players like Hayward would have adapted themselves to it, but Hayward would have been a bit better than most to-day. I think I might have adapted myself. I do not see why I should not also have scored runs."

There was fast bowling in the old days. "A fast bowler to-day is an event. They tell you the wicket is too easy paced, but a fast bowler is a necessity; he is always likely to get a wicket at the beginning of an innings. Pace bowlers are still the same type, but they have lost a bit of their devil. If Trueman keeps free from injury he should 'make the grade.'"

The game is more commercialized now, he says. There must be good gates and lively cricket is necessary. Surrey played lively cricket last summer and had some handsome gates. He did not want to compare the team of last year with that in which he played when Surrey last won the county championship in 1914. "I do not think we were inferior, but they played magnificently last summer and gave me a thrill or two. There is such a good spirit in the side."

The difference between players then and now is not so much of quality as of quantity. "There were more stars then; many good amateurs are lost now because of high costs and taxes." But English teams have been improving since the war. "With young Len Hutton as skipper we have the best chance of beating the Australians next summer that we have had for years. The Australians seem to be in the doldrums now; with an even break in the luck, we should win. They do not seem to have as many good players as in the Bradman era.

"Bradman was a team in himself. I think Don was too good; he spoilt the game. He got too many runs. The pot calling the kettle black? No, I was human; he got hundreds every time he went in. I did cheer the hearts of the bowlers even in my most palmy days. He was mechanical; he was the greatest run-getting machine of all time. I do not think we want to see another one quite like him. I do not think we ever shall."

Hobbs spoke of his favourite strokes. "We always liked to hook a good ball. Then I liked a good square cut, you could get a lot of power into it, it was a beautiful shot to make. I liked a cover drive, but . . ." he paused and gave a slow smile, "you like them all when you can hit them hard."

Of all the bowling he faced he preferred the googlies above all. "They put you on your mettle and there is always a loose one – and then you crack it." Sydney Barnes was perhaps the best bowler of all and would have been even better on present wickets.

Hobbs qualified two comments that have been made on his game – his improved fielding, and a tendency to be l.-b.-w. It was said that he developed suddenly from a comparatively poor fielder into the most brilliant cover-point of his generation. He denies he was ever poor. "I had a minor injury – I had thrown my arm out – and nobody knew about it at the time." The way he used often to be out he explains on the ground that to play a straight bat he had to stand behind the flight of the ball. Sometimes he missed it. "If you miss a straight ball, you get out. Some people get bowled, I was l.-b.-w."

He really enjoyed the Tests, but it is not always the big occasions that are fixed in his memory. His most enjoyable innings was in a private match in 1921 when he played for Lionel Robinson's XI against a side captained by MacLaren which included Australians. Everything went right and he felt he could not get out. After making 87 he retired hurt, having pulled a muscle going for a desperate run.

Hobbs remembers every innings he played on a bad wicket. There was the terrible "sticky" at Melbourne on the 1928-29 tour when he and Sutcliffe put on over 100 for the first wicket after people had prophesied that England would be out for under 70. England won by four wickets. He considers his most valuable innings was that at the Oval in 1926 when he and Sutcliffe each made centuries on a bad wicket and England won the rubber against Australia for the first time for 14 years.

He will never forget the game against Kent at the Oval in 1919 when he and Jack Crawford, batting against the clock, made 90-odd in 35 minutes and the crowd went mad. He remembers the excitement when he needed a hundred to equal Grace's record of 126 centuries. It was a long time coming; then he scored 91 one day at Taunton and had to make nine the next morning. "We started a quarter of an hour late while they let the crowd in. I remember feeling a bit jittery waiting." He recalls his highest score, 316 not out at Lord's in 1926 at the age of 43. "I did not get tired. I never got tired batting, though cricket is a game of intense concentration."

When Jack Hobbs retired in 1934 after making 197 centuries, regret was expressed universally; but he was certain then, as now, that he was right. "I gave up before my 200th century because I thought I had outstayed my usefulness with the Surrey side. You cannot go on for ever keeping people out of the side. Also I did not want to be an object of sympathy. Some people said I was playing as well as ever, but I knew how I felt, what I could and could not do. Looking back, though, it is a pity I did not get the 200; I should like to have been the first."

Jack Hobbs was a cricket idol then. To-day he is a sporting legend.

The Fight for the Ashes

Australian Hopes for Coming Test Series

BY SIR DONALD BRADMAN

21 *February* 1953. In 1926 an Australian team went to England to do battle for "The Ashes." Since then it has been my good fortune to be a member of every Australian team which has followed in their footsteps until now, when it is my turn to be on the side-lines. That period of history covers 27 years, and so I confess to a slight feeling of nostalgia at staying behind, for I love England and her people.

When a touring team is chosen critics usually find several good reasons why the selection committee should be sacked. This year is no exception. However, for once I was not on the committee and could afford to smile. After the team had been announced and I was returning to my hotel I accosted three strangers and out of pure devilment said to them: "What do you think of the team?" The first simply said, "Horrible"; the second, "Too old"; and the third, "We'll lose the Ashes with that selection." These opinions rather shocked me, so I sat down and made a quiet analysis to myself of my miniature private Gallup poll. If the team is "horrible" it must be conceded that it contains the best 11 cricketers in Australia, even though we may argue about some of the remainder. If it is "too old" at least it includes the youngest player ever to be selected for Australia. Whether we lose or not still remains to be answered.

The South African team which has just toured Australia won two, lost two, and drew one Test in the series. This is being used as an argument to discredit Australia, for at the beginning of their tour the visitors were not conceded any chance of winning. But let me say at once that these South Africans moulded into a combination of formidable strength. They were young, full of enthusiasm, and remarkably fit. I never once saw a man sit down on the field when a wicket fell, even towards the close of the hardest day. No greater fielding team has ever been seen in Australia, according to even the oldest spectator. Their batting improved until finally, without having a shining star around whom to build, they had an even quality down to number ten which merited comparison with true international standard. Only in bowling did I feel they were below it. The lack of real speed was evident at once and was sadly missed in spite of lionhearted efforts by the medium pacers. A vicious leg spinner would have been invaluable on many occasions. Marvellous fielding, including some of the most incredible catching, helped to hide these deficiencies, but to the discerning eye the attack was very limited.

Here, then, to my way of thinking, we come to probably the most important question about Australia's potential weakness. Our batsmen (in the selectors' eyes the best we have), under conditions more suitable for run-making than they are likely to find in England, did not collectively make enough runs against South Africa. The same players will need to improve if they are to make higher scores against Bedser, Trueman and Co. Our touring team has only two regular openers. The older and more experienced of the two is Arthur Morris, and a great deal will depend on whether he can recapture his 1948 form.

If the openers fail to provide a good start heavy responsibility will fall on Hassett (should he elect to bat first wicket down) or Harvey. The latter was positively brilliant against South Africa. His powerful hitting, aggressive attitude, and at times unorthodox methods made him stand out above his colleagues. He is at the peak of his form and should play many grand innings on the tour, but it will be flirting with providence to have him at the crease while the ball is new and the bowlers fresh. Possibly Hassett will prefer to trust his own greater experience and more sedate methods to try to lay the foundations for the attackers. Come what may, Hassett is no longer cast in the role of the aggressor but Harvey is, and in that category is best likely to serve his team even though in defence he is now tighter and sounder than ever before.

Of the other batsmen, it will be interesting to see who develops most quickly. In Hole, Craig, and de Courcy we have a trio who are very different in method but all very talented. Perhaps attention will first be focused on Craig because of his youth. In a country where youth is rewarded sometimes more than experience it was thought remarkable that a boy of 17 could be good enough to play for Australia. The selectors believed he was, and his batting in the fifth Test against South Africa probably surpassed even their high expectations. Surely here is a great player in the making.

Australians think highly of Graeme Hole, whose offside play possesses a fluency and grace of the classical variety. He also bids fair on recent form to remedy a weakness in our slip fielding. The West Indians were surprised that de Courcy was not chosen in the Tests against them. He is a versatile, quick-footed batsman who should benefit from continuous play and the knowledge that he is in the team. These things have been denied him in the past. Englishmen know the debonair, unpredictable Keith Miller. He will thrill them again when the mood strikes him, but recurrent back trouble has caused grave fears as to how much longer he can be a star fast bowler without being unfair to himself. Anxious eyes will be on him those first weeks.

In young Benaud will be found a cricketer who could easily be mistaken for Miller as he moves lithely after a ball. Their movements, build, and mannerisms are similar. Benaud is a lovely field and a batsman who can hit with tremendous power, but strangely enough in bowling he reverts to slow leg spinners. He may easily be called upon to do a lot of work and if so will obviously enjoy it. There are two other leg spinners. Of these, Ring is well known to Englishmen and is regarded as our number one. The second is Jack Hill – the surprise choice of the 17. He bowls faster than the orthodox leg spinner but on our pitches does not turn to any extent. His length is usually impeccable and without any doubt his inclusion is an insurance against the failure of our other leg spinners, coupled with the thought that he may force his claims to a place in the eleven on his own prowess.

In Bill Johnston Englishmen will find a stout-hearted bowler who from the pavilion appears just the same as the 1948 vintage. He laughs even more, and his infectious joviality on the field even makes fun of a bumper which might from anyone else cause resentment. His understudy is Davidson – a glorious fieldsman, a more than useful hard-hitting batsman, and a left-hand bowler of the Johnston type. If the opportunity presents itself Davidson could easily join the top flight.

Of Lindwall one can say that his bowling against South Africa had not quite the fire of earlier years, except when he deemed it necessary to put forward a special effort. Nevertheless it was at all times intelligently directed and his absence from the attack in the fifth Test was sorely felt. Here again, unfortunately, there is the lurking fear of a leg injury, and Hassett will certainly take all precautions to keep Lindwall fit for the important occasions. He, too, has an understudy in young Ron Archer – a lad of 19 summers. Perhaps Archer would admit he was a lucky boy, on his limited experience of first-class cricket, to catch the selectors' vote, but they have shown courage in trying to develop a young virile athlete who shows distinct promise in all departments of the game. As yet he can scarcely be termed fast, and this tour should decide whether he can find the extra pace to lift him beyond the realms of fast medium.

Of wicket keepers it is enough to say we have two reliable stalwarts, both tested and proved in the crucible of international cricket. Tallon is still a great artist, and even if Langley has not the polish, do not be misled. Wait until someone touches a swinger. Our bowlers are confident that no safer pair of hands exists to-day. As for courage, he is a real bulldog. There, in a brief review, is Australia's team.

I am not going to forecast the result of the series. All signs point to a very even struggle. However, I think England may very reasonably contend she has at least an equal chance, on the grounds that Australia's batting appears to be weaker than in 1948, and her bowling and fielding no stronger. On the other hand, England's claims that her own bowling, fielding, and batting have improved seem to be well founded. These variations in strength can, of course, be quickly altered by the luck of the toss, a sudden storm, or even an umpire's decision.

Irrespective of the result, I may perhaps make a plea in the interests of cricket and on behalf of the general public. It is just simply that the teams endeavour to play a bright, attacking game, and not shut out by defensive strategy those glories of stroke play which are exclusive to our national game. Cricket in Australia was stimulated by the South Africans. Their whole attitude to the game was delightful, and their departure is regretted on all sides. I, for one, hope our players and those of the Mother Country will in the forthcoming series do still more to popularise a sport which is unquestionably an invisible asset in the Empire balance-sheet.

THE AUSTRALIAN TEAM

*A. L. Hassett, aged 39, Victoria (capt.)   *A. R. Morris, 31, N.S.W. (vice-capt.)
 R. Archer, 19, Queensland   R. Benaud, 22, N.S.W.
 I. Craig, 17, N.S.W.   A. Davidson, 23, N.S.W.
 J. de Courcy, 25, N.S.W.   *R. N. Harvey, 24, Victoria
 J. Hill, 29, Victoria   G. Hole, 21, South Australia
*W. A. Johnston, 31, Victoria   G. Langley, 33, South Australia
*R. R. Lindwall, 31, N.S.W.   C. McDonald, 24, Victoria
*K. R. Miller, 33, N.S.W.   *D. Ring, 34, Victoria
*D. Tallon, 37, Queensland

* Member of 1948 touring team.

The party will sail from Perth, Western Australia, in the Orcades on March 22, and is due at Tilbury on April 13.

Lights Up at Lord's

12 *March* 1953, *Leading Article*. With everybody tumbling over themselves to be thought up-to-date and progressive, last ditches to-day are unoccupied areas, but surely a few stalwarts will man them and make their protest against the alterations which have now been made to the scoreboards at Lord's. The numbers one to eleven have been added, with the letter S for substitute, and then the ball is caught or fielded the scorer will press a button and a light above the player's score-card number will shine out on the board. Lord's, indeed, will be more like Piccadilly Circus than a respectable cricket ground, and gone will be the favourite occupation of the expert onlooker, that of gently but firmly correcting the erroneous notions of his neighbour. When the man in the row in front has loudly applauded a piece of fielding and confided to his impressed companion that Dash is the best cover-point in the country, no longer will he be able to remark, with an air of mild yet unmistakable superiority, "That, sir, was not Dash, the ex-Cantab., but Blank, the old Oxonian."

Besides, to carry through such a reckless revolution at this particular moment is to surrender a point in the psychological warfare which is now the recognized prelude and accompaniment to all respectable games. Even when the Australians were rolling us in the dust, there was always comfort in the thought that at least we did things in our own and, therefore, the superior way. If Sydney and Melbourne chose so to conduct their business that the crowd could turn its back on the game and watch its progress on boards huge in size and correspondingly lavish with information, that was their own affair and we had no intention of following suit. In the good old days of not so very long ago it was part of the fun to bamboozle the paying spectator and keep him in a stage of comic ignorance as to what was going on. If it rained and then stopped, he was seldom told when play was likely to begin again, and, on some grounds, score-cards before luncheon were a treat. He, stout fellow, stood it all with the utmost good humour but now all is changed. The man is positively pampered, a decent anonymity is no more, and cricketers, to all intents and purposes, are as the poor footballers who carry numbers as though they were horses or articles at an auction sale. Still, last ditches are uncomfortable places to linger in, the Oval and Trent Bridge have already gone part of the way with Sydney and Melbourne and the hope is that this summer the lights of Lord's may shine out as brightly as the sun itself.

Butterfingers

6 *April* 1953, *Leading Article*. The comparative shortness of the present school holidays before the long vistas of the summer term does not excuse those parental duties which the young expect to be performed. He who has cricketing offspring is fortunate indeed if he has been sufficiently old-fashioned to have a quiverful, for he may then delegate some of the burden of "hardening up" for the season. There were famous cricketing families in the good old days in which father, mother, sisters, and even well-trained fielding dogs were enlisted to give practice to the son or sons of the house. But in these modern times smaller families are more usual, so that an unwarranted strain is likely to fall upon father – mother is too busy in the home; sister despises cricket and is playing lawn-tennis; dog is, maybe, a dachshund of a serious turn of mind, and, in spite of springing from a stock once famous for badger-hunting, is now more interested in a five-year plan for the storage of bones rather than in any form of sport.

If the cricketing offspring has reached double figures in years he has probably also outgrown the home ground on the lawn, and, for fear of the neighbours, father is forced to agree to practice on the nearest public open space, perhaps a corner of the village green or local pitch, still uncut and unrolled, and from which the ball is likely to rise at any angle. Woe to the parent who has given his son a new ball as a part Christmas present. There was a time when that same parent probably prayed to be asked to go on to bowl when the shine was still on the ball, but now the vicious-looking unworn seam is apparently only there to lacerate the palms. Having contracted that the son shall retrieve everything within moderate range – in other words, father must not hit too hard during his own innings – the parent cannot resist making his one scoring stroke, a chancy slash through the covers from which the ball indubitably ends up in the pond. Its pristine loveliness muddied, there follows a torrent of protests from its young owner.

As the single wicket match progresses through one of the bleaker April afternoons, father goes on to bowl, and has to stop some stinging returns. It is little comfort to him that soon those tougher types, the Australians, will be experiencing an English spring on the field of Worcester. Father tries to remember some of the more pleasant interludes of his cricketing past – the smell of hay from the paddock by the leg-boundary, the pavilion flag just stirring in the lightest of breezes, and the whole white and green rhythm of a cricket match on a perfect summer's day. Suddenly he realizes that the ball is descending upon him from a height; one of those deceptive, spinning catches that usually seem to go to mid-on from a mishit. As in the days of long ago the ball falls feebly to the ground, and, borne on the east wind, father hears a reedy, scornful, but still unpleasantly familiar cry of "butterfingers."

"The Final Test"

Mr. Rattigan's Film about Cricket

[BY DUDLEY CAREW]

13 *April* 1953. The ultimate feeling left by *The Final Test* (London Pavilion) is one of deep admiration for the consummate cleverness of Mr. Terence Rattigan as a playwright – *The Final Test* is a film, but the word is apposite and must stand.

Cricket is a game for the contemplative, and, as its literature shows, for the poetic. It reveals character, certainly, but through the medium of action on the field; it is blessed with both emotion and humour, yet, here again, these qualities belong to the actual pitch and are not easily transferable to stage or screen. And yet Mr. Rattigan, who is a good cricketer himself [*opening batsman for Harrow 1929-30*], has so contrived that in the 90 minutes the film takes to run, character, emotion, humour, and the essence of the game itself shall all have their innings, and in this he has been greatly helped by the director, Mr. Anthony Asquith.

His story is cunningly thought out and the film gets off the mark in the first scene. Mr. Rattigan has decreed that Sam Palmer – a batsman of Sutcliffe-Leyland calibre – shall be playing his last match for England against Australia at the Oval. Sam has a son, Reggie (Mr. Ray Jackson), who has, however, no intention of following in father's footsteps. Reggie writes poetry and hero-worships not Hutton – who, incidentally, has a not so very small part in the film and acts it admirably – but an advanced poet, Alexander Whitehead. Reggie, on the morning he should be watching his father play his last innings for England, goes instead to visit Whitehead only to find. . . . Only to find, of course, that Whitehead has no thoughts for anything but the Test match and, on hearing that Reggie has a spare ticket, rushes him to the Oval. Add to this neat contrivance the fact that Sam is in love with Cora (Miss Brenda Bruce) who is a barmaid and who, through her calling, can introduce on to the screen the solemn Englishness of a public-house crowd listening to a Test match on the wireless, and it will be realized just how clever Mr. Rattigan has been.

The scenes at the Oval, both on the field and in the dressing-room, have the stamp of authenticity and realism, and if, with Whitehead, Mr. Rattigan allows himself a degree of farcical exaggeration, it is, perhaps, because Mr. Robert Morley is so very willing to play. He makes the poet a most endearing eccentric, and the scenes he shares with Mr. Jack Warner's solid, likeable Sam, who, in spite of his lack of accent, must have played for Yorkshire, are the most delightful in a delightful film. Miss Adrianne Allen runs up a not inconsiderable score as Sam's sister, and Miss Bruce makes Cora a pearl among barmaids.

Eightieth Birthday Tribute
to S. F. Barnes

BY OUR SPECIAL CORRESPONDENT [JOHN HARTLEY]

14 *April* 1953. Sydney Barnes, the former England Test cricketer, will be 80 on April 19, and to celebrate his birthday he will bowl at the beginning of a match in his honour at Stafford on April 26. As the tall, erect figure runs slowly up to the wicket and delivers the ball from the outside edge of the crease, cricket lovers will be seeing one of the greatest cricketers of all time.

It is many years since Australian mothers frightened naughty children with the name of Sydney Barnes. It is years since Australian and South African crowds sat stunned into horrified silence as Barnes shattered the might of their batsmen on their own perfect wickets.

But Barnes's reputation has lived on. It tells of devastating bowling; of an attack that came like summer lightning, impersonally destroying wherever it struck.

In 1901, when Barnes was 28, A. C. MacLaren dropped a bombshell into the cricket world when he announced that S. F. Barnes would go on the next Australian tour.

Yet after two Tests the Australians were hailing him as the finest hard wicket bowler ever sent from England. Six years later, after another tour, M. A. Noble was describing him as the finest bowler in the world, and P. F. Warner said that Barnes was the best bowler he had played against.

But Barnes did not reach his peak for another six years – during tours of Australia and South Africa in which his performances have moved into legend. He was then widely acclaimed as the finest bowler the world had ever seen.

At 80 Barnes is neither frail nor infirm. Anyone seeing him striding easily and quickly each day up the long flight of steps to his office in the Shire Hall, Stafford, must be impressed by his vigour.

His manner is courteous and gentle. It is only when an incautious word is uttered that one realizes that the internal fires are not completely banked down, that age will never entirely mellow this rock of a man. The fateful, kindling word is "batsmen." At its sound a frosty look overtakes the bright blue eyes, and a hard edge comes into the Staffordshire accent. Mention of the ancient enemy takes Barnes back in his memory through the stages by which his attack was built up.

He began as a fast bowler, playing occasionally, but without much success, for Warwickshire. He was taught the off-break, but decided that the ball moving away from the batsman was more difficult to play. He developed a leg-break which was spun with the third finger so that it could be whipped down from the same height as the off-break. "It is speed off the pitch that counts." The "Barnes ball" was a leg-break that pitched on the leg stump and came off very fast to hit the top of the off stump. The action was very similar to that of the off-break, and Barnes never bowled googlies – "I did not need to."

He learnt much about swing in his first Test tour, and on a later tour Charles Macartney, in his first innings for Australia, saw Barnes bowl Victor Trumper. The ball was fast on the leg stump, but just before it pitched it swung suddenly to the off. Then it pitched, broke back, and took Trumper's leg stump. Macartney said afterwards: "It was the sort of ball a man might see if he was dreaming or drunk."

Barnes could make the ball swing one way and break the other and he could do it for both off- and leg-breaks. What is more, through variation of pace and flight alone, he could change both the spot at which the swing would become effective and the amount of the break. Finally he decided to bowl from the outside edge of the crease to make the line of flight of the ball more deceptive.

He was accurate and kept a perfect length. His bowling was directed against the weaknesses of batsmen. "I never bowled at the wickets: I bowled at the stroke. I intended the batsman to make a stroke, then I tried to beat it. I tried to make the batsman move. The time a batsman makes mistakes is when he has to move his feet."

Barnes's field was meticulously set. He would stand impassively, sometimes being barracked for delay, with long forefinger flicking every fielder to the exact spot. After a few balls he might move a man just a yard and a half – where he would take the catch straight to him.

The bowling to-day makes him impatient. "The l.-b.-w. rule is mainly responsible. It has shut out the lovely off-side strokes; there is too much defensive bowling outside the leg stump and too much playing off the back foot. If you are going to get wickets you must attack the batsman."

Barnes thinks we have one good bowler – Bedser – and a very promising bowler – Trueman – and that we can beat the Australians. "We should have beaten them years ago if we had attacked them." He would like to have bowled at Bradman. "He did not like one going away."

Barnes could bat, and once, with a 38 not out, including the winning hit, saved a Test for England. But he often threw his wicket away. "Why don't you try to make runs?" asked C. B. Fry. "If I make a century and took no wickets, would the selectors pick me for my batting?" was the reply. He once undertook to make 50 if allowed to go in first. He opened against Tasmania, but made only 47.

Barnes is not prepared to say who he thinks was the best batsman of his day – "there were so many really good men then." He would sometimes "just plug them down at Jack Hobbs and hope he would have a fit or something." Clem Hill was probably the most difficult to get out.

Although he had an immensely long playing career – from 1893 to 1936 –

Barnes played little first-class cricket. After his Test *début* he played two seasons for Lancashire – 1902 and 1903 – and thereafter played no first-class cricket except representative matches. In 22 seasons for Staffordshire he took 1,432 wickets for an average of 8.03 runs, and in 38 seasons of League cricket he took 3,741 wickets for an average of 6.68 runs.

The battles with the Australians provide his most treasured memories. Of these the most vivid is the classic occasion at Melbourne in 1911 – one of the finest feats of bowling in Test history. Australia with a powerful, triumphant side had won the toss and went in first on a perfect wicket. The crowd settled back happily in expectation of a huge score. F. R. Foster bowled the first over, then Barnes, who had been ill all week and was scarcely recovered, took the ball.

His first ball swung in to Bardsley, hit him on the toe and went on to the wicket. "He would have been l.-b.-w. if it had not." Shortly afterwards Kelleway stepped in front of the wicket and did not attempt to play a ball going past his legs. "It dipped into him and he was l.-b.-w." Clem Hill, the left-hander, was next. "I gave him one that was an off-break to him and then an in-swinger. Then I sent him one going away and he let it go. The last ball of the over pitched on his leg stump and hit the off. Clem said afterwards he had never had such an over."

The crowd was thunderstruck. But worse was to follow. Trumper and Armstrong, grim and determined, seemed to be making a stand. "Then a leg break to Armstrong went across nicely and very quick off the pitch. He played back, snicked it, and was caught at the wicket. I turned to Douglas, who was captain. Everything was going round. I said: 'I'll have to chuck it. I can hardly see the other end.'" He came off, having bowled nine overs with six maidens and taken four wickets for three runs. He did not bowl again until after lunch.

Then, in his first over, three runs were scored. In the next Minnett played forward to a leg-break, did not get it in the middle, and was caught by Jack Hobbs at cover-point. Barnes had taken five wickets for six runs.

In spite of his successes Barnes was not a popular idol. He was then too stern, too reserved, and he played too little first-class cricket. There was never any national tribute paid him, and though the game on Sunday comes for his eightieth birthday it is gratifying that Barnes is now as able as at any time in a distinguished career to appreciate the feelings of regard that cricket lovers everywhere will feel for a very great player.

Cricketers' War Memorial

28 *April* 1953. The Duke of Edinburgh yesterday opened the Imperial Cricket Memorial, constructed at Lord's to commemorate cricketers who died in two world wars. The ceremony was attended by High Commissioners

of Commonwealth countries and representatives of many cricketing organizations, among them members of the visiting Australian team.

The DUKE of EDINBURGH spoke of the almost universal delight in cricket throughout the British Commonwealth, and said that as a result it attracted a wide and devoted following, bound together by ties of affection for a wonderful game. They formed a great brotherhood of kindred spirits from every corner of the world.

It was appropriate that the memorial should have been provided at Lord's to cricketers from many different walks of life. Many would have been commemorated by their regiments, services, or in their home towns. Their friends would rather remember them as cricketers.

The DUKE of BEAUFORT, president of Marylebone Cricket Club, said that an emergency committee recommended in 1945 that the disused rackets court at Lord's be adapted for use as a cricketers' war memorial composed of a picture gallery and library. Mr. J. H. Markham was commissioned to prepare plans to provide gallery space on two floors.

Responsibility for the cost of the building was borne by the M.C.C.; no appeal for funds was made to the general public, but one was sent to M.C.C. members, and copies were addressed to county clubs and other cricket organizations that might wish to be associated with the scheme.

In response, about £4,200 was subscribed. The fund was still open, and donations were being made in a fairly steady volume.

The Duke of Beaufort referred to presentations of pictures by Sir Jeremiah Colman and cricket bodies overseas. Those from overseas were displayed on the ground floor in a small gallery that housed the commemorative tablet.

A notable exhibit, on view for the first time since the war, was the original urn that contained the ashes presented to Ivo Bligh during the successful tour of an English team in Australia in 1882-83.

The memorial was dedicated by the Bishop of London.

With the Gloves Off

5 *June* 1953, *Leading Article*. The rules of cricket were simply defined by Brigadier Gerard when he was a prisoner of war in this country. It is, he reported home to France, a brave pastime, a game for soldiers. Each tries to strike the other with the ball, and it is but a small stick with which you may ward it off. Three sticks behind show the spot beyond which you may not retreat. "I can tell you," the Brigadier exclaimed, "it is no game for children, and I will confess that, in spite of my nine campaigns, I felt myself turn pale when first the ball flashed past me." But he had reason to look back with complacency on his introduction to this stern sport. His aim was so true that he struck the batsman, a brave man who fell upon the wooden pegs behind him and, even in that moment of anguish, was sporting enough to confess

that there had been no accident in the victory. Again and again he cried aloud, "He did it a-purpose, he did it a-purpose!"

No such balm of righteous self-indignation soothed poor MR. REVILL, the Derbyshire batsman who was given out "hit wicket" after being struck on the hand so that he shook off his glove in pain and it removed a bail. That grand and genial sportsman MR. A. V. BEDSER must have been the sorriest man at the Oval when he took the wicket by this freakish and unprecedented chance. Nothing so odd has happened at the Oval for more than eighty years. A certain J. SOUTHERTON, playing for Surrey against the M.C.C. in 1870, skied a ball and, being evidently of a pessimistic turn of mind, unusual in batsmen, hurried off to the pavilion without waiting to watch what seemed to him a certain catch. The fielder dropped it, but MR. SOUTHERTON did not return, and so he is recorded as having "retired, thinking he was caught." MR. WARD, in a Lancashire against Derbyshire match at Old Trafford, half a century ago, was given out "hit wicket," when a ball knocked a shoulder off his bat on to one of the stumps.

More fortunate, and well within living memory, was MR. PEARCE, whose experience has its memorial in the Long Room at Lord's. A ball bowled to him by MR. JAHANGIR KHAN killed a sparrow in flight which, the batsman having played his stroke, fell dead against the wicket, but without removing the bails. Presumably, even had the wretched bird taken a bail off the verdict would have been "Not Out." The rule confines itself to the hitting down of the wicket with bat or any part of the person and the sparrow was not, and had no wish to be, in any way connected with MR. PEARCE. The law may have been fulfilled at the Oval, but the spirit of the game was certainly flouted. Would a batsman struck in the stomach by a viciously rising ball and caused to sit down, winded, on the stumps, be given out? Tough old gentlemen in the pavilion, their playing days safely behind them, may, here and there, mutter that the bat is provided to hit the ball with and that to miss with it lays you open to all the consequences. But most cricketers will join in a chorus of "Bad luck, Revill."

England Have Last Word
Three Yeomen foil Australia

FROM OUR CRICKET CORRESPONDENT [GEOFFREY GREEN]

1 *July* 1953. Out of darkness, through fire into light. Thus did England yesterday rise like some Phoenix from the ashes of apparent defeat to save the second Test match at Lord's and so gain a remarkable draw against Australia with a final score of 282 for seven wickets, just 61 runs behind their original aim for victory.

The age of miracles it proved was not yet past, nor could all the ranks of

Tuscany scarce forebear to cheer this most dramatic and most honourable ending to a match already full of the oddest twists. But within the climax there came the longest and most agonizing last half-hour of a match it is possible to imagine, for in that last span Australia stood to snatch back with leg-spin bowling all that three yeomen of England had denied them for nearly the whole of this last gruelling day.

The yeomen, the heroes, stood apart. They were Watson, Bailey, and Compton, and the greatest of them was Watson. The left-handed Yorkshire-man, in the centre of the batting order, was the soul and the pulse of England's rearguard action, and he now became the twentieth man in history to score a century on his first appearance in an England v. Australia Test match. From six o'clock on Monday evening, when the desperate peril of England was shown in her 12 runs for three wickets, he held the crease until 10 minutes to 6 last evening. A moment before he finally left, mentally and physically exhausted after a personal battle of five hours and three-quarters against all the odds, England stood at 236 for four. Therein lay the measure of his triumph, though mere figures alone can never disclose the heart of his achievement.

But he was not alone. First at his side there stood Compton. Theirs has been a happy association in the past. Three times against South Africa in the summer of 1951 they fashioned century partnerships. But none could now compare with the 61 vital runs that were born of an hour and three-quarters struggle that first turned back the Australian assault. Compton for the second time in this perplexing exciting match batted finely and for the second time it took a really good ball to claim him. It was at 20 minutes to one yesterday that the bounding, left-handed Johnston, loose and long of limb, suddenly had him l.-b.-w. with a ball, a yard quicker through the air, which kept low.

England then were 73 for four and a long, long way yet from any harbour of safety. But already Compton and his partner, footballers both, had achieved something. They had lit a tiny flame of hope. More practically Compton, with three crashing off-drives to the boundary in a single over, seemed to destroy all Benaud's confidence in his own length and leg-spin that lasted far into the day. That was of considerable importance.

So with four hours and 50 minutes left Bailey walked down the pavilion steps. Each stride to the crease took him nearer his part in what was to prove an epic achievement of courage, concentration and will power, not to men-tion skill. For all but three-quarters of an hour of that wide ocean of time did he and Watson stand firm in the face of all that Hassett and his Australians could hurl at them. Together they fanned that first tiny flame of hope until it spurted up into a sturdy fire. Their fourth-wicket partnership of 163 runs was the greatest of all this great match. And it has been a great match, worth every penny of its world record receipts of over £57,716, a match that day by day took one by the hand down new and unexpected paths.

There were four crises on this last desperate day. The first came at the beginning as Watson and Compton faced Lindwall and Johnston. This crisis at last was passed as Hassett turned to the leg-spin of Ring and Benaud. It was now that Compton set Benaud back with an attack that saw 52 runs arrive in the first hour, three overs costing Benaud 22.

The second critical moment came with Compton's dismissal. This, together with a third anxiety – the arrival of a new ball in the hands of Lindwall and Miller at 3 o'clock with the score 149 for four – was neutralized by the glowing courage and concentration of Watson and Bailey as the bowlers tore at them with pace and lift. Twice indeed at this last point in mid-afternoon Bailey suffered the sharpest of blows on his knuckles from Lindwall that searched out the tendrils of his spirit.

For 40 minutes they met the barrage, scraped together 10 runs and won through. So tea came with England almost miraculously 183, still for four wickets, with Watson 84, Bailey 39 and a 100 partnership already under their pads. The runs had ticked up at a declining rate of 52, 44, 35, and 29 through succeeding hours which showed the intensity of the struggle and the fact that Hassett by now was clearly a worried man. Things had slipped through his fingers slowly, largely because the spin of Ring and Benaud had failed him when most he needed it.

Through all this long span Watson had been passed on the forward stroke once each by Lindwall and Miller and once had snicked Davidson just short of the slips. But mostly he had been firm in his stroke play, turning the ball beautifully off his legs to the on side, whence most of his runs came. Bailey, also beaten once by Miller, again, as he had done before, got his head down well and his bat along the strict line of the ball to present a teasing barrier, sweeping every now and then any loose ball that was offered and, on one occasion particularly, cutting Johnston beautifully for 4.

The Australian bowling, when faced by this growing problem, seemed strangely out of gear. Its sharp edge of earlier was now surprisingly blunted, though Ring, who occasionally worried Watson, Johnston, and Miller, tried everything from both sides of the wicket to various combinations of close fielders outside the leg and off stump.

It was all to no avail until Ring, in a long, last spell after tea, finally began to get some work on the ball down the hill from the Nursery end. But by half-past 5 Watson was past his great hundred, nearly out incidentally at long leg, as he swept Ring for 4 to a mighty cheer; Bailey, too, was beyond his 50. Together they had all but piloted England to safety.

But at 10 minutes to 6 things suddenly began to happen. Watson, almost on his last legs, snicked Ring's googly to slip, to receive a wonderful ovation on his return home; 236—5—109. Then, just short of 6 o'clock, Bailey loosely tried to drive Ring's away spin, pitched well outside the off-stump, and holed out at cover-point; 246—6—71. He, too, another footballer, received the applause of a hero.

Now came the last fearful half-hour as Australia, suddenly revitalized and on tiptoe, strained every nerve for a dramatic breakthrough. How Brown and Evans at times survived the spin of Ring and Benaud none could truly tell. But Brown at least showed himself a man for this last crisis. With no little sense of discrimination, and some thumping drives, he hit the spin away for four telling boundaries that helped to preserve all that had been built up so patiently through the long hours.

Every ball played was now met by nervous applause as the assembly sensed the tingle of the fading battle. Though Brown, with five minutes left, finally fell to Benaud in the slips, the battle at last was over. The enemy had been deprived of his prey.

AUSTRALIA 346 (A. L. Hassett 104, A. K. Davidson 76, R. N. Harvey 59; Bedser 5 for 105, Wardle 4 for 77) and 368 (K. R. Miller 109, A. R. Morris 89, R. R. Lindwall 50, G. B. Hole 47; F. R. Brown 4 for 82)
ENGLAND 372 (Hutton 145, Graveney 78, Compton 57; R. R. Lindwall 5 for 66) and 282 for 7 (Watson 109, T. E. Bailey 71)
Match drawn

Test Cricket Triumphant

20 *August* 1953, *Leading Article*. Some of the players in yesterday's Test Match were unborn when England last won the Ashes at home, and the oldest of them was no more than a small schoolboy. It is natural, after so long and at times so bleak an interval, for lovers of English cricket to rejoice. But looking back over the exciting – and even the nerve-wracking – ups and downs of this season, victory once again at the Oval is seen to be only one reason why hearts should be light to-day. Test cricket, like other traditional institutions, reflects social change. A game that has its roots in a more leisurely age than the present has been thought by some loyal supporters of past glory to be in danger. The bloom of freshness, it has been said – more often privately than in public – must wilt in the hothouse atmosphere of daily and, indeed, hourly publicity.

So fierce a concentration of limelight was, according to this pessimistic view, bound to lead to demand for "brighter" play, to disputes about selection, and to new and worse outbreaks of ill-feeling between the countries. The tireless pens of the critics and the ceaseless voices of the commentators could be taken, with the ominous, slow hand-clapping of the crowds, as "noises off," sounding the death knell of cricket as the special summer's pleasure of those who understand it. A wider, casual public was being brought in to transform a glorious game into a branch of high pressure and highly professional sport.

The genius – it might almost be called the imp – of cricket has now stepped in to confound these prophets. Australia sent over a side less formidable, or at least less fortified with terrible names, than she has sometimes done before, and England was no better placed. The robot quality of skill that, in other seasons, has made a finish a foregone conclusion, temporarily vanished. Scores were low. Neither side reached four hundred in any innings and there were only six centuries – two of them from HASSETT and one from HUTTON – in the series. Each of the struggling and changing elevens was lucky to escape decisive defeat. The fortunes of the players rose and fell so unpredictably that honours were spread, and no single man towered to HOBBS or BRADMAN height.

This, had the melancholy thesis proved sound, would have led to a season of discontent and frustration. Instead, it has been a bumper season and everyone, including the players, has enjoyed almost every moment of it. HASSETT and his men will go home knowing that, though they leave the Ashes behind them, they leave, too, as happy memories with their hosts as did any of the sides that came before them. They and our own men have triumphantly survived ordeal by stop-press, loudspeaker, and television camera. No cricket season in history has seen a series of Test matches between England and Australia played more closely in the spirit of the clubs and villages from north of the Trent to south of Sydney on which the health – and the fun – of the game depends. Is there an Englishman who, putting his hand on his heart, can swear that, when he went to bed on Tuesday night, he knew for certain that all was over bar the cheering round the pavilion? Eleventh hour upsetting of probability is the salt of cricket and 1953 has brought it in full measure.

Lord's Turns to Lacrosse

BY OUR SPECIAL CORRESPONDENT

7 *October* 1953. There is a place for Lord's Cricket Ground in the hearts of all lacrosse players, for besides its congenial surroundings and excellent turf, it has a long historical connexion with the sport. Indeed, a history of lacrosse at Lord's covering the last 70 years would make fascinating reading.

Although the appearance of the players of to-day and the form of their equipment have changed since the Canadian pioneers of 1833 played at Lord's, the skill, teamwork, and character have been maintained. This Saturday Kenton and Old Thorntonians, meeting there in a championship match, begin a new chapter in this history. Other games will follow every Saturday until November 14.

In First Ball

10 *April* 1954, *Leading Article*. Breathes there a man with past so dead that not even an ember in it is made to glow by the window display, currently on

view, of a "Junior Cricket Set," complete for fifteen and fourpence? Completeness consists of one bat, one ball, four stumps, stuck into a stand, and a string "carry bag." That, shockingly though the prices of sports gear have risen, is bumper value for money to-day. Seeing the complete set, shiny and immaculate, in the window is to be reminded that the seasons come stealthily on city dwellers with always a surprise in store. Let the countryman keep his familiar nests and flowers bravely trying to avoid the staleness of annual repetition; it is only the townsman who gets such a novel reminder as this that the time for cricket is round the corner.

How diverse will be the fates of those complete sets when they go out into the world. All will lose their present look of being as neat and clean as choir boys on Sunday mornings. Many will quickly be divorced from their stand. It will be useful, indeed essential, on asphalt but, wherever there is turf to be punctured, the three stumps will go in at one end and the singleton at the other. Bat and ball may be the first of their kinds ever to be handled by their new owner. They cannot guess, until they leave the shop, in whose fumbling fingers they will be made, dramatically speaking, to serve the masters of the game. Hutton will hit a six (and wreak havoc in the process among out-of-bounds flowers) with the bat. The Bedsers will take turns with the ball and, between overs, it will be thrown at the smallest fielder to remind him not to lose interest in the proceedings because he has just been given out leg-before-wicket.

The first taste of cricket is, for many men, the sweetest. Played on recreation grounds, on the sands and in back gardens, it is free from umpires and other spoil-sport conventions. All players can and do loudly refuse to admit that they are out or that they have been bowling for too long. Competitive instinct and little or no nonsense about the old school tie reign supreme. We are all little Graces when we first play cricket. White flannels, net and fielding practice and all the mature glories of the game come later and are not, by every one, loved as much. The holidays enjoy for embryo cricketers what the lawyers call privilege. Then, and only then, can the Hutton and the Rabbit of to-morrow join in an uninhibited shout of "Got your off stump! Give Bill the bat." If, as is highly unlikely, Bill is given the bat there and then, what matter that it may take some time before his dog can, by chasing and persuasion, be induced to disgorge the ball?

Jet Cricket

17 *April* 1954, *Leading Article.* The full results have not yet been made public of an experiment, fraught with interest for the British race and indeed for most of the British Commonwealth, which was carried out the other day. A jet aircraft engine was used to dry out a cricket-pitch and naturally did the job much quicker than Dame Nature, even at her most cooperative, could

have done it. The unreliability, often verging on malice, of our climate constantly menaces the best interests of our national game, disappointing crowds, playing havoc with averages, and perverting the ends of justice by saving the other side from defeat (occasionally, of course, it is the other way round and we remind ourselves complacently that there is no game quite like cricket). Nothing will do more to reduce frustration and delay and to lessen wear and tear on the gramophone records which enable the B.B.C., when rain stops play, to substitute for the commentator's voice a medley of intensely unpopular tunes, than a device which will dry out a pitch many times quicker than the brightest of bright intervals.

Reactionary voices will no doubt be heard complaining that the balance of Nature is being upset, and wet-bobs will take pleasure in concocting, only in order to rebut them, rumours that oil is going to be sprayed over the course at Henley in the event of rough weather during Regatta week. But most people will welcome anything that will make it possible for more actual cricket to be played during cricket matches. One pleasing feature of the new device is that it is absolutely useless to foreigners. All too often in the past British pioneering in the field of sport has been requited in the long run by national humiliation. Other races have learnt our rules, borrowed our equipment and some of our vocabulary and come back to trounce us. There is no danger of this boomerang process happening this time, and it is comforting (though possibly a shade mean) to reflect that – within, so to speak, the family – a means of drying the pitch quickly is not nearly such an important requirement in Australia as it is here.

It will take a little time to get the hang of the new device, and the M.C.C. will have to draw up very carefully the rules governing its use. Will captains, between innings, have the choice between the light jet and the heavy jet? Problems of finance will obtrude themselves, for grounds equipped with this new gimmick will, like cinemas equipped with 3D, offer spectators something of which they have never before had the advantage, and no enterprising club will be able to dispense with one. Who will operate them? What should they be called? If the final results of the recent experiment turn out satisfactorily, the coming cricket season may be full of surprises – unless of course there is just one surprise, the biggest of the lot, in the shape of a really fine summer.

George Hirst

11 *May* 1954, *Leading Article.* Posterity's memory being the wayward and parsimonious thing it is, it can easily be said that cricket has already too many "immortals" for so comparatively young a game. But it can be said with equal certainty that the newest comer to the Elysian fields will last with the longest. GEORGE HIRST was more than a great cricketer. He was a great character. Already in his lifetime he had begun to be a legend. Not that the

deeds of the cricketer should be forgotten. They are remarkable enough for any man. The *Wisden* of 1922, marking his fiftieth birthday and also his impending retirement from the game, records a page of astonishing figures. In thirty-one years of first-class matches HIRST batted in 1,211 innings, scored 36,196 runs, with an average of 34.14 an innings. In those same years he bowled 122,592 balls, and took 2,723 wickets at an average of 18.75 runs a wicket. But what no figures can give was the wonder and the beauty of his fielding at mid-off. Whatever credit he deserved for the swerve, it was one of the lesser parts of the fame of this very all-round player.

There are many men – and indeed women, for HIRST was the idol of all Yorkshire – now advancing in years, who can remember the joy of seeing HIRST in his prime. It was not merely the joy of achievement – he could on occasion fail as humbly as any other man – but he brought to everything he did a courage, an integrity, a vigour and a tenacity that meant that no game in which he took part was decided until the last ball had been bowled and the last stroke made. One of the few remaining links with W. G. GRACE, he belonged to cricket's Homeric age. At least, so those who ever saw him in the field must now think. No doubt the Homeric days of cricket are always with us, and there are probably small boys at this time building pedestals for their own idols of the future. Fortunate indeed will any generation of them be that can count upon seeing the peer of HIRST.

18 *May* 1954. Sir Francis Meynell writes:–
  In 1904 when George Hirst took his Benefit I sent him from my preparatory school a hard-saved half a crown; and I asked him how to make the ball swerve. His reply – in his own round and careful hand, for Benefits had no first, second, and third secretaries in those days – was as follows:
  "Dear Sir [and this alone was worth the money to a schoolboy] thank you for the 2s. 6d. I cannot tell you how to make the ball swerve, hold the ball with the seam between the first two fingers. Yours faithfully, George Hirst." But that was not the end. There was a gap of an inch and then, generously, another "George Hirst" – detachable, as a "swop."

Complacent Masters Beaten by Their Pupils

FROM OUR CRICKET CORRESPONDENT [JOHN WOODCOCK]

18 *August* 1954. The young cricketers from Pakistan had their finest hour, and England one of their less glorious, at the Oval yesterday when the fourth and final Test match was won and lost there by 24 runs. Pakistan gained a victory which carried with it a sharing of the rubber and England

suffered a defeat which came as a rather unwelcome awakening within a month of sailing for Australia.

Some may say that the full strength of England was not in the field, some that the losers had the worst of the wicket, but first and foremost all should acknowledge a performance of great merit by Pakistan, and one upon which they are to be congratulated most warmly. By seizing their chance with both hands and winning this Test match on English soil on their first tour they have achieved in less than four months what it took Australia two years, South Africa 28 years, and West Indies 22 years to achieve, and what to this day has eluded New Zealand and India.

Pakistan's particular hero was Fazal, who brought his tally of wickets in the match to 12, and who throughout the series has established himself as a bowler of medium pace fit to rank near our own Bedser. Next to Fazal one would put Wazir and Zulfiqar, whose ninth wicket partnership of 58, when all seemed lost, gave birth to the recovery from which victory sprang. Kardar, when suddenly he saw the heel of Achilles exposed, captained his side in every respect as astutely as he has done all summer, and there was an alert response from those under him.

Much of England's play, from the moment that Wazir and Zulfiqar came together on Monday morning, was almost too bad to be true. The bowling of Loader and Tyson became lifeless and inaccurate; the fielding became casual; and the inadequacy of the batting on a good wicket is reflected in the score-book. May and Simpson played well, but they got themselves out, and Compton's 29 would have been nearly 50 had he made the most of the loose balls he received. Graveney failed in the crisis, as he had in the first innings, and the tail proved to be no shorter than one had feared. Nor, should Bailey by some mischance be out of action, and if five bowlers are played as they surely must be, will it be any shorter in Australia.

The odds, when play started yesterday with England's last four wickets needing 43 runs, seemed to be slightly in Pakistan's favour, and one simply hoped that England would put up a fight. Their main chance rested with Wardle, who has made a good many runs against Pakistan this year. Given the opportunity he could have won the match off his own bat in 10 minutes, but Kardar sensibly chose Mahmud to bowl with Fazal, and speed does not suit Wardle's book so well as spin. The result was that Wardle was prevented from using the long handle and never flourished.

There was an impartial cheer for anything of note from the small crowd, and the sense of strain in the middle was soon shown in an injudicious single. Then at 129 Wardle was dropped at second slip off Mahmud, a none too difficult catch as slip catches go, and presently the same batsman survived two leg-before appeals from Fazal. After 25 minutes only six had been scored, but by then Tyson seemed to be finding his feet, and Pakistan badly needed a wicket. It came just on noon, when Tyson felt speculatively for an out-swinger from Fazal and gave Imtiaz his seventh catch of the match. Loader now came in ninth instead of his usual eleventh, and at once forced a 4 to long-on, followed by a quick single which took the score to 138.

With 30 needed from three wickets it was anyone's game, and yet within a quarter of an hour the end had come. At 138 Wardle was caught round the corner turning Fazal off his legs, and Loader, hitting out desperately, immediately sent a steepling catch to cover-point, where Waqar, after an agony of suspense, held it and threw it aloft. There remained only some missing and snicking, a run out escape, and then a fatal call by McConnon, who underestimated Hanif's quickness and accuracy of throw from cover-point to the bowler's end. Hanif hit the stumps, umpire Davies adjudicated, and Pakistan, who had come to learn, had come and conquered.

> PAKISTAN 133 (Tyson 4 for 35) and 164 (Wazir Mohammad 42 not out; Wardle 7 for 56)
> ENGLAND 130 (Compton 53; Fazal Mahmud 6 for 53, Mahmud Husain 4 for 58) and 143 (P. B. H. May 53; Fazal Mahmud 6 for 46)
> *Pakistan won by 24 runs*

COURT OF APPEAL
Professional Cricketer's Tax

D. E. Moorhouse (Inspector of Taxes) v. Dooland

BEFORE THE MASTER OF THE ROLLS, LORD JUSTICE JENKINS, AND LORD JUSTICE BIRKETT

20, 22, 23 *November* 1954. The COURT reserved judgment in this appeal by the Crown from a decision of Mr. Justice Harman on May 27, 1954, confirming a decision of the Commissioners for the district of Blackburn, Lancashire, that benefits received by Mr. Bruce Dooland, professional cricketer, were not liable to income tax.

Mr. R. E. Borneman, Q.C., and Sir Reginald Hills appeared for the Crown; Mr. F. N. Bucher for the cricketer.

The respondent was the cricket professional to the East Lancashire Club, a member of the Lancashire Cricket League. In August, 1949, he entered into a written agreement with the club to act as their professional for the seasons 1951 and 1952, at a salary of £800 a year.

A clause in the agreement provided that "collections shall be made for any meritorious performance by the professonal with bat or ball."

In 1951 the respondent became entitled on 11 occasions to have a collection made on his behalf, and £48 15s. was so collected. The question in the case was whether the money so received was a taxable profit within the wording of schedule E as being "salaries fees wages perquisites or profits whatsoever" from the exercise of an office or employment of profit for the year of assessment.

MR. BORNEMAN, in opening, submitted that the money received by the respondent was not a mere token of esteem but was payment for services rendered. A professional footballer's benefit was taxable; and if a cricketer's was not there was an anomaly which the Crown considered should be removed.

The MASTER OF THE ROLLS said that he was quite unmoved by the assertion that there was an anomaly; whether there was or was not was immaterial. Cricketers had had many things to put up with, including summers like that of 1954. Cricket was the only game which distinguished us from all others.

Counsel argued that while the tax anomaly remained footballers, parsons, who had to pay on Easter offerings, and taxi drivers, who were taxed on tips, might feel that they were being dealt with harshly.

LORD JUSTICE BIRKETT. – You could remove the anomaly by saying that they should not be taxed. The tax in this case would be something trivial.

LORD JUSTICE JENKINS. – I hope this is being done at the Crown's expense.

Counsel replied that, if successful, the Crown would not ask for costs. He could imagine nothing more generous than that.

LORD JUSTICE BIRKETT. – I can.

Counsel said that Mr. Justice Harman took the view that as only some £20 was involved the matter might well have been left alone. The Crown felt, however, that it had to administer the law. There was no question of sympathy for anybody.

The MASTER OF THE ROLLS. – If you bring this sort of case you expose yourself to this sort of bowling.

LORD JUSTICE JENKINS. – Do they never have a collection for an umpire?

The MASTER OF THE ROLLS. – For rejecting five or more appeals?

The MASTER OF THE ROLLS, later referring to the tax on clergymen's Easter offerings, said: "I regard it as the gravest case of misplaced fiscal enthusiasm. When one thinks of the expenses the unfortunate clergy have to bear I cannot understand it." On the taking of tips, he said that the inspectors taxed every person suspected of getting them. "How on earth is the amount of the tip ever discovered?" he asked. "Presumably only the honest pay."

LORD JUSTICE BIRKETT said that the law became rather absurd if it could not be observed in a uniform way.

During further argument the MASTER OF THE ROLLS said that if the Crown indulged in its "passion for uniformity" Christmas boxes ought to be taxed.

MR. BORNEMAN, continuing his argument, submitted that the words in the schedule could not be wider: all "profits whatsoever" included money received from any persons, not only from persons with whom the recipient had a contract. The remuneration of the respondent was to be partly in the form of collections, and was liable to tax. It might be said that the law was too harsh, but that was a matter for the Legislature to consider. Whether a payment was made in pursuance of the terms of a contract or was a gift independent of contract must depend on the particular facts of each case, and on the facts of this case he submitted that the finding of the Commissioners could not be supported. The only cases where such payments were not liable to tax were cases where the payment was on some exceptional occasion, such as the end of a career, which could not recur, and was not in respect of the performance of the duties of an employment.

SIR REGINALD HILLS, following, said that the money was received by the respondent because he had played well in a match in which he was employed to play. It was plainly a profit from his employment.

The MASTER OF THE ROLLS asked what the position would be of a young man employed by the club whose father gave him a shilling for every run he made. Would that gift from his father be liable to tax?

SIR REGINALD HILLS submitted that the right to have collections was part of the respondent's contract.

The MASTER OF THE ROLLS told counsel in the next case (Prescott v. Birmingham Corporation) they could go away since Sir Reginald was not out yet and the other side had to go in.

MR. BUCHER, for the cricketer, submitted that for money to be taxable it must be a payment made in return for services rendered by the payee to the payer. Where there was no service relationship the payment was spontaneous, and was not within the scope of "emoluments." There was no certainty about the amount to be raised by a cricket collection, and the cricketer could not claim any sum at all as a right. Easter offerings were taxable because they were not a personal gift to the incumbent for the time being but were a tribute to the office. The real question here was whether the money came to the respondent as the club professional, or as Mr. Dooland. It did not come to him as the professional for the time being, but it came to him in his personal capacity. Whether a particular case fell on one side or other of the line was a question of fact for the Commissioners; and their finding here should not be disturbed, unless it could be held to be such a conclusion as rational men could not have reached. The yield from the collections was so small that the Commissioners, as local men, could hold that the right to such collections was not an inducement to Mr. Dooland to serve his club. They were a spontaneous sign of appreciation from the spectators.

Solicitors. – Solicitor of Inland Revenue; Messrs. Gibson and Weldon for Messrs. Crockford and Anderson, Nottingham.

The appeal of the tax inspector was allowed, in the judgment delivered the following month, on the grounds that the collections constituted part of the earnings of Dooland's profession under the terms of his contract.

Commentary before Breakfast

26 *November* 1954, *Leading Article.* The thoughts we entertain in the early morning remain for the most part unrevealed, for as a nation we are notoriously uncommunicative until the breakfast things have been cleared away. Whatever may go on behind those inexpressive features as they greet the new day it is certain that to-day the thoughts of many will have been with our Test players in Australia. Before daylight has asserted itself the hand of the cricket enthusiast emerges from the bedclothes to grope for the switch on his wireless set and to satisfy a powerful curiosity. For weeks he has followed the triumphs and failures of our players. The last time they were in Australia he was plagued by news of injuries. If it was not COMPTON's knee it was WRIGHT's neck or BAILEY's shoulder. This year the casualty list has been shorter and the achievement already substantial, but he has been kept on tenterhooks by the in-and-out form of the English batsmen. Now the rehearsals are finished. The captains, the teams, and the umpires have been picked; the pitch has been appraised for the last time, the coin has been tossed, and in the cold light of breakfast time speculation gives way to fact.

The news may not always be to the audience's liking – in 1946 BRADMAN was already on his way to a double century after the first day's play – but the score is not everything. The hard figures of the day's play may be heard in later bulletins, but nothing can quite destroy the fascination of listening to the ebb and flow of the commentator's voice as he describes, from the other side of the world, LINDWALL running in to bowl or a sweep to leg by COMPTON. So absorbing can this become that the whole routine of a household may temporarily be set at naught. The listener wanders about distractedly, carrying cups of tea and listening for the quickening of the commentator's voice as it tells of a boundary or the muffled roar that greets a fallen wicket. Sustenance is taken not necessarily at the breakfast table but wherever the loudspeaker stands. Children are hushed into silence. Sooner or later the passage of time forces the listener back into the rhythm of another working day, but before he slips on his overcoat he will have relished the sound of cheers from an Australian crowd on whom – or so he imagines – the sun is beating pitilessly down.

A Cricket Lover's Bequest

Local Ground the Pride of Darley Dale

FROM OUR SPECIAL CORRESPONDENT [PHILIP URE]

20 *December* 1954; *Darley Dale*, 19 *December*. A village cricket club that in these stringent times is bequeathed the sum of £5,000 must be accounted

fortunate indeed. But Mr. Alfred Smith of Darley Oak was a lover of cricket, and the club and ground of this his native village near Matlock gave him all the pleasures of the game that he ever desired. He died last summer at the age of 82 and under his will, which has just been published, Darley Dale Cricket Club comes into £5,000.

Alfred Smith first played for Darley Dale in 1887 at a time when he had to borrow the club subscription of half a crown from his mother. He continued to play for 50 years and in his prime was acknowledged the club's best bowler. He became a wealthy man – his estate is valued at more than £200,000 – and during his lifetime spent much money in making the cricket ground of Darley Dale one of the finest in all the Midlands.

His most intimate surviving friend says of Alfred Smith: "He had two drawing rooms – the cricket pavilion in summer and the billiards room in winter." He is said to have been an exceptionally shy man, and it is pleasant to think of the cricket field and the cricket club as the places where such a man felt most at ease with his neighbours.

Outside his devotion to the cricket club he was frugal in the spending of money, in spite of his substantial fortune. But no one in Darley Dale thinks of Alfred Smith as ever having been mean; it was just that he had been brought up strictly. This showed itself in a lifelong opposition to Sunday play, and in his will he expresses a wish that there shall continue to be no Sunday play at Darley Dale. But his wish was not written as a cast-iron stipulation, for he recognized how feeling on this question was changing with the march of time.

Now that he is gone, the field that was his great pride will remain the pride of Darley Dale and, through his beneficence, can be kept in the first-class condition that he would wish.

Tyson Levels Test Series for England

FROM OUR CRICKET CORRESPONDENT [JOHN WOODCOCK]

23 *December* 1954; *Sydney, 22 December.* At Brisbane, tragedy; at Sydney, triumph. Here this afternoon England won a memorable victory by 38 runs after one of the most exciting Test matches for many years. At 10 minutes past three Tyson and Statham, heroes at the head of England's team, were cheered from sight through one pavilion gate, and through the other went little Harvey, undefeated after a masterly effort to steer Australia home.

There have been many Test matches in which the technical standard has been higher, and, for that matter, several in which the margin of victory has been smaller. But few can have followed a more winding course or reached so great a climax as did this one. And in few can there have been so courageous and sustained a piece of fast bowling as Tyson's to-day. For four days England's cricket alternated between the pit of depression and, very occasionally, the heights of expectation, until this morning it seemed that Australia would most likely win.

Indeed it had seemed that way since England were bowled out for 154 in their first innings. But Tyson, with a bump on the back of his head the size of an egg, swung the balance after 15 minutes to-day with two shattering yorkers in an over. Thereafter England fought like lions, paralysing all Australia's batsmen except Harvey. Statham supported Tyson with great heart and determination, Appleyard got a valuable wicket, and Evans took a staggering catch. Nor must one forget the batting of May and Cowdrey or England's last-wicket partners. Yet the match should be remembered more than anything for Tyson's fast bowling to-day on an easy wicket.

Only last week at Melbourne he changed to a shorter, more controlled, run. Now he has also learnt the value of a full length by watching Lindwall, and 10 wickets in a Test match is the result. He is strong, and it is difficult to see how a man can bowl much faster than he did at times to-day. Within a fortnight he has acquired for himself a considerable ascendancy over Australia's leading batsmen through being genuinely too good for them.

M.C.C. can thank him for being able to spend Christmas with happy hearts, and England are in the elevating psychological position in which Australia found themselves after Brisbane. Had this match gone the other way, however, as it came within an ace of doing, much of the interest might have gone from the series.

Now it is ablaze with possibilities, with Hutton's side restored to confidence and their doubters faithful again. Hutton captained calmly and with judgment to-day. It was not easy for him with runs so precious and with Tyson and Statham to be conserved and yet released.

Nor is Harvey an easy man to keep down. This innings of his was altogether better than his century at Brisbane, and it would have gone down to posterity had he somehow won the match for Australia, as there was a chance he was going to during a, to English eyes, torturing last-wicket partnership of 39 with Johnston. For the first time on this tour Harvey looked a great player. Never before has one seen him so scrupulously behind the line of the ball, and never has one seen his bat have fewer edges. Almost always before when playing against England he has looked brilliant but unsound; to-day he played hardly a false stroke.

When Harvey and Burke made their way to the wicket in cool and sunny weather this morning it needed only an over apiece from Statham and Tyson to reveal that the pitch was dead and remarkable things would have to happen if England were to win. Remarkable things did happen in Tyson's second over, for off the third ball the obdurate Burke was yorked, and off the seventh Hole met a similar fate.

Benaud was struggling, Harvey was hemmed in, the bowlers' length was checking many drives, and for almost an hour the battle went slowly yet tensely on with 29 runs being secored. Hutton soon had Bailey on from the

M. A. Noble stand end, with Tyson and Statham in short bursts from the other, but it was Appleyard who made the next vital contribution to England's day when he replaced Bailey. Appleyard is forever likely to beat in the air someone to whom he has not bowled before with the ball he holds back, and sure enough in his second over he caused Benaud to sweep too soon and send a high swirling catch to Tyson off the top edge of the bat. Tyson was at backward square leg half-way to the boundary, and he caught the ball so far from his body that for an awful moment one feared the catch might go to ground.

Australia's innings, if not now open as England's would have been, was at least ajar and Archer survived until luncheon, when Harvey had passed his 50 in 165 minutes. During the interval nobody could make up his mind who was going to win. Some said two to one against England, some said even money, few yet favoured England, but the first half-hour of the afternoon virtually settled the issue. Tyson and Statham began the bowling and the former bowled Archer in his second over. The ball fairly whipped back off the pitch and Australia, with four wickets to go, still needed 101 to win. One had lurking fears of Davidson and Lindwall, both of whom are highly inflammable drivers, and yet before Harvey could get at the bowling to shield and prepare them they had gone. Davidson was the victim of Evans's resilience, for he flicked at an out-swinger and there was Evans throwing himself to the ball in front of first slip.

The crowd savoured the meeting of Tyson and Lindwall after Tuesday's accident and at 136 Tyson got ample revenge with his one stroke of luck to-day. He pitched one well up outside the off-stump and Lindwall, trying to chop it, dragged it on. Four times had Tyson hit the wickets and he deserved all the praise his colleagues gave him. But the game was by no means over yet, for it was now that Harvey began to rule it while he had the chance. He pulled Statham for four and hooked Tyson for three before losing Langley, bowled by Statham in trying to keep a half-volley out of his stumps with a shot of his own.

Surely all was as good as over and, one felt, Hutton thought so too when he called for drinks to let victory linger on the palate. Nor did Johnston do anything to destroy the feeling of exultation when he missed his first three balls and escaped an l.-b.-w. appeal off his fourth. These were the last four balls of Statham's over and 78 were needed with one last wicket to fall. But for 40 minutes Harvey and Johnston tortured all Englishmen present. Women in the crowd began to get hysterical and the spectator in front of your Correspondent mistook his dark glasses for his pipe. In seven overs Johnston had only nine balls to face. He ran where there was no run and got away with it. He hooked over Bailey's head at long leg when Bailey would have had a catch had he been where he should have been, on the fence. He drove and he glanced and all the time Tyson and Statham were wearing themselves out.

There were terrible visions of anticlimax as the lead dwindled and the fielding became ragged. Finally Bailey had to replace Statham, who had been playing an important part by bowling most gallantly into the wind for 85 minutes, and Harvey hit Bailey for two fours. Tyson, too, after 90 minutes' bowling since luncheon, was almost on his knees when at last he had Johnston before him on the first ball of an over. Johnston maddeningly hit a four one-handed to fine leg off the fourth ball but off the fifth he glanced a catch down the leg side to Evans and the umpire's finger was up.

ENGLAND 154 and 296 (P. B. H. May 104, M. C. Cowdrey 54)
AUSTRALIA 228 (R. Archer 49, J. Burke 44; Tyson 4 for 45, T. E. Bailey 4 for 59) and 184 (R. N. Harvey 92 not out; Tyson 6 for 85)
England won by 38 runs

Wit and Wisden

Centenary of a Versatile Writer on Sport and Stage

FROM A CORRESPONDENT [ALAN PITT ROBBINS]

23 *September* 1955. Tribute is paid on the front page of *The Times* this morning to the memory of Sydney H. Pardon, who was born a hundred years ago to-day. Although it is a few months short of thirty years ago since he died his name is remembered with affection and gratitude wherever cricket is played, and wherever *Wisden's Cricketers Almanack* is studied by lovers of the game who look upon it with awe as one of the most complete reference books ever placed upon the market.

"S. H. P.," who combined for some years the positions of Editor of "Wisden's," Cricket Correspondent of *The Times*, and a partner in the Cricket Reporting Agency, established a unique individual position in cricket. As far as his closest friends knew, he had never played the game in his life. But he became the recognized authority on the game whom county captains and even the M.C.C. were glad to consult. His descriptive writing was admirable and he had an uncanny knack of picking out the promising young player. To be selected as one of the five hopefuls of the season in "Wisden's" was an honour greatly prized. On the first occasion that Pardon saw Victor Trumper his innings consisted of six balls only, but at the end of it Pardon was convinced that he had seen the greatest bat that Australia had ever produced. When Sir Jack Hobbs made his first appearance for Surrey Pardon wrote in "Wisden's" that there was a new player "from whom a great deal can be expected and who can be regarded as the best batsman brought forward for years."

In those days writers on cricket had not to face the competition of commentators on the air. Pardon would not have made a success at broadcasting. His voice was too gentle and his sight was so poor that he could not follow cricket without the most powerful glasses. He would probably have been impatient with those who were compelled to take snap decisions on a meritorious batting, bowling, or fielding performance. He preferred to form more leisurely judgments, and events rarely proved him to be wrong, as any who care to read the Editor's notes in successive issues of "Wisden's" will discover. It is a coincidence that John Wisden first opened his "cricket and cigar depôt" in London in the year of Pardon's birth. He launched his Almanack in 1864. Pardon took over the editorship in 1891 and held it until his death in 1925. One of his greatest friends, happily still with us, was Sir Pelham Warner, who wrote after his death that on all questions which agitated the cricket world his views were always balanced and judicious and that he never wrote an unkind word about a cricketer because, although criticism was sometimes imperative, the charitable touch was never wanting. Nor was his sense of humour. His quiet but piercing wit always entertained, and he had a wonderful memory for the lighter incidents of the game.

But, although cricket was both his business and his hobby, it was always Pardon's proudest boast that he had written special articles for *The Times* on four widely different subjects – cricket, the drama, opera, and horse racing.

Touring Cricketers

29 *February* 1956, *Leading Article*. No sportsmen have earned, over the years and on and off the field of play, a better reputation than have English cricketers. When they go oversea they have been counted upon not only to give a good account of themselves in the game but also to win the friendship of their hosts. Unfortunately the hooliganism – no ligher word fits – of some members of the M.C.C. team in Pakistan has blotted this record. It would be comforting to be able to say that their breach of decent manners was without precedent. But it is common knowledge that a recent touring side left a bad impression behind them in the West Indies. This, it may be hoped, will be corrected by MR. SWANTON's eleven, which will shortly begin a West Indian tour. Meanwhile, the Peshawar affair cannot be dismissed with the apologies that have been given and accepted.

This is an affair in which the M.C.C. must, and, no doubt, will, intervene as soon as a full report has been received and considered at Lord's. Rough horseplay, of which an umpire is a victim [*as a prank Idris Begh had been doused with cold water*], would be quite beyond the bounds if all concerned were here at home, Englishmen among themselves, at Old Trafford or the Oval. But our men are guests in an Eastern country, and they should have known better than to forget themselves as they evidently did. Old stagers will certainly say that such a thing would not have happened in the palmy days of captains who, while remaining on the friendliest terms with their men, kept discipline and stood no nonsense during games or in the intervals between them.

But the control of a touring cricket side, as of other bodies that need authority set over them, can no longer be exercised in the traditional way. The greater freedom now given to the individual imposes on him a stronger obligation to be self-disciplined. Every man involved in this sorry business must be aware that, in the fullest sense of the phrase, he has let England's side down. When our men are booed by a crowd oversea, as has just happened, and we at home have to admit to one another that they had brought it on themselves, matters have come to an ugly pass. The air will not be cleared until the M.C.C. has spoken, and spoken in no uncertain voice.

The President of M.C.C., Lord Alexander of Tunis, offered to cancel the rest of the tour, but it was completed. On the team's return M.C.C. laid responsibility for the incident on the captain, D. B. Carr, who had been present.

Hutton's Refusal

2 *May* 1956. Mr. L. Hutton, former England Test captain, has declined an offer by East Bradford Conservatives to be their prospective Parliamentary candidate.

Memories of Watching Cricket since 1878

BY SIR HOME GORDON

10 *May* 1956. It would seem reasonable to believe that I am the last surviving spectator of the game between Gentlemen of England and the Australians played at Prince's (now Cadogan Square) in June, 1878. The feature of a low-scoring struggle, in which no batsman made 30, was that the crowd surged into the playing space. I, a startled child in his seventh year, was removed. It was an odd commencement to my prolonged career of an unwearying onlooker.

Probable also is the presumption that I alone among those still alive watched the first Test match ever played in England at the Oval in 1880. Some may be surprised to learn that there was an open-air skating rink at the Vauxhall corner. It was a fine gesture of Lord Harris to accept the captaincy, because, during the preceding winter, he had been the victim of a violent mob attack at Sydney, burly George Ulyett defending him with a stump.

Though Spofforth was not playing, the contest was tremendous. W. G. Grace amassed a magnificent 152. The Australian captain, W. L. Murdoch, bet him a sovereign he would surpass this and actually compiled 153 not out. Subsequently, wearing it on his watch chain, he showed it to me when captain of Sussex. Those he led at the Oval were crude bats so far as style was concerned, but they revolutionized cricket in the placing of the field. Blackham came here as second string wicketkeeper to Murdoch, but was at once recognized as supreme. It was not he but diminutive Henry Phillips, of Sussex, who led to the dispensation of long-stop.

One feature of this historic match was a phenomenal catch. Bonnor, who stood 6ft. 6in. in his socks, hit such a terrific skier that two were run before the ball was beautifully judged by G. F. Grace. There has been controversy as to where the fielder took it. I am certain he ran at top speed to grasp the ball in front of the second gasometer. A month later he was dead, due to sleeping in a damp bed at Chichester. At the final fixture of the tour at the Crystal Palace, the Australians wore black bands on their left sleeves.

In the Test match of 1882 W. G. Grace, when bowling, put down the wicket beside him because the batsman, S. P. Jones, was backing up too eagerly. In 1924 so much was said about this by Australians to A. E. R. Gilligan, leader of our side out there, that he cabled me to know the facts.

England's cricket sank to its lowest in that game, which we lost by seven runs in trying to get 85. C. T. Studd – later a missionary in China – that year had made more than a thousand runs. Yet he was put in tenth by A. N. Hornby and never received a ball because Peate was bowled in attempting a reckless smite. Horan, who always batted in brown pads, has related that in the desperate tension one spectator dropped dead and another gnawed pieces from the handle of his umbrella.

Often I am asked what Spofforth was like. Long, lean, with flying arms and running at great speed, he came like a whirlwind towards the batsman, using cleverly varied pace and direction. Subsequently, when he was manager of a tea company, I knew him well. He was pleasant but very conceited, persisting that he was the fastest bowler ever.

This was sheer nonsense, for he never acquired the pace of E. Jones – who bowled through Grace's beard – nor of N. A. Knox, Kortright, or the South African Kotze. In the later nineties many Australians regarded C. T. B. Turner as a better bowler.

The first Test match at Lord's was in 1884. I have seen all played there since, as well as others at Old Trafford, Headingley, Edgbaston, Trent Bridge, and Kennington. A. G. Steel amassed a superlative 148, the sort of effort Neville Cardus would ascribe to a d'Artagnan of the game. Alfred Lyttelton afforded invaluable support. He was the only man I ever saw keep wicket wearing a hard straw hat. This was for Middlesex against Gloucestershire at Clifton in 1880.

The rubber was instituted in 1886. Shrewsbury was at the wicket at Lord's for seven hours for 164. Both Sir Aubrey Smith and W. Newham told me that, when touring with them in Australia in 1887, he wore a wig which did not fit and insisted upon eating all his meals with a hat on his head. Lohmann declared him to be the most difficult bat to bowl at he ever opposed.

Turner and Ferris showed us how to disregard the state of the wicket when bowling. Between them they claimed 514 wickets for 6,195 runs in one season. After the first war J. M. Gregory and McDonald transformed cricket by starting any match under any conditions with fast bowling at both ends. The last-named had the most beautiful rhythmic delivery I have ever seen.

The partnership of "the pair of midgets," as S. E. Gregory and Graham were called, completely demoralized England at Lord's, arousing wild enthusiasm by their smart running between the wickets. How different from the stolidity of Iredale and Darling, which provoked onlookers on the Mound to whistle the Dead March in Saul, quite harmoniously.

It was because Sir F. S. Jackson and some Yorkshire professionals preferred to play for their county rather than for England that selectors were appointed. At Leeds "the governor-general" Macartney scored a dazzling century before luncheon. During that interval Mrs. Sutcliffe, with a baby in her arms, explained that she had brought her son so that when he grew up he would be able to say he had seen his father's first Test in Yorkshire. To-day that infant is captain of Yorkshire and I had the pleasure of proposing him for M.C.C.

Frequently it is put to me: what has been the greatest innings I have watched. Perhaps it was that of J. T. Tyldesley at Birmingham in 1902 on a rain-soaked wicket unfit to play on. Or was it that supreme demonstration of "pulling it off" by Gilbert Jessop – 104 out of 139 in 75 minutes? He assured me that the more accurate the bowling the easier he found it to hit in every direction.

Or could there be more glamorous batting than that of Victor Trumper – "perfecting the dexterity of MacLaren"? Most modest of men, it may be that he foresaw his early death, for it was curious, as Doctor Rowley Pope pointed out, that he never made plans but existed from week to week.

Was batting ever more controlled than that of K. S. Ranjitsinhji? He told me repeatedly that he himself had only begun where W. G. Grace left off and that his own success could be ascribed to exceptional concentration as well as numberless nets. In the field he always wore his shirtsleeves buttoned round his wrists. Hammond occasionally did so. As my host in India for the Durbar, the Jam Sahib was superlative. But he would not praise the perfection of his nephew Duleepsinhji for fear of turning his head – which was absurd.

I remember an Indian prince – the beloved Duleep – when twelfth man in a Test match at Trent Bridge, taking out a sweater to an English professional, Maurice Tate. Both those great judges, Ranjitsinhji and P. A. Perrin, said they regarded Maurice as an inferior bowler to his father, Fred.

Superfluous to dilate on the wonder of the batting of Bradman, Hobbs, or Hammond, academic to discuss whether Clem Hill or Frank Woolley was the greater left-handed bat. Bardsley lacked the grace of either, though so difficult to oust. Of the many masters behind the stumps Oldfield comes first. All honour to him for the unselfish way in which for so long he was second string to Carter.

No more pleasant pastime can be cited than picking representative teams.

It entails temerity because the inquiry is provoked: "How can you leave out So and So?" My answer is that there are only 11 places to be filled. Whom would you omit? Anyhow, here are my selected sides, past and present, for others to consider. Australia – Bradman, McDonnell, Trumper, Macartney, Clem Hill, Keith Miller, Turner, Noble, Oldfield, Mailey, Spofforth or Lindwall. England – W. G. Grace, Hobbs, Ranjitsinhji, Hutton, Rhodes, Lohmann, Larwood, Ames or Evans, Maurice Tate, Sydney Barnes. How invidious to choose so few out of so many that have afforded delight. How keenly do I anticipate watching the Test at Lord's next month.

Sir Home supplied the name of his eleventh English player – Woolley – in a letter to the Editor published four days later.

All Ten Australians Wickets and 19 in the Match

FROM OUR CRICKET CORRESPONDENT [JOHN WOODCOCK]

1 *August* 1956. England won the fourth Test match against Australia at Old Trafford yesterday by an innings and 170 runs, so retaining the Ashes, and Laker made the achievement possible by taking all 10 wickets in Australia's second innings. Either feat is notable enough; but when one leads to the other a mockery is made of all laws of probability. Last Friday Laker captured nine wickets in Australia's first innings and his remarkable tally of 19 wickets for 90 runs must always make this one of the most memorable games of cricket ever played. Indeed, it is unlikely that Laker's performance will ever be equalled. Cobden's match and Fowler's match and many others have their own place in history. This one will always be remembered as Laker's match for the way in which his off breaks paralysed Australia.

There are many tedious records which have singularly little meaning, but those which the 34-year-old Laker surpassed yesterday were all of considerable significance. In the first place he became the first bowler ever to take 19 wickets in any first-class match, let alone a Test match. In Test matches S. F. Barnes headed the list with 17 for 159 against South Africa in 1913. Against Australia, H. Verity and W. Rhodes both took 15 in a match, and for Australia F. R. Spofforth took 14 in 1882. But Laker's crop leaves all these far behind and now with 39 wickets in the series, he has equalled the number established by A. V. Bedser as a record against Australia in 1953. At the Oval, Laker will almost certainly exceed Bedser's total and the whole affair, which is already stranger than fiction, is made even more incredible by the fact that Laker also bowled out the Australians on his own for Surrey in May.

Now he has enabled England to hold the Ashes on three successive occasions for the first time since five matches in a series became the rule in 1897. It is also the first time since 1905 that England won two matches at home in one summer against Australia. And to make Laker's achievement all the more extraordinary is the fact that Lock, who is generally so irresistible when the ball is turning, plugged away for 69 overs in the match for one wicket. That to some extent is a comment on the state of the pitch. Lock did not bowl particularly well, nor did things go his way, and Laker bowled magnificently. But the pitch was very far from being a travesty.

This match will always be talked about as much as any of the 171 played between England and Australia before, not only because of Laker's analysis but also because there arose on the second day a widespread controversy over the condition of the pitch. Then the ball spun from dry turf. Yesterday it did so after persistent rain and the batsmen's task grew progressively harder. Yet for a long while it seemed that the grass would not dry sufficiently or quickly enough for England to win and as nothing was foregone the play was full of tension. One knew that the turn would not have to be ridiculously awkward for England's purpose and during the long partnership between Craig and McDonald the batting was so good that the art was made to seem perfectly feasible. As soon as Craig was out, it was made at times to look impossible. In reality it was somewhere between the two when the game finally hurried to its conclusion.

McDonald's innings was a triumph for his fighting spirit. He is no great technician, but once he is entrenched he is as stubborn as they come. To score runs he waited for a chance to cut. For the rest of the time he played forward or back in a way too open to please the purists, but he was wonderfully watchful and there could have been no better example of unyielding concentration. Craig, who was his partner for so long, played an innings of almost equal value. He could hardly have had a fiercer baptism in Test matches against England, but the experience of it will always stand him in good stead.

Craig is still only 21, yet he had a long time in the wilderness awaiting a chance to show his skill. Now his patience and perseverence in the face of all manner of disappointments have been rewarded and there are many series ahead for England to appreciate his beautiful method. Two hall-marks of class are stamped on his play. In the first place he has plenty of time in which to make his strokes, in the second his judgment of length is extremely sound, and not until Laker dislodged him yesterday did England start striding towards victory.

Play was begun only 10 minutes late, although it had rained heavily through the night until 5 o'clock, and before luncheon the pitch was too saturated to be of any use to anyone. May explored every move. He began with Bailey, who was inclined to bowl too short, and later he gave Oakman a turn. Statham, too, tried with the new ball to hammer some life from the pitch. But of course the attack was based primarily on Laker and Lock, and what they wanted most of all was some sunshine to dry the turf. There was a stiff wind, which sent the many lowering clouds scudding over the ground, but that was not enough, and towards the end of the morning some blue sky began to appear. And with it the pitch perked up and the ball showed signs of misbehaving.

At luncheon McDonald and Craig were still together. They had then added only 59, but the important thing was that they had each been batting for more than four hours. Ahead of them stretched another four and only 15 minutes of these had ticked away when Laker struck his first blow. Craig, still showing a full sense of duty after 259 minutes, played back where he might have been better advised to go forward, and was leg-before. Several other Australians were to do the same and the departure of Craig revealed a hollow middle to Australia's innings. Mackay splashed about in deep water until he sank pushing forward at Laker and being caught off the edge of the bat at second slip. Miller undermined himself, by choosing to take everything he could on the pads. One has never seen him so completely dispossessed and he was out at 130 lunging myopically at a ball he might have made into a full pitch. Archer at once was caught by the middle of three backward short legs playing back to Laker and the day was not yet half run. The sun, too, was now blessing the scene, the threat of showers was fading and as Laker's spin quickened it seemed that there might be a collapse of the kind that had been witnessed on Friday.

Perhaps if Benaud had fallen at once there would have been, for Mackay, Miller, and Archer had not scored a run between them and between 25 past two and five to three four wickets had gone for 16 runs. But McDonald stood immensely determined amid this crumbling world, and now Benaud stayed with him until tea. That was for 80 minutes, and it began to seem again as though England might be thwarted. Benaud carried gamesmanship almost to an extreme by asking for guard in every over, and slowly and deliberately taking a botanical interest in the pitch after every ball. It is fair enough to repair each divot mark which the ball makes, but Benaud's way of doing it irritated the crowd, just as his admirable powers of resistance must have worried England.

When the final two hours of the evening started, whichever side was to win still had a long way to go. Someone was going to be denied and the likelihood that it would be Australia increased when McDonald's monumental vigil of 337 minutes was ended by the second ball after tea. He pushed forward at an off-break and Oakman at backward short leg took his fifth catch of the match. The next two balls from Laker must have settled any doubts that had been sown in English minds. Both of them turned viciously and now it was only a matter of time and a question of whether Laker could take the last three wickets himself.

This was suddenly a fabulous possibility, and three-quarters of an hour later it was an accomplished deed. First Benaud was forced back on to his stumps and bowled by a generously flighted off-break, then Lindwall was snapped up in the leg trap, and finally Maddocks was trapped leg-before. Australia were beaten, the crowd flooded the ground, there were smiles and handshakes, and the hero jogged off as though nothing very much had happened. Close behind him was May, who could feel justly proud at having led England to the Ashes at his first attempt. His splendid efforts must not be overlooked, but this now was Laker's hour, and here to end with and for all time are his figures. In Australia's second innings he took 10 for 53, in the match 19 for 90 in 68 overs, and yesterday eight for 26 in 36 faultless overs. Surely there may never again be anything like it.

ENGLAND 459 (Rev. D. S. Sheppard 113, P. E. Richardson 104, M. C. Cowdrey 80, Evans 47, P. B. H. May 43; I. W. Johnson 4 for 151)
AUSTRALIA 84 (Laker 9 for 37) and 205 (C. C. McDonald 89; Laker 10 for 53)
England won by an innings and 170 runs

Memories of Old Wicket-Keeper

FROM OUR SPECIAL CORRESPONDENT [A. P. RYAN]

3 *May* 1958. Mr. Herbert Strudwick is beginning his sixtieth and – so he says – last season in the service of Surrey cricket. But you would not think it as you watched him darting across his little score box by the side of the Oval pavilion to show you how a ball, low on the leg side, should be taken behind the wicket. His hands would be diagnosed at a glance, even by Dr. Watson, as those of an old wicket-keeper. Every finger bears honourable proofs of what happened when gloves were thin ghosts of their present plump and well-protected selves. His memories, keen and racily put, go back to his native Mitcham in the eighties, when he and the other village boys would hurry to the station to watch the Australians arrive in a special saloon coach for practice on the famous common.

You cannot pin him down to the past. For he rushes off from it in conversation as quickly as he used to leave the wicket and career towards the boundary. ("You had to; we didn't have all those men on the on side – often only one. That's why I always used the smallest pads I could get hold of. Ernie or I had to chase all the balls played to square leg. Not much above the knee. With them you were light on your feet.") First-class cricketers, he says, are as good and – allowing for changes in the wicket and laws – as fast scoring as ever they were. The crowd, he thinks, know less of the game than they once did. ("Almost everybody who watched played a bit. There were more to choose from at the top. We could have the county, the second eleven and two club and ground teams playing on the same day. Spectators didn't expect every batsman to be a Jessop or a Woolley. If he were they'd soon get tired of seeing boundary after boundary. You chaps on the Press are partly to blame. What I'd like to see (and here Mr. Strudwick plays with his fingers on the buttons he presses to light up the numbers of the fielders on the score board) is more reports of who did a good piece of ground fielding. If all the members in a team to-day got their fair share of praise it would encourage them no end. They are putting up as good a show, by and large, as any men have done in my time. There have always been slow scoring patches in any well fought game. They are part of the excitement.")

Back to wicket-keeping and Mr. Strudwick, leaving the buttons and his chair, crouches to make his points. ("Hands matter more than pads. Once, when I was a youngster at Dorking, all the chaps started chucking balls at me as fast as I could take them, before the start of a match. I did not realize that I had no pads on until I was taking the first ball of the match. The chaps had been trying to hit me on my shins. But my eye was in and they hadn't. Stand nice and comfy, drop the hands with the fingers pointing down. Watch the ball from the bowler's hands and then off the ground. If you don't you can't tell what it's going to do next. Above all don't stiffen as the ball leaves the ground. If one part of the body is stiff, it'll all be stiff.")

Did he, as has often been said, put raw meat inside his gloves? ("Never. Most of them did. But I thought it too messy. So I was glad when the gloves and the inners got better. At first I had only brown leather round the fingers and inners with nothing much to them. For my first two years I hadn't a box protector. When it did come in it was like cardboard. It didn't save you but it gave you confidence. I never had a long-stop. Hardly any of them did except Harry Butt and he only for Vine. Albert Trott used to turn round and try to hit the ball past the wicket-keeper's head when the ball was outside the leg stump. He used a very heavy bat and it was not a nice feeling when you felt this bat somewhere near your face. I remember Trott hitting Butt a nasty blow from a ball pitched outside the leg stump. You didn't dare to drop out even if you had a groggy finger. There were two or three waiting to take my place. Once the middle finger of my right hand was so swollen that I wanted to rest. I reported to the doctor. He said 'Let's see your tongue.' I told him it wasn't my tongue that was sore. He said again 'Let's see your tongue.' I did. He glanced at it and told me 'You're quite fit. Out you go on to the field.'")

What is the most awkward bowling to take? ("A slow bowler is trickier than a fast one. Razor Smith was about the worst. He could turn the ball so sharply from the off. Kirk, our Surrey left-arm swinger, delivered the ball with his feet at all angles across the popping crease. Tarrant of Middlesex once came out to play here, padded as high as he could get them, and with towels wrapped round his body. He told me there wasn't a chance of being given out l.b.w. So he meant to stand in front of his wicket. I said 'What about me? I can't see round you.' I had a word once with Kirk for having made an l.b.w. appeal he shouldn't have done. His answer was 'Well I get 'em out like that in club cricket.'

("Simpson-Hayward was another tricky one with his underhanders. He was the only bowler I ever kept to who could twist the ball in his hand as though it were a billiard ball. When we were in South Africa one of their batsmen, Zulch, put a bit of white paper to mark where Simpson-Hayward's good length ball would pitch outside the off stump. His idea was to play any ball from further out with his legs. But I wasn't having that. The paper would have put me off and so I picked it up.")

Mr. Strudwick admits that all fast bowlers were not easy. ("N. A. Knox was the hardest of the lot. You never knew what he was going to do next. He did not know himself. As the ball whizzed past the batsman's head our captain would say 'Well bowled Neville.' Richardson was faster but safe to take. He was one of our heroes when I was a kid. I used to see him on Saturday morning down at Mitcham after I'd helped my mother and then gone for a day's watching. We used to shout 'Hullo, Curly' at Richardson, and he always gave us a smile. I got into a bit of trouble in those days through sitting right by the sight screen so as to be as near behind the wicket-keeper as I could get. When I came to keep to Richardson there was one ball of his that *was* difficult. He could make them go past the off-stump in such a curve that I had to take them far away to leg. I believe Richardson would be pretty well unplayable with the bigger stumps of to-day and with this new l.b.w. rule.")

"Batsmen," says Mr. Strudwick, "can make a lot of difference to a wicket-keeper. I noticed Jack Gunn when standing back to the bowler always fell flat down if the ball was pitched very short, and out of his ground. So I asked Mr. Crawford to 'Send him down a short one as fast as you can bowl it.' He did. Jack Gunn went miles out to it and fell flat. And I stumped him. As he was going back I said, 'Jack, I've been trying to stump you for years.' He was very cross with me. W. G. Grace was a tricky one. He never stopped talking or muttering. I've heard him at point keep on saying 'Get him in a minute, get him in a minute.' " Four visits to Australia and two to South Africa have left him with pleasant memories of playing on matted wickets. ("They give you a better chance. They're faster and truer. Turf wickets are much slower than they used to be. Balls got up above stump high much more than on these modern wickets – and much faster – I used to think after the first ball, I will never be able to stop them to-day. But during the last years of my playing I was taking the ball below my knees.")

The last has, it seems, not been heard of Strudwicks behind the stumps. There is a grandson, beginning his first term at Brighton and his grandfather, who has coached him in the garden, says he shapes well as a wicket-keeper.

Cricket has not been Mr. Strudwick's only game. He broke his nose at football, he was a keen hockey player. ("They wanted me to keep goal. But I wasn't having that. No thank you.") He took up golf in his early days and at 78 still plays it. He and Sir John Hobbs have a round at West Hove regularly once a week. The conversation then must, surely, be the best cricket talk to be heard in the world to-day.

Mr. D. R. Jardine

24 *June* 1958. L. E. J. [Sir Lawrence Jones] writes:–

It is always a little disconcerting to the friends of great players of games to read obituary notices which confine themselves to the field of play. Jardine himself always regarded cricket as "only a game." He never wanted to talk about it. His main preoccupation, in the years when I knew him both in a City office and in my own home, was Hindu philosophy. He had a speculative mind, intent on ethical and religious problems. Kindly and high-minded, he had in those years an antipathy to Christianity, to which he always referred as "Rewards and Fairies," equal to Gibbon's. Nor, in his manner and bearing, was there the faintest trace of the stern, aloof, decisive cricket captain. He was gentle and diffident in all his ways; slow and hesitant in speech, and, as it seemed to us, in thought; he chewed things over and came to cautious and tentative conclusions, except when attacking "Rewards and Fairies." Then he could be trenchant, and we realized how this mild-mannered philosopher could have been the instigator of "body-line" bowling.

It must be seldom that a great cricketer can have played the game so seriously and yet, on retirement from it, have put cricket so firmly in its proper place.

Former Test Cricketer Fined

19 *September* 1958. Herbert Sutcliffe, the former Yorkshire and England cricketer, of Tubham Rise, Ilkley, Yorkshire, was fined 20s. at Bow Street Court yesterday for passing a traffic signal at red in the Strand. In a letter to the court, he wrote: "I have no wish to doubt the accusation made by the police, but I should like to state that my eyesight and concentration are almost as good now as when I had the honour of playing for England along with my old partner Sir J. B. Hobbs. I must confess I find it difficult to think I have proceeded through traffic lights at red."

Quite Like Old Times
Lindwall Scourge of M.C.C.

FROM OUR CRICKET CORRESPONDENT [JOHN WOODCOCK]

1 *December* 1958; *Brisbane*, 30 *November*. M.C.C. got a thoroughly bad day out of their system here yesterday when they were dismissed by Queensland for the miserable total of 151. Up to a point it was quite like old times, for Lindwall took five wickets for 57 runs and it was his bowling alone that

distinguished the day. The old warrior's arm is lower than it was – the surprising thing would be if, at the age of 37, it were not – but of all the bowlers in Australia he is still the finest craftsman and England's batsmen must be relieved that he will not be playing against them on Friday.

The great natural cricketers of this world can go on for years if they remain as fit as Lindwall, and in his case guile compensates for any loss of speed. Moreover he is as keen as he has ever been, so that his ambitions even now comprehend a return to the Australian side, and, from what we have seen in the past few weeks, he remains a better bowler than either Davidson or Meckiff, who have been chosen for the first Test match.

Australian selectors are always reluctant to fall back on a favourite once he has been discarded. Lindwall's last Test appearance was two years ago. Since then he has been overlooked for a South African tour, even when a replacement had to be sent for, and, until yesterday, he has not seemed a candidate for this series. But now he found a useful wicket to bowl on, with sufficient grass to help the seam and enough humidity in the air to encourage swing. Certainly it was the best seam bowler's wicket we have come across on this tour, and, even when he returned after tea to finish off the innings, Lindwall was still moving the ball about.

Four years ago this corresponding match started in the same way, with Lindwall sending back Cowdrey and Bailey in a fine opening spell before Compton and Simpson retrieved the situation with a century apiece. Now Lindwall had Watson caught at the wicket after half an hour and Milton at forward short leg 10 minutes later. May was taken low down at slip off Mackay's first ball, and after that M.C.C.'s innings was a tedious and, at times, humilitating struggle.

It has been so for some time that when May fails runs are scarce. Things are made worse at the moment by Cowdrey's inhibitions. Cowdrey is such a fine player that he is sure to come good, as they say, in the Test matches again, but since Perth he has become increasingly diffident and subdued. He pens himself in, allowing the bowlers to take the initiative, and is reluctant, it seems, to go through with his strokes. It is sad to see a player with such an outstanding talent becoming the butt of the barrackers.

Bailey, of course, is entirely different. He is in such a defensive groove that if he can possibly lie doggo he will do so. Yesterday he saved an ugly situation when M.C.C. were 39 for four, having just lost Milton, Watson, May, and Cowdrey for 17 runs in 35 minutes, and by the time Subba Row was bowled the score had reached 112. Bailey then was well set and, on Subba Row's departure, he should have made some effort to get the bowling away. Instead he contributed precisely three runs in 70 minutes before tea and not for the first time on the tour a good Saturday afternoon crowd were baffled by his refusal to play what appeared the right game for his side.

The remaining batsmen inevitably suffered from watching Bailey make the bowling look so difficult, and it was a mercy when the innings was over at a quarter past four, having lasted for four hours and a half. Lindwall revived old memories again when he found an immediate yorker for Laker, and Bailey was denied the not out which he seemed so intent on achieving when Lindwall made a ball lift to have him caught in the gully.

The Australian spectators, delighted as they were at Queensland's excellent showing, must have been mystified that this was the strength of England, for, apart from Milton, who is in encouraging form, and Subba Row, whose determination is beginning to find some reward, there was nothing to cheer. No doubt M.C.C. would have been seen in a more favourable light had they been bowling rather than batting, for Statham, Bailey, and Tyson would have been a nasty proposition during the morning when traces of moisture were to be found. By half past four the pitch was more placid than the man who tends it.

He had been in evidence at the tea interval but half an hour later, when the wicket was being rolled between innings, he had resigned over the employment of one of his assistants. His resignation was accepted and a former Woolloongabba groundsman, now nearing 80 and watching the play as a spectator, was called in and entrusted with the preparation of the Test wicket. That was until the groundsman put an end to the pantomime by withdrawing his resignation. Whether or not his wicket will be so temperamental on Friday no one knows. At present it is heavily grassed and everything may depend on how closely it is shaved, a matter which, as a writer of detective fiction, the groundsman is keeping a closely guarded secret.

MCC 151 (R. Subba Row 51; R. R. Lindwall 5 for 57) and 71 for 4
QUEENSLAND 210 (R. G. Archer 83; Laker 4 for 27)
Score after first day: M.C.C. 151, Queensland 30 for 1
Match drawn

The Decay of Initials

17 *February* 1959, *Leading Article*. Various reasons have been given for the present rather dull and depressed state of English cricket. Some are technical and others fanciful and nostalgic. Among the latter is the lack of players having three initials. Where are the great three-deckers of yesteryear? The most illustrious player in England at this moment is properly dowered but his initials do not run trippingly off the tongue as they would once have done. No one talks of P. B. H. MAY. It might be said of him as of the Bishop of Rum-Ti-Foo in the *Bab Ballads*

> They called him Peter, people say,
> Because it was his name.

He is rapidly become Petermay in a single word in the manner of Peterloo.

It is hard to lay a finger on the cause of this deplorable phenomenon. It is probably this odious familiarity of Christian names which has overflowed the world in a great vulgar tide.

One who laments it has written down without the book some five and thirty examples of the trebly endowed and they make a rich feast. Here are just a few of them: S.M.J. and L.C.H., H.D.G. and B.J.T., A.J.L. and D.L.A., F.G.J., P.G.H., A.P.F., and, should something, as Sherlock Holmes would say, a little more recondite be wanted, what will the reader make of P.J.T. and S.A.P.? And this is but a small selection; our memory man has plenty more up his sleeve. He finds modern times miserably poor by comparison. Being a Sussex man he remembers first G.H.G. and then from Warwickshire – just to pass the reader a hint – M.J.K.

It may be simply that parents have gradually grown more niggardly at the font, although they have on the whole fewer children to christen. Again it may be that to-day far fewer amateurs can afford to play cricket and it was they that used to have the larger number of initials. Once upon a time indeed professionals had no initials, at any rate on the programme. If by some fortunate accident he learnt their Christian names the adoring small boy could hug to himself knowledge of Luke or Ephraim, Saul or Mordecai; but such things were to be thought, not uttered. It is all a little sad but there is some strange comfort in compensation. If some columnist of to-day had flourished in the days of W. G. he would never have been satisfied with those initials to simply and severely great. He would have called him GILBERT or, even, gracious powers! have shortened him to GILLIE.

Walking by Himself

20 *June* 1959, *Leading Article*. A fair minded man might well assert that the most composed of all those who have taken the field at Lord's during the past two days was the resident cat – the cat which, in the middle stages of India's first innings and in fine full view of the spectators and the television camera, fielded for a short period at square leg, changed comfortably to mid-off at the end of the over and then stalked majestically off the field. Though he was unable to improve on his pause before the last ten yards by taking off a cap or waving a bat, many a player must have envied him the easy grace and the absence of self-consciousness with which he made the long walk between the wicket and the pavilion. That walk, whether it is at the school fathers' match or at one of the more skilful if less exacting contests that take place at Lord's or the Oval, tries even the strongest nerves. The difficult thing, on a lone public occasion, is to have nothing to do except just walk. The occasional century-maker has, it is true, various gestures of acknowledgment as well as his inner joy to sustain him. Even the duck-maker can indulge in some comic by-play – provided his ducks are rare enough. The poor wretch who has

made about five, and usually does, has no saving grave.

But the real test is the walk to the beginning of a performance, whether at a wicket or, say, a rostrum. Slow speed, like that of the Lord's cat, is certainly the essence of the technique – confident slowness, conveying the impression of knowledge that the crowd is expectant and that the walker has something so good to bestow that he can well keep them waiting. Mr. Pickwick would never have kept such a grip on the Club if he had not "slowly mounted into the Windsor chair." Of nobody less than a Beatrix Esmond can it be said that their "motion, whether rapid or slow," is "always perfect grace." It is useful to keep to a practised standard gait and mien; though this is little help to the hardest tested of all solitary walkers – the young athlete who is called up successively at the school sports prize-giving to receive the trophies of, say, the 100 yards, 220, 440, long jump, high jump, hurdles, and Victor Ludorum. In all these things cats have it over human beings. They are used to walking slowly and by themselves, and they are creatures of habit. A long, solitary walk suits them, and they share with all animals the lack of self-consciousness which creates public dignity. They gain by the facility for doing a bit of what comes naturally. At which point truth compels us to admit that the Lord's cat directed his stately walk from the wicket not to the Pavilion but to the Bar.

Pain in the Neck

29 *June* 1959, *Leading Article*. We have so long been accustomed to irreverence in biography that such works of piety as FORSTER's *Life of Dickens* or MORLEY's *Gladstone* seem farther back in time than actually they are. Even so we are, where venerable figures are concerned, still capable of being shocked. LORD CHANDOS certainly administered a blow the other day when he revealed that when, as a child, he asked an uncle what it was like to play with W. G. GRACE, he received the crisp reply "The dirtiest neck I ever kept wicket behind."

The words are as vivid as they are unexpected, and on the instant the bearded formidable figure who bestrode the cricket field, and, if it comes to that, the later Victorian era, like a Colossus is reduced to the stature of a small and grubby boy. A man is not a hero to his valet, but a great batsman has the right to expect a measure of admiration and respect from an opposing wicket-keeper, and was it not the REV. A. P. WICKHAM, one of Somerset's clerical wearers of the gloves, as the old sporting journalese had it, who, after "keeping" to W.G. during an innings of mammoth proportions, recorded that not a single ball had passed the bat? No pat on the back for technique, however, can make up for the comment that soap and water had neglected to work backwards from the face, and if W.G. were alive to-day there is no doubt that he would regard the whole race of wicket-keepers with the gravest suspicion.

On the other hand he would, if possible, be even a greater hero to the juvenile members of the population who, when the state of their ears and the back of their necks came in for public criticism, could cite the great man in defence and, what is more, point out that he was a doctor as well as a cricketer. The medical attitude towards what is sometimes breezily called a little healthy dirt was, in truth, more liberal then than it is now, and the masculine neck, when all is said and done, is nothing to make a fuss about. Female necks, on the other hand, were highly thought of at the time the DOCTOR was breaking the hearts of bowlers, and to own one which could, with no more than a moderate degree of poetic licence, be described as "swan-like" was as good as possessing a pair of eyes like twin stars. CALIGULA amiably wished that his subjects had one collective neck so that he could dispose of them with a minimum of inconvenience, and small boys – and, as it seems, W.G. – are inclined to forget that they have them at all. To be reminded that they do and that they are in need of attention is a pain in the neck indeed.

Keep Your Shirts On, Please

17 *August* 1959. About 30 men sitting shirtless in the sun watching the Middlesex-Yorkshire cricket match at Lord's on Saturday were asked by an M.C.C. attendant to replace their shirts. The attendant said this move was a result of complaints from women spectators during the recent hot spell. "After all, Lord's is Lord's," he added.

Later, a Lord's official said there was no ground rule enforcing the wearing of shirts, "but we do have regular complaints from ladies who object to seeing men with bare chests. We do our best to comply with their views and to persuade men to wear shirts."

Unforgettable Words

26 *October* 1959, *Leading Article*. MR. GEORGE LYTTELTON'S letter about HIRST'S immortal words to RHODES, "We'll get them in singles," sheds at first sight a gentle melancholy upon the soul. HIRST seems to have denied all knowledge of them. It is true that he only said he had no recollection of using them and that is some comfort. So is MR. LYTTELTON'S suggestion that if he had but said not "singles" but "wuns" (which appears to be the Yorkshire idiom) memory might have come flooding back. Still, it is saddening and makes us wonder what we can believe. Did TOM EMMETT never say of W. G. that he ought to be made to play with a littler bat? That is a dreadful thought. Did WILLIAM PALMER not say, "It was the riding that did it," nor JACK MYTTON, after setting light to his nightshirt, "The hiccup has

gone, by God"? Most tragic of all, what of "Up Guards, and at 'em"? CROKER asked the DUKE in a letter whether he had used those words, and the DUKE, in his reply, did his best for posterity. He wrote: "What I must have said or possibly did say was 'Stand up, Guards' and then given the commanding officers the order to attack." We must be content with what we can get.

Yet perhaps it does not really matter so very much, save for the sake of pedantic accuracy, whether HIRST said it or not. To the younger men coming in at so tremendous a crisis he would have addressed some reassuring words, and what could be better than those long since enshrined in our faith – if he did not say it he ought to have. After a time it is surely more important that history should be romantic than that it should be precisely true. There ought to be a statute of limitations about great words whereby, after a certain period, they should be unquestionably accepted, and we may feel sure that, at the bottom of his heart, MR. LYTTELTON would agree. For all we know, CAESAR's memory about "*Veni, Vidi, Vici*" may have become a little shaky, but he did his duty in remembering it. We should abolish from all our admirable dictionaries the sceptical letters "attr." Let there be no attributions! At any rate, we may thank Heaven that HIRST did not say in the words of a most uncricketing poem, far too often quoted: "Play up, play up, and play the game." He would have known better than that.

Prince Duleepsinhji

7 *December* 1959. Prince Duleepsinhji, the former Sussex and England cricketer, died at Bombay on Saturday at the age of 54. His cricketing career was cut short by illness, but it lasted long enough to establish him as one of the great batsmen of his generation.

Kumar Shri Duleepsinhji was born on June 13, 1905. He was a nephew of Ranjitsinhji, with whose style his wristy elegance and attacking spirit had some affinity. When he came to England to be educated, he made his mark on the cricket-field almost at once. He was in the Cheltenham XI in 1921 when he was only just 16, and in his last season at the college he was probably the best school batsman of the year. For the Lord's schools against the Rest, he scored 108 and took five wickets for 41 runs.

He went up to Cambridge in 1924, and was awarded his Blue the following summer, making 932 runs during the university season, with two centuries. In 1926 he became qualified for Sussex, and showed himself as great a run-getter in county as in all other classes of cricket. It was in 1927 that the first interruption took place, for early in the season he was pronounced to be seriously ill, and after May he played no more. A winter spent in Switzerland set him up, and he came back to England with restored health. Then began an even more notable run of success. His highest score for Sussex, which he captained with tact and ability, was 333 against Northamptonshire at Hove. He scored two separate hundreds in a match three times, and a hundred and two hundred once in a match against Kent in 1929. He made four hundreds in successive innings in 1931. Outside the county championship he was particularly effective in Gentlemen and Players, making three centuries. And finally, in the first of his 12 Test matches, against Australia at Lord's in 1930, he distinguished himself with a splendid innings of 173. In his three golden years of 1929–31 he scored over 2,500 runs each season.

The curtain fell all too soon. In 1932 his health again gave way. This time his visit to Switzerland did not have the desired effect, and the pulmonary disease from which he suffered grew worse. In 1933 he retired from the Sussex captaincy, and towards the end of the summer he knew definitely he would not play first-class cricket again.

He joined the Indian foreign service in 1949 and was appointed High Commissioner for India in Australia and New Zealand. After his return to India in 1953 he became chairman of the public service commission in the state of Saurashtra of which his brother was Rajpramukh. He married in 1936 Shrimati Jayaraj Kumari, who survives him.

"The Greatest Test Match of All Time"

FROM OUR SPECIAL CORESPONDENT [MICHAEL DAVIE]

15 *December* 1960; *Brisbane* 14 *December*. The first Test match between Australia and the West Indies ended here at four minutes past six tonight with the first tie and the most sensational finish in the history of Test cricket.

After the game, with sweat pouring off his brow, the Australian captain, Benaud, said that this had been "the greatest cricket match I have ever played in and the finish could only be described as fantastic". The West Indies captain, Worrell, took the same view: "I have never played in a game like it before." And to Sir Donald Bradman it was "the greatest Test match of all time".

Overnight the West Indies had been 207 runs ahead with one wicket standing, and this morning and afternoon there was much palpitating cricket as they finished their innings and Australia set out after a total of 233. But it was at the tea interval that the tension really began to mount.

At tea the game could scarcely have been more evenly balanced. Australia, 109 for six, needed 124 to win in exactly two hours. The wicket was the colour of pale straw, scarred with black patches around the crease: though anything but easy, there were still runs in it.

The Australians, plainly and characteristically, decided to go for the runs. Valentine bowled to Benaud and Benaud hit him high over mid-on's head for four. Hall, who had wrecked the start of Australia's innings with a fine, sustained spell of fast bowling (his figures were 12–3–38–4) came back for his second spell and Davidson clipped him easily into the covers. Ramadhin replaced Valentine and with his first ball baffled Davidson completely. But the Australians kept on the attack, driving firmly and running quick singles.

At five o'clock, with an hour to go, Australia needed 61 with the new ball between them and victory. Davidson picked Ramadhin off his stumps and hit him a colossal blow in the air to the mid-wicket bounday to put up his 50. If he were not the best new ball bowler in the game, Davidson would be in the Australian side for his batting. When Worrell now took himself off and put on Sobers to bowl his left arm tweakers over the wicket, it seemed to be the critical moment to the entire match. Benaud seemed to think so too, for he watched Sobers on to the bat with deepest concentration before he swung him out to midwicket for four off the last ball. The Australians were keeping in exact step with the clock.

Davidson drove Ramadhin straight for four and swung him round to the fine leg boundary to bring up the 100 partnership in 95 minutes. Forty-three minutes to play and 40 wanted. The West Indies fielding hereabouts was magnificent and so was the Australian running of safe, quick singles. Benaud hit Ramadhin straight for one run and Australia had reached 200. With half an hour to go, with Hall taking the new ball and the crowd alight with excitement, Australia needed 27, still with four wickets intact.

Benaud hit Hall in the air not far short of Hunte at square leg, and Davidson hooked him first bounce to the midwicket boundary. With 20 minutes left and 19 runs to get Worrell brought back Sobers at the other end bowling his faster ones, but Benaud, looking now more sallow than ever, drove him to mid-on for four. Benaud had his 50 in just over two hours. With 15 minutes left Australia needed 10, and then nine in 10 minutes after Hall had bowled a long over for one run.

At last, with seven minutes left, Benaud pushed Sobers to mid-wicket for one quick single too many. Solomon hit the stumps and Davidson who had made 80, was run out. Six minutes left, seven runs to win and three wickets remain. Grout was hit on the leg and the whole crowd seemed to appeal. But he was not out and he then took a single to mid-on. So, as the last over of the match started, Australia needed six to win and Grout faced Hall. Grout was hit in the stomach and Benaud dashed through for a run when the ball dropped at Grout's feet. Benaud swung at the next ball with all the power at his command, got a touch, and Alexander caught it: the crowd went through the roof. Six balls to go, five runs to get and two wickets to fall.

Meckiff kept Hall out on his first ball and gave a nervous smile. The next one went through to the wicketkeeper, who threw it to Hall, and if Hall had hit the wicket when they took another quick single, Meckiff would have been out. Four balls to go and four to get. Grout struck the next ball high and straight up in the air; everyone rushed forward and Hall, knocking Kanhai out of the way, got under it and, to roars of ecstasy, dropped it while the batsmen went through. Three balls left for the three runs wanted.

Meckiff got hold of the next ball and it soared out towards the midwicket fence looking like six and the end of the match. But Hunte cut it off on the bounce as the batsmen, running like men possessed, went through for a third run and now Grout was run out by a foot. The sides were level with two balls to go.

In came Kline, looking pale and drawn. He took guard and not a bird moved. He lashed out like a man in a nightmare fighting off phantoms: the ball flew to midwicket, there was a flurry of desperate fieldsmen, Solomon flung at the wicket and to an incredulous shout of joy and anguish, scattered the stumps. The umpire's finger shot up and Meckiff was out. It was a tie. Four wickets had fallen in 13 balls, three of them run out, and three of them in seven balls.

The day had started with an hilarious stand between Hall and Valentine who kept out Davidson and Benaud in full cry for nearly 40 minutes to add another 25 runs to the West Indies overnight score of 259 for nine. The time they took was as important as the runs they made, for they left Australia 233 to win in 312 minutes, or a rate of 45 an hour. Even so, it had seemed well within Australia's power to get them with time to spare.

But the Australians got off to a bad start. Simpson, who showed little sign of liking Hall in the first innings and was even less comfortable in the second, when Hall was bowling up to his reputation, tried to pull the sixth ball of the fast bowler's second over and was caught by the forward of three short legs. Harvey took a four off his first ball and then played back, got an outside edge and Sobers dived unbelievably to pick up the ball an inch from the ground in his right hand. He dislocated a finger doing so and left the field grimacing with pain to have it strapped.

At luncheon Australia were 28 for two. Then, a quarter of an hour after the interval, O'Neill was caught at the wicket off Hall and Australia seemed on the run. They were 49 for three. Favell was nearly out to the next one, and from the next ball of the new over McDonald played forward to what seemed a straightforward ball from Worrell and was clean bowled. The West Indies were then right on top. When a quarter of an hour later Favell turned Hall straight into Solomon's hands at short leg and Australia were 57 for five it seemed all over.

The next wicket went to Ramadhin. He came on at three o'clock, just about the time Australia needed 150 in even time with Mackay getting dug in. His first ball to Mackay was a googly. Mackay, wholly baffled, followed it to give a catch to slip which, agonizingly, was dropped. But this affected Mackay's temperament and it was not surprising shortly afterwards when Ramadhin got one to turn a little more sharply to hit the leg stump.

That brought together Benaud with Davidson for a stand of a lifetime. But it nearly never began, for the second ball Benaud got from Ramadhin he never saw and he could scarcely believe his luck when he found it had somehow missed the stumps. Then both batsmen began to settle down and Benaud off-drove Valentine just before the tea interval to bring up the Australian 100 in 175 minutes.

Until that interval, and its extraordinary sequel, it had scarcely seemed possible that Australia could win the match. Subsequently it seemed impossible they should lose. There seems every likelihood, indeed, that historians of the game will decide that this was not only the first tie in Test cricket but one in which, of all Tests, the expectation of victory most frequently oscillated between two teams. The second Test match of the series, which starts in Melbourne on December 30, should fill that airless and mammoth stadium.

WEST INDIES 453 (G. Sobers 132, F. M. Worrell 65, J. S. Solomon 65, F. C. M. Alexander 60, W. Hall 50; A. K. Davidson 5 for 135) and 284 (F. M. Worrell 65, R. Kanhai 54, J. S. Solomon 47; A. K. Davidson 6 for 87)
AUSTRALIA 505 (N. O'Neill 181, R. B. Simpson 92, C. C. McDonald 57, L. Favell 45, A. K. Davidson 44; W. Hall 4 for 140) and 232 (A. K. Davidson 80, R. Benaud 52; W. Hall 5 for 63)
Match tied

Lord's Will Have Music

3 *June* 1961. For the first time in memory there will be music played at Lord's during a county cricket match. The Middlesex Regiment's band, in this country during a summer for the first time since the last war, offered its services and the Middlesex club accepted. So musical selections will be played during the lunch and tea intervals at the Middlesex and Warwickshire match today. Bands do play at Lord's during the season, but only when Services teams are taking part.

Seven Runs Decide Exciting Knock-out Match

[BY GORDON ROSS]

3 *May* 1962. In a finish which would have gripped the most unemotional and carping critic Leicestershire beat Derbyshire by seven runs in the one-day Midlands knock-out competition at Leicester, and thus qualify to meet Northamptonshire at Leicester next Wednesday.

This absorbing day's cricket – which clearly stamps the experiment with considerable success, a happy augury for the future – produced 493 runs in a little under seven hours, yet at no time did the proceedings give the impression of prostituting the basic skills of the game.

There was no suggestion of a carnival. In fact only three sixes were struck.

It was just a question of bowlers bowling a liberal ration of overs in the time and batsmen getting on with it by playing strokes and using their pads only for protection.

This enterprising experiment arises from a desire expressed by all the counties to acquire a practical knowledge, before 1963, of just how one-day cricket can operate successfully, and how different is its image from the accepted format for county cricket. The Leicestershire secretary, turning this over in his mind, discovered that Leicestershire, Derbyshire, Nottinghamshire, and Northamptonshire had these available dates and took swift action.

The geographical position of these four means that no hotel accommodation is involved and, as it turned out, the fees received from the Independent Television Authority defrayed all the expenses of the competition, including the purchase of a cup – the Midlands Counties Knock-out Cup – to be competed for annually.

Laws framed for this match limit each innings to 65 overs, prevent any one bowler from bowling more than 15 overs, restrict the off side field to six players, and authorize the umpires to be the sole judges as to whether or not extra time shall be played in order to finish the match. The technique of this sort of cricket has yet to be evolved. Carr made one obvious point when, on winning the toss, he put Leicestershire in. The side fielding first have more manoeuvrability, since they know exactly what they must do in the batting time allotted to them.

Kirby and Hallam, for instance, opening for Leicestershire, feeling the pulse of something foreign to them, took 10 minutes to score their first run before a crowd which barely constituted a quorum on a bitter morning. The rash discarding of early wickets would be folly; some heavy artillery must be kept in hand for an all-out assault when the end of the 65 overs is in sight.

After 20 runs in 10 overs the pace of the morning soon quickened and in due course showed a brisk acceleration upon the old formula. After two hours' cricket and 41 overs Leicestershire had made 148 for one, so that practically all their resources were still available to mount a blistering attack from a position of strength, with Hallam 85 not out and batting beautifully.

Plans, however, went awry at this point when Hallam was run out and Wharton was stumped. Carr, having worked out this process with his customary shrewdness, had kept half a dozen overs apiece from Jackson and Rhodes up his sleeve. This, as it transpired, produced the remarkable sight of Jackson being hit by Jayasinghe for three fours in one over, not quite as Carr had intended, but in the main it did stop any undue high jinks. Leicestershire finished with 250 for five in three hours and 20 minutes off the prescribed 65 overs.

Derbyshire began like a house on fire. Carr (who apparently has always had a sneaking feeling for opening the innings) and Lee put up 50 in the twelfth over and 100 in the twentieth, Carr hoisting the hundred with a six.

He also hit seven fours.

Barratt enjoyed a spell of seven overs, four maidens, five runs and one wicket, yet many a captain has shown consistent reluctance to put a spinner on when wickets are wanted, for fear of his being hit. Barratt, who is 19, was an economic proposition. The real excitement came at the end when Derbyshire seemed to be sailing home with a score of 229 for 6, but they failed to get there.

LEICESTERSHIRE 250 for 5 (65 overs) (Hallam 86, Wharton 50, Jayasinghe 49 not out)
DERBYSHIRE 243 (61.4 overs) (D. B. Carr 62, Lee 50, Oates 46)
Leicestershire won by 7 runs

Day of Memories at Lord's
Old England Win Lightheartedly

FROM A STAFF REPORTER [BRIAN MOORE]

18 *June* 1962. "Go on, Keith, bowl him a bumper", came the cry as Compton took guard with the shadows beginning to inch their way across Lord's on Saturday evening. Miller, ever the man for such a moment, tossed that fiery mane of his, an action still capable of chilling English blood, and duly parted Compton's hair with what can only be called a fizzer. Howls of laughter from all sides.

In that moment there was crystallized the whole purpose of this day's sparkling cricket between an Old England XI and the Lord's Taverners. For, corseted within an agreeable wrapping of good humour and pure farce, the not-so-old heroes (some of them it is sad and surprising to find, already greying) evoked memories for all.

There was something for everyone, in fact, even the captive tea lady who said she had managed to abandon her urn long enough to watch "that smashing bit of nonsense between Norman Wisdom and Roy Castle", the Taverners hilarious ninth wicket pair. And wasn't that Roy Castle a good bowler, too, she gravely opined, getting that chap out like that. That chap being no less a batsman than Robertson, stumped far from home for 51, and not worrying over much about it either.

But for the most part it was the Comptons, Edriches, Browns, and Wrights in the cast who made the more genuine and lasting impact. And about the only concessions that they made to the growing number of Wisdens that stand between 1962 and their own great deeds were perhaps a certain reluctance to bend and chase in the field and to bowl off a shortened approach.

Wright, for example, no longer runs up as though hotly pursued by a swarm of angry bees, all flailing arms and kangaroo hops, although he still turns over a most respectable leg break at some pace off four or five yards;

Gover shuffles fussily over the same distance, with enough nip still to quicken the stroke (54 years old? Impossible); Brown's right arm looks a good deal lower than once it was; and little Edrich, for a time after the war an impoverished England's fastest bowler for half-a-dozen overs, now trundles down some improbable, looping off breaks.

There were more authentic touches, too: Bedser's clockwork toy run up, for example, with its efficiency unimpaired, and still he finds Evans's red palms, eager and impeccable as of old, with a resounding thud; Washbrook, too, brooding in the covers waiting to swoop.

And, of course, there was the dynamic Miller. He came in when the Taverners ("a cheerful collection of cricketers, cricketing actors and acting-cricketers", the programme said) were 28 for three. A situation ripe for such a showman. In a twinkling he had hit Compton for four sixes, one of them, a massive blow, scattering the unsuspecting as well as the "Read Compton on Cricket" signs in St. John's Wood Road. He smacked 53 in half-an-hour.

Subba Row (too young for Old England?) aroused painful reminders that he has retired too soon with a well struck 82, Barnett made a prim 92, and the Taverners, after scoring 257 for six *by luncheon*, declared with 319 for nine at three o'clock.

Washbrook and Robertson soon made inroads into this score with 100 in 45 minutes, having seen off Miller and the new ball, a point that would have had a much more satisfying ring about it some 10 years ago. Even so it was a dazzling start, with Washbrook matching Miller's six into the road in his pugnacious 73.

Robertson, Edrich, Ikin, and Compton then played their full part – although what a pity we were denied the last tantalizing glimpse of Edrich and Compton at the wicket togehter – so that Old England, to everyone's delight, overhauled their truly cheerful opponents with two wickets standing. Lord's had been revisited to be sure, worthily and with splendour.

> LORD'S TAVERNERS 319 for 9 dec (B. A. Barnett 92, R. Subba Row 82, K. R. Miller 53)
> OLD ENGLAND 321 for 8 (C. Washbrook 73, J. T. Ikin 63, J. D. Robertson 51)
> *Old England won by 2 wickets*

A Chance to Win in 1963

BY SIR LEARIE CONSTANTINE M.B.E.,
HIGH COMMISSIONER FOR TRINIDAD AND TOBAGO

31 *August* 1962, *Supplement on Trinidad and Tobago*. The Summer of 1963 will find the stage all set for one of the most interesting struggles in the history of test matches between England and the West Indies.

Many have wondered at the effect the breaking up of the West Indies

Federation would have on West Indies cricket, sad as this must be for all of us. West Indies cricket existed long before anything was done to create Federation, and its eventual dissolution can only mean that cricket is one of the essentials of common services.

I am by now noted for sticking my neck out, and I begin with the prediction that the West Indies will defeat England in this series [*They won 3-1*]. It is important to go into a few details to confirm this first impression, and I begin with the West Indies tour of Australia two winters ago.

Worrell as captain threw out a challenge to Benaud the Australian skipper; Benaud accepted it and cricket the world over benefited by this enterprise. I stated without hesitation that if Worrell could only improve the West Indies fielding from what hitherto had been its most backward department, we could defeat Australia. The fielding did improve, in fact it reached a high standard, and considering the farewell that Australia gave to Worrell and his men, the lawyer could be forgiven for noting, so far as results were concerned, the disparity between the *de jure* and the *de facto*.

England has of late been developing along the proper lines and the counties have been trying to revive the old tradition of bright play. It takes a Robins as chairman of the English Selection Committee to encourage a player of the calibre and outlook of Dexter as captain as against a more cautious and exact scientist. He would do a good job in Australia; he will create a brightness hitherto absent from the English batting. This would be good for the English players, but I do not believe that it could be developed sufficiently to thwart the efforts and stratagems of the West Indies players. On the other hand, the England bowling is and will remain suspect, and although the West Indies batting will be "tops", it is their bowling that should pave the way for their eventual victory. To talk of Hall as being the fastest bowler in the world today is to talk in terms of real speed, and there are other fast bowlers too who could be included in the side to keep Hall a terror right up to the end of the series. The job of the West Indies selectors, therefore, is to pick such a bowling combination that Hall could be spared the ordinary chores of county matches.

In that connexion, I would like to feel that whatever were Ramadhin's failures in Australia, he would be considered for the tour of England as I believe that he is and will always remain a mystery to the uninitiated.

Sobers is one of the finest bowlers in the world, a left-hander bowling the wrong-un and the top spinner with such facility that the captain would have a difficult job to determine whether his bowling or his batting should predominate. West Indies batting should be strong with McMorris, a disciplined opening batsman, Kanhai, Solomon, Sobers, Worrell, Hunte and a few others who should give the England bowlers some long, tiring days in the sun.

Worrell has been selected as captain. I am usually accused of bringing up the subject of colour in my deliberations on this great game. I do not need to make any excuses for so doing because the fact that it is the first time that a black man has been selected to captain the West Indies side in England leaves the field wide open for other people to make the excuses. Worrell is a student of the game. He knows it inside out. He has had a lot of experience, including a close study of present-day players, and I would wager that he makes a contribution in tactical manoeuvring equal to some of the greatest masters of the game. He will, I imagine, outwit Dexter; and if he does not, then like the Yorkshireman I say "it would be a glorious draw".

One aspect that must not be omitted in considering the relative merits of the side is that most of the West Indies are achieving independence. To us this means self respect and an opportunity to make, among other things, our characteristic contribution to this great game. It will have a psychological effect on the West Indies side and it is bound to reflect itself in their play. The motto of the newly independent Trinidad and Tobago – "Together we aspire, together we achieve" – is apt in the circumstances. Do not underrate it. I am happy that I shall be present to watch this great battle between my country and my almost adopted country.

Cricket Breaks with the Past

End of the Distinction between Amateur and Professional

27 *November* 1962. The 17 first-class cricket counties decided at Lord's yesterday by a clear majority to do away with the amateur status. In future, all players will be known as cricketers. Approval is necessary from M.C.C. before this can come into force, but it is expected that this will be forthcoming when the M.C.C. committee hold their next meeting at the end of January.

Lawn tennis has for three years been deliberating upon whether or not to make their Wimbledon championships an open meeting. Cricket, along with table tennis, will now be the only sport without recognized amateurs, although cricketers can continue to play without accepting payment if they wish.

This means the end of the Gentlemen v. Players match, which dates back to 1806. It is expected that M.C.C. will substitute another representative match in its place at Lord's next summer, possibly the former North v. South game, and there will have to be an alteration in the Scarborough Festival games which also include a Gentlemen v. Players match. . .

The committee have accepted a block grant of £6,500 by the Gillette Razor Company, who will sponsor the new KNOCKOUT CUP COMPETITION which starts next season. Apart from the grants, a trophy will be presented to the team winning the final at Lord's. It will be known as the Gillette Cup or Trophy, and there will also be awards in respect of each of the 16 ties on the basis of meritorious individual performances. The Gillette awards will be made to the "man (or men) of the match". There will be two rounds, a semi-final round and a final, together with a bye round to be arranged between the two counties occupying the bottom places in the county championship. The draw for the knock-out competition will be made today.

England and West Indies have accepted an offer by Wisden to provide a perpetual trophy for the winners of the Test series between the two countries. This is in celebration of the Wisden Cricketers' Almanack centenary edition in 1963, when the West Indies tour England. It is hoped that the WISDEN TROPHY will play a similar role in the matches between England and the West Indies as the Ashes do between England and Australia.

Our Cricket Correspondent [John Woodcock] cables from Brisbane:–

The abolition of the distinction between the amateur and the professional in cricket is a realistic decision. For some time the borderline between the two has been spurious and E. R. Dexter's admission in Melbourne recently that he made a good deal more from cricket than business emphasized the anomalous situation.

In principle the amateur outlook is a fine thing. It charms away routine. Yet the day of the genuine amateur who cultivated the game purely as a pastime has gone. The attitude now among the leading amateurs is becoming increasingly mercenary. Without making money from cricket they could not afford to play, so that they advertise and write and receive liberal expenses, which amounts in some cases to considerably more than a professional's salary. The distinction is therfore largely theoretical. To remove it is at once a break with a tradition which has, in its day, been a great strength to cricket and an acceptance of changing times.

Yet I see no reason why a cricketer, if he chooses, should not remain unpaid and thereby retain his independence. The change might attract new blood to the game. It might draw in a part-time player who has the potential of a top-class cricketer but lacks the time or the inclination or the resources to devote a full summer to the game. The "amateur spirit" would still be there. Many young men can introduce this by their natural way of playing. It is in their character or the upbringing and it always will be, whether they are called Gentlemen or Players or just cricketers.

Wisden's Century

17 *April* 1963, *Leading Article*. The little top-hatted figure of JOHN WISDEN, a Brighton builders' son, is familiar to all lovers of old cricket prints, and in his day he was a terror to batsmen. Although he stood 5ft. 4in. and weighed seven stone his prowess as a fast bowler, who, among other feats, once took six wickets in six balls, has become legendary. But his lasting claim to fame rests on his almanac – that hardy annual which this season reaches its century.

JOHN WISDEN, like THOMAS LORD, was a man of many interests outside cricket. He kept a tobacconist's and sports shop in Leicester Square and had a shrewd eye for advertisement. What would this businesslike sportsman make of the current issue of the almanac and of the state of play of the game it so faithfully records?

As one who had played overseas – though in Canada and the United States – he would be pleased to find an article, rich in good stories, by SIR ROBERT MENZIES, the Prime Minister of Australia. Inevitably he would be out of it when he came across MR. NEVILLE CARDUS choosing as the six giants of the Wisden century, GRACE, HOBBS, BRADMAN, RICHARDSON, BARNES, and TRUMPER. But remembering the rivalries and arguments of his own day he might sympathize with MR.CARDUS for nervously and promptly following that list with: "I can already hear in my imagination a thousand protesting voices (including my own)." What might well give him most satisfaction would be to learn that the sale of the almanac is now steady, averaging 21,000.

How far does this reflect healthiness in cricket? Certainly it is proof of keenness in a large minority of followers. Loyalty shown to the Cricket Society points the same way. But the quick eye of WISDEN would, we may be sure, light on MR. JOHN SOLAN's look "Through the Crystal Ball", in which it is noted that the attendance paying at the entrance at county matches last year was 933,000, compared with nearly two million just after the Second World War. Six-day cricket, MR. SOLAN reminds us, has no future. "It is one of county cricket's most melancholy anomalies that the dullest day's play is almost invariably reserved for Saturdays." The future pattern, he argues, must have at its centre a "virile and satisfying spectacle on that important day". It is a measure of *Wisden*'s contemporary vitality that such plain truths appear in its centenary number. If this interest in the personalities and statistics of cricket is to be kept up at past level, imaginative reform cannot much longer be delayed.

Talking of Cricket

13 *June* 1963, *Leading Article*. It must have interested elder listeners when they recently heard one of the B.B.C.'s fluent commentators on Test match cricket call the wickets the timbers. There was a time when the sports reporters on papers of widest appeal took a professional pride in avoiding the obvious word. Simile and synonym were unremittingly pursued. In Rugby football no try could be simply converted; the oval had to be propelled through the uprights and players were not tackled but grassed. In descriptions of cricket there was an even greater practice of this habit. The ball that kept low had to be a daisy-cutter although a first-class cricket pitch has surely been sufficiently mown to lose all likeness to a flowery meadow. The timbers,

recently restored to favour, were constantly appearing. A series of pulls which ended with a catch at the wicket would appear in this form: "After several cow-shots into the Great Beyond, Basher was neatly pouched by the timber-watcher." The wicketkeeper was also the custodian of the woodpile. Fielding was leather-hunting and the bat was always the willow. The weather had its own lingo, in which traces of a classical education, though possibly limited, were on view. It was Old Sol and not the sun that shone. If rain stopped play it was Jupiter Pluvius who intervened.

The custom dwindled, partly because it grew tiresome and partly because reporting of games was taken up by authors of repute, critics of the arts, and other servants of the Muses. A remarkable salute to culture was made in a paper of large circulation which headed its accounts of cricket-matches with "Poet and Novelist" after the writer's name. Now plain speaking is the general rule. But the jargon of games retains some curios. Much has been written of the origin and naming of the googly, which has its Oriental cousin, the Chinaman, attached to a similar form of deceptive spin. The commentator who was restoring the timbers to use mentioned this twister; he implored viewers not to drench him with letters of inquiry about the word. It was a natural precaution, but at least he could assume that mention of the timbers would get by without attracting massive correspondence. He might have included the willow in his arboreal references. This makes one wonder whether any of the aforetime Latinists ever called a bat a salicaceous implement. They might have done. Those were the days.

Close, Cricket's Enigma, Now a Hero

Unforgettable End to Lord's Test Match

FROM OUR CRICKET CORRESPONDENT [JOHN WOODCOCK]

26 *June* 1963. The second Test match between England and West Indies had, as it deserved, a finish of unforgettable, unbearable excitement. When Cowdrey came to the wicket with two balls to go, his left arm encased in plaster, any of four results was technically possible. England needed six to win, West Indies had one wicket to take, the light was fading fast, the crowd could scarcely cast their eyes upon the scene. That Allen settled for a draw was understandable and took nothing from the drama.

No sooner had he done so than hundreds of West Indians poured across the ground. They besieged the pavilion and called for Worrell as though it was election night. It was the epilogue to one of the greatest Test matches Lord's has ever seen. England, requiring 234 to win, were 228 for nine when time was called. From 2.20, when play began, until six minutes past six, fortunes had swayed this way and that, and while Close was playing his finest innings England looked the likelier winners. As the result of it all, the series is established. By the interest that it will engender the next instalment at Edgbaston is a success in advance.

West Indies sought victory with the battering ram. For three hours 20 minutes Hall bowled from the pavilion end without relief. His energy was astonishing, his stamina inexhaustible, his speed awesome, from the first ball to the last. Forgetting the fact that he took an unconscionable time about his overs, it was a stupendous piece of bowling. His partner for all but five overs was Griffith, likewise a man of the fiercest strength. Standing against them until 20 minutes from the end was Close, the enigma of English cricket.

Barrington stayed for a while; so, too, did Parks and Titmus. And without Allen, who braved the flames of the last three-quarters of an hour, England would probably have lost. But England's hero of the day was Close. There were those, when he was out, who blamed him for losing his head. It was more gracious to acclaim him for having kept it through a struggle as tense and unrelenting as any he will know.

Through the afternoon Close played with a sense of responsibility with which few have credited him. After tea he was obliged to take a risk to keep England abreast of the clock. He chose to do so by running out to the fast bowlers before they had delivered. This is a recognized way of distracting a bowler and upsetting his rhythm. That it was Close's downfall in the end was a venial sin, reckless though it may have appeared.

At the start of play Close was seven not out and England were 116 for three. When he was caught by Murray, heaving mightily at Griffith, they were 219 for eight. Perhaps if Close had been prepared quietly to glean the remaining runs, England would have won. It is a reasonable line of argument. Had he done so the misdemeanours of his career, if you can call them that, would have vanished in the evening air. As it was they mostly had, for without him there would not have been the climax that there was.

Fifteen runs were wanted when Close departed and Shackleton joined Allen. With only Cowdrey to come they kept the winning chance in mind without daring to attempt too much. Thus, when the last over started, England were still eight runs short. From the balcony came instructions for a death or glory bid, and Shackleton threw his bat at the first ball without making contact. He and Allen took a short single off the second, with Hall in his follow-through making a spectacular attempt to run Allen out. The third ball was glanced by Allen for one, leaving six to make in the remainder of the over.

At the fourth ball Shackleton lunged in vain; it went through to Murray, and Allen ran for a single without Shackleton's knowledge. By the time Shackleton was aware of what was happening Murray had thrown the ball to Worrell at forward short leg, and Worrell, remaining inscrutably calm, raced for the bowler's end and took off the bails before Shackleton made his ground.

It was now that Cowdrey emerged, cheered for his bravery. He had a long consultation with Allen, deciding in the course of it that six runs off two balls from Hall with the fielders scattered far and wide was not a proposition. No one could blame them for reaching this conclusion. The run-out had left Cowdrey at the bowler's end, which was merciful, and Allen lay doggo for the last two balls. Both were straight and fast, and Allen moved resolutely into line.

In spite of morning rain there had been thoughts of resuming play as early as 12 o'clock. The covers were removed and there was to have been a start at 12.15 had there been no further rain. In the event the rain hung about until half past one. An early luncheon was taken, and at 1.50 the umpires announced the pitch as fit but not the light. Soon after two o'clock the sky cleared, and at 2.20 the match was on. The pitch was unaffected, having been protected all night, and the field was surprisingly dry. There was no need of a towel for the bowlers, and the piles of sawdust remained unused.

Barrington, who had played so well on Monday, never picked up steam. In 55 minutes he managed only two scoring strokes. The first, after three-quarters of an hour, flew to fine leg off the shoulder of the bat, the shot being a protective one against a short-pitched ball. The other was a boundary to square leg. Barrington was persuaded ultimately to spar at a short off-side ball from Griffith, which led to his being caught at the wicket.

Most of the scoring during these opening exchanges was done by Close, and there was not much of it. Parks was freer with his strokes after surviving, off his first ball from Griffith, a concerted appeal for leg-before. He lived for long enough to add 28 with Close and to display two ravishing cover drives off Griffith. Close, by now, looked as much at ease as could be expected in the circumstances. He was being hit about the body a good deal by Hall, but already we were revising opinions about his temperament for the big occasion.

Parks was beginning to look positively happy when he was leg-before to a short ball from Griffith which bounced less than most. Parks was trying to push it away past the short legs. At tea, 20 minutes later, England were 171 for five. In one hour 55 minutes West Indies had bowled 28.1 overs. Apart from the last over at the Nursery end these had been bowled exclusively by Hall and Griffith. Of the 55 runs England had added Close was responsible for 28.

So long as Titmus stayed with Close England had their noses in front, and he did so until only 33 were wanted. The first four overs after tea took 20 minutes to bowl, which was an unconscionably long time. Close now was looking for runs more eagerly than before. Care turned to urgency. He began to swing at balls down the leg side which earlier he had allowed to pass. He gathered a four to fine leg off Hall and would have had another but for a brilliant save by Butcher. At 182 for five, with 65 minutes left, Gibbs replaced Griffith.

With an hour remaining and four effective wickets standing England needed 48 to win. A few minutes later word came through that Cowdrey was changed. The England dressing room must have been a place of shattered nerves. Titmus was clinging on like a burr and running well between wickets, and at 196 he joined the applause for Close's 50, reached with a hook to fine leg for four off Hall. The pavilion was filling up as businessmen arrived in bowler hats from the city.

This, then, was the position when Titmus pushed Hall firmly to the middle of three short legs where McMorris held an excellent catch. Next ball Trueman was taken at the wicket and England in a trice had their backs to the wall. It was Close or no one now and he continued to edge England forward. Two more hooks brought two more fours, with Allen hanging on for his life.

Once, perhaps twice, an over Close was charging down the wicket. The first time he did so Hall pulled up before delivering the ball, clutching his back as though in pain. A gentle word from Worrell wrought a miracle of healing. Griffith returned in place of Gibbs. Twenty minutes later Close was out and as he made his way in the pavilion rose to receive him. We had endured already an agony of suspense, and there was still more to come.

WEST INDIES 301 (R. Kanhai 73, J. Solomon 56, C. Hunte 44, G. Sobers 42; F. S. Trueman 6 for 100) and 229 (B. Butcher 133; F. S. Trueman 5 for 52, D. Shackleton 4 for 72)
ENGLAND 297 (K. F. Barrington 80, E. R. Dexter 70, F. J. Titmus 52 not out; C. Griffith 5 for 91) and 228 for 9 (D. B. Close 70, K. F. Barrington 60; W. Hall 4 for 93)
Match drawn

Sussex Achieve Success through Attrition

FROM OUR CRICKET CORRESPONDENT [JOHN WOODCOCK]

9 *September* 1963; *Lord's.* Manifest in the final of the one-day knock-out competition were several of the best features of this type of cricket and a number of the worst. Sussex, the first winners of the Gillette Cup, achieved their success through attrition rather than attack, which is, of course, contrary to the aims of the competition.

Because of the loyalties involved and the great gathering of supporters who had travelled from Sussex and Worcestershire, the atmosphere was full of excitement. It was like Yorkshire and Lancashire with the lid off. There was some of the ribaldry of Eton and Harrow before the war; and at times devotees from Dudley and *aficionados* from Angmering found themselves reacting to a boundary hit more like West Indians than Englishmen of traditional reserve. From this point of view it was only a pity that the ground was far from full, in spite of all the tickets having been sold and all the private boxes taken.

In the matter of weather the organizers were remarkably fortunate, as they have been all along. The groundsman had excelled himself in producing a table dry enough for play, and although the last hour of Worcestershire's innings took place in Stygian gloom and occasional rain there were no interruptions. If Worcestershire had appealed against the conditions the umpires could hardly have turned them down; instead, they struggled on against Dexter's protective fields, and thanks in the end to Booth they made an exciting finish of it. The anticlimax of leaving a few overs to be bowled this morning was mercifully avoided.

There is not much doubt, I think, that those who began the day with an open mind mostly turned sooner or later to supporting Worcestershire. In the first place Worcestershire bowled 34 overs of spin, which was a welcome break from the season's motto theme. It was their clear intention to get Sussex out. Sussex, on the other hand, went into the field after making 168 with the main purpose of containing Worcestershire. Where Kenyon had, for the opening overs, placed two slips, a gully and a short leg. Dexter had only one close fielder, a slip, for Thomson and Buss. This made for a hard match and a slow rate of scoring.

For Sussex, only Parks played with the dash and distinction of other rounds. Oakman and Langridge provided a good beginning, with Langridge the more forceful. Their opening stand of 62 had a big influence on the match. After Gifford had dismissed them both in the same over wickets fell with regularity. Dexter was caught at slip off bat and pad, the umpire being more sure than the batsman that ball had made contact with bat. Suttle was out before luncheon and Lenham soon afterwards, both to Gifford, whose four wickets for 33 runs in 15 overs earned him the special prize for the best individual performance of the day.

Sussex scored their runs at 2.8 an over as against 4.7 in their three earlier matches. The pitch was inevitably slow; the ball would turn, and only Parks's handsome driving gave impetus to the innings. Worcestershire in the field were shrewdly directed by Kenyon. With the bat the initiative eluded them.

Although the pitch had dried out a little by the time Worcestershire went in, it still frustrated all but the finest drivers. Sussex's tactics were unashamedly defensive and insidiously effective. Once Kenyon was leg-before to a break back and Horton had been brilliantly caught and bowled it was up to Headley and Graveney to mount the challenge.

This was a crucial phase in the match, and it was by their successful suppression of Headley for two hours and a quarter that Sussex settled the issue. Headley played any number of good strokes for nought, the ball hit hard and straight to a fielder. It seemed not to occur to him to try to upset Sussex with the short single on the off side. Eventually Graveney got himself out in the effort to accelerate and at 103, Headley skied Bates to mid-on. Thereafter it was a race against the light, the rain and, for Worcestershire, against time.

After a few lusty hits by Broadbent, Snow took three quick wickets which reduced Worcestershire to 133 for nine. With eight overs left and the last pair together, Worcestershire still needed 36. That they got 21 of them was due largely to Booth. In every era there are a number of worthy cricketers who do yeoman service for their counties without ever quite achieving fame. Booth is one of these. He batted now with unexpected ease and quickness of foot and not until Carter, his partner, was run out a few minutes before seven o'clock were Sussex assured of victory. Had Carter beaten Suttle's throw as he went for a second run, Worcestershire would have required 14 to win off 10 balls. The end, in fact, was close enough for anyone, even if the means on the way had, at times, been a perversion of positive cricket.

No doubt the one-day knock-out match, contested by first class cricketers, has come to stay. A knock-out draw, with all reasonable entries accepted, provides, to my mind, enough yet not too much of this type of cricket. Perhaps next year Saturdays will be put aside for the competition: the final, too, may be played earlier in the season when the days are longer and less of a premium would be put on winning the toss.

This inceptive tournament, generously sponsored, has come through un-scathed by the weather, and that is miraculous. It has provided, with its brilliant fielding and interesting tactics and fast running, a happy diversion from three-day matches. It was won, however, by a side which bowled, in four rounds, only 23 overs of spin and deployed their fielders with unremitting caution. That, in itself, exposes an undoubted weakness of this kind of cricket in our kind of climate.

SUSSEX 168 (60.2 overs) (J. M. Parks 57; N. Gifford 4 for 33)
WORCESTERSHIRE 154 (63.2 overs)
Sussex won by 14 *runs*

Sir Jack Hobbs

30 *December* 1963. Mr. J. W. Chance writes:–

Some years ago I bought a cricket bat at Sir Jack Hobbs's shop in Fleet Street. This was required for a raffle as part of a programme to raise funds for repairs to a church in Buckinghamshire. Having completed the purchase I asked Sir Jack Hobbs whether he would do me the honour of autographing the bat. On learning the charitable nature of the request he immediately agreed to do so, and then asked whether I would care to collect as well the signatures of the Surrey XI, at that time in the middle of their reign as champion county. I said that I would be only too grateful, but how should I set about it. He then produced his own Oval pass and told me to use it to introduce myself to Mr. Surridge, the captain. I did so one afternoon when Surrey was playing Cambridge University at home. Within a short time I had all the team's signatures on that bat. including the twelfth man and the umpires.

But that was not all. A day or two later I received £1 from Sir Jack for tickets in our raffle. I have subsequently heard from another Surrey cricketer that anything to do with the church always evoked his sympathy and support.

Apology to Cricket Captain

Wheatley v. Beaverbrook Newspapers Limited and Others

BEFORE MR. JUSTICE SACHS
HIGH COURT OF JUSTICE: QUEEN'S BENCH DIVISION

1 *August* 1964. The settlement was announced of this libel action by Mr. Oswald Stephen Wheatley, the well-known cricketer and captain of the Glamorgan County Cricket Club, against Beaverbrook Newspapers Ltd. and the Daily Sketch and Daily Graphic Ltd., in respect of reports in the *Daily Express* and *Daily Sketch* of July 18, 1963, of an incident at Colchester on Wednesday, July 17, 1963, when Glamorgan were playing Essex.

Mr. Brian Neill appeared for the plaintiff; Mr. Douglas Lowe, Q.C., and Mr. David Hirst for the defendants.

MR. NEILL, for the plaintiff, said that on Tuesday, July 16, the plaintiff had been playing at Dover for Glamorgan against Kent. He was due to attend the annual dinner of the Hawks Club in London that evening, but he realized that it would be impossible for him, if he left Dover at the close of play, to reach the restaurant where the dinner was to be held in time if he were to change into his dinner jacket in London. For this reason he made the change in Dover. All the plaintiff's clothes were sent with the club bags direct from Dover to Colchester.

The plaintiff left the dinner about midnight, went to bed shortly thereafter and left next morning dressed in his dinner jacket. He arrived at Colchester in time for the toss, which took place well before the start of play, with only a few people at the ground and with the plaintiff still in his dinner jacket.

The *Daily Express* and *Daily Sketch* on Thursday, July 18, reported this incident. The plaintiff would have had no objection whatsoever to their doing so had they confined themselves to the facts, but the articles in both newspapers were so worded as to suggest that the plaintiff, instead of going to bed, had attended an all-night party. The plaintiff regarded that quite unfounded suggestion as most damaging to his reputation as a professional cricket captain, and had felt it necessary to bring these proceedings. The defendants had agreed to express their apologies to the plaintiff in open court and to pay him a sum of money appropriate to the injury to his reputation, and also his costs.

MR. LOWE, for the defendants, said that the defendants fully accepted what had been said by counsel for the plaintiff, and sincerely regretted that the articles were worded so as to convey the imputations suggested, which they fully accepted were untrue.

The record was, by leave, withdrawn.

Solicitors. – Messrs. Norton, Rose, Botterell & Roche, for Messrs. Bickley, Wheatley & Co., Birmingham; Messrs. Oswald Hickson, Collier & Co.; Messrs. Swepstone Walsh & Son.

Tricky Wicket for Mr. Dexter

Caution on Politics

FROM OUR SOUTH WALES CORRESPONDENT

2 *August* 1964; *Cardiff*, 1 *August.* Mr. E.R. Dexter deserves more net practice before he faces the demon bowler of Cardiff South-East, Mr. James Callaghan. This morning England's cricket captain held a press conference after his selection by the divisional Conservative Association as prospec‐ tive candidate to fight the seat now held by Labour's shadow Chancellor.

This morning England's cricket captain held a press conference after his selection by the divisional Conservative Association as prospective candidate to fight the seat now held by Labour's shadow Chancellor.

Mr. Dexter agreed that he had never before spoken for the party from a political platform or been a "physical member" of the Conservative Party or a Young Conservative. Much of his life had been spent out of the country, he explained, and it was now that he was settling down with a growing family that he had the opportunity of helping the Conservative Party. By conviction he had always been Conservative.

Mr. Dexter was reminded by a questioner that he had put down one of his interests as economics and that Mr. Callaghan might also have something to say on this subject. What did Mr. Dexter think about the problems of inter‐ national liquidity?

He wisely took his bat away. "I would rather not tangle with Mr. Callaghan on that one", he said. Those were specialized things with which he had not had time to get seriously acquainted. As from October (after the end of the cricket season) his time was going to be his own. He would then get better acquainted with Cardiff and with such specialized fields.

As a captain Mr. Dexter was able to answer with some fellow feeling a question about his views on the Conservative succession. "I would align myself behind Mr. Macmillan", he said. "If he thought we should have a successor then I would align myself behind him."

When asked what he did have strong views about (coloured immigration, perhaps) Mr. Dexter stonewalled. He did not really want to be tied down to such matters of policy, he said. He obviously had personal feelings about these things, but did not want to make comments on them at this juncture.

Would not the electors of Cardiff South-East expect him to? When he was knocking on doors in October, he said, he would give them his own considered views. A reporter wondered what Mr. Dexter would specialize in. That, he replied, would emerge in his visits to Cardiff, but he thought he would specialize in the particular problems of Cardiff South-East. "I do not pretend to know those in detail at the moment." But he hoped to put that right in the future.

Mr. Dexter was drawn into saying he would be against renationalization of steel and that the Government was remarkable in what it had achieved in education, thus deserving a further term of office.

In an introductory statement Mr. G. V. Wynne-Jones, chairman of the local association, said those people who had met and known Ted Dexter would realize it was Dexter the man and not Dexter the cricketer who had been chosen.

At the General Election Callaghan scored 30,129 votes, Dexter 22,288.

Graveney 15th to Achieve Century of Centuries

FROM OUR CRICKET CORRESPONDENT [JOHN WOODCOCK]

6 *August* 1964; *Worcester.* This is an encomium, or an acclamation, of a famous player rather than a commentary upon a successful side. Worcestershire's total of 309 for eight declared was a fine one, on a dry pitch emitting puffs of dust. But yesterday belonged not to Worcestershire but to Graveney, who became the fifteenth cricketer to score a century of centuries.

Here is the constellation which Graveney joins, with the number of hundreds they have made. – J. B. Hobbs (197), E. Hendren (170), W. R. Hammond (167), C. P. Mead (153), H. Sutcliffe (149), F. E. Woolley (145), L. Hutton (129), W. G. Grace (126), D. C. S. Compton (122), D. G. Bradman (117), A. Sandham (107), T. Hayward (104), L. E. G. Ames (102), and E. Tyldesley (102). Graveney became one of them just after half past five, towards the end of a scorching day.

He had played, characteristically, an innings of distinction and grace. Most of his 19 boundaries were drives, beautifully made with a flowing swing of the bat. We shall remember him for the high stance, the tanned face, the long peak to his cap, and the shoulders slightly rounded, the right rather lower than the left. When we are old we shall recall, nostalgically, the charm and rhythm of Graveney's stroke play. "Ah," we shall say, "you should have seen Graveney: there was elegance for you."

Yes, Graveney expresses as well as anyone the beauty in batting. Whether he is leaning on his bat between overs or playing a feathered glance or a delicate cut, he *looks* a cricketer. All the strokes are there, they have given pleasure in all the cricketing countries of the world. And now, at 37, Graveney is as good a player as he ever was.

That should be an example to those who think of giving up too soon. And let it be an encouragement to them that Hobbs scored more than 100 hundreds after he was 40. Graveney has many more to come, I hope. It is only a pity that someone of such infinite gifts should not have given more to England. As a Test match cricketer the best has seldom been got out of him, and now, it seems, the selectors have set him to one side.

Another large crowd watched yesterday's cricket. The game has the whole county by the ears at present, and by the middle of the afternoon there was scarcely a seat unfilled. For a long time the play was predictably slow. With the pitch likely to worsen, and the ball already turning, Worcestershire set cautiously about their business. In the two hours and a quarter of the morning they made 76 for two. Kenyon lost his off stump to Watts and Headley forced Scott to mid-on. Andrew soon had his spinners on, both of them slow left-arm over the wicket. After luncheon P. D. Watts had three overs of rather extravagant leg breaks.

Steele, who is a cousin of Crump, had much the longest stint of his career, without proposing himself as a strong spinner of the ball. He bowled an accurate line, on and outside the off stump, and well deserved his wickets. Scott stands fifth in the bowling averages with 81 wickets. He has a nice high build for a bowler of his type, though the action itself is square. Of the four orthodox left-arm spinners in the match, I imagine Gifford turns the ball the most. Today it will be interesting to see what he and Slade achieve.

Apart from Graveney, the best of Worcestershire's batting came from Horton, Richardson and Booth. Horton is a good, four-square player in his own right. Batting for so long in Kenyon's presence has brought him on. S. M. Brown learnt a lot from watching Robertson at close quarters, as Lowson did from watching Hutton, and Sandham must have done from watching Hobbs. Horton now made 54 solid runs before Milburn at silly mid-off, caught him off Steele, anticipating the stroke and diving to his right. Somewhere, I am sure, a seismograph must have recorded Milburn's fall. Horton and Graveney had added 75 and laid the basis of the innings.

By luncheon Graveney was installed. From the start his defensive technique was proof against the turning ball. Gradually the strokes began to flow, liquid as a mountain stream. He was never missed; he was seldom beaten; he was never hurried. During the afternoon he made 52 with an ease and a style that concealed the problems of the pitch. For half an hour Ormrod used his feet as Graveney's partner. And then Booth came to see him pass this great milestone in his career, and stayed on to share the celebrations. A sixth wicket partnership of 108 ensured a powerful position for Worcestershire in, to them, a vital game.

Graveney went to three figures with a succession of hooks off Larter. Everyone congratulated him, as is customary on these occasions. Graveney acknowledged the cheers to the manner born. I was at Canterbury when Ames reached his hundredth hundred. Here was another glorious natural batsman. Hutton was the last to do so, in 1951. May could be the next if he chose, his tally being 85. Cowdrey, with 69, probably will be. In any day and age, to achieve such a feat is a sign of abundant ability and the outcome of many years delightfully spent.

WORCESTERSHIRE 309 for 8 dec (T. W. Graveney 132, M. J. Horton 54, R. Booth 51; D. S. Steele 4 for 65) and 112 (J. D. F. Larter 5 for 44, B. Crump 4 for 39)
NORTHAMPTONSHIRE 212 (P. D. Watts 91, B. L. Reynolds 50; M. J. Horton 4 for 59) and 142 for 5 (P. D. Watts 48)
Score after first day: Worcestershire 309 for 8 dec, Northamptonshire 0 for 1
Match drawn

Cricket for Russians

15 *August* 1964, *Leading Article.* A gallant effort is made by *Anglia*, the official British magazine in Russian that circulates in the Soviet Union, to add to NIKITA SERGEYEVICH'S well-known store of proverbs and popular sayings. Quite rightly *Anglia* draws its offerings from Britain's national game *kriket*, otherwise cricket. First it gives a scholarly explanation of the game itself, telling all about the *betsmeny, boylery, fildery* and the two commands of eleven men apiece. Having set the field, the talented author then goes on to give what all Marxists would call a valuable generalization based on experience and with a just application to the tasks for today. He points out that cricket has enriched the English language with many very popular phrases, each with a moral. Pride of place he properly gives to "That is not cricket", *Eto nye kriket,* and explains it means "That's not fair", *nye po-sportsmensky.*

The good work is taken up in yet another article in the magazine, this time in English. If, as one may confidently expect, MR. KHRUSHCHEV is given a translation he will find it hard to resist the cricketing metaphors which it lists. He may not go so far as to complain to MAO TSE-TUNG that the Chinese are always trying to get him "on a sticky wicket". But there are the British. The Russians frequently assure us that they wish relations to be excellent – or, next on the list of *Anglia*'s examples, "on a good wicket".

There would be no better way of warming and softening SIR ALEC DOUGLAS-HOME'S cricketing heart than by Moscow's assuring him in a friendly letter that, though NIKITA SERGEYEVICH may occasionally "send down a fast one" in negotiations, he recognizes that (relying on *Anglia* again) it is SIR ALEC'S job to try to "hit it for six" – "a phrase commonly used to describe the complete frustration of an opponent in almost any context". On the other hand MR. KHRUSHCHEV, having read on, may feel it no less right to point out that if an opponent has "no fit reply to an apparently unanswerable question" he may be said to be "clean bowled" or "stumped". There are many new opportunities for enlivening diplomatic correspondence along such lines. *Anglia* is certainly on a good wicket.

Personal Column

24 *November* 1964. A first class County Cricket Club [Lancashire] invites applications from persons with first-class cricket experience for the position of Captain of the County XI. The position will carry a salary in accordance with experience and an allowance to cover expenses. – Write Box J.961. The Times, E.C.4.

Mr. Wilson Plays Himself In

15 *December* 1964. Mr. Wilson yesterday forced a draw – or should it be tie? – between himself and Sir Alec Douglas-Home. The Prime Minister whipped off his own green tie at Lord's and replaced it with a Lord's Taverners' tie.

He was accepting honorary membership of the Lord's Taverners, an exclusive charitable cricket club established at the famous tavern. Earlier this year Sir Alec, who has played in first-class cricket, brought roars of approval when he slipped off his own tie in favour of the club's. As Mr. Wilson did likewise yesterday, a wag among the cheering members called out: "Pull it tight."

Mr. Wilson said: "The first time I was here was one of the grimmest evenings in British cricket. We had lost three for 14 before nightfall, including Hutton, in the second Test of 1953. But all was saved next day by Willie Watson.

"I was a very bad cricketer, but I did get into my house team for Huddersfield – I was last man in", Mr. Wilson said. He recalled a match when the opposition were all out for 15. "We were 15 for nine. I went in; there were three balls, bumpers, and blinding light."

His partner came half-way down the pitch and said in "Yorkshire language" that he should not try to score but keep his end up. "I swiped at the first one and missed, and the same thing happened to the next two balls. Then my partner got the bowling and was clean bowled. He was Willie Watson."

Lord Reith was also made an honorary member of the club.

Mr. Raymond Robertson-Glasgow

6 *March* 1965. Mr. Raymond Robertson-Glasgow, who died on Thursday at the age of 63, was a man of many parts, scholar, athlete, wit, and first-class conversationalist. All these talents were focused on his favourite subject in life, cricket, and made him a notable and in many ways a unique figure among the brotherhood of cricketers.

His career as a performer started at his preparatory school, developed at

Charterhouse and came to full power on going up to Oxford. He played for Oxford in four University matches but, having bowled Hubert Ashton in the first, failed to take a wicket in his following three appearances. This was one of many unusual and original performances for which he had a most endearing flair. It was the more remarkable for he was a fine bowler of fastish pace who made the new ball leave the bat. His bowling career with Somerset and Oxford from 1920 to 1935 brought him almost 500 wickets, and many of these were defended by the greatest professional batsmen of a prolific age.

He was no mean batsman himself when called upon to exert himself to the full but his normal attitude, as a member of the lesser half of the order, was one of immense if ephemeral enjoyment. The most serious engagement of this extremely unserious but wholly devoted cricketer was one appearance for the Gentlemen (at Lord's) in 1924.

His time with Somerset was spent among some gay and colourful companions, such as Sam Woods, John Daniell and "Farmer" White, whose friendship filled him with great joy, and whose feats and foibles gave him a wealth of reminiscence which he retailed by spoken word or pen with a touch and gusto unexcelled in sporting talk or writing.

For 10 years from 1923 Robertson-Glasgow taught at St. Edmund's School, Hindhead. He entered journalism as golf and then cricket correspondent for the *Morning Post* in 1933, later working for the *Daily Telegraph*, *The Observer*, and *The Sunday Times*. He also contributed to *Punch* and other magazines.

His autobiography, *46 Not Out*, was published in 1948. Among his other books were *Cricket Prints* (1943), *More Cricket Prints* (1948), and *The Brighter Side of Cricket* (1951).

His writings were a departure in cricket journalism. His practical knowledge made him a dependable and informative observer, but the immense fascination of his work sprang from a warm and kindly wit which lay close beneath the surface of every sentence he spoke or wrote.

To those who knew him it came as no surprise that the open scholar of Corpus Christi College, Oxford, should later have written a wartime book *I Was Himmler's Aunt*.

Much of his writing was achieved against a background of ill-health, and there can be little doubt that but for this his talents would have been more widely known. He was the unrelenting enemy of all humbug and solemnity in sport; to him the brighter side of the game, whatever it might be, was all-important. This made him the perfect chronicler of cricket matches far below his own standard of play, and of such golfing pleasures as the meetings of the Oxford and Cambridge Golfing Society and the Halford Hewitt.

He married, in 1943, Elizabeth Edward, widow of P. Y. Hutton.

9 *March*. Our Cricket Correspondent [John Woodcock] writes:–
Raymond Robertson-Glasgow, known to his countless friends (with great

affection) as "Crusoe", possessed a warm and wonderful way of delighting his companions. He had, for one thing, a laugh which was as infectious and uninhibited in its enjoyment of the jokes of other people as of those he made himself. He had the background of a classical scholar, combined with a riotous imagination and a sense of humour which lit bonfires of good will. You had only to cross the threshold of a pavilion to hear and to know whether "Crusoe" was there.

In 1950, on the M.C.C. tour to Australia, I drove through the country with "Crusoe", and with his wife, Elizabeth, and watched them while they made a trail of friends. He reported the tour for *The Times*. Subsequently, his appearances dwindled. Ill health had much to do with that, for he would suffer long periods of depression when, to all but those who knew him best, he seemed in cracking form.

From 1953, when he retired from regular cricket writing, "Crusoe's" influence on the cricketing scene and his generous nature were badly missed. To him, cricket at every level was a game to be enjoyed. In his reporting of it there was an understanding of the difficulties involved, and a knowledge of the finer points which commanded everyone's respect. Solemnity was scorned. It is no coincidence that first class cricket has tended to become a more serious business and a less amusing one since "Crusoe" no longer inhabited, as a chronicler, and a sportsman, a humorist, and a wit, the grounds where it is played.

10 *March. From our correspondent, Reading, 9 March.* A widow said at an inquest here today that her husband, who had been suffering from melancholic depression, became depressed at the sight of the snow last Thursday and took an overdose of drugs.

Mrs. Elizabeth Robertson-Glasgow, of Lime Tree Cottage, Buckhold, Berkshire, said that usually her husband, Mr. R. C. Robertson-Glasgow, aged 63, author and former Somerset cricketer, was first downstairs to make the morning tea. On this day she was first down. She had swept the snow away from the kitchen door when she saw her husband. He told her: "Please telephone the doctor. It's urgent, darling. I am sorry for what I have done."

He said he had taken about 20 tablets.

A verdict of Suicide while the balance of the mind was disturbed was recorded on Mr. Robertson-Glasgow, who died in hospital at Reading. Dr. Frank Hampson, a pathologist, said that an analyst's report showed that he died from barbiturate poisoning.

M.C.C. Plan for Tavern Bar at Lord's

6 *May* 1965. Beer-drinking spectators of cricket outside the Tavern at Lord's this summer will need to order an extra pint to drown their nostalgia. For at

their backs, as they drink, time's winged chariot will be drawing near in the form of a redevelopment plan which will obliterate their century-old haven behind cover point, or mid-wicket, depending on which end is bowling.

M.C.C. yesterday published the details of the comprehensive £1m. redevelopment plan for the south-west corner of cricket's headquarters. In the plan the Tavern will be demolished and rebuilt with an added restaurant next to the Grace Gates and out of sight of the wicket.

A new stand, seating about 2,000 spectators, will be built on the site of the existing Tavern, members' dining room, and clock tower. In the background a 12-storey block of flats will be erected, partially overlooking the ground, and presumably in great demand as a vantage point during Test matches.

But thirsty spectators can sip their pints in security all this summer and next, while they watch the run-stealers flicker to and fro; demolition of the existing Tavern will not start until September, 1966, when the new Tavern will be ready for them.

M.C.C. have also realized that there is a need for some therapeutic haven with a view of the cricket in which their customers can find liquid inoculation against bitter weather and tedious stone-wallers. So on the site of the present Tavern they will build a smaller Tavern bar. And from here in the future, as in the past, hearty cries of comment and advice will be hurled at any batsman who tries to put the shutters up in the last few overs before luncheon.

McKenzie and Hawke Rout West Indies

FROM OUR SPECIAL CORRESPONDENT [C. L. R. JAMES]

18 *May* 1965; *Port of Spain*, 17 *May*. Australia gained an astonishing victory here today in the fifth Test match against West Indies and with it they lessened the disappointment of having already lost the series. They won by 10 wickets with three full days to spare, having dismissed West Indies in their second innings for 131. Simpson and Lawry scored without difficulty the 61 runs which Australia needed for victory, thereby underlining the memory of a beautiful day, a large crowd, and some notable bowling.

Of the 11 wickets to fall today the fast bowlers claimed ten, Griffith setting the fashion by getting rid of his opposite number McKenzie, with the last ball of his only over this morning. Australia's first innings thus ended without addition to the starting score of 294 for nine. When West Indies batted, Sincock, with his unorthodox medley of left arm chinamen and googlies, played an important part. Although he bowled many bad balls – there was not a single maiden among his 18 overs – Simpson never took him off, once he was on, for he unsettled all the batsmen except Hunte.

But it was McKenzie, with five for 33, and Hawke, with three for 31, who set Australia on the way to their remarkable victory. Only Hunte, who carried his bat for 60, saved West Indies, with their great batting strength, from total rout in their second innings. Butcher, who helped Hunte to add 41 for the third wicket, was the only other West Indian batsman to reach double figures.

At the start of the day the groundlings had been out for a good time, their setbacks unforeseen. They applauded Hunte straight driving McKenzie for three and doubled the applause when Booth returned that ball over the bowler's head straight into Grout's hands. Davis showed his strength by a perfect off drive from Hawke and was then leg-before to one that squatted.

Kanhai at once made vintage strokes and played Hawke watchfully forward. Hawke was moving the ball into the batsman in the air. Apparently one did not move in the air and Kanhai's stumps were spreadeagled. The ball did nothing awkward off the pitch. At 27 Sincock bowled some dreadful long hops and presumably strategic full pitches. Butcher hit one of each for four, but seemed over-anxious to hit Sincock about and achieved a number of would-be potent but ineffective hits. Not so Hunte, who was very much the anchor with 16 to Butcher's 20 at luncheon when West Indies were 53 for two.

Butcher hit a high full pitch from Sincock straight into the hands of mid-wicket. Nurse was leg-before to Hawke, and four wickets were down with West Indies still four runs short of the deficit of 70.

Sobers seemed comfortable but was not. He missed quite a few leg hits at Sincock. Then, trying to force McKenzie off the back foot, he was convincingly beaten and bowled. McKenzie was going all out and the crowd hummed awesomely at the pace he was making off the pitch. The Australian fielding, always of a high order, was giving nothing away. The 100 came with Hunte 39. Allan scored only seven; but he showed a readiness to resist and the crowd made much of him.

Sincock is not only master of the deadly full pitch. His long hops, pitched half way, possess the faculty of evading the most carefully aimed cuts. What prevents an unvarnished statement of how bad the West Indian batting was is that it would diminish the merit of the Australian bowling and fielding.

Hunte's 50 came out of 121 and he celebrated by digging out two creepers in an over from McKenzie. McKenzie bowled Hall and Griffith. Gibbs gained applause by stopping the hat trick but was bowled next ball.

WEST INDIES 224 (R. B. Kanhai 121) and 131 (C. C. Hunte 60 not out; G. D. McKenzie 5 for 33)
AUSTRALIA 294 (R. B. Simpson 72, R. M. Cowper 69; C. C. Griffith 6 for 46) and 63 for 0
Australia won by 10 wickets

Festival Cricket

27 *August* 1965, *Leading Article.* All too soon now festival cricket will be taking over from the Test and championship variety, a familiar sign that the season is at its last gasp. The word "festival" in connexion with the technical intricacies of the contest between bat and ball may seem a little out of place. It suggests clowns and false noses, whereas cricket, if it is to have any meaning or attraction, must be played seriously – which does not mean solemnly.

Festival cricket has interpreted this basic truth genially, with Scarborough, which has over the generations established itself as the leader in this particular field, setting the example. Much excellent and exciting cricket, the real, as against the spurious, kind, has been seen on that friendliest of all the Yorkshire grounds with Trafalgar Square at one end to attract the attentions of such hitters as C. I. THORNTON, whose name is so intimately linked with the place. The gentlemen v. players match is no longer played and it is now under the name of T. N. PEARCE and not H. D. G. LEVESON-GOWER that teams go out to do battle. But the knack of combining light-hearted enjoyment with earnest endeavour has been preserved.

Other places have had – and still have – their cricket festivals, but not always with Scarborough's success. At Blackpool, understandably enough, the accent was too much on the holiday spirit. At a match there in the twenties the umpires announced that they had been instructed to be "very generous about l.-b.-w. decisions". The characteristic comment of GEORGE GUNN on this, was, according to R. C. ROBERTSON-GLASGOW, "And I suppose if anyone's bowled (rhyming with 'scowled') it's just a nusty accident?" Folkestone has seen some good games, although the wide open spaces there, in the absence of large crowds, have sometimes seemed a little intimidating. Hastings, now back in favour, is compact enough with the castle guarding the ramparts overlooking the sea, and always has, as it were, a festival atmosphere. Festival cricket all the season is a horrid thought. So is the idea of a summer without any at all.

Marylebone Cricket Club

18 *October* 1965, *Personal Column.* Full members should attend special general meeting 5.30 p.m., Wednesday, October 20, 1965, to oppose proposals to provide funds for grandiose building programme. Proposals include increasing members' subscriptions by 50 per cent, pledging property, selling investments and building site lease. Members have received no explanations. Financial justification very large expenditure seems very slender. – Inserted by a member of the Club.

The Seamy Side of Cricket

8 *March* 1966, *Leading Article.* If SIR ALAN HERBERT – that dauntless stormer of seemingly impregnable strongholds and doughty tilter at windmills – were given to saying, "I told you so", he has now good reason for saying it again. What is more, he would be justified in doing so to the wise men of Lord's. Nestling modestly and to a large extent undetected among their latest layings down of the rules of cricket is a paragraph headed, "Polishing ball". This strikes with revolutionary thoroughness at bowlers who polish their missiles or rub the shine off them. They must in future find other ways of taking a wicket, and even wiping and cleaning will be allowed only under the supervision of the umpire.

At first sight this may not appear as earth-shaking news. Those unhappy people for whom cricket is no more than a game may greet it in the Johnsonian spirit of – In a world bursting with sin and misery, you come prating to me of string. But opening a parcel by cutting instead of untying the knot is surely an offence far more trivial than that of tampering with a ball before bowling it. Like so many insidious lapses from virtue, the habit grew up slowly.

It is part of the *mystique* of the "seamer" of whom so much is heard in cricket reporting. He has brought his verbs in with him. He "seams" and is "seaming". The once fashionable "swing" bowler has been made to take a relatively back seat in the idiom of the sports commentators, and, as for "fast", it has almost become a dirty word. If the new rule leads to more spin bowling and to wicketkeepers less often standing half-way back to the boundary, it will cheer those who are tired of some recent trends. It will certainly gladden the heart of SIR ALAN. He has had to wait for his triumph. As long ago as 1959, he denounced in these columns the rubbing of the ball as "inelegant and laughable" and called for an amendment of the law. Were his letters, one wonders, read aloud lately to this august sub-committee of the M.C.C.?

Successful Sunday for Essex and Somerset

FROM OUR CRICKET CORRESPONDENT [JOHN WOODCOCK]

16 *May* 1966. If the first objective of first-class cricket on Sundays is to make it more accessible to the public, the experiment got away to a notable start at Ilford yesterday. For the second day of their match with Somerset, Essex had one of their largest home crowds for years. The cricket itself was less auspicious.

On Saturday 21 wickets fell for only 259 runs on a pitch which allowed the ball to move readily off the seam. Yesterday there was no such movement and

Somerset, who were 54 runs behind on the first innings, spent the four hours and a half of play easing their way back into the game. Clayton, the night watchman, gave them a good start by making 42 and Virgin played nicely for 51. After tea G. Atkinson and Kitchen made sure that Somerset's recovery became well established.

It was a pleasant family scene, mother being there with the best of them to see whether it was all worth while. The ground, set in a park, was a congenial place for the outing, and the afternoon was warm and sunny.

East, recruited straight from village cricket (he joined the Essex staff from East Bergholt), showed promise as a left-arm orthodox spinner, and Hobbs had the luxury of a long spell. Bailey, on the field as player and off it as secretary, was happy to take a part in the launching of a new scheme.

Not many years ago people were saying that Sunday cricket would "never come in our lifetime". Now it is here – to stay, if there are many more days as congenial as this.

SOMERSET 102 (B. R. Knight 6 for 36) and 343 for 6 dec (M. Kitchen 76, G. Atkinson 76, R. Virgin 51, G. Clayton 42)
ESSEX 156 (B. R. Knight 56; B. Langford 4 for 10) and 286 for 7 (B. Taylor 77, K. Fletcher 73)
Score after second day: Somerset 102 and 239 for 3, Essex 156
Match drawn

Definitely Not Cricket

2 *January* 1967, *Leading Article*. Indian cricket fans will have been disappointed by yesterday's newspaper placards about the second Test match against the West Indies in Calcutta. "Riots stopped play" was the news from that sprawling, uncontrollable city.

By now the world has become used to rioting students, intransigent Sikhs, no less determined defenders of the cow, and crowds that turn to violence at almost any railway station for almost any reason. This troubled Test match might seem only another proof of India's growing taste for violence. Others might take a different view. Was it not Britain that gave the game to India? And was it not an enthusiastic crowd, cramming the ground to a capacity of 80,000, with more trying to force their way in, that started the rioting?

But what of the scene at the holy of holies – the pitch? There a small tragedy was enacted. Some cricket-lovers tried to save it, but these brave fellows were overcome by angrier sportsmen who set about the most fiendish desecration of the pitch.

Come to think of it, the Calcutta police might find a cause of the rioting in a wily anti-imperialist of the Sukarno type. "Was not cricket an imposition of the British imperialists?", he would demand. And here, he would go on, in this Test match between the West Indies and India was a most subtly corrupting trick of neo-colonialism.

Happily the game has its built-in defence. If Britain is saved from the destruction of yet another of its missions overseas it will be because Indians would find it not cricket thus to turn on the importers of the game. All credit to the ordinary, workaday Indians that their anti-colonialism does no more than occasionally chip the nose from the statue of some long-departed viceroy.

Sir Frank Worrell

14 *March* 1967. Sir Frank Worrell, the great West Indian cricketer, died yesterday in Kingston, Jamaica, at the age of 42. His death will come as a profound shock to cricket lovers around the world for it is little more than three years since he ended his first class career as captain of the triumphant West Indian touring team in England. He was one of the finest all-rounders in the history of the game, but he will be remembered as much for his leadership as his play. It was he who moulded the West Indian Test team from a group of talented, entertaining but erratic individuals into what it has now become – probably the finest side in the world. In doing this he not only won personal fame but raised the status and dignity of the West Indian coloured cricketer.

Frank Mortimer Maglinne Worrell was born at Bridgetown on August 1, 1924. As nearly a natural cricketer as may be – for he was never coached and rarely practised – he was a leading figure in the remarkable upsurge of Barbadian cricket in the 1940s. He was an outstanding player from boyhood; at Combermere School he was primarily an orthodox slow left-arm bowler and as such – and a number eleven batsman – was first chosen for Barbados – when he was 17. A year later while still at school, sent in as "night watchman" he went on next morning to make 64 and to establish himself as a batsman. In the same West Indian season he scored 188, the first of his 40 centuries against Trinidad. In 1943-44 at 19, he made 308 not out in an unfinished partnership of 502 with John Goddard, a record for the fourth wicket which he and Walcott broke two years later with an unbroken 574, also against Trinidad. When world cricket recommenced after the Second World War, he and his fellow Barbadian batsmen, Walcott and Weekes, were the legendary "three Ws".

Worrell was the most orthodox of the three; his self-taught technique was so correct that he seemed incapable of a crooked stroke. Lithely built and superbly balanced, he was a stylist with an elegantly unhurried air, although his wide range of strokes, off front or back foot, was based on rapid movement into correct position. His cutting was delicate, his driving, for all its easy execution, powerful; he was strong on both sides of the wicket; and he combined ability to relax when not actually playing with the unremitting concentration of those who build long innings.

The demands of League cricket changed his bowling method from slow to fast-medium left arm; he exploited English conditions in sharp movement off the seam and his pace from the pitch was so hostile as at times to be little short of genuinely fast. Latterly his speed declined but to the end of his Test career his experience and control enabled him to seal up an end. He was a safe fieldsman and a clean catcher anywhere and latterly his fielding at silly mid-on was a considerable tactical asset for his bowlers.

As a young man he was markedly sensitive to criticism and some schoolday bitternesses rankled so deeply that, in 1947, he made his home in Jamaica. So it was as a Jamaican player that he established his Test place in the series of 1947-48 against England.

His performances brought him the offer which few West Indian cricketers have found it financially possible to resist and in 1948 he joined the Central Lancashire League club, Radcliffe. There, and subsequently with Norton and Church, he spent some dozen happy and successful years as a league professional. Meanwhile, he read first Optics and then Economics at Manchester University. He contrived, however, to take part in all the West Indies' Tests of that period except those of 1958-59 in India which coincided with the final terms before he took a B.A.(Admin.) degree. He made three tours of India with Commonwealth sides.

For the team of 1950, which was the first from the West Indies to win a Test, and a rubber, in England, he was top of the batting averages with 539 runs at 89.93 and made an important contribution to team-balance by his fast-medium bowling. At Trent Bridge after taking three important English wickets he scored 261, then the highest innings by a West Indian in a Test in England.

In the West Indian side which was beaten in Australia in 1951-52 he emerged as a genuine all rounder of Test standard. Apart from his technical ability, the quality of his temperament was strikingly apparent in Goddard's defeated and dispirited team of 1957 in England, when he made good the lack of an opening batsman and opened the bowling. He took seven English wickets in the innings at Headingley and finished second in the batting and first in the bowling averages for Tests.

It was now apparent that only internal politics could prevent him from captaining the West Indies. He himself wisely took little part in the occasionally acrimonious controversy which ended when he was asked to take the 1960-61 team to Australia; the first time a coloured West Indian had been appointed to the captaincy of a touring side.

On that tour, which included the famous tied Test at Brisbane, cricket in Australia was raised to such heights of public esteem as it had not reached since the days of Bradman. Australian opinion was reflected in the institution of the "Worrell Trophy" for all future series between the two countries.

When he captained the touring side of 1963 to England, he was almost 39, a veteran by West Indian standards; indeed, all his famous contemporaries of the 1940s had retired from Test cricket. He himself was no longer the player he had been but, as batsman, bowler and fielder, he was still useful and he was one of the few men whose captaincy was so outstanding as to make a major contribution to a side's strength. He declared his purpose as not merely to win the Test series, but also to make such an impression as to bring West Indies to England again appreciably before the 1971 season of the Conference schedule. He achieved both his aims. The West Indies won the rubber three-one.

Worrell's captaincy was outstanding. Sharp in tactical perception, astute in attack and defence, quietly spoken, yet firm to the brink of ruthlessness, he outwitted his opponents and sustained his colleagues. As lately as 1957 a West Indian team had crumpled psychologically in face of defeat. Now, at one crisis after another, Worrell, with what sometimes seemed exaggerated calm, held them steady. His achievement may best be described as instilling in his players a professional attitude and stability which has endured. As in Australia, his side's cricket roused such immense public interest as achieved his second design. In the following winter the tour programme was revised, bringing another West Indian team to England in 1966.

By the time that decision was taken, Worrell had returned home to a magnificent public reception, the Post of Warden in the University of the West Indies at Kingston and a seat in the Jamaican Senate; a knighthood followed in the New Year Honours of 1964. In 1966 he was appointed Dean of Students for the branch of the University of the West Indies in Trinidad.

He was a non-smoker who kept enviably fit with a minimum of training. Convivial and conversational, he would talk gaily far into the night in his pleasant, slightly husky voice; he was quick and flexible in debate, fond of England and his many English friends, courteous in manner and he only rarely revealed the depth of his feeling on racial matters.

In 51 Test Matches he scored 3,860 runs at an average of 49.48 and took 69 wickets at 38.37.

He married Velda Brewster of Barbados in 1948; they had one daughter.

Magic of Lord's – Even Without the Tavern

BY JOHN WOODCOCK

17 *June* 1967. It is no use arranging to meet a friend on the Tavern forecourt, as it used to be called, or under the Clock Tower boxes during next week's Test match against India at Lord's. If you do, you will find yourself hidden by boarding from a view of the play and in the way of men working on the new stand, which it is hoped will be finished by the start of the 1968 cricket season.

The Tavern today means the new pub which has just been opened to the west of the Grace Gates, complete with banqueting facilities. For old times' sake, the M.C.C. were keen to erect a temporary bar in front of where the original tavern stood; but the contractors resisted lest it should delay their progress. As things are going, it will be possible to watch next year's Test match against Australia from where the workmen's sparks now fly.

That, of course, is a great occasion. England against Australia at Lord's, like the Royal meeting at Ascot, has nothing quite to match it. Yet for any touring side this particular Test match is the showpiece of their tour. It will be the same for the Nawab of Pataudi's side next Thursday, in spite of the steel girders and the building operations, and happily the Indians have found the form which should enable them to enjoy themselves.

May is now a bad and costly memory – for the majority of counties as much as the Indians themselves. I shall always remember, though never willingly, the lugubrious expressions of Mr. T. Tarapore, who is their manager, and his treasurer, Mr. Chinnaswamy, who was always huddled at his side, in those melancholy weeks. Only at Headingley at the beginning of this week did they allow themselves a smile as India, against all the odds, made their highest total against England.

Each touring side brings to Lord's its own distinctive cricketing character. And in some felicitous way they generally manage, when they come there, to be at their best, at least for a time. The Australians are still the toughest of them all and their feathers the most prized. Only a pair of Australians would spend the day on their feet, barracking from the stand reserved for Members' friends. And only Keith Miller, two of whose many friends they were, would have put them there in the first place.

Only an Australian, too, would pay off a taxi at the Grace Gates a quarter of an hour before the start of play on a Monday morning when he was the "Not out" batsman. Richie Benaud, having been caught in the traffic on the way, did so in 1956, and in the next two hours he increased his score from three to 97. Yet the Australians are the first to say that no other ground in the world has the same quelling atmosphere as Lord's, that great "cathedral of cricket" as Sir Robert Menzies has called it.

The New Zealanders offer more homespun methods, and a modesty that is inhibiting except when they have a Donnelly or a Sutcliffe in their side. Of all the fine innings played at Lord's since the war, Martin Donnelly's double century in the second Test of 1949 is among the very best. Donnelly had the irresistible qualities, when they are allied to one another, of greatness and humility. You will find him now, unchanged except that his hair is grey, fishing the mountain streams of Australia or boating with a large family in Sydney harbour.

South Africans have a special affection for Lord's as being the scene of their first Test victory in England. In 1935, when leather jackets lived in the wicket, Xenophon Balaskas, a Greek chemist from Johannesburg, destroyed England with his leg breaks. Sir Pelham Warner described Lord's that season as looking like "the sand on the sea shore".

It was at Lord's, too, that the West Indies beat England for the first time over here. That was in 1950, when the calypso writers set Ramadhin and Valentine to music, and gaiety and passion broke loose. It was the start of the West Indies' rise to power. On their next tour, in 1957, Everton Weekes played so magnificently on a flying wicket that Mr. Ronnie Aird, secretary of the M.C.C., wrote on the club's behalf to congratulate him.

In 1963 came the epic match which ended in a draw, with England three runs short and West Indies needing only the wicket of Cowdrey, whose arm was encased in plaster. Several West Indians who got drunk that night were excused the next day by a magistrate. "I don't blame you", he said. "It was worth it."

Now it is India and Pakistan whom people will go to Lord's to watch; and many of the pleasures will be the same as if the Australians were there. Planters from Assam will arrange to meet sheep farmers from Victoria in the Long Room Bar, as they did when last they were at home. Whoever the visitors, it is always a full and beautiful time of year, with the hay being mown, strawberries in the Memorial Garden, and the buttonholes matching the members' complexions.

Next week the Indians may feel with a sense of relief that they have already proved themselves after their great recovery at Leeds. Their bowling is critically weak, and at any time, as Trueman had a way of proving, a genuine spell of fast bowling tends to find them out. Probably they have too many weaknesses to win.

But if all goes well they will show with the bat those gifts peculiar to themselves – of quickness of foot and eye, and flexibility of wrist – that can make them so attractive at the crease. If Pataudi, Chandra Borde, Hanumant Singh and Farrokh Engineer feel the sun on their backs and a firm and true wicket at their feet, the grazier and his friend will soon leave the bar.

Surrey's Great Effort Fails

FROM JOHN SILCHESTER [JOHN ARLOTT]

1 *July* 1967; *The Oval.* In an hour of sharp, well-organized out cricket, Kent came from prospective defeat to beat Surrey and move to second in the championship table.

A little before five o'clock Edrich and Stewart, batting better than anyone else in the match, were in command, and Surrey needed 111 to win with nine wickets and 95 minutes in hand.

In the next half-hour Underwood and Graham broke through. Cowdrey caught Smith at slip in a fashion to recall Hammond, and only Edrich remained to dispute the issue.

But it was resolved by Underwood. He achieved little turn, occasionally he spun enough to straighten, but largely by steady line and slight variations on his slow-medium theme, he took five wickets for 28 in his last nine overs. After the best innings of his life in the morning, his day was happily complete.

The Kent innings was a curious, uneasy affair of fits and starts, as one batsman after another tried to create the position for a declaration. Prodger fretted in rigid orthodoxy: his eight runs took, altogether, 80 minutes. Meanwhile, in strong contrast at the opposite end, Underwood, sent in on Thursday as night watchman, sensibly, and without any apparent difficulty, made the highest score of his career.

Cowdrey's 27, at a run a minute, was like a Turner watercolour sketch, tiny perfection in its own right, but only the outline of a major work from such a hand. He obviously considered the life of an orthodox batsman precarious on this pitch, an opinion he emphasized by declaring at lunch-time, and asking Surrey a scoring rate of less than 63 runs an hour.

As if this were their cue, both batsmen began to make aggressive strokes. It was a triumph of mind over marl: the pitch which hitherto had inhibited all who batted on it suddenly seemed full of runs. Had it dried a little?

Suddenly it still had no real pace but Edrich's bat made a rich noise when he drove, Stewart hooked the faster bowlers jauntily: the field retreated farther, and, by tea, Surrey were 120 for one, nearly halfway home, as nearly as made no matter up with the clock, and holding advantage for the first time in the match.

The pair were gathering momentum again after tea and their partnership had made 133 when Stewart, changing his stroke to a ball from Underwood which straightened, sent an awkward catch to cover where Shepherd, a lithe, prehensile fieldsman, held it. The remainder of the day belonged to Kent, and then still had half-an-hour of it to spare at the end.

> KENT 220 (B. W. Luckhurst 96; S. J. Storey 5 for 47) and 161 for 8 dec
> (D. L. Underwood 47)
> SURREY 132 (J. H. Edrich 55) and 177 (J. H. Edrich 92, M. J. Stewart 61;
> D. L. Underwood 5 for 59)
> *Kent won by 72 runs*

'Hello! Is There a QC on the Ground?'

BY DENZIL BATCHELOR

23 *August* 1967. Olympus broods over the case of Brian Close after his acquisition of what *The Times* described as "two dishonourable points" in last week's match against Warwickshire. No doubt, had he not resorted to the more questionable tricks of the trade, he would by now have been appointed England's captain for the West Indian tour.

His case would be *sub judice* were the M.C.C. Committee a court of law. Public opinion observes, not for the first time, that morality can be a matter of geography: just as, if you have several wives in a man-depleted tropical island you are the best of citizens, though you would hardly be rated so highly in a London police court.

In this case, the Yorkshire columnist of a Sunday paper believes "Close's tactics to be entirely justifiable" though one, possibly without the advantages of his background, openly wished that Mike Smith, rather than Close, had been chosen to captain England in this season's last Test.

Even Richie Benaud, outstanding as a broadcaster and critic as he was as a player, took sides against him, saying that such tactics would kill cricket within a year. And Benaud fully realizes the flexibility of cricket's morality. When he came to England as Australia's captain in 1961 he announced that he had given orders to his team to "walk" when they knew they were out, without waiting for the umpire's decision. [*In a letter published two days later Benaud said that, as a result of a team meeting, it was their general policy to walk but that the matter was left entirely to the individual.*]

On the same day his book *Way of Cricket* was published, in which he told how in the Lord's Test of 1956 he had been caught at the wicket when three, had been given not out, and, according to the Australian custom at that time, had stayed on to score 97, which many of us thought had a great deal to do with Australia's victory in the match.

Time-wasting tactics are, I think, a modern invention. W. G. Grace, accused of most forms of sharp practice, never attempted them: he believed, like Mrs. Battle, in the rigour of the game – or perhaps he never thought of them. They are an off-shoot of one of the greatest evils cricket is heir to, the fact that at the highest level games of cricket are not played – only rubbers. In this case, of course, it was participation in a league table rather than a match against Warwickshire that was to blame. C. B. Fry told me that when England won the famous Oval victory in 1902 nobody grieved that the rubber and the Ashes were already lost: all rejoiced in victory in a match against Australia. In those days people knew no better than to suppose that a game was a game.

But the fact remains (though Mr. S. C. Griffith points out that M.C.C. has previously dealt with two cases of alleged time-wasting this season) this trick of the trade has come to be a recognized tactic today. You might say that it is all part of gamesmanship – to potter and not quite cheat.

My feeling is that we have only touched the fringe of the art. What have spectators to complain of: a bowler's practice run, walking back to bowl slower than ever, changing over languidly and repeated consultations due, according to Mr. Close, to the noise the crowd was making, rendering him inaudible?

Pretty primitive stuff surely. What about gaining time with a slip fields-man's broken shoelace? Or a bowler sending to the pavilion for his lucky cap (to be given to the umpire as soon as it arrives)? Or a cover-point who pleads that the crowd's noise has made him deaf and has to wait while the captain writes out instructions for him, possibly in triplicate, to provide the county committees with a copy apiece?

Then – telegrams. They used to be part and parcel of cricket, but seem to have gone out of fashion. What is to stop an imaginative captain from sending two or three to players – it always takes a valuable couple of minutes to open, read, and say there's no answer? A really thoughtful captain could send fielding orders to members of his team by telegram, if the crowd was really booing.

Then there is the wicketkeeper. Is the captain satisfied with his performance? Why not change wicketkeepers, especially if the bowler is of the pace of Hobbs, who, of course, would take a 20-yard run to the wicket to send down the slowest ball of the season?

You can try anything once, and at least puzzle the umpires. I can hear the announcer asking: "Is there a Q.C. on the ground?"

Wilfred Rhodes Reaches 90

BY A. A. THOMSON

28 *October* 1967. Mr. Wilfred Rhodes, who celebrates his ninetieth birthday tomorrow, is one of the surviving great figures of cricket's golden age. He has lived long, travelled widely, and has always been a shrewd observer of the human scene, but it is fair to say that cricket has been his life.

He and his lifelong friend, the late George Herbert Hirst, came from the same tiny hillside village in the West Riding and when, in their heyday, the question arose, "Who is England's greatest all-rounder?", the local worthies would nod sagely, murmuring enigmatically: "He bats right and bowls left; and he comes from Kirkheaton". No two men, in character and outlook, could have been more different – Hirst, dashing, exuberant; Rhodes, cool, relentless, technically a perfectionist – but, together, for Yorkshire and England, they were the consummate pair.

Rhodes's career reads like that of the industrious apprentice, blessed with a fairy godmother. In 1898 he came into the first class game as heir to Yorkshire's line of slow lefthanders, Peate and Peel; he retired 32 years later, after taking his regular 100 wickets up to the age of 50 and, more astonishingly, after enjoying a middle period as England's No. 2 batsman, opening with Hobbs, England's greatest No. 1. In the historic tour to Australia in 1911-12 these two set up a first-wicket Test record, only surpassed by Hutton and Washbrook 37 years later.

The old Yorkshire cricketers called W. G. Grace a "nonesuch" and, by any standard, Rhodes has been a nonesuch, too. In cricket there has hardly been a prize that he has not won, an objective he has not attained; 16 doubles, over 4,000 wickets, nearly 40,000 runs. His first Test match in 1899 was W.G.'s last. In his year of retirement he bowled against Bradman, who, he thinks, was the finest of all batsmen.

His career has touched the high peaks of cricket history. In the first match of the epic rubber of 1902 he and Hirst crushed the Australians for 36, and in the last – Jessop's match – he joined his fellow-Yorkshireman when 15 runs were needed. Whether they "got them in singles" or not, get them they did in an electrifying finish which brought triumph to England by one wicket.

His exploits in Warner's Australian tour of 1903-04 ranged even higher. In the second Test he exploited a Melbourne "glue-pot" to take fifteen wickets, while in the first, at Sydney, he had shared what is still a record last-wicket stand with R. E. Foster and bowled all day on a billiard-table pitch at the brilliant Victor Trumper, who hit 185 not out, but not many of them off Rhodes. Before the day's last over Trumper begged, with a rueful smile: "Now, Wilf, give us a bit of mercy."

Whereupon Rhodes bowled him the most diabolical maiden over of the day, which no one but Trumper could have survived.

Heads were shaken when in county cricket Rhodes started to score runs. "Now, Wilfred", said Lord Hawke, "no more than 20". But his scores multiplied; soon he was opening for Yorkshire and then for England. That perfect understanding between partners which we associate with Hobbs and Sutcliff sprang to life with Hobbs and Rhodes. Asked to explain the secret of this remarkable harmony, Rhodes replied with his own gruff humour: "Here's the secret: if I'm coming I say Yes; if I'm not, I say No."

In the 1914-18 War he worked on munitions, playing League cricket at the weekend. When county cricket restarted he was over 40 and the Leagues tried hard to entice him away. ("They sat on my doorstep with their contracts," he told me.)

But Yorkshire retained his allegiance, and, season after season, in devastating fashion, he headed the first class bowling averages until in 1926, another Australian year, he was dramatically recalled.

"Can you", he was anxiously asked, "still pitch them there?"

"There", he replied, "or thereabouts".

He was two and a half months away from his forty-ninth birthday and three members of the England side, including his captain, had not, at the time of Rhodes's first Test, been born. Yet it is history that in the last Test at the Oval England won the rubber and regained the Ashes. It is also history that in Australia's second innings Rhodes clinched the issue by taking four for 44.

Thirty years later he told me: "The pitch was improving. They should have put me on sooner."

That was the last of his 58 Tests, but he went on four seasons longer, taking 100 wickets in both 1928 and 1929. After his retirement in 1930 he played a season with a Scottish county and here the shadow of tragedy fell.

"I got bowled by a slow full toss", he said, "and I knew something was wrong with my eyes".

Twenty years passed before total blindness overtook him. Its onset was a double blow, for his keen, clear eyesight was the envy of all cricketers.

"Is it true", he was asked, "that when you batted with Jack Hobbs you could see the seam on the ball?"

"Ah", said he, "you should have played with Ranji. He could see the stitches."

In the years following the Second World War his sight grew worse but he faced the enemy indomitably. Seeing the ball as a small white blur, he played a remarkable game of golf. ("I've no trouble keeping my head down. I don't have to watch the ball.")

In the 1950s I watched him tending his garden. "It's no trouble", he said, "I can work between those two big white stones".

For many Septembers his friends have greeted him at the Scarborough Festival, and apart from the war years I do not think that, as player or patron, he has missed a trip to Scarborough between 1898 and 1966. He sits on the bench outside the Yorkshire dressing-room, "watching" the play by ear, criticizing the sound of an edgy stroke, holding court among old admirers.

In his blend of inflexibly firm character and splendid skills, he has been the complete cricketer. No bowler before or since has matched his classic art, his rhythmic action, his supreme command of length and flight. To the impatient batsman he was the subtlest tempter since the Serpent of Eden. His batting lacked the sheer beauty of his bowling. ("The cut was never a business stroke.") It was utilitarian, but massive, and you cannot score 39,797 runs without gifts of the highest order.

In old age and blindness there is pathos, but in Wilfred Rhodes at 90 there is no pathos, but something far, far from it. He has attained the highest reaches of his profession, which happens to be an English way of life; he retains his dry humour, his acute intelligence, his delightfully youthful complexion and, above all, the unaffected dignity of a life well lived. No pathos, indeed, but a kind of human grandeur.

Cockney with Melody in his Name
and Poetry in his Action

BY ALAN GIBSON

8 *November* 1967. It is 50 years this month since Colin Blythe was killed in action, in one of those pointless attacks at the end of Passchendaele. His name was a melody in itself, his bowling action by every account was a poem; he played the violin; people who saw Rhodes, Peel, Peate, Briggs, Parker and

Verity averred that Blythe was the best slow left-arm bowler cricket has ever known.

This is probably still true. The only modern contender, I suppose, would be Lock – a great bowler, without doubt, but so different in style from Blythe as to invalidate close comparisons.

Nevertheless, Rhodes – and, later, Woolley – usually kept Blythe out of the English team. In a career lasting 15 years he played in only 19 Test matches. This was not just because Rhodes and Woolley were better batsmen. It was held that Blythe's temperament too often let him down upon the big occasion.

The figures do not bear this out. In 19 Tests he took exactly 100 wickets. This is a higher ratio of wickets to matches than any English bowler (who has reached 100) except Barnes. It is true that 59 of Blythe's wickets were taken against South Africa, but they were a strong side in that period. His 41 wickets against Australia, in nine Tests, were taken at an average of 21. His average for all Tests was under 19.

His greatest triumph was against the formidable South African side of 1907. On a turning wicket at Headingley only his bowling, and Fry's batting, won England the decisive match of the rubber. Blythe took 15 for 99 in the match, and England had 53 runs to spare after being out in the first innings for 76. According to Fry, in this match Blythe never bowled a bad length ball. But he was a sick man for days afterwards. He was one of those in whom nervous strain produces severe physical reactions.

He was perfectly happy bowling for Kent, and in all first-class matches took 2,506 wickets at an average of 16.81. Of the 11 bowlers who have taken more wickets, only Rhodes has a better average – by .10 per cent.

This aversion to Tests was rather a strange thing, since in those days county matches were usually considered almost as important. In 1893, for instance, F. S. Jackson declined to play for England against Australia, preferring to play in an important match for Yorkshire. But it was undoubtedly so, and after the first Test in 1909 Blythe was left out of the England team on the advice of a nerve specialist. He had taken 11 wickets in that Test, his best performance against Australia. He came back for the fourth, taking seven more wickets, but was unfit again for the fifth. His absence may well have cost England the rubber.

Blythe was born in Deptford in far from luxurious circumstances, and Sir Neville Cardus has recorded his astonishment at discovering that this man of the poetic run-up and musical tastes talked with a broad Cockney accent. He first played for Kent in 1899. He had gone to watch Kent play Somerset at Blackheath.

"I don't think", he said, "there were many more spectators than players. Walter Wright came out to practice and asked me to 'bowl him a few'. Captain McCanlis happened to be present and took my name and address." The following year he headed the bowling averages for the county.

From then until the outbreak of war, in spite of some fine performances from Fielder and the advent of Woolley (who modelled himself upon his forerunner), Blythe was Kent's principal attacking weapon. His most remarkable single achievement was against Northamptonshire in 1907 when he took 17 wickets in a day, for 48; all 10 for 30 in the first innings.

He was deadly on a turning wicket, but contemporaries praised as highly his ability to keep runs down when the wicket was plumb. Flight, rather than spin, was his principal ally.

He took a lot of wickets with the ball that moved on with the arm, and could make the new ball swerve (he often opened the bowling). He varied his pace subtly, kept his arm high, and often surprised batsmen out with the ball delivered from a yard or two behind the crease.

Blythe seemed an improbable soldier. Sir Home Gordon commented: "How he ever passed the medical examination must be dubious." But he became a sergeant in the Kent Fortress Engineers. At the time of his death he was attached to The King's Own Yorkshire Light Infantry, in which one may see a pleasant irony, since it was against Yorkshire that he had obtained some of his greatest successes – always a test of a cricketer. In 1903, for instance, when they were not far from their peak, he took 13 for 61 against them at Canterbury. The same season he took 11 for 97 against Lancashire at Old Trafford. I wonder if anyone else has achieved such a double as that?

He was 38 when he was killed. His powers had shown little sign of decline, and it seems probable that he would have played for England again after the First World War, since slow left arm bowlers do not usually wear out easily. It was a loss comparable to that of Verity in the Second World War. It seems singularly bitter that the fates, in succeeding generations, should have struck down so savagely two thoughtful, gracious practitioners of so delicate an art.

Rain Stops Film

28 *May* 1968, *Diary*. The film debut of Gary Sobers yesterday wasn't. Sobers was to have been performing at Vincent Square, Westminster School's pleasant tree-lined ground near Victoria, for a film called *Two Gentlemen Sharing*, but – thanks to Saturday's rain – was engaged instead in the Gillette Cup at Worcester.

Cricket may be, as they say, too leisurely for this bustling age, but – without Sobers anyway – film-making couldn't survive one summer as a spectator sport. Infinitely slowly, a camera backed before Robin Phillips and Esther Anderson, two of the stars, as they walked by slumbering extras in front of the pavilion, and Phillips fumbled with two deck chairs. Again and again. Film executives – major and minor – buzzed about.

Sobers – who should now be making his debut today – will in fact be merely an expensive "double" for Hal Frederick, an American negro actor, who plays a cricketing West Indian law student in *Two Gentlemen Sharing*.

Frederick is not a cricketer. But, said Mr. Ted Kotcheff, the genial Canadian director, he does have a coach. "Alf . . .". He turned to a knot of executives: "What's his name?" . . . "Glover" . . . "Grove" . . . "Alf Grover" . . . "Alf GOVER", one read from a list. "The Surrey" . . . "English" . . . "Test" . . . "bowler, I think" . . . "COACH".

In Sobers's absence, Frederick did face up to a couple of deliveries from John Snow, the England fast bowler, "We hired him because he can land the ball on a sixpence", said an executive. Snow landed the ball on Frederick's bat, and then thigh. "It's an Indian ball. It swings about like a pebble", Snow explained. Bad light stopped filming.

The Woman Behind the Hailstones

24 *June* 1968, *Diary*. Cricket and the occult make strange companions. But last Thursday a woman telephoned Lord's when the ground was covered in hailstones, and said: "I'm responsible for this storm. And there will be more such storms until the Australians pay their debts." Mr. Donald Carr, assistant secretary of Lord's, told a colleague of the incident at the dinner which the M.C.C. gave on Saturday night to commemorate the 200th Test match between England and Australia.

The Lord's switchgirl, he said, asked the caller for a little more information about herself. "I have occult powers so far as the weather is concerned", said the voice. "Several years ago I used these powers to break the drought in Australia. The Australians have not yet paid me for my services. My spell over their matches will continue." The Australian fast bowler, Graham McKenzie, received a similar call during the rainy second match at Leicester, evidently from the same person. Again the drought debt was her main theme.

"This woman said she wasn't fooling", continued Mr. Carr, "and she proceeded to put a spell upon our Jean over the telephone. At the end of a few seconds, Jean felt so dizzy that she cut the caller off."

In fact, using my own highly developed occult powers, I can tell Mr. Carr precisely who the sinister caller was: Mrs. Doris Munday, of Applegarth Road, W.14.

"I've been doing this for a long time", she confessed, clearly not in the least rattled at being discovered. "It was three years ago when the Australians asked me to break up their seven year drought and when I did it, they gave all the credit to the aborigines.

"They also promised to take up a collection for me, and didn't; not that I wanted the money, but I was annoyed. So I started off by smashing the Brisbane Test in 1966. I've been bashing them ever since."

Mrs. Munday, who is 49, broke into the psychic business a long time ago as a hypnotist; then about four years ago she was told by a hypnotist friend that she was a "weather manipulator".

"I was so shocked I told him to leave at once. But then I took a few tests in psychic phenomena, and sure enough I found I could do it", she recalls. Since then she claims to have broken droughts in India, China and the United States, brought freak storms throughout Britain and given countless friends sunny holidays.

Cowdrey 100 Not Out

BY JOHN WOODCOCK

10 *July* 1968. At Edgbaston tomorrow, Colin Cowdrey plays in his one hundredth Test match. It is a landmark reached by no other cricketer and one which Cowdrey will pass without thinking for one moment that a bottle of champagne is called for. He is too unassuming and abstemious for that.

Such a vast collection of "caps" is possible only in these days of regular touring. W. R. Hammond, whose Test career spanned 20 years, compared with Cowdrey's 14, made 85 appearances for England. Godfrey Evans, who is next in line to Cowdrey, made 91. Len Hutton made 79 and Denis Compton 78, with the war years intervening.

Neil Harvey, with 79, is the leading Australian; John Waite, with 50, the leading South African, Gary Sobers, with 65 the leading West Indian; John Reid with 58, the leading New Zealander, and P. R. Umrigar, with 59, the leading Indian. Of Pakistan's 53 Test matches Hanif has played in 51.

In 19 years "W.G." played in only 22 Test matches. S. F. Barnes took his 189 Test wickets in just 27 matches. Fred Trueman's 307 wickets came in 67 Tests, Don Bradman's 6,996 runs in 52.

Cowdrey so far has held 112 catches and made 6,940 runs. No one has taken more catches; only Hammond, Bradman and Hutton have made more runs. As things are going Cowdrey will soon have left them all behind with only Barrington and Sobers on his heels.

Cowdrey's baptism was in Brisbane in 1954, as the youngest member of Hutton's side. England lost that match by an innings and 154 runs, though Cowdrey's own batting was more auspicious. He made 40 in the first innings there, and 23 and 54 in the next Test at Sydney. His 102 at Melbourne, immediately after that, is, to this day, as fine an innings as he has played.

I can see him now, driving England out of trouble in the classical manner, on a green wicket with Keith Miller's mane escaping in all directions as he made to destroy England. Cowdrey was then 22: an undergraduate at Oxford on an extended vacation.

In the years that have followed, he has filled us at times with sheer delight and at times with utter despair. At his best he is such a superb batsman that one wonders why he should ever become, as he sometimes does, so deeply introspective. The answer lies somewhere in his makeup.

His modesty is a drawback to his batting. If he had ever realized just how good he really is he would have been, to an even greater extent, the despair of his opponents.

Of Cowdrey's 99 Test matches, I have seen all but a few in New Zealand. This has meant sharing the pleasure of success, the disappointment of failure, and the anxiety of the big occasion. To play in an important Test match is not the fun that many people may imagine it to be, especially for a batsman carrying the chief burden.

In Melbourne at the beginning of 1963, when England had just won a Test match, I congratulated Cowdrey on his considerable part in the victory. It was some hours after the match had finished and he had made 113 and 58 not out. I said how relieved he must be that it was all over. To which he replied: "Yes, but now there's the next one to worry about."

The strain of Test cricket, in these days of mass publicity and exaggerated criticism, is great, especially for the captains and the kings.

It is one of Cowdrey's worthiest achievements that he has stuck it for so long. While others have retired before their time, and when England could ill afford to lose them, Cowdrey has battled on, through triumph and setback, because of his love for the game and the life that goes with it.

His players admire him for this, and it is a fine reward for his perseverance and keenness that his stock stands higher now than ever before.

If he retains his form there is no reason why his remaining years for England should not be his most influential. What he would like to do, I think, is lead M.C.C. to South Africa next winter and to Australia in 1970-71 before retiring from Test cricket.

After that he should still be fit enough, and young enough in spirit, to play another three or four years for Kent, leading, one would like to think, a crusade for bold, unselfish play.

Cowdrey has four children, three of them boys who are encouraged but never forced to find fun in games. From a large house set in a beautiful garden on the borders of Kent and Surrey, he leads a busy life. His appointments book is invariably full, even when he has a match off.

Last Friday, for instance, he followed a few holes of golf with Brian Huggett in the early morning with his daily correspondence. He lunched at his old prep school, where in the afternoon he played against the boys in a match organized to raise funds for a new playing field. Having made 50 and a short speech there, he moved on to the Sports Day at his daughter's school.

I am often amazed by the things he finds time to do and the number of letters that he writes and lessons that he reads. He loves the simple life, has a quick sense of humour, a wonderful eye for ball games, a lot of friends, a stubborn streak, a rare gift for organization, and a hundred "caps" as well as a healthy desire to see the Ashes regained.

Test Selectors Win an Apology

Insole and Others v. Parkinson and Another

BEFORE MR. JUSTICE NIELD
HIGH COURT OF JUSTICE: QUEEN'S BENCH DIVISION

26 *July* 1968. Apologies were offered to Mr. Douglas Insole and his fellow Test selectors over suggestions, in an article in *The Sunday Times* of June 25 last year critical of the dropping of Geoffrey Boycott from the Test team, that in choosing it they had been actuated by "unworthy and discreditable motives".

Mr. Insole, Mr. A. V. Bedser, Mr. Donald Kenyon, Mr. Peter May and Mr. Brian Close had brought an action for libel against Times Newspapers Ltd., publishers of *The Sunday Times*, and Mr. Michael Parkinson, the writer of the article.

Mr. Michael Kempster for the plaintiffs; Mr. Brian Neill, Q.C., for the defendants.

Announcing a settlement of the action, Mr. Kempster said that Mr. Parkinson had written a long and highly critical article concerning the plaintiffs' decision to drop Mr. Boycott from the Test team notwithstanding the fact that in the previous match he had scored 246 not out. Mr. Parkinson considered that the selectors had done Mr. Boycott a very considerable injustice.

Had the matter ended there the plaintiffs would have had no wish to complain since they fully accepted that their decisions as selectors had to be open to full discussion and criticism in the press. Unfortunately certain passages in the article went considerably farther and were such as to suggest that in choosing the team the selectors had been actuated by unworthy and discreditable motives.

After the matter had been drawn to their attention the defendants had published in *The Sunday Times* an express disclaimer to the effect that it was not their contention that the selectors were actuated by any such motives, although they did not accept that the article complained of conveyed those imputations.

On further consideration, however, the defendants had realized that the article was capable of such construction. They therefore attended by counsel to withdraw the suggestions.

As the plaintiffs' object in bringing the action was to clear their names, they were content to let the matter rest. The defendants had agreed to pay their legal costs.

Mr. Neill, on behalf of the defendants, said that he associated himself with all that had been said. Without withdrawing or departing from their criticisms of the selectors' decision to drop Mr. Boycott, they were happy to make it clear that they accepted that, in reaching that decision, the selectors had not been actuated by any improper or unworthy motive and were seeking to further the best interests of the game.

The Sunday Times and Mr. Parkinson apologized to the plaintiffs for the distress which the passages in question had caused them.

Solicitors. – Halsey, Lightly & Hemsley; Theodore Goddard & Co.

Test Bowled Two Maidens Over

BY RITA MARSHALL

27 *July* 1968. In a room with three cricket photographs on the wall, and a view of St. Pancras station, sit some of the most telephoned girls in London.

They are the G.P.O.'s "Test team", and thousands of people ring them every day – dialling UMP – to hear the latest Test match score. During the present series with Australia more than six million calls have been made.

Four girls provide the voices on a continuous commentary, Miss Margaret Woodin, Mrs. Ellen Moelly, Miss Pamela Hawes and Miss Yvonne Biddulph, who comes from Guyana. Miss Biddulph said: "It got exciting when the West Indians played here. But we didn't exactly come to blows."

The girls work in teams of three. An editor is in direct link with the ground on which the Test match is being played, and two telephonists take it in turns to record the score or to check the telephone commentary against the information from the ground. The average time between getting a new score from the ground and putting it on record is 25 seconds.

Most of the girls are cricket enthusiasts, and two who were "not all that interested" are now fascinated by the game. Miss Hawes and Miss Woodin have never seen a Test Match, but said: "We are going to try and get to the Oval for the last match if we can get some tickets".

The two editors, Miss Pat Weighall and Miss Sheila Keogh, both Post Office telecommunications traffic officers, are self confessed cricket addicts. "We've offered to take our equipment to the ground", Miss Keogh said. "We have even said we would not mind the overseas tours, but we are still here".

Although they have no favourite cricketer, all the girls speak affectionately of "Uncle" Tom Graveney. Mrs. Moelly, who supports Sussex, thinks Ted Dexter is "lovely".

The Post Office Test team "reserve" is Mrs. Thelma Cumberbatch, a mother of two, who comes from Barbados and is something of a cricket expert because "I used to play it back home". She is learning the job, but said: "I haven't done very much yet. Every time it is my turn rain seems to stop play."

Bards Rejoice

Eisteddfod in the Wings

BY DAVID PARRY-JONES

6 *August* 1968. Yesterday was the first day of the 1968 national Eisteddfod in Barry, but even the bards carried transistor radios tucked under their robes as they strove to keep up with the fall of wickets 30 miles along the coast. The sheer elation when the final news came through was such that all 11 Glamorgan men must stand a chance of election to the Gorsedd.

Of course, this is the second time running that the Australians have fallen to Glamorgan, and if there were any Ashes at stake between Wales and Australia, they would now be firmly enshrined in the Guildhall at Swansea 100 yards or so from St. Helens. Sooner or later some nationalist wag is sure to say that Australia should now drop the weaker cricketing countries, such as England, from their Test engagements in order to concentrate properly on a series with Wales.

Not that Glamorgan are quite the Welshmen that they were six or eight seasons ago. Like many other counties, they are starting to resemble a Commonwealth side. Though I would be inclined to say that only Cordle, a West Indian, is a real odd man out; the other West Indian, Bryan Davis, has a name that is as Welsh as the Mumbles; while the exciting No. 4 batsman, Majid Jahangir comes from Pakistan but boasts an accent identified as mid-Rhondda.

The foundation of this victory though – and Glamorgan achieved it without their captain, Tony Lewis, who has a throat infection – was laid on the first morning with a fine 99 by Alan Jones, the left-handed opening batsman, who is a real local boy.

Now entering his 30s, Jones has served his county well, and it both puzzles and saddens us in Wales that he has never represented England (which sounds paradoxical, but you know what I mean) or toured with M.C.C. His average is at present over 40, in a low scoring season, and surely he deserves a place on the winter tour of South Africa.

Don Shepherd, the veteran off-spin bowler who acted as Glamorgan's captain, said that yesterday was one of the greatest days of his life. That is roughly what Keith Catchpole said two years ago when he led Australia to a surprise Rugby victory over Wales at Cardiff Arms Park. Revenge is very sweet.

League at Cost of Cavaliers

BY JOHN WOODCOCK, CRICKET CORRESPONDENT

21 *August* 1968. The International Cavaliers, who have given so much pleasure to cricket watchers, both around the country and on B.B.C.2, may have to go out of business next season because of the ruling, made by the counties and announced from the Lord's yesterday, that the only Sunday cricket to be televised live in 1969 will be the new one-day league. This is bad luck on the Cavaliers, who, after appropriating the name by which they are known, themselves pioneered this popular form of Sunday cricket.

A sponsor has been found, though not yet named, for the Sunday League, and both B.B.C. and I.T.A. have been invited to tender for the television rights. It is hoped that between them the new sponsors (who are not, in fact, dependent on television) and one or other of the television channels will contribute about £80,000 compared with £40,000 which the Cavaliers, in conjunction with B.B.C., had agreed to pay. This would make the Sunday League the game's richest source of income.

Of the money available, a large share will be used for making direct payments to the players who take part. It will amount, for them, to a fairly substantial pay rise.

Each county will meet the remaining 16 once in the new competition, and there will be no Sunday play in three-day championship matches.

The regulations for the Sunday League will be made known in October. It will involve an uncomfortable amount of extra travelling, though to offset this the county championship will be reduced from 28 to 24 three-day matches.

The Sunday League will be conducted on the lines of the present Cavaliers' matches – with a limited number of overs for each side, a limitation of the bowler's run-up, and special rules for days when rain takes a part. It should, in fact, be just as much fun to watch on television as the Cavaliers' matches have been, with a greater competitiveness between the sides compensating for a reduction in the all-star quality of the cast.

Sponsored by Rothmans, the cigarette company, the Cavaliers have presented the world's leading players to the English cricketing public. The large sums paid for the right to televise their matches have been ploughed back into the game; the gate money has been given either to charity or to cricketers whose benefit year it has been. Last Sunday, for instance, Don Bates, of Sussex, received a cheque for £1,200 from the match between Sussex and the Cavaliers at Hove.

To encourage the Cavaliers to continue their good work. I had thought they might be admitted into the Sunday League as the eighteenth side, so that their matches could still be televised. They were prepared to import three or four overseas players to replace those who will in future be regularly engaged with their counties. But that is not to be.

The Cavaliers have not yet committed themselves as to whether or not, in the absence of television they will fulfil their provisional programme for 1969. But a joint statement with Rothmans last night said that: "There must now be considerable doubt whether these matches can take place as envisaged."

Free Lunch for Cricket Watcher

30 *August* 1968. Loudspeakers at the Hampshire and Nottinghamshire county cricket match at Portsmouth yesterday warned a schoolboy on the ground: "Don't eat the sausage sandwiches – the sausages are off." It was from his father. The boy, Paul Brown, of Clay Hill Drive, Gosport, was then invited by loudspeaker to lunch in the members' room at Hampshire Cricket Club's expense. Afterwards he confessed: "I was so hungry that I had three of the sandwiches before I heard the warning. But I feel all right."

Mr. Vorster v. M.C.C.

19 *September* 1968, *Leading Article*. To the outside world Mr. Vorster's speech about Mr. D'Oliveira was one more indication of the mental weakness of apartheid, which is a fetish rather than a policy. To hear it said that Mr. D'Oliveira had been chosen by the anti-apartheid league sounded like the murky justifications of Pravda or Izvestia. No one ever thought that Mr. Vorster or his Government wanted a South African born man of colour to show his equality in a touring side. Nevertheless, faintly permissive noises had been made about him at the time when South Africa still hoped that its mixed team would be accepted at the Olympic Games. If the Olympic decision had not been reversed, Mr. D'Oliveira's inclusion in the M.C.C. side would have been swallowed. And even after the Olympic rejection. Mr. Vorster could not easily have objected to his initial selection on merit, without exposing himself to the charge of political interference in sport which he levelled at the Olympic committee and now levels at the M.C.C.

The offer of a contract for Mr. D'Oliveira to go to South Africa as a sports writer, and the unfortunate havering over his inclusion in the side when a vacancy occurred, gave Mr. Vorster his chance to justify exclusion to his own people. Sensible South African cricketers will not accept his absurd allegations, but they will be accepted by the mass of Afrikaner opinion which is sore about Mexico but not so keen on cricket. There may be trouble over the All-Blacks Rugby tour, which touches the Afrikaners more closely. The M.C.C. is the perfect Aunt Sally.

Mr. Vorster is thus able to give a sop to the right-wing malcontents in his party, the "Verkramptes". They denounced the racial concessions made to the Olympic committee, and exploited the ensuing humiliation. They would have opposed the relaxation of the rules of "petty apartheid" at social occasions for Mr. D'Oliveira, just as they do relaxations in favour of the black diplomats whom Mr. Vorster's "forward policy" will supposedly bring to Pretoria.

These extremists are not dominant, but Mr. Vorster has shown he is willing enough at times to appease them. The fact that they have won another point should caution those who think political principle has been vindicated now that the M.C.C. is virtually precluded from touring South Africa. Among Afrikaners the way this issue has emerged is a political defeat, not victory, for liberal ideas.

Sport is possibly not a "bridge" into South Africa that can bear much ideological traffic. It did carry some. It was worth preserving because contacts with South Africa cannot be ended, but they will be less beneficial when they are confined to diplomacy and business. More and more cut off from reality and the world, South African society will increasingly accept the paranoid decisions and dogmas of the ruling party and that party's inner clique. A hunger for respect and recognition by the world nevertheless remains – as was shown by South African pride in Dr. Barnard's achievements. So long as South Africa retains any sensitivity to outside opinion, so long as its conscience can be kept alive by any means, the loss of contacts must be regretted.

Freddie Trueman Retires

BY JOHN WOODCOCK, CRICKET CORRESPONDENT

11 *November* 1968. Frederick Sewards Trueman, now in his thirty-eighth year, has announced his retirement from first-class cricket. "Time marches on", he said. It takes with it a character who has enriched the game and a fast bowler of monumental achievement.

Trueman holds the record bag of Test wickets. Between 1952 and 1965 he took 307 in 67 appearances for England. These are figures which tell well enough of a wonderful natural talent.

He was born with a rhythm for bowling and a strong physique which assured him of cricketing success. But what marked him out from other cricketers, apart from his ability, was his temperament, which was forthright, and his sense of humour, which was basic.

His best years were from 1958 until 1964, though right from the start he was attended by success. His first series for England was in 1952, when he took 29 wickets in 119.4 overs and put the Indians to flight.

In 1953 he had a part in England's at last regaining the Ashes, and in 1955 he established a partnership with Brian Statham which became as famous and as fecund as that between Larwood and Voce or Lindwall and Miller. Both Trueman and Statham were superb fielders, and the years of their prime coincided with a period of English ascendancy.

But it was Trueman's personality as much as his prowess that made him star quality. Wherever he appeared – from Bradford to Brisbane, via Bridgetown and Bombay – he was cheered on sight.

Of England's fast bowlers since the war, Tyson, for a short time, was the fastest, Statham the most accurate, and Trueman the most volatile. He emerged from the coal face, as it were, of a mining village – rough hewn and with a strong disinclination to compromise his character. Because of this he blotted his copybook in the West Indies in 1953-54 and was left out of M.C.C. teams to Australia in 1954-55 and South Africa in 1956-57.

I am reluctant to believe that characters are many fewer now than they were; but it may be a long time before another comes along of Trueman's calibre. Last year he took only 66 wickets, so that he is wise to give up before his powers fail and to accept a lucrative offer from the International Cavaliers.

Undoubtedly, Trueman goes down as one of the greatest of all fast bowlers. Sometimes with spectacular success he wielded a bat like a pickaxe, and had he put his mind to it he could have made many more runs than he did.

Because of who and what he is, many of the best cricket stories are attributed now to Fred. That is a compliment initself. But here, as an example, is an authentic specimen.

During the M.C.C. tour to Australia in 1962-63, at a civic reception in Perth, a bishop mounted the platform. Trueman to David Sheppard, wearing a dog collar for the occasion: "Is that your senior pro?" This, for once, is an unexpurgated version.

Wilson's Hitting Fails to Save Yorkshire

BY JOHN WOODCOCK, CRICKET CORRESPONDENT

28 *April* 1969. Considering the weather, which was cold but dry, and the fact that the sides were short of confidence and practice, the Player's Sunday League got away to a most encouraging start at Lord's yesterday. Middlesex beat Yorkshire by 43 runs, in one of the lower scoring matches of the day, and I am sure the 5,000 spectators who watched them do so will look forward to coming again.

Yorkshire were without Trueman and Illingworth. But for a swashbuckling effort by Don Wilson, who made all but half their score, they would have been humbled rather than merely beaten. None of their bowlers was anywhere near as accurate and lively as Price, and their five main batsmen managed only 21 runs between them. Where Yorkshire excelled was in their fielding, which was splendid. But so, too, was the Middlesex fielding.

For Yorkshire there were some brilliant saves by Wilson, and Balderstone threw Hooker out from mid-off in just about a perfect piece of work. Sharpe, too, made his usual blinding catch at slip. For Middlesex, Parfitt started the Yorkshire rot by a fine diving catch at second slip in Connolly's first over in his new colours, and Price, whether bowling or fielding, was in irresistible form.

Price found it about as easy squeezing that long and stuttering approach into 15 yards as he might do trying to fit himself into a baby's cot. But once he had done it he worked up a good pace, and following through to his own bowling he ran out Boycott, who had been called for a sharp single by Padgett.

For most of the time the wicketkeeper stood back. For much of it the field was far flung. Yet the overall impression was one of urgency. There is really no time for much else in a match beginnng at 2 o'clock and scheduled to end by 6.30. Yesterday's game was over by 6.10, by when Wilson had earned himself three shares of £1,000 – the sum to be distributed among all those who hit a six in the competition.

Middlesex were indebted to Parfitt and Radley for pulling their own innings round after a rather wanton start in which Smith and Russell cast away their wickets. Parfitt got things going with some brisk running and a succession of spirited strokes. Radley picked up the idea, and later on Keith Jones, an all rounder from Shepherds Bush, played uncommonly well.

Yorkshire's chance of winning was virtually gone within a dozen overs. Price saw to that. There was Parfitt's catch and Price's run out, and then Padgett and Hampshire were both out to balls that lifted. There followed a partnership between Wilson and Binks which added 48 and was ended by Hooker just as it was getting dangerous for Middlesex.

> MIDDLESEX 137 for 8 (40 overs)
> YORKSHIRE 94 (32.2 overs) (D. Wilson 46)
> *Middlesex won by 43 runs*

Milburn May not Play again in Tests

BY JOHN WOODCOCK

26 *May* 1969. With his spirit unimpaired, Colin Milburn was receiving visitors and messages and gifts at the General Hospital, Northampton, yesterday. He has already got fruit enough to open a stall, though when I saw him on my way to Leicester he was wanting a newspaper so that he might catch up with Saturday's scores. Not surprisingly, none was delivered with his morning tea.

Having spent 24 hours feeling quite sick at the news of Milburn's accident, I left him encouraged, as everyone will be, by his cheerfulness. He was never unconscious following the crash, and when the ward sister told him after the operation of the loss of his eye, he was not surprised. A shattered windscreen did the damage, and he does not believe that a seat belt would have saved him. He has several nasty cuts about the forehead and face, and there are seven stitches in his right knee; but on his right eye there is only one slight scratch.

It is hard to believe, even with such unquenchable spirit, that Milburn will ever play Test cricket again. He, bless him, has no doubt that he will. "Buster" Nupen played for South Africa with one eye, but he was a bowler; and more recently, the Nawab of Pataudi has batted wonderfully well after having an eye badly cut, also in a motor accident.

But in Pataudi's case it was the right eye that was injured, and, as he has written himself, the light which the bad eye let in was a great help to the good one. He tried unsuccessfully to bat with a pirate's patch. These are worn sometimes in the shooting field to counter a master eye, but they create their own problems of judgment and timing. It is necessary only to put a hand over one's right or one's left eye to realize this.

Again, to a right-handed batsman, which Milburn is, the left eye, even when it is not the master eye, is still the less dispensable of the two. To play with his right eye only would necessitate an unnaturally open stance. A specialist at the hospital thought that Milburn's master eye was almost certainly the right one, which would, of course, be a help. It generally is, apparently, in the case of good right-handed games players. In the specialist's view, the extent of a man's adjustment to such a handicap depends first of all on the individual; and if anyone can overcome it and still be a first-class batsman, I am sure Milburn will.

That the accident should have happened to him of all people, at a time when the game is short of characters, is particularly cruel. He is looked upon with genuine affection by friend no less than foe and by everyone who meets him. In the last two or three years he has played a number of innings of incredible devastation, and he is still only 27. Only last winter he scored 181 between luncheon and tea playing for Western Australia against Queensland, and in his only championship match this season he made 158 against Leicestershire.

Before his accident he was English cricket's greatest asset and its most lovable personality. If surgery permitted it, I am sure thousands of cricketers would gladly present him with an eye, and in an effort to disperse the gloom it would be nice if his first-class colleagues were all to have a Milburn day – when they played the game for fun and not for figures. He hopes to leave hospital within a fortnight's time and to have a false eye fitted within a month or two of that.

Glamorgan Have a One-sided Victory

BY ALAN GIBSON

18 *June* 1969; *Bournemouth*. "When the umpire shall call 'play,' the party refusing to play shall lose the match." This, referring both to the state of play, and to intervals (including the fall of a wicket) was set down in the Laws of Cricket as revised by the Marylebone Club in 1830. It has always been, and remains, the basic assumption of any match at cricket.

I suppose the result of this match should be recorded as: "Glamorgan won because Hampshire refused to play." Not that they refused in any deliberate sense. They had simply gone away under the impression that the match was over.

To set the scene: at the beginning of the day Glamorgan faced with Hampshire's declared total of 337, had scored 256 for seven. A. R. Lewis, the Glamorgan captain, slightly surprisingly, decided to bat on. He was presumably hoping for a few more quick boundaries from E. Jones, who indeed got a couple of lusty ones. But when Jones was caught and bowled, after 20 minutes, Glamorgan declared, which was sad for Williams, who was just beginning to get his eye in.

The Hampshire second innings had not really begun to take shape when the rain started. It was slow, persistent, dismal rain. Lunch was taken early. The rain drizzled on. We longed for a storm to end the futility of hanging around. Duty, not hope, kept us miserably waiting.

The public, such as them as were present, was given no indication of what decisions might be taken about the future of play, and gradually drifted away. At four o'clock, sitting in the little pavilion and contemplating a cold, flat beer, I saw the Hampshire team leave, changed and off to the next engagement. I concluded that all was over, and ordered a taxi.

Perhaps five minutes later the Glamorgan team came out of their dressing room, also changed, packed, and ready to depart. A. R. Lewis spoke, casually but sensibly enough, to the senior umpire, Wight. Lewis said: "I suppose it is all off?" Wight replied to this effect: "There are more than two hours to go, the rain is not heavy, the wicket will be playable almost as soon as it stops. It is far too early to abandon the match." Someone said: "Does Marshall know?" Wight replied: "I have not been asked."

In this decision Wight was, in my view, unquestionably right, and his fellow umpire, Budd – a former Hampshire player – was strong in agreement with him.

So Glamorgan stayed on the ground. Efforts were unsuccessfully made to contact the scattered Hampshire team. At 5 o'clock the rain had almost stopped. The umpires made an inspection and ordered mopping up operations. Satisfied with these, they decreed a resumption of play at 5.30.

Glamorgan, unnecessarily, changed back into flannels (or thereabouts Walker was partly revealing a fetching pink undergarment) and took their places on the field. Budd, the bowling umpire, called "Play". It was all quite properly done. There was no unseemly hurry, Cordle marked out his run.

And then, at 5.31 – believe me I do not exaggerate – the flimsy drizzle developed into serious rain. A batsman might have been justified in walking off, but there were no batsmen. Glamorgan stoicly stuck it out in the field (Walker had taken up an aggressive position within the return crease), Wight looked at his watch, measuring every agonizing second, and after the necessary two minutes turned back towards the pavilion.

Glamorgan had taken 10 points for a win, because the other party had refused to play. This gave them 12 points to Hampshire's seven, though I suppose it is arguable, and will be argued, whether a side failing to come up to the scratch is entitled to any points at all.

No criticism can be made of the umpires. The weather was good enough at 5.30 to resume play, and though it rained shortly thereafter both sides had played through heavier rain in the morning. The question why Marshall, the Hampshire captain, was so confident that the game was over, is more difficult. I was assured by the umpires that they had said nothing whatsoever to give him such an impression. My own guess is that it started from one of those well meaning busybodies who are sometimes found at cricket grounds. A glance at the foreboding sky, a wave of the hand, and "all off!" they knowingly say. And the rest of us, also liking to be busy and knowing, pass it on to our neighbours – "All off! All off!" – and it percolates to the dressing room. Still, it is a captain's job to make sure.

HAMPSHIRE 337 for 5 dec (R. M. C. Gilliat 114, B. A. Richards 80, P. J. Sainsbury 66) and 28 for 1
GLAMORGAN 270 for 9 dec (E. Jones 85, Majid Jehangir 74; D. W. White 6 for 58)
Glamorgan won by default

The decision was later overturned and the matched declared a draw.

A Great Day for the Irish

BY RICHARD STREETON

3 *July* 1969. Even the Duke of Wellington – the Iron Duke of Napoleonic fame, that is – who played cricket for Ireland in his youth, never quite achieved a comparable victory. A hard man to please, he would have been proud of his successors yesterday. For the mighty West Indian cricketers, straight from the Lord's Test match with England, were routed for 25 runs in their one-day game against Ireland.

This piece of cricket history will scarcely be credited in the sugar cane fields of Barbados or the rum shops of Kingston. But they know differently in Sion Mills, a village some 15 miles outside Londonderry, where it all happened. The little people were in good humour yesterday morning and the rest was inevitable.

Now, of course, Sion Mills will appear for ever in Wisden. But the staid prose of the cricketers' Bible will hardly tell the whole story. There is little scope between the covers for mention of the part played by the leprechauns in Ireland's triumph. Wisden will mention how reaction after the stress of a Test match affected the West Indians. Wisden will also speak of a tiring journey from London and the difficulties of batting on a wicket both green and wet from overnight rain.

The West Indians actually lost their first six wickets for eight runs, and they heard the howling of Irish wolves. Clyde Walcott, the team's manager, making a rare appearance, then called on all his experience to thwart his opponents – both seen and unseen – to the extent of making six runs. Grayson Shillingford, from Dominica, where it is too hot for leprechauns, did even better and made the top score of nine. The West Indians at least reached double figures as the fairies relented a little.

When Ireland batted they established a lead of 100 runs and then declared with two wickets in hand – an imperious gesture but an opportunity not to be missed. It had the added advantage of letting the crowd see the touring team bat again.

The official result under the laws of cricket goes down to posterity as a win for Ireland by nine wickets on first innings. The details will be pasted in many a scrapbook in Sion Mills, described by a helpful assistant in the local library as having one street, 1,569 souls at the 1966 census and with linen mills providing the main source of employment. In the Caribbean the same details will be regarded with awe for a long time.

Emmott Robinson

19 *November* 1969. Mr. Emmott Robinson, the Yorkshire all-rounder, died on Monday.

Emmott Robinson was 35 before he first played for Yorkshire. Between 1919 and 1931 he scored nearly 10,000 runs and took just over 900 wickets, helping to form, with Rhodes, Waddington, Macaulay, Kilner and E. R. Wilson, one of the two strongest county attacks in cricket history. In such a powerful side his chances of shining were limited, yet year after year he would bat creditably and take his 60 or 70 wickets, never quite achieving the double, but coming near to it several times, notably in 1928, with 926 runs and 113 wickets. In 1926 he shared with Leyland Yorkshire's record sixth-wicket partnership of 276 and for a dozen seasons he fielded with prehensile audacity in the close positions.

Though not a cricketer of princely rank, like Hirst or Rhodes, Sutcliffe or Hutton, he was as true a Yorkshireman as any; indeed, the Yorkshire terrier might have been his symbol: tenacious, belligerent and slightly shaggy. For him the smoking chimneys of Bramall Lane were as happy a background as were the green trees and bright bannerets of Canterbury for Frank Woolley. To him Yorkshire cricket was everything; victory for Yorkshire was a law of life; defeat an outrage. He tried with heart and soul to capture a wicket with every ball he bowled and from his fine grey head to his turned-in toes, he was Yorkshire incarnate.

North-country crowds knew him well and savoured his image with a kind of wry affection: his concertina trousers, the Christopher Robin hoppity-hop in the middle of his run-up, the wicked outswinger that took the batsman's breath (and bails) away. They chuckled over his uncanny judgment of a wicket's texture, which enabled him to advise his captain on matters of declaration in terms of minutes rather than hours ("No, Mr. Wilson, not twenty-five past – twenty past.")

He held high place in Yorkshire's long line of rich comedy characters, which stretches from Tom Emmett to Freddie Trueman. Anecdotes of his pugnacity are innumerable and, even when apocryphal, highly characteristic. Fielding at suicidally silly mid-off, he was warned by a dashing but humane batsman to step back out of mortal danger. "Thee get on with thi lakin', Mr. Foster", said Emmott austerely, "and I'll get on with mine".

A Cambridge batsman, after a few flashing hits, was bowled by a superlative ball which pitched on the leg-stump and whipped away his off-bail. "By jove", he murmured, as he passed on his way out of history, "that was a beauty."

"It was an' all", said Emmott. "It were wasted on thee."

In his later playing years he nobly served the game by the encouragement and cunning coaching he gave to the youthful Bowes and Verity. Not for them the cinema in the evening; in their hotel bedrooms, with the aid of shaving sticks and tooth-brushes, Emmott would demonstrate just how badly they had bowled that day. To refrain from obloquy was his only praise. And they loved him for it.

Race Vindication for Yorkshire

21 *November* 1969. Yorkshire cricket club's policy of allowing only Yorkshire-born players to represent the county is not a breach of the Race Relations Act, our Race Relations correspondent writes.

This was stated yesterday by the Race Relations Board, who said that the 76 M.P.s who have signed a Commons motion on the subject appeared to have misunderstood the Act completely. The motion urges that the Act be amended to allow the club to continue its policy.

The board said: "To be born a Yorkshireman is undoubtedly a distinction. But merely being born in Yorkshire does not in any way distinguish a man by colour, race or ethnic or national origin – and that is what the Act is all about."

Rhodesia Snubs Asian Boy

15 *December* 1969; *Salisbury*, 14 *December*. A 17-year-old Asian schoolboy cricketer, Haroom Ismail, who won the prize for the best batting performance at the national school trials last week, has not been selected for the Rhodesian team which is to play in South Africa. He was not allowed to eat in the same room as his white team mates.

Mr. A. I. Kassim, chairman of the boy's league club, said: "If we had known he was going to be subjected to all this humiliation, we would have asked him not to go. Rhodesian sportsmen have always boasted that politics does not enter sport."

Six Killed in Stampede at Test

FROM OUR CORRESPONDENT

17 *December* 1969; *Calcutta*, 16 *December*. Six people were killed and at least 30 seriously injured in a stampede outside the Eden Gardens stadium in Calcutta this morning, three hours before play began on the fourth day of the fourth Test between India and Australia.

A large crowd had been waiting for tickets at the stadium since last night and an hour before the counters opened this morning, many people broke away from the queues and tried to force their way through the gates. Police used tear gas and batons to disperse them and they retaliated by throwing stones.

Seized by panic, the whole crowd started running and a stampede resulted.

The situation was soon brought under control and play began on time. Australia won the match with all its wickets intact.

It was inside this stadium three years ago that a day's play in a Test between India and the West Indies was disrupted by rioting because more people had been sold tickets than could be accommodated.

The trouble today occurred because the demand for tickets exceeded the available accommodation.

Hobbs's Home Goes

28 *January* 1970. The terraced house in River Place, Sleaford Street, Cambridge, where Sir Jack Hobbs grew up and learnt to play cricket is to be pulled down under a slum clearance order.

Graeme Pollock without Peer

FROM JOHN WOODCOCK

31 *January* 1970; *Cape Town*, 30 *January*. Graeme Pollock, South Africa's greatest batsman and regarded by many as the best in the world, has no army of supporters or aircraft of his own, no fetish for fitness or yearning for retirement. He is just a mild, straightforward, easy-going fellow with a gift for batting, which it pleases him to use.

He enjoys living in Port Elizabeth, where he was brought up, because it's "away from the rat race". He is very much a home town boy. His father was editor of the *Port Elizabeth Herald* until he died last year; his wife is a Port Elizabeth girl and his young son is being nourished on Port Elizabeth air. When Graeme has some spare time from his new job as sales manager of a large group of clothing companies, he likes to round up two or three friends for a few frames of snooker at the club. It's a game with a tempo that suits him. Anything for the quiet life. In the field he likes to stand at slip. This involves a minimum of running and there is always someone close by with whom to discuss the less important matters of the day.

On the afternoon before a Test match when the teams are at practice you will see Eddie Barlow or Graeme's brother, Peter, or Trevor Goddard with their shirts clinging to their backs. Graeme will scarcely break out of a canter if he can help it. When last summer he was in England playing for the International Cavaliers, he and his wife rented a flat within a long iron shot of Lord's but it would never have occurred to him to go there for a net. He played for me in a village match in Hampshire and produced the perfect innings. In the evening he drank beer with the village side without the least embarrassment either to himself or them.

Graeme's grandfather was a Scottish Presbyterian minister. His own father had a year or two at Heriot's before the family came to South Africa to settle. The ability to play games is inherited though not until the present generation has it been so marked. Graeme and his elder brother, Peter, who is still South Africa's opening bowler, are the sons of a father who kept wicket for Orange Free State and a mother who played tennis for Natal.

Graeme could walk when he was eight months old and he was making centuries by the time he was nine years old. Just before he was 17 he became the youngest South African cricketer to score a first class 100 and just after he was 19 he scored a double 100 at an earlier age than any other South African. "For a long time," says his brother, "I thought he was sure to be found out. He was always so much better than the rest of us and we were all quite a bit older." But it has yet to happen. Graeme is still, at the age of 25, in a class of his own. But he is old enough now to worry about it. The more that is expected of him the more nervous he becomes. This is never evident but he assures me it is so.

He was at Grey High School in Port Elizabeth from the age of six to 16. The coach there at the time was George Cox, of Sussex, himself a true son of nature. Realizing that he had a rare talent in his hands Cox left well alone. I wish Graeme could have seen George on one of those days at Hove when his cap grew more faded in the sun and the shots he played were too brilliant to have come from any text book. A year after leaving school Graeme visited England with his parents and, at Cox's suggestion, he played half a dozen matches for Sussex second eleven.

By the time he was 18 he had decided to concentrate on cricket. It was not as rough a game as rugger, at which he excelled as a stand-off half, and it was less strenuous than tennis. Like Cliff Drysdale, with whom he played a lot of tennis, he had a two-handed backhand and at one time there was nothing to choose between them. By 1962 the New Zealanders were returning home from a tour to South Africa and saying that they had seen in Port Elizabeth the player of the future. And when the late Ron Roberts took a side to South Africa at the end of that year he came back with reports of a prodigy who had made 209 not out for Eastern Province.

A year later Graeme began his Test career. It was in Australia on a tour which started with his making nought and one against Western Australia in the first match. In the following week, after he had scored a century in 88 minutes against a combined eleven, Don Bradman said to him: 'If you ever play an innings like that again I hope I'm there to see it." Well, he has been doing so ever since – the last of them was against the Australians at Port Elizabeth recently when he made 105 in 102 minutes. On that tour of Australia he treated Bradman to an innings of 175 at Adelaide (he and Barlow added 341 for South Africa's third wicket) and another of 122 at Sydney. On his only tour to England his 125 at Trent Bridge ranks among the finest innings of post-war cricket.

But if Bradman applauded Pollock's style of batting I am not sure that he can have approved of his view of records. In the Don's heyday there used to be a general exodus from shops and offices to watch him bat. If he was not out at lunch it was a safe bet that he would be there well into the afternoon if not the evening. When he made 309 in a single day against England at Leeds he described it as "a nice bit of practice for tomorrow". With Graeme Pollock it is different. Once past his 100 he is happy enough for someone else to take a turn.

As a captain he receives only moderately good notices. It may be that he is too phlegmatic for the job or not sufficiently dedicated, or perhaps because he has never really had to work at the game himself, he finds it difficult to comprehend the problems which lesser batsmen have to contend with. The most successful captains are not always the most talented and popular cricketers.

From his colleagues in the South African side come, quite independently, much the same observations . . . "Just a nice uncomplicated guy. . . ." "If he were twice as ambitious they'd never get him out. . . ." "Tricky to run with because he's always after the strike. . . ." Bill Lawry, the Australian captain, is less enthusiastic – "A good bad ball player – but he's always giving the bowler a chance." Richie Benaud on the other hand puts Graeme on a pedestal partly because of the caning he got from him in Australia. Bobby Simpson does the same and so I fancy does Gary Sobers.

When Sobers joined Nottinghamshire he was asked whether there was anyone else he'd particularly like the county to try to sign. The name Sobers gave was Pollock, who was approached and for a while thought seriously about it. What the struggling bowlers of other counties would have said I am not sure. I doubt whether the seam bowlers would have liked it, for they are Graeme's favourite dish. "Good fast bowlers and good spinners are a challenge. The easiest to attack are the medium pacers."

But Sobers and Pollock will never play for Nottinghamshire together. After one more visit to Australia in 1971, Graeme intends, though he will be only 28, to confine his cricket to South Africa. If so, South Africa's forthcoming tour to England may provide English cricket lovers with a last look at a splendid batsman. He is not the most elegant player of the day, as with his considerable height he might be, and he is certainly not the fittest. But with less fuss and effort than the rest he inflicts the greatest damage on a bowler's pride.

Champion County Face Giant Bolster too

BY ALAN GIBSON

25 *April* 1970. Cornwall today at Truro make their first appearance in the Gillette Cup. They will be the fifteenth of the 19 Minor Counties to play in the competition, and they have every intention of becoming the first to beat a first-class county, and the champions [*Glamorgan*] at that. Certainly they can expect a large and enthusiastic crowd to watch them try.

Cornish cricket has never made much of a stir in the world; nothing comparable with Cornish rugby. They earned their place in the cup by finishing third last season, and only narrowly missed being able to challenge Bucking-hamshire for the championship. But that is the highest position they have ever held. Yet there is considerable enthusiasm for the game in the county, and much care in its organization.

For many years league cricket has been popular among Cornish clubs, and the approach has been strongly competitive; more so than, for instance, in the gentler if more polished atmosphere of club cricket in Devon. I have spent many afternoons watching Cornish league matches which were not only pleasant (for some of the grounds are lovely) but compelling.

I remember particularly a perfect day at Mullion, and a fine innings, which just failed to win the match, by the professional Billy Strauss (who won wider fame as a footballer with Aberdeen and Plymouth Argyle). There was much excitement at the climax. Crowds used to be quite large at these matches, the holiday visitors swelling them in season, though I gather that – as with other forms of cricket – there has been a decline in recent years. Still, this familiarity with competition ought to help a minor county to make a respectable showing in the Gillette.

One attractive feature of the game in Cornwall is that quite small places, little more than villages, are able to compete effectively against the sides of the larger towns. Mullion always used to have a good side. Troon has pro-duced some fine cricketers, and Gorran, and St. Just-in-Penwith, as well as the more obvious places such as Falmouth and Camborne and Penzance. Cornwall's captain last season, G. R. Harvey, came from St. Columb. A former captain of Blundell's, he averaged 58, which put him at the top of the Minor Counties' averages.

From St. Columb, too, came Jack Crapp, who is, I suppose, the best cricketer Cornwall has produced, at least in modern times (though R. T. Weeks was in the Warwickshire championship side of 1951). He joined the Gloucestershire staff in the mid-thirties, and when in 1938 he scored 1,700 runs, it was clear there was a good one on the way. Wisden commented that year that he "would have improved further by the more general use of his natural aptitude to force the game", which reads oddly to those of us only familiar with him in his latter years, when he used frequently to get out through genial attempts to hoick the spinners over long on. Crapp was a left-hander, who played with credit against the terrible Australians of 1948 and again for England in South Africa the following winter. In his career he scored 23,500 runs at an average of 35, with 38 centuries. His warm and tranquil personality was, and remains today in the umpire's white coat, a splendid advertisement for Cornish character and Cornish sport.

Harvey's predecessor as captain was R. W. Hosen, a capable all-rounder, and one of the many rugby players who have also represented Cornwall at the summer game. R. A. W. Sharp, a wicket-keeper who was in the running for a blue at Oxford, is another.

I am sure that the improvement in Cornish standards of play must owe a good deal to the end-of-season tours undertaken in recent years by the Crusaders XI, organized by Mr. Ross Salmon, and containing many of the best cricketers in the country. These matches have not only enhanced the popularity of the game, but given Cornish cricketers experience against top-class players. Lack of such experience has always been a handicap: they play only eight matches in the championship, all in the south-west. They used to venture further – Cornish sides have played at the Oval – but the difficulties of geography and finance have become too severe. Thanks to the Crusaders, the mountain has come to Mahomet, or, more appropriately one might say, to the Giant Bolster, who once reigned over west Cornwall.

I think it was Edmund Blunden who put forward the theory that the first known cricket match was played between the Giant Cuchullain and a hundred Colts of Ulster (score: Colts, b. Cuchullain, o; Cuchullain, not out, 1). Now Cuchullain and Bolster were not only contemporaries but in all probability relations.

What more natural than that the Irish giant should have passed on a few tips to his Cornish cousin? Let Cornwall therefore take the field this morning confident in the knowledge of an illustrious and venerable history. Surely old Bolster will be there, six miles high, one foot on Carn Brea and one on St. Agnes Beacon, peering down over the Truro ground to urge them on.

Why Not to Cancel

2 *May* 1970, *Leading Article*. The Times has expressed the opinion that the M.C.C. should have called off this year's tour by South African cricketers immediately after the refusal of the South African Government to admit Mr. D'Oliveira as a member of the M.C.C. party to tour that country in the winter of 1968-69. The reason for doing so was not the objection that is taken here to the South African manner of selecting their players, for that would have been to offer South Africa the very discourtesy that was complained of in their case, namely interference in the other people's prerogative to select whom they want to. The 1970 tour should have been cancelled in order to make it absolutely plain to the South Africans that we will brook no inter-ference of that kind. That was a sufficient reason in itself. There was a further reason for withdrawing at that stage in that Mr. Vorster's action made it inevitable that the 1970 tour would not pass without a great deal of bitterness.

The M.C.C. took a different view. Primarily in the interests of cricket, also in the belief that the maintenance of links with South African cricketers is more likely than their severance to promote the cause of multiracial sport in South Africa, the M.C.C. decided to proceed with the tour. Though in our opinion wrong, the decision was reasonable on both counts, and it was one which the M.C.C. was fully entitled to make. It is of the essence of a free and plural society that persons and organizations may make decisions and act lawfully upon them, however vehemently other persons and organizations may hold those decisions to be wrong. That is toleration, a principle with difficulty established and precariously preserved during the long course of British civil history.

In the meantime explicit and credible threats have been made to bring about the unlawful disruption of the matches by physical means. These threats make it more difficult for the Cricket Council (to which responsibility has been transferred from the M.C.C.) to reverse the decision. They also make it imperative that it should not. For there is now at stake something of more importance than the disputable question whether playing with the South Africans does more than not playing with them to dent apartheid. We are now posed within our own society with the proposition that one section of people may, in what seems a good cause, forcibly impose their view on another section of people by unlawful means. That is to substitute mob rule for the rule of law.

The disorders that may be expected to occur could be ridden out, and would be worth riding out in order to indicate the principle of civil toleration. But there is another dimension to the affair which causes some who would otherwise concur with that to withdraw and demand that the tour be now cancelled. They are deeply and justly anxious about the effect of disorder surrounding these matches on race relations.

It is possible to share these anxieties to the full without concluding that it would be expedient to cancel the tour. In the first place its enforced cancellation at this stage and in these circumstances would be deeply resented by some non-demonstrating sections of the community, and the resentment would be directed if not against coloured people at least against the fervent propagandists of racial integration. Secondly, it needs to be asked precisely how racial disharmony is likely to be provoked by the tour. It will not come primarily and directly from resentment on the part of the coloured communities at the presence here of white South African cricketers. The main impetus of the campaign to stop the tour has not come from them; their organizations have entered the lists at a fairly late stage in the agitation. The damage will be done by mass demonstrations, menacing or violent at the fringes, by battles with the police, by disorders in or around the grounds on which the games are played – all having at their root a conflict of ideas about racial policy. They will not be race riots (if riots they become) but they will be riots concerning race, which are almost as poisoning and polarizing in their effect.

It is said that the whole blame for this prospect rests with the Cricket Council for its "provocation" in persevering with the tour. It is almost as if to demonstrate or go in for disruption in the face of this provocation were an incontrollable impulse. It is not. It is a calculated act. And if it is a reasonable calculation that mass demonstrations will provide cover for disorders, and that disorder will lead to a deterioration of race relations in our cities, then those whose primary concern in the matter is not to seek release for their moral indignation but to prevent the hardening of racial antagonism may be asked to draw the conclusion that they had better not turn out on the streets and had better use their influence to persuade others not to do so. Of all the advice which has been so freely given by important people to those among whom they have influence, that of Mr. Victor Feather is the most sensible: if you disapprove of these matches, have nothing to do with them.

Plan to Disrupt Cricket Tour with Locusts

11 *May* 1970. A London University student said yesterday that a plan had been devised to wreck the South African cricket tour with an army of locusts. By the time the tourists arrived 500,000 would be ready for release on cricket pitches so that they would eat the grass, he said.

Mr. David Wilton-Godberford, a biology student aged 20, already has 50,000 of the insects at his home at Colwyn Bay. He said that friends were also breeding them in secret in other parts of North Wales.

The breeds he intends to use are the desert locust and African migratory locust. They will be up to $1\frac{1}{2}$in. long, harmless to human beings, and unable to fly.

In a brick building behind his home rows of small glass-fronted cages contain thousands of locusts, kept warm by the heat from electric bulbs. There are also scores of bottles containing eggs.

Mr. Wilton-Godberford, who said he was against violence, explained: "I abhor apartheid and this is to be my personal protest. Anything up to 100,000 locusts will be let loose at a particular ground and I think the plan is foolproof. They will ravage every blade of grass and green foliage. The greatest care will be taken to ensure they are in the correct physiological stage. So that their insatiable appetites will not be impaired they will not be fed for 24 hours before the moment of truth.

"It takes 70,000 hoppers 12 minutes to consume one cwt. of grass. The crack of a solid army of locusts feeding on the grass will sound like flames. The South Africans are going to dread this trip; they will see more locusts than they have ever done back home."

He said the insects would probably die within a month because of the climate and certainly before their wings developed.

The tour was called off on 22 May following a request from the Home Secretary.

Sobers Gets Ovation in Rhodesia

FROM IAN SMITH

14 *September* 1970; *Salisbury*, 13 *September*. Gary Sobers, the West Indian cricketer, left Salisbury tonight after a two-and-a-half day visit to Rhodesia, during which he won the hearts of Rhodesian cricket fans.

After he had made a short, farewell speech today at the end of play on the police ground, 7,000 fans gave him a standing ovation and three cheers and then sang "For he's a jolly good fellow".

Throughout his visit, Sobers played the diplomat, avoiding comment on the political issues which have bedevilled Rhodesia's sport with the outside world since the Unilateral Declaration of Independence (U.D.I.) nearly five years ago.

He told the crowd today that his visit had given him "something to think about", adding, "I enjoyed it very much indeed". His partner in a $1,000 single-wicket competition, Ali Bacher, the Springbok captain, said he would like to see Sobers play again – further south.

Sobers said in an interview that he would like to see the Rest of the World XI play in Rhodesia and South Africa.

Gary Sobers is the first world-class non-white cricketer to visit Rhodesia since U.D.I. When he arrived on Friday he was cheered by a large crowd on the balcony at Salisbury airport and members of the Indian community put a garland of flowers around his neck.

This morning he met Mr. Ian Smith, the Rhodesian Prime Minister, and his wife. He sat beside Mr. Smith watching the competition, won by Mike Procter, of Rhodesia, and Lee Irvine, of South Africa, who gained full points from their three games. Each of the other pairs won one of their games.

India's Three Exciting Hours to Fame

BY JOHN WOODCOCK, CRICKET CORRESPONDENT

25 *August* 1971; *The Oval*. India's victory, received amid scenes of great enthusiasm, stands as one of the finest achieved by a visiting side to this country. It is something they have been striving for since they first played Test cricket 39 years ago, and it came from an apparently hopeless position.

Just think of it. They had been saved from defeat at Lord's and Old Trafford by rain, and last Friday evening no one gave them the slightest chance of winning. With a first innings total of 355 England, it seemed, were secure from defeat. With Australia, West Indies, New Zealand and Pakistan already under their belt, they were moving to another cold and calculated victory. Or so we thought. But, Chandrasekhar fooled us all, and yesterday India kept their nerve where Pakistan and Australia have recently lost theirs.

England fought, as they have been guaranteed to fight. Never was a match more reluctantly conceded, and this was all to England's credit. It was a desperately slow pitch, so slow that Illingworth gave Price not a single over and Snow bowled only six. He relied upon himself and Underwood to win the match, and for once there were too few runs to play with. Hardly a ball turned, and Snow might as well have bowled a poached egg as a bouncer.

Yet when Wadekar was run out without a run added to the overnight score of 76 for two, it looked as though England might get away with it again. D'Oliveira, from cover point, took advantage of a moment's hesitation to beat Wadekar's dash for safety after Sardesai had called him for a single. For some time after that Underwood, Illingworth and D'Oliveira probed away, hopefully, thoughtfully, patiently, persistently. And with the luck they needed through the slips Viswanath and Sardesai survived.

For the most part Illingworth gave Underwood the pavilion end, from which the ball was more likely to turn, and Underwood, for all his accuracy, lacked the flight or spin to win the day. Laker and Lock would have fancied their chances no doubt, but Locks and Lakers are few and far between. Illingworth ringed the bat, to try to delude the batsmen, and his fielders gave him all they had. But Sardesai and Viswanath, and then Engineer, were too good for them.

When Underwood got a ball to turn at Sardesai and Knott took a good catch, there was still a chance for England. So there was when Underwood stuck out his left hand to take a spectacular return catch from Solkar. That was 134 for five and, as Illingworth said afterwards, he believed then that England could win if they made short work of Engineer, which they failed to do.

Sardesai defended stubbornly for two hours, 40 minutes, and with great skill Viswanath kept England at bay for almost three hours. Without these two India would not have won. And without Engineer they would have won less comfortably. He came in with 39 still needed, and of these he made 28 himself.

Having got out going for the winning runs, Viswanath was not there to be garlanded as Engineer was. He was caught by Knott off Luckhurst, brought on by Illingworth as a last desperate throw. It had taken India three hours to make the 97 they needed when the day began; three tense, exciting hours which culminated with an invasion of the field by the Indians of London.

So, at last, the tightrope snapped. England have walked it several times this year. During the winter they did so at Sydney and then at Auckland; and again this summer at Edgbaston, Headingley and Lord's. They are not a good side, as England sides go, and their performances this summer have reflected, quite starkly, the hapless state of Australian cricket. But their way of playing makes them devilishly difficult to beat.

Both India and Pakistan have appeared to enjoy their cricket more than England. They have contributed more liberally to our summer's pleasures. In Illingworth's time as captain, England have now won eight Test matches, drawn 12 and lost only one. Before that, under Cowdrey, they played seven more without defeat. But an unbeaten record has its complications. Now that England have lost they should think in terms of building a side which plays the game with more of a smile and less of a frown.

This, of course, was a wonderful result for Indian cricket. Always they have bred fine, natural players, whose temperament has been suspect. Yesterday was their festival of Ganesh, which is one of the great Hindu festivals. Ganesh, a god with an elephant's face, comes to the succor of the distressed.

Well, it was England who were in need of his help. And if, as they should, they proclaim their readiness to tour India this winter, they may need it again. For in a short time Ajit Wadekar has made this Indian side into a match for anyone. Within six months they have beaten West Indies and England away from home – and climbed the highest peaks in the cricketing world.

ENGLAND 335 (A. P. E. Knott 90, J. A. Jameson 82, R. A. Hutton 81, J. H. Edrich 41) and 101 (B. S. Chandrasekhar 6 for 38)
INDIA 284 (F. M. Engineer 59, D. N. Sardesai 54, A. L. Wadekar 48, E. D. Solkar 44; R. Illingworth 5 for 70) and 174 for 6 (A. L. Wadekar 45, D. N. Sardesai 40)
India won by 4 wickets

Wilder Notes than
Sweet Music of Ball on Bat

BY PHILIP HOWARD

15 *September* 1971. No gaudy celebration or victorious pennant fluttered over the ancient sporting arena in south London yesterday. One of the gasholders was at half-mast. Surrey, the champion county for the first time since 1958, were still finishing their last match of the season at Southampton.

Old scorecards blew around the gutters, urban autumnal leaves that show that summer is over in Kennington. Groundsmen were refreshing the famous turf, which is battered, brown and hard after a season of attrition for bonus points. And workmen were carrying huge chessmen into the ground for Saturday's pop concert.

At the Vauxhall end a stage was being hammered together from which new echoes will startle the ghosts of the Oval, and provoke more vigorous approval than the customary sleepy ripple of applause from the members' stand.

The Oval is full of shades and echoes of golden summers long ago:

Richardson flashing down balls so fast that even before they became ghostly they beat the eye; Hobbs stroking the ball past cover; Hayward and Abel, Lohmann and Lockwood; Strudwick and Sandham; May, Bedser and other names that are incantations.

But a larger crowd than watched any day's cricket there this summer will take the Underground and the No. 3 buses to the Oval on Saturday to sit on the grass and listen to The Who, the Atomic Rooster and non-cricketers so withered and so wild in their attire that look not like the inhabitants of the Oval and yet are about to make history by being on it.

The staff were up till midnight last night dealing with requests for tickets. They have already sold more than 5,000 and are prepared for a crowd worthy of Bradman on Saturday. The square will be covered by coconut matting; and not many of the crowd are likely to be wearing shoes that tear the turf as roughly as cricket's spikes.

Cricket has always been a leisurely, backward-looking obsession, glorying in ancient paladins and Old Wisden. The great days of cricket, when summers were golden, it never rained and Hayward was permanently at the wicket, always have been 50 years ago – even 50 years ago.

In the golden days at the Oval, before 1939, club membership was never as high as it has become since the war. It was always relatively few people who went to the Oval even when Hobbs was batting.

In the golden days the managerial and professional classes who belonged to the club left the office for the Oval at four, and at close of play caught steam trains to Camberwell and Croydon, where they employed two servants and lived in respectable style on £500 a year.

Vast oil paintings and yellowing photographs in the pavilion show them posing in silk hats, mutton-chop whiskers and sporty expressions all over the playing area, with a formidable 11 of dukes and earls at their head.

Anyway tradition is always changing. Hobbs would have been as startled by the absence of trams rattling past the wall and by the need to provide parking space for motor cars as he would have been by the pop concert.

In the nineteenth century the FA Cup Final and England-Scotland soccer internationals were played on the Oval; in those days 20 groundsmen were employed all the year instead of four today, Mr. Geoffrey Howard, secretary of Surrey County Cricket Club, says: "We have to adapt to the demand of the times, just as the old cricketers would have adapted to the demands of modern cricket.

"It is better that people should use the Oval than that it should be empty. We badly want to go on providing cricket here, because we love it. We cannot force the new generation to love cricket. But if we can make a little money by promoting what people enjoy, it must be a good thing for cricket."

In his office in Curzon Street, full of hubbub and beautiful people moaning from behind dark glasses about having been up late last night, Mr. Rikki Farr, the producer of Saturday's show, said that he aims to provide a form of circus relevant to 1971. "If rock and roll can help to salvage the financial situation of the Oval, then cricket should be in awe of rock and roll and not the other way round.

"The astonishing thing about Saturday is that thousands of the generation that is the whipping donkey of the establishment will be paying £1.25 each, knowing that the profits from the concert will go to the relief of refugees from East Bengal.

"What cricket needs is some new rules to hype [derived from high-power] it up as a change from all this boring old nonsense with batsmen prodding about. I should love to do a concert in the true bastion of the old days, Lord's."

Commentators and Credibility

BY JOHN HENNESSY

6 *January* 1972. If there is anything more depressing than a cricket field guarded by covers against the summer rain it is the spurious attempt to create Test matches out of a computer. This is the brainchild of the BBC, who now regularly tell us how Boycott, who can hardly even have seen Bradman play, is setting about outwitting the old master. The bats really do seem to have gravitated from the bag to the belfry.

Foreigners (which for this purpose include the Scots) have always regarded cricket as an English disease. They must now see it as a form of madness, when a sham excitement is breathed into a run-out that never was or a wicket that never stood let alone fell.

There seem to be two ways of looking at this form of sporting charade. Either the BBC know their business, which does not say much for those on the other end of the transmissions. Are they in such a pathetic state of deprivation, in spite of the proliferation of Test matches nowadays, that they must dream impossible dreams in their dotage to keep body and soul together during the long winter months?

Or is it the BBC who have taken leave of their senses? No doubt a "spokesman" will leap forward with a set of statistics to prove that the transmissions are a roaring success, that people turn off their electric razors or television sets, according to the time of day, by the millions to hear Bradman bowled for a duck by Bedser. But who is to say that the statistics themselves have not been regurgitated by a computer programmed by a madman in quartered cap and multi-coloured blazer?

These words, I should add, are not the ravings of a cricket hater. Certainly a disenchantment has set in with the antics of the governing body (under whatever name) in recent years and the drift towards thud-and-blunder cricket, but I still demand the blood of the Australians as vociferously as the next man and will do so through the coming summer. What blood, though, can anyone extract from a computer, with a transistor where the heart should be?

The series does, however, raise one important issue – the credibility of the commentator. It may be recalled that John Arlott declined to comment on matches involving the South Africans on the ground that broadcasting was a matter of mutual enjoyment and there could be none on his side. I could not quite understand his position then, but I think I can now.

Brian Johnston does such a remarkable job in simulating the real thing that it is hard to tell that the bails are not flying before his very eyes. But what happens when he takes his place at Lord's or Leeds with 13 men of flesh and blood paraded before him? How shall we know that the excitement he is displaying is genuine and not vamped up at the behest of some voiceless producer talking through an instrument thrust in his ear?

Some commentators switch from one mood to another so quickly that it is impossible to believe that the transformation is genuine, arising solely from deeds of derring-do being performed before them. Mr. Johnston is of a different breed, or has been until now. However irritating his digressions into matters of laundry or bird-life may be, he has generally seemed to be a man honestly trying to convey to the listeners what he feels and thinks. It will be hard to take him on trust in the future.

It is surprising to find Arlott himself and Sir Neville Cardus associated with this tomfoolery. But whether either has so lowered his professional standards as to offer a commentary I could not say. If so, it has been my good fortune to be otherwise engaged at the time.

To be fair, the BBC is not alone in its midwinter madness. One paper, not particularly distinguished for its cricket coverage, not only gives the full ghostly scoreboard but also a fairly lengthy report. There we learn that Bradman was bowled by a "late inswinger pitching middle-and-leg and cutting away to bowl Bradman off his pads". It must be suffering from a touch of the sun.

Duncan Fearnley

Cricketer and Bat Maker Who Works Hard at his Pleasure

BY ARTHUR OSMAN

17 *January* 1972. The river Severn is running fast and high, five miles away the Malvern Hills are lost in rain clouds, and the view from the cricket ground to the cathedral has a veil of rain across it. It is hardly a day for daydreaming about cricket prospects. But the thoughts of one man, who works a couple of six hits from the county ground, are occupied with little else.

Duncan Fearnley admits to devoting his working life and leisure to cricket. He works hard at his pleasure. At the age of 31 he has tasted success as a county professional and is now emerging as one of the world's few individual makers of high quality cricket bats.

He can claim to be the only cricketer playing today who makes for himself, and for a growing number of world batsmen, the most valuable tool of their trade. All are fashioned from selected clefts of Suffolk and Essex willow which have been seasoned and dried for up to 14 months.

The affinity between a cricketer and his bat has a certain mystical quality. Mr. Fearnley knows this well and insists that no bat leaves his workshop which has not been case-hardened, spliced and balanced by himself.

Players at professional and club level treat a bat with the sort of respect that a weekend motorist gives to the family car.

Mr. Fearnley's life has revolved around cricket since he was a child, which is not surprising, since he was born at Pudsey, Yorkshire, played for England as a schoolboy and hoped to follow illustrious fellow townsmen such as Sutcliffe and Hutton into the Yorkshire team.

As events turned out this was not to be, and in 1961 he moved to Worcestershire, where he soon established himself as a notable opening bat. In 1968 the county engaged Turner, the New Zealander, and Mr. Fearnley moved on to Lincolnshire to play in the Minor Counties. This season he will captain Worcestershire second eleven.

When he left school he had learnt the batmaker's craft at a one-man shop in Bradford, and later he always kept equipment at home.

His family had a tradition of working in wood, his grandfather having partnered Ray Illingworth's in a cabinetmaking business and his father being a woodwork teacher at a local school.

The turning point for Mr. Fearnley came at a party at Ilkley for the England and Rest of the World teams in 1970. He had in his pocket several rough drawings of a suitable marque to put on his bats, and after some hilarious suggestions it was decided that only one would do – a perspective view of a set of bails and wickets.

The sign has become known as the Black Wicket, and from a distance it looks like a large black triangle on the back of the blade. It has intrigued many armchair viewers of the game, has kept Mr. Fearnley's wife, Mary, busy this winter cutting out 4,000 of them, and all in all has proved a potent asset.

John Snow took three of the first 12 bats produced to Australia, and another, which was a spare in the bag of a player, produced five centuries. It is now the centrepiece of what Mr. Fearnley hopes will be a distinguished collection.

Its impact was sufficient to produce an order for 3,000 bats from Australia during the 1970-71 tour, and another order for 1,000 received in the past few days will be shipped out this summer. New Zealand is another developing market, as is the West Indies.

He says: "My involvement as a player has been an invaluable asset, because

I know what batsmen are looking for. I have been through it all myself. When I watch cricket on television I feel like a split personality, for I am watching the performance of my bat just as much as that of the player." When Mr. Fearnley lifts a bat, his highest praise for it is "Aye, it's not a bad stick". When he adds "It taps up nicely" one feels that nothing short of a crisp 100 on its first outing will do.

Greek Translator Required

20 *March* 1972, *Diary*. The Cricket Society is looking for a Greek scholar to translate the laws of cricket into Greek. The society's chairman, Christopher Box-Grainger, is offering a cash prize for its completion. The translation is required by the members (and, more particularly, by the umpires) of the two local cricket teams in Corfu – Gymnastikos and Byron – both of which can claim seniority over The Cricket Society. (Corfiot cricket was begun, it is thought, by Lord Byron.)

This year at least three English teams are going to Corfu to take part in a cricket festival in September – Lord Orr-Ewing's XI, H. P. F. Forster's "Cricketer" XI and The Cricket Society's XI. The society has prepared a handbook which has a glossary of local cricketing terms such as *bombarda* (full toss), *pintz* (Yorker) and *apo psila* (caught).

An Eastern Potentate Who Became Prince of the English Game

BY ALAN GIBSON

6 *May* 1972. We are now so accustomed to the fact that many of the world's best cricketers are of other than English stock, that it is hard to realize what a surprise it was when Ranjitsinhji, born a hundred years ago, appeared on the sporting scene in the early eighteen-nineties. In 1892 he was clearly one of the best batsmen at Cambridge, but was not given his Blue. The captain was F. S. Jackson, who later readily admitted his mistake, but who had by his own account made very little attempt to find out how good a cricketer this Indian prince was. Jackson was captain of Cambridge again in 1893. In the winter he had been on a cricket tour of India, and this broadened his horizons. That summer Ranjitsinhji was given his Blue.

There were many who felt that an Indian, however high-ranking, had no business in a cricket match between Oxford and Cambridge. Sir Home Gordon, who was very far from being a wild radical, recalled in later years that he had been abused by a committee-member of M.C.C. for having "the disgusting degeneracy to praise a dirty black". The outcry did not last long, partly because it was soon apparent that Ranji (the abbreviation rapidly became popular) was an astonishingly good cricketer. The further question remained: should he be picked for England?

In 1896, the Australians were here. At the time the England side was chosen by the authorities of the ground on which the match was played. Ranji was not chosen at Lord's, it was said, because of the disapproval of Lord Harris. The Lancashire committee asked him to play at Old Trafford, and he said he would be delighted, if the Australian captain had no objection. Harry Trott cheerfully agreed.

This was one of the best matches ever played between England and Australia. Ranji scored 62 and 154 not out. His second innings, when his side was in a losing position, against Ernest Jones on a fiery wicket, was considered by many the best he ever played. That season he was at the head of the first-class averages, and scored 2,780 runs. It was the highest aggregate ever recorded, beating W. G. Grace's 2,739 (in 1871).

But his greatest years were 1899-1901. In 1899 he broke his own aggregate record, scoring 3,159. In 1900 he scored 3,065. At this point, therefore, the three highest aggregates ever made stood in his name. No wonder men called him a marvel. Most of these runs were made for Sussex, with C. B. Fry at the other end. In 1901 Fry reached the 3,000 mark, and so did Tyldesley. Ranji was not so successful, with 2,468 runs. But he only batted 40 times (to Tyldesley's 60) and his average was 70.51.

His other occupations, and in later years his duties of state, often limited his appearances. In some seasons he was out of the country altogether. When he made an occasional return he did not always easily find his touch. In his last appearances, after the First World War, he had only one eye. In spite of these handicaps, during his career he scored 24,567 runs at an average of 45, with 72 centuries.

In the seasons 1899-1901 he scored 8,692 of those runs (Fry 7,838 in the same three seasons). Against Australia, he also averaged nearly 45, despite the astounding events of 1902, when his Test match average was 3.75 (which was nevertheless a notable triumph over Fry, who averaged 1.25 for the same number of innings).

I have given this statistical outline of his career because to a later generation he became a legend as much for what he was as what he did, and we need to remember that in those early dramatic years he surpassed, even in terms of figures, what any batsman had ever achieved. But, of course, it was the way he made the runs that also caught the public's imagination, and set the press-men scratching their heads ("magic of the east", and "Oriental conjuror" are only good phrases once). Nobody, not even W. G. Grace or Bradman in their heydays, ever filled the grounds as Ranji did. He developed new strokes and new variations of old ones.

There have been many technical analyses of his batting, none entirely satisfactory, even that by Fry. The action photographs of him were taken too

late to show him at his best. He put on weight early. We have to content ourselves with tantalizing glimpses. For instance, once when he was playing a
fast bowler to leg, that stroke something between a hook and a leg glance, he
missed, and the ball broke the skin of the lobe of his ear: his left ear.

He explained that when playing short balls to leg, it was necessary to get
an entire sight of the ball (with both eyes). No doubt he had marvellous eyesight. Indeed, he was responsible for the belief, widespread among cricketers
for many years, that all Indian cricketers had marvellous eyesight. I played
some cricket in university days with M. J. Kalyasunderam, a distinguished
scholar with a rich talent for a song in the evening, but not – he will forgive
me for saying – a formidable cricketer. As soon as Kalyasunderam went in
the field would spread, and when his first off-drive went to long-leg (his most
productive stroke) be sure an elderly spectator would say: "Wonderful eye
these chaps have."

Ranjitsinhji was a prince and potentate, and only subordinately a cricketer.
The monarchs of the Raj lived in a peculiar tension, between the lures of the
western world, and their own long habits and glories. This is why they sometimes seem to us, unimperial Englishmen of 1972, so odd.

None can have suffered this strain more acutely than Ranji. He became,
in one aspect, so much the English gentleman, that there is an occasional note
of pained surprise in the comments of his English friends. Sir Home Gordon,
for instance, who knew him well, and received many favours from him,
wrote: "When we all met him, the Jam Saheb was thoroughly western, apart
from due assumption of his dignity as an Indian prince when occasion arose.
But I have been told that out there he had phases of going entirely native, not
speaking English for weeks and subsisting then solely on rice with some condi-
ments in the curries." Imagine it! A Cambridge Blue, an England cricketer,
not speaking English for weeks and subsisting on curries!

In 1912, Ranjitsinhji was of much value to the King-Emperor at the Delhi
Durbar, and was rewarded with an increase in the number of his guns, which
gave him much delight. He attended the Durbar in a silver coach, which he
wished to present to the King-Emperor. The offer was declined.

His income at the time was £75,000, and his entertainment for the fortnight
of the Durbar cost him £36,000, even though his palace was not then built,
and he had to put up his guests in huts. Afterwards, the special train in which
he was taking his party back to Nawanagar was held up for five hours, because
he had no money to pay for it, and the railway company insisted on cash in
advance. He had not expected to succeed to the throne of Nawanagar, which
goes by nomination of the ruler (though within the family), and this must
have been an additional strain for him. He is often referred to in English
accounts as a model prince, but there does not seem much evidence for this,
apart from what he told his friends. However, he was made Chancellor of the
Princes, and was an Indian representative at the League of Nations, and
there is no doubting the quickness of his intelligence, any more than of his

eye. There is a remarkable book waiting to be written about him by someone better versed in Indian affairs and the politics of the 1920s than I.

He was always, in England, the English gentleman, no more eccentric than an English gentleman of the period might legitimately be (a good deal less eccentric, for instance, than MacLaren). He much enjoyed the part, and entertained lavishly at his home at Staines, though possibly it took the Staines tradesmen some years to recover from the shock.

He died in 1933. His death was sudden, but cannot to him have been unexpected, for the night before he had given to his British political officer, urgently summoned, a special copy of his nomination for the succession. An autopsy found no traces of foul play, or apparently of any other cause of death. His mother and sister observed strict purdah.

How Cricket Came to Argentina

FROM RICHARD WIGG

8 *June* 1972; *Buenos Aires, 7 June.* A typical Buenos Aires Taxi driver asked "Cree-ket? You mean that English sport?" as he took me, one hot summer afternoon in January, to watch the North versus the South game, the principal fixture of Argentina's cricket season.

The familiar smack of bat hitting ball and the appeals to the umpire were sufficient to make any Englishman homesick.

Everyone that afternoon was speaking English as a mother tongue, but it was accent-less and a fine ear noticed that the vocabulary was occasionally old-fashioned. These are all the distinguishing marks of a remarkable breed of men, the Anglo-Argentines.

This month the Argentine Cricket Association is sending the first fully Argentine side to play in England and Wales, concluding with a match against the MCC at Lord's.

Last century, when the British gave this South American country the biggest sustained economic development it has ever enjoyed, they threw in as a bonus the introduction of football, rugby, tennis, golf, rowing, boxing, and polo. All these games have since become native sports, several of them developed by Argentines to world standards, as in the case of football and boxing.

Cricket has proved a sport idiosyncratic enough to fascinate only the already highly idiosyncratic Anglo-Argentines.

The team is captained by Mr. Frank Forrester, a 28-year-old broker in a Buenos Aires insurance business; several members have the Anglo-Saxon surnames of Anglo-Argentine families. One of the players was born in Brazil of British parents and one of the best bowlers, who works for a local British bank, was born in England. Of the rest of the team, some are farmers, engineers, accountants, business executives or students.

Englishmen and Anglo-Argentines, were playing cricket more than one hundred years ago. Sometimes under unusual conditions. In 1859 when General Justo Urquiza was besieging Buenos Aires during one of the frequent civil wars the cricketers insisted on their game going ahead and obtained from the fiery general permission to cross the lines to get to their pitch. They played their game – in spite of a dead horse on the pitch.

The North versus South matches date back to the 1880s when British staff ran the Argentine railways and much of the country's meat producing industry.

In 1926, when British prestige reached its zenith, the Argentine President (accompanied by the Army general who was to succeed him in a coup) thought it proper to attend a first "Test match" at the Hurlingham Club (the Anglo-Argentines' holy of holies) against a visiting MCC side.

But then came Perónism and difficult times for Britons, Anglo-Argentines and, of course, for cricket.

In 1948 "Evita", wife of the former dictator, allegedly disgusted at her cool reception in Britain, caused "difficulties" to be made for the Buenos Aires Cricket Club and for its famous cricket ground in the high class suburb of Palermo.

The British Ambassador managed to stave off a showdown with General Perón. But the final blow came when one night Perónists burnt down the club house, removed the fences, and drove bulldozers all over the pitch.

Cricket is played regularly at weekends from November to February by enthusiastic Anglo-Argentines and younger members of the surviving British community (the "Ancient Britons" in diplomatic circles).

The coming British tour is important to Argentine cricket. It should raise the sport's prestige sufficiently to encourage efforts to "graft" cricket into the Argentine school curriculum, and so make cricket a fully national sport.

Clash over Cricket Money Back Offer

BY A STAFF REPORTER

13 *June* 1972. Wilfred Wooller, secretary of Glamorgan County Cricket Club, took an unusual step to register a protest at the way Somerset were conducting their innings at Swansea yesterday. He announced over the public address system that if any spectator felt he was not getting value for money an application for a refund would be sympathetically considered.

At that point Somerset, standing at 245 for four at luncheon on the second day, elected to continue their innings into the afternoon. Welsh resentment, already stirred by Somerset's slow play on Saturday, welled over.

Brian Close, the Somerset captain, met the situation in the most effective way possible. Having scored a century himself, he set his bowlers to scatter the Glamorgan batsmen and before close of play Glamorgan were batting again, having followed on 169 runs behind Somerset's 314 for seven wickets declared.

Wooller said: "The spectators are the people who matter in this. They pay the players' wages, and Somerset's tactics in batting on after lunch seemed to be quite unreasonable. It is a very pleasant afternoon but I doubt if we have collected £20."

Close's immediate comment was "bloody ridiculous". He promised another forthright statement by close of play, but in the event he confined himself to saying that Somerset had given their answer on the field of play. "I am not", he said, "going to get as cheap as he [Wooller] was."

Three Question Marks over England Team

BY JOHN WOODCOCK, CRICKET CORRESPONDENT

26 *June* 1972. Those who left Lord's on Saturday evening despondent at having seen a Test match lost – and there were a lot of them – could, with advantage, have looked at things from a different angle. For they had seen a summer made. If Australia win today, as they surely will, the series will be level, and the last three Tests (at Trent Bridge, Headingley and the Oval) should be worth going a long way to watch.

I confess to having had a dread of seeing England sitting on a lead of two matches before decreasing crowds. But if Australia win this one there need be no fear of that. In three days they have discovered a gifted bowler and established some faith in themselves. It is the England selectors who have the worries now, and fairly substantial ones they are. Illingworth has been reappointed as captain for the last three Test matches, but Price, Gifford and Luckhurst all have question marks above their names.

How has it all happened? How, on a pitch that is basically firm and sound and of a good pace, did England come to lose nine wickets for 86 runs in 48 overs? Especially after Australia's last five wickets had added 107 runs, with Marsh, their wicketkeeper, making an entertaining 50 in an hour and a quarter against an England attack armed with a new ball. It amounted to a day's cricket which many must have been at a loss to understand.

While great credit is due to Greg Chappell for a wonderful innings of 131, to Edwards for his part in steadying Australia's innings on Friday, to Lillee for making the first breaches into England's innings, and to Colley for lending valuable support, the man who has put Australia into an apparently invincible position is Massie. So far he has taken 15 wickets for 122 runs in 56.5 overs. He is the first Australian to have taken 15 wickets in a Test match, and only Jim Laker (19 for 90 against Australia at Old Trafford in 1956) and S. F. Barnes (17 for 159 for England against South Africa at Johannesburg in 1913) have taken more. That is in over 700 Test matches, at all times and in all places.

But who *is* Bob Massie? And where has he been hiding his light? He is 25, a bank clerk from Perth in Western Australia, and what the Australians call a "Bonzer bloke". He had three seasons (1969, 1970 and 1971) in Scottish cricket, playing for Kilmarnock, the arrangements for that being made by Tony Lock, who was then captain of Western Australia.

In his first match for Kilmarnock, in the Western Union competition, Massie took all 10 wickets against Polock, who had Sadiq Mohammad, now with Gloucestershire, playing for them. In his time up there Massie married a Kilmarnock girl.

Last December, while having varying success for Western Australia in the Sheffield Shield, he worked the scoreboard in the Test match against the Rest of the World at Perth before playing in the last two Test matches of that series. By taking the first six wickets (Gavaskar, Ackerman, Zaheer Abbas, Graeme Pollock, Sobers and Asif Masood) for 27 runs in the match at Sydney, he earned his place for the present tour.

Those who played both at Sydney and on Saturday say that he moved the ball rather more at Sydney than at Lord's. He has also been known to swing it quite prodigiously into the breeze that blows off the Swan river in Perth.

At Worcester in April he showed signs of doing it, with six for 31 in Worcestershire's second innings, and he was looking like it again at Lord's in May against MCC when he strained a muscle in his side. This kept him out of the first Test at Old Trafford, where he could have been well nigh unplayable, and when he returned to play against the Combined Universities on June 14 he had trouble with his control. It was partly this which has led to his bowling round the wicket at Lord's with such astonishing success.

It was decided that he should do so at a team meeting before the match, Neil Hawke, who came to England in 1964 and 1968, being cited as a bowler making the switch to good effect, unlike most bowlers who go round the wicket as a variation to their normal style. Massie has no trouble in avoiding the pitch in his followthrough. Neither Constant nor Fagg, the umpires at Lord's, have needed to warn him about this.

With eight for 84 in England's first innings, Massie was suddenly a name to be reckoned with, and on Saturday he held the whole ground in thrall. England began their second innings half an hour after luncheon, 36 runs behind Australia, with Massie bowling from the nursery end and Lillee working up a genuine pace at the pavilion end.

At 6.30 Massie was still at it, having had a break only for tea and taken seven for 38 in 24 overs. At 6.15, when feeling sick from the effort of it all, he sent for a tablet, and had the rest of the Australian side chaired him off the field it would have been no surprise. It was as though he had worked a miracle for them. The clouds had lifted from the hill and the long, cold night was over.

In having a humid, overcast day to bowl on, Massie was fortunate. It helped to accentuate his swing. The ball moved at times as though radio-controlled, and the fact that seven catches were taken at the wicket or in the slips shows how much he made it leave the bat. His pace is a brisk medium, his action economical, and for the rest of the tour he must expect to find himself treated with the care of a crown jewel.

As for England's batsmen, they were up against a superb piece of bowling, which they never looked remotely like containing, although between them they have scored 36 Test hundreds. Boycott was out unluckily, when the ball dropped off his body on to the stumps, with just enough impetus to remove the off bail.

Luckhurst never looked up to it (his scores in four Test innings this season are 14, 0, 1 and 4) and Edrich failed for once to stick it out. With no rescuing act from D'Oliveira or Knott, the score was 52 for six soon after 5 o'clock. Standing among the ruins, needing all his resolution to survive, was Smith, and when Illingworth, after holding on for 45 minutes, left him, it was 74 for seven. With Smith's own departure soon afterwards went England's last chance of leaving Australia a total to test them today.

What we all wondered, would Hammond have made of the bowling, or Compton, or Hutton, or Hobbs and Sutcliffe? It is difficult, indeed impossible, to say. But from some there would have been an attempt to hook and cut when Lillee pitched short. And these great players of the past were more accustomed than those of today to playing the ball that leaves the bat. The bowler saw more of the English left shoulder than he does now, and felt more of the cover drive. For sheer determination Smith's was a fine effort. But it was not enough to steal the thunder from a bank clerk from Perth.

ENGLAND 272 (A. W. Greig 54, A. P. E. Knott 43; R. A. Massie 8 for 84) and 116 (R. A. Massie 8 for 53)
AUSTRALIA 308 (G. S. Chappell 131, I. M. Chappell 56, R. W. Marsh 50; J. A. Snow 5 for 57) and 81 for 2 (K. R. Stackpole 57 not out)
Score after third day: England 272 and 86 for 9; Australia 308
Australia won by 8 wickets

Cricketers Told to Get their Hair Cut

11 *July* 1972; *Singapore*, 10 *July*. Zealous immigration officers told two Oxford University cricketers here today to get their hair cut or face deportation.

They confiscated the passports of Mr. Simon Corlett, aged 22, and of Mr. Bryan Hamblin, aged 20, and gave them three days to comply with the order.

Mr. Corlett, one of 15 members of an Oxford-Cambridge team which arrived here today for a tour, said they had no choice but to visit the barber tomorrow.

Tourists Keep Steam in the Dressing Room

BY JACK FINGLETON

19 *August* 1972. It was a happy part the Australian cricketers had in the Oval dressingroom last Wednesday, Ian Chappell, the most casual of all Australian captains, wore a yellow and blue track suit and a gay tam-o'-shanter from Scotland. Most, with draped towels, were in their birthday suits and champagne corks popped with musical rapidity. Malcolm Chappell, whose third son, Trevor, could also one day play with Ian and Greg in the same Test side, quietly and proudly packed the Chappell gear.

I much appreciated being invited to join in the conviviality. As an old cricketer, I am a bit of a fogey when it comes to the privacy of dressingrooms, which belong exclusively to players, and I have purposely not stayed at the same hotels as the Australians. If players on a tour as long as this want to let their hair down occasionally, they are entitled to do so in privacy and it would be more than odd if fit-to-busting young athletes did not want to go on the rampage occasionally with a few drinks and songs.

This Australian team has had some severe, but most isolated, criticism of its behaviour on tour. Incidents happen on any sporting tour when tensions are released and this Test series has known plenty of tensions. Dressing-room incidents can be written of any team. Bats are flung, feelings are got out of the system.

Possibly a reason why one or two critics have turned to "team behaviour" this tour could be because, forecasting that the Australians were a poor side and would not win a Test, they have gone off at a tangent. Cricketers of any country are not parlour saints. The Australians did not emerge with flying colours from Scotland and Northampton. They were careless in their approach to both games and at Northants apparently offended the shop steward of the waitresses by helping themselves to cheese and biscuits.

Manager Ray Steele, a splendid manager with discipline but no stuffiness, dressed them down in no uncertain terms over their playing approach. He did not mention the cheese and biscuits.

In an interview he gave me in his Adelaide club before he left Australia, Ian Chappell said he would not tolerate any suggestion by any of his players of disagreement with an umpire's decision. Nor has there been an instance of this. I wish I could repeat what Chappell said to Mallett at the Oval the other day when umpire Rhodes gave Mallett his final warning over running down the pitch after delivery. There have been other occasions, when a bowler has been warned for intimidation or pitch trespass, when a skipper has argued the point for his bowler with the umpire.

Not so this time. Umpires Rhodes and Spencer have said that this was the easiest touring team they have had to handle. That's nice, for Australians, to know. It could not have come from a more informative source.

The dominant feature of this Australian team, apart from its friendliness, has been its youth, yet it could well be that not many of them will come again because the Australians, due to some odd itinerary quirk which happened many years ago, are not due to come to England again until 1977. Many of them will have given their bats away by then. There is talk of some World Cup series in England in 1975 but, as the huge gate takings have shown – and that despite the disadvantages of weather – no game appeals like an honest-to-goodness Test match between England and Australia. Officials of both countries should sort this one out. I would think England will want us again in the four years usual time. We certainly would like it that way.

Now comes the hardest part of the Australian tour. There is inevitable reaction after a Test series and these one-day games, with all their rushing and scurrying, are not only comparatively new to the Australians but are the very deuce for the players. Fitness does not go off on a long tour. It is the mental attitude that gets blunted.

I do hope my fellow Australians see it through. Coming as a young, un-tried side, I think they have done magnificently, although I could be biased. My hackles rise when I think they are criticized unfairly and it often strikes me as odd how the bare one or two, who were possibly no plaster saints on the field themselves, are so eager to dip their pens in vitriol against Australians. You would think we are not of the same stock; that hundreds of thousands of Britishers have not, in recent times, made Australia their home.

Of course, a healthy young Australian has fire in his belly and red blood in his veins. Field Marshal Montgomery did not find anything wrong with the Australian Ninth division in the Middle East. (The team before this one was rocked to its haunches when the Field Marshal walked into the Australian dressingroom at Southampton and asked: "Were any of you chaps with me in the Desert?")

Once again, I say I am proud of these young Australians, even if they do not ask for the biscuits and cheese to be passed. I hope the sun will shine on them for the rest of their tour and especially when they sing the chorus of their song: "And the rain, rain, rain comes pouring down; on the Aussie cricket tour." The word, by the way, is not pouring!

One fashion – or domestic note – to end. Those evil looking, drooping Chinese moustaches that Messrs Sheahan and Edwards wore for most of the tour disappeared overnight when Mesdames Sheahan and Edwards arrived in England. Which proves that the word is mightier than the pen.

Social Joys of an Off-duty Cricketer

BY JOHN WOODCOCK

30 *December* 1972; *Delhi*, 29 *December*. I am often asked which of the cricket tours that one undertakes is the most enjoyable. Is it to Australia, West Indies, South Africa or India and Pakistan?

The answer I think is that they are all enjoyable and yet all different.

From a purely cricketing point of view there is nothing to equal a visit to Australia. To sail from Tilbury as we used to do and three weeks later to see Fremantle through one's port-hole, having watched the team become a team on the voyage, was wonderful fun. Even now, when the journey is made by air, there is something very special about arriving in Australia to fight for the Ashes. And except for Lord's the players will say that the best Test ground in the world is Sydney.

Round the crescent from Perth to Brisbane the entertainment seldom ceases: from the first of the civic receptions and the first of a thousand speeches. Where else can a cricket team in its off moments sign for a dozen oysters or be given the courtesy of so many beautiful golf courses or enter so many welcoming homes or by their identity stir so many memories? Nor on the field of play can there be anything quite to compare with routing an Australian side.

In the days when we went to South Africa, to sail into Table Bay and to watch cricket at Newlands was the introduction to a tour when the hospitality was every bit as lavish, yet the glare of publicity less fierce. At the time of the last MCC tour there in 1964-65 South Africa were not quite the cricketing force they would be now, but they were not far from it.

There, as in Australia, the players were never left to fend for themselves.

It is the same in the West Indies. A steel band is there to serenade them when they arrive, and life thereafter is as exotic as they choose to make it. On the field this is a hard tour, with lighter interludes in lovely places like St. Lucia or Nevis or St. Vincent or St. Kitts. Where we are now, in India, the enthusiasm for the game is even greater than in the West Indies, and the matches are even harder to win.

In Bombay every open space it seems is given over to cricket. Sometimes on the pavements one has to wait for an over to end before passing on. In Hyderabad 100,000 people watched a three-day match. In Indore a monument in the shape of a bat 145 feet high and bearing a replica of the signatures of Ajit Wadekar's side has been erected to mark their victory over England in 1971. In Delhi where a Test match has just been played every day was a sell-out.

Yet nowhere else is a touring side so dependent upon its ingenuity for its recreation, or so acutely uncomfortable when it is uncomfortable, or for that matter more comfortable when it is comfortable. If less than it was, India is still a country of extremes: of poverty at the palace gates, of finery and filth.

In Indore where this present team were assigned to rooms like prison cells, they sang like an army on the march to sustain their spirits. In Delhi they spent 10 days in a tower of luxury. Instead of singing themselves they listened in smoochy restaurants to Indian singers "dreaming of a white Christmas".

On the Tuesday following their Test victory, the team made the pilgrimage to Agra to see the Taj Mahal. The week before they went to the Golden Temple in Amritsar. To visit such places is one of the delights of an Indian tour. There is golf too for the declining number of cricketers who play it. In Delhi there was a fine course – well kept and with caddies to get one out of trouble if they could. With their toes they perform prodigies of manipulation in the way they provide a lie for a wooden club, even in the densest country.

Besides a lack of opportunity, what holds the Indians back from making a mark at golf is the cost and shortage of equipment.

I played recently with a merchant of great wealth who can lay his hands on only one new ball a month due to import restrictions.

This week it is Calcutta, next week Bangalore, the week after that Madras. And so it goes on. For one reason and another there has developed on this tour the best spirit I have known and it was this not least which led to England winning in Delhi. Through there being fewer diversions the team are usually together and therefore working out their cricket. There is more of this here than in Australia, South Africa or West Indies.

A day for the players goes something like this. A coach to the ground at nine o'clock with a net for those not playing in the match. Play starts at 10 a.m. or 10.15 a.m. and lasts until 4.50 p.m. or 5.05 p.m. More often than not there will be a warm bath at the hotel after play followed by a beer in the manager's room (thanks to a British brewery whose supply of cans makes for a great saving, with local beer at the equivalent of 50p a bottle). The evenings are passed either at a reception in a gaily lit garden, the curry taken standing up, or more often in the hotel. There are few British homes to go to any more except in Delhi where the High Commission is based.

A massage being a good way to pass the time, the physiotherapist is seldom idle. It is he who insists upon the team doing their teeth in soda water, and allowing no water to pass their lips unless it is known to have been purified. The team's bill for soda water on this tour will come to something in the region of £250.

On the last tour they were said by one of the Indian authorities to have eaten over £150 worth of bananas, mostly in lieu of a cooked lunch on the grounds. There is as you will see less sophistication than on most tours, more making do. But going into the New Year with a victory behind them, Tony Lewis and his side are happy at the moment to settle for that.

Ward Sent Home and Coloured Bats Are Out

BY RICHARD STREETON

19 *June* 1973. The image of cricket as a tranquil sport, free from acrimony and purely routine away from the field, was a little dented yesterday by a series of incidents and announcements in a variety of places. Easily the most momentous event was the sending home of Alan Ward, the Derbyshire and England fast bowler, for seemingly disciplinary reasons before play ended. Next, perhaps, for rapidity of action and drama came the banning by the authorities at Lord's until the full implications are studied of coloured bats. An enterprising manufacturer had introduced them only on Sunday as a sales gimmick.

Cricket is unused to people being sent off and nobody at Chesterfield was saying very much after Ward left the ground with the game against Yorkshire still in progress. Brian Bolus, the former Yorkshire and Nottinghamshire player now captaining Derbyshire in his first season with them, can hardly have dreamt when play started that by the close he would have joined Lord Hawke (Yorkshire) and Lord Tennyson (Hampshire) as the only English captains previously to have deprived their side deliberately of the services of a player before a match was completed. Peel and Newman respectively – both bowlers – were the men "sent off" in the past.

All Bolus would say afterwards was: "You saw what happened. It is up to you to put your own interpretation on what you saw. I have nothing further to say on the matter. This is the concern of the Derbyshire County Cricket Club."

Onlookers had seen Ward savagely punished by the Yorkshire batsmen early on, being hit for 19 in one over by Hampshire and after one further over in the afternoon, finishing with figures of one for 56 in nine overs.

Later, as Yorkshire's total continued to grow, Bolus approached Ward and then left the field. He returned and approached Ward again only to turn to the pavilion and beckon the 12th man to take the field, at the same time waving Ward off.

Major Douglas Carr, the Derbyshire secretary, would not confirm that Ward had been sent off but he did say: "I can confirm that he has been told to go home and that I will be seeing him formally in the morning. He is not injured as far as I am aware." He confirmed that Bolus had sent a message from the field asking to see him but he declined to say what was discussed and what had gone on between Ward and his captain. Ward also declined to comment on the matter before leaving the Chesterfield ground.

Meanwhile, the last comparable uproar over cricket bats before yesterday's issue of coloured bats was in 1771 when one Thomas "Shock" White of Reigate "arrived with a bat which completely covered the width of the stumps". The quotation is from the minute book of the Hambledon Club, who at the time governed the game, and almost overnight they instituted the first regulations governing the size of the bat.

In the 200 years since nobody has found it necessary to think much about the bat's size, or anything else and certainly not its colour until on Sunday Richards used an orange bat for Hampshire and Roope a blue one for Surrey in John Player League games. Roope was quoted as saying that he would use his blue bat in the Lord's Test match this Thursday. The complications which might arise from, say, the use of a bat coloured the same red as the ball or the distastefulness of manufacturers and their contracted players from trying to outdo each other in public are obvious.

One of those lengthy solemn statements that give the impression of having been drawn up by a bevy of judges and Queen's Counsels at Lord's was immediately forthcoming and most people's sympathies are with the officials. One does hope, however, that the appropriate committee meets and acts quickly – as their forebears at Hambledon did. Just occasionally cricket committees tend to defer problems too long.

The text of yesterday's broadside read: "Coloured bats shall not be used in matches under the control of the Test and County Cricket Board. This includes the Test match against New Zealand at Lord's on Thursday. While in general principle the board has never sought to restrict the type of equipment used by players, it is considered only right that the board have the chance to consider the implications of using equipment to which the opposition might justifiably object, or which could conceivably make the task of the umpires more difficult." All fair enough, perfectly reasonable and no doubt a compromise will be reached in the usual way of English cricket.

The Skill is Undiminished

BY JOHN WOODCOCK, CRICKET CORRESPONDENT

21 *June* 1973; *Cricket – A Special Report*. It has been said before that cricket never was what it used to be. Pick out, at random, any one of the 110 *Wisdens* contained in a full set, and somewhere the game or those who play it will be under fire.

This is worth remembering when taking a look at the contemporary scene. The young shavers sitting on the boundary's edge at Trent Bridge during the recent Test match there, will be saying in 30 years' time how no one compares with Amiss, Greig and Congdon. They will hold their children spellbound with the story of New Zealand's great recovery.

In English cricket there can seldom have been a greater wealth of skill, but only a small part of it is English skill. In the golden age of batsmanship, so incomparably described by Sir Neville Cardus, I doubt whether there were so very many finer batsmen playing in the county championship than there are now, but they were all English then.

To Sir Neville, Barry Richards, Gary Sobers, Mike Procter, Clive Lloyd, Rohan Kanhai, Majid Khan, Geoff Boycott, Asif Iqbal, Mushtaq Mohammad and the rest are not to be compared with "Ranji" and Charles Fry and Gilbert Jessop, and Tom Hayward and Archie MacLaren and Stanley Jackson. Whether or not when stood side by side they are as good, I believe they are playing a more difficult game not a better game, but a more difficult one.

Just as in football, more emphasis is being placed on saving goals than scoring them, so, in cricket, captains and bowlers think increasingly in terms of containment rather than attack. To some extent this is the outcome of limited-over cricket; but it is a development which was taking shape before the one-day game was introduced on anything like its present scale. There is no way in which it can be for the best, and no way, so far as I can see, in which the trend can be reversed.

To get an idea of how much the game has changed it is worth wondering what would have come of "Tich" Freeman, the second leading wicket-taker in the history of cricket, had he been starting today. Between 1914 and 1936 he took 3,776 wickets, 1,122 of them in four seasons between 1928 and 1931, with leg breaks and googlies.

In 1973 it is most unlikely that he would have found a county to give him a start. He gives too much away, they would say. Wickets are not bought any more, as Freeman used to buy them. From Test cricket down to the village green the game is dominated by bowlers all of much the same pace. For this reason much of the technical variety has left it, to be replaced by variety of a different kind.

Whereas a dozen years ago the championship was the only domestic competition in which first-class cricketers took part, there are now three others, all of them sponsored and designed to appeal to a public which no longer has much time or the inclination to watch the three-day county game.

There is not a single spectator sport that has not been faced in the last decade by falling gates. Rugby and soccer, racing, boxing, tennis and golf have all had the same worries as cricket. Only the great traditional fixtures can still be sure to draw the crowds: the Open Championship, the FA Cup, the Derby, a fight for the heavyweight title of the world, or the battle for the Ashes. This is a fact of life to which different sports have reacted in different ways and at different speeds. Cricket has not, on the whole, been dilatory.

First as a gimmick, then as a lifeline, the one-day game has been developed. The players accept it as a necessary expediency; it makes their life more hectic but financially more rewarding. Television accepts it as a sellable product, and that is vital. There is between television and sport a love-hate relationship. To cricket the liaison is worth £150,000 a year; yet in the course of a season there is no knowing how many would-be spectators it keeps at home.

A good many more, no doubt, than it encourages to come.

Sponsorship extracts less of a price for its patronage, and it is doubtful whether without it all 17 first-class counties would still be in existence. Last year more than £400,000 was invested in the game by almost everyone from cigarette manufacturers to the makers of toys and prams. It is not least because of them that the best overseas cricketers migrate each year to England, to play their game and make their living. It is a migration which has been insufficiently curbed, but which, overall, has been of undoubted benefit to the English game.

Take Lancashire, for instance. In 1968 they were joined by Clive Lloyd, the West Indian left-hander. At once he brought a revival in their fortunes. His fielding and batting and zest for cricket were as much of an example to the side as an attraction to the public. Yet the fact that Lloyd went to Old Trafford, to be followed almost immediately by Farookh Engineer, the Indian wicketkeeper, has kept Frank Hayes, one of England's bright young men, waiting longer than he would otherwise have done for a regular place in the Lancashire side.

All round the country, except in Yorkshire, there are examples of this. It is no use anyone who is not a Yorkshireman applying to play for Yorkshire. Other counties must soon insist on a tighter control of imported players, as well as on no further increase in one-day cricket at the expense of the championship programme.

I think cricket holds as high a place as ever in an Englishman's affections, in spite of all its ups and downs. When England played Australia last year the Post Office dealt with 15 million telephone calls from people asking for the Test score. Opinion polls have shown that, next to football, cricket has by far the largest readership of any game in the newspapers.

At the grass roots the game is healthy enough, except that it mirrors the imperfections at the highest level. Driving through the countryside on a Saturday or Sunday evening you will see as many games as you ever did, many of them with a new competitive element. If fewer boys now play cricket at school those who are lost to other sports are mostly those that would simply have been making up the number.

To some extent the enthusiasm for taking a bat and a ball to the park, rather than the infernal football, varies with the success which England's footballers or cricketers are having at the time. When England beats Australia cricket does well for recruits, and for those who choose it as their summer pastime it continues to provide as happy a way as there is of making the friends and memories of a lifetime.

The Art of Captaincy

BY MICHAEL BREARLEY

21 *June* 1973; *Cricket – A Special Report.* The effects of the changes in the structure of county cricket have been and are being discussed *ad nauseam*; but it is perhaps worth mentioning the differences these changes have made to the captain's job.

It is widely believed, I think, that the arts of captaincy are among those numerous skills which disappear as soon as limited-overs cricket starts. Tactics are thought to be unnecessary and absent.

In all types of cricket there have been captains, no doubt a majority, who work to rule, following whichever book happens to be fashionable at the time. They merely set things in motion and await results. And it is especially tempting to think of the job along these lines in limited-overs cricket. As usual, if he has a good side under him, the captain who follows a rigid pattern will usually achieve adequate results; but this approach is a pale shadow of proper captaincy.

It is of course essential to have some sort of plan or outline of policy. But situations vary enormously; no simple formula can fit all contingencies. The perfect captain will have a feeling for the moment when a batsman has taken the measure of one of his bowlers. He will know which of his bowlers is least likely to be heaved to the short boundary on the leg-side.

He will gauge accurately the time to stop worrying too much about saving singles and to concentrate on saving fours. In the midst of impending chaos he remains calm, juggles his bowlers sensibly, and keeps weak fielders out of the way.

From the batting point of view, the tempo of the side's approach requires constant reappraisal. In 40-over matches one must, I am sure, go for one's strokes from the start of the innings. At the same time the batting should almost never be reckless. Every batsman has to play himself in a little; the special skill lies in doing so without destroying the momentum of the innings.

Team selection and batting order call for clear-headedness. Many of the most successful Sunday league players have been young enough not to have founded their whole game on three-day cricket. Yet one-day cricket can easily induce bad habits among the less experienced. It is often hard to weigh the contribution of a steady batsman against that of a chancy all-rounder. What, one must ask, is the average value of X's fine fielding or Y's ability to bowl a few overs in a pinch?

I personally like one-day cricket and enjoy captaining Middlesex in their games. I find myself totally absorbed in what is going on. I have always found the tactical aspects of the game as intriguing and fulfilling as batting. This absorption is, for me, the main attraction of the job.

A danger, for me, is the tendency to a sense of omnipotence which tempts a captain to exaggerate his own responsibility both for success and failure. Others rarely help, for one receives, as captain, as little sensible praise as sensible blame. There are, of course, the trials and rewards of positions of responsibility in many areas. But it is rare that the overall assessment appears to be so easily calculable or so publicly available.

Different captains are temperamentally suited to different forms of cricket. For this reason, and to dilute the pressures which many captains fell, it would be feasible for a county to appoint different players as captains for three-day and one-day competitions. There was a certain irony in the choice last year of Brian Close to captain England in the one-day internationals. For in one-day cricket the guiding principle is to restrict the opposition, whereas Close is by nature an attacking captain, who, I suspect, took some time to come to terms with the challenge of limited-overs cricket.

One last point on this subject. Twelve years ago there was only one inter-county competition, the championship. Now there are four. One entirely happy result is that most counties have something to play for during at least some stages of the season. Middlesex, so far, have done little in the championship or in the Benson and Hedges Cup. But we are, touch wood, doing well in the John Player League. Last year we had a chance in the last two; the year before, in the championship. The increased range of potential success keeps up the morale of players and members alike.

Changes in social structure, though less tangible, have had no less an influence on the role of the captain. The aristocratic tyrant has to some extent given way to the collaborating foreman. Some older players yearn for the old-style discipline. Cricket still provides a locus for both snobbery and inverted snobbery.

At the same time the administrators of the game have brought into the committees of the Test and County Cricket Board several current players, mostly county captains. The captain can find himself betwixt and between. He is often the only representative of the players on the county committee, yet he is also a member of that committee.

The biennial captains' meetings at Lord's, under the persuasive chairmanship of Doug Insole, have been represented as the voice of the cricketers. This picture may with justification be resented by the players, as happened this year over the issue of fines for county sides who fail to average 18.5 overs an hour. The rise of the Cricketers' Association may in retrospect appear to have been as important a development of the 1960s and 1970s as the introduction of one-day cricket.

Prince Ranjitsinhji wrote beautifully about the duties of a captain in *The Jubilee Book of Cricket*. Much of his sensible and sensitive account of this complex job in personal relations, administration, tactical sense and leadership still applies. Shall we see, in the next few years, a dividing-up of these functions?

Will there arrive in county cricket managers and trainers, the apparatus of soccer and, for that matter, of American sport, to plan and dictate policy, and to lay down rules and procedures for training and discipline? Tentative steps in this direction have been made. I am doubtful about how far they can profitably go. I do feel, however, that there is room for greater professionalism, in the best sense of that tarnished word, in cricket.

This professionalism will have to extend to the running of clubs. I will end with one illustration of the success this can produce. Two of the most improved sides of the past five years, Leicestershire and Northamptonshire, owe their improvement largely to the powerful and incisive influence of their secretaries, Mike Turner and Ken Turner. It will, I think, increasingly become clear that success will require secretaries (call them managers if you will) among whose tasks will be the finding and signing-on of players.

Adventure in Each Ball Bowled

BY BEN TRAVERS

21 *June* 1973; *Cricket – A Special Report*. Mystique, my dictionary avers, is a "secret known to its inspired practitioners"; a definition to be treasured by anybody confronted with the challenge: "Why on earth do you give up all that time and thought to cricket?"

"Ah", he can reply, "that is my mystique." The trouble is that the true reason for his obsession remains a secret even from the inspired practitioner himself.

Thousands of his lifetime's precious hours he spends with his eyes glued on other men playing cricket or on the rain which has stopped them doing so. Why? Is the love of the game born in him, lurking in his system from the outset among the lesser but delectable natural appetites? Or is it, as the dictionary seems to think, an inspiration stimulated by early hero-worship and maturing into the insistent bigotry of the mystique?

In my case, I honestly suspect it was inbred. Although, as a boy, I sat enthralled watching W.G. and Ranji making a hundred apiece in partnership and, a few years later, Jessop's classic century at the Oval, the love of cricket was deeply implanted in me long before it embraced such glorious revels.

But the game's survival and prosperity depend not upon the fanatic but upon the normal discriminating supporter. His first reason for going to see cricket played is to see the players who play it. His interest lies in the performance or promise of individual players, to be appreciated, criticized, argued about.

And in every generation along come hundreds of cricketers of swingeing ability and entertainment value with, here and there, some star performer whose outstanding abilities are enhanced by a personality which makes him a

compelling attraction for the regular worshipper and tickles the curiosity of
the sceptic – Grace, Ranji, Jessop, Hobbs, Hammond, Bradman, Compton,
Dexter, Trueman and who you will beside.

Suddenly, not so long ago, the cricket-lover, like everybody else, found
himself caught up in the whirl of the speed age. Life is now one perpetual
rush-hour. The long-drawn-out three-day county match soon felt the strain.
Somebody had to do something pretty drastic. Somebody did. He was inspired to institute and sponsor the one-day, result-guaranteed contest. It
caught on.

The Test match still thrives with a glamour and box office value of its own;
meanwhile the authorities struggle to recapture the interest of the preoccu-
pied public in the three-day county game. But their well-intentioned system
of bonus points appeals only to the faithful county partisan; the hardened
old bigot ignores it as beyond his comprehension or concern.

Yet, so long as cricket endures, he and his progeny will likewise endure;
still creating upheaval and protest in the crowded railway carriage in an effort
to glimpse just one ball being bowled in the club match alongside; dawdling
on the seafront promenade to study the form of the little boy on the sands
wielding a spade one handed as a bat and with the outsize bucket for stumps.

The basic question remains – why do I love cricket? First, I think it is the
allurement of keen continuous anticipation which makes every ball bowled a
fresh, isolated adventure. I love, too, the whole setting and atmosphere, the
traditional dignified amplitude. For me, the moment of the umpires' emer-
gence from the pavilion at the opening of a Test match (preferably against
Australia) is one of unparalleled bliss. I relish it in silence, merely turning my
head to exchange a wink with another old inspired practitioner in the row
behind me.

This Special Report *on Cricket was an eight-page supplement to* The Times
of 21 June 1973.

Close of Play at the Lane

BY BRIAN CASHINELLA

4 *August* 1973. The last county cricket match ever to be played on the historic
turf of Bramall Lane, Sheffield, starts this morning. Fittingly, the ground's
professional career ends with (what else?) a Roses battle between Lancashire
and Yorkshire.

More than ever before, if that is possible, Yorkshire will want to win this
one and offer the victory to the memory of the surroundings which have
witnessed some of their finest successes.

Messrs Boycott and Lloyd, the captains, will be aware that, whatever
happens, their names will forever be linked with one of the most famous

cricket grounds in the world and lodged firmly in the knowledgeable memory banks of the local cricket fraternity.

The demise of Bramall Lane is the cricket equivalent of a state funeral and who is to say that the ghosts of the famous – Rhodes, Makepeace, Duckworth, Verity, Lord Hawke, Leyland, Jackson, Tyldesley and many others – will not patrol the boundary rope and watch the latest chapter in the deadly serious clash between the great rivals.

It was alleged to be in the old "grinders' stand" there that a man was complaining about the slow scoring rate in an earlier confrontation between the red and white roses. "Is thee from Yorkshire?" he was asked roughly. "No", he replied. "Well, is thee from Lancashire, then?" Again "No." . . . "Well, what th' 'ell's it got to do wi' thee?"

While Yorkshire and Lancashire have had their fair share of cricketing punch-ups at the Lane, few of the players down the ages were likely to remember their reception with any regret. On the other hand, Surrey's memories are somewhat different.

For just over a century ago, one of their teams was almost lynched by the irate Sheffield crowd after a thunderstorm had apparently put an end to a tightly-balanced game with Yorkshire. The Surrey skipper was William Caffyn who accepted the umpires' decision that further play was impossible and began preparing his team for the return to London.

No such luck. The Sheffield crowd had decided the game must go on and the Surrey players, already on their way to the railway station, were confronted by an angry section of the spectators and threatened with a fate worse than death if they did not resume immediately.

It was an offer they could not refuse. The unfortunate Surrey players literally paddled their way back on the pitch and slopped the ball down until Yorkshire clouted enough runs to win by two wickets.

Douglas Jardine, the Bodyline tour captain, much criticized by some sections of the cricket community, was loved at Sheffield, and so was "Big Bill" Bowes, another fast bowler. Both players and the crowd had one thing in common: they played to win.

For it is the crowd, rather than the ground itself, that players remember. F. G. Mann, the Middlesex captain, will always recall the Lane as the place where he put Yorkshire in to bat on what proved to be a good wicket. The home batsmen proved difficult to move and a wag in the crowd bawled at the fielding skipper: "Tha put us in, nah get us aht!"

Herbert Sutcliffe scored his 100th century for Yorkshire there and, as Cyril Washbrook describes in his autobiography: "The whole vast crowd stood up, and it was the finest reception given to an English cricketer I have heard anywhere in the world."

But, you can take any match you like, load it with as many exciting boundaries as your mind can muster, fill it with bowling like you have never seen before, and it will not compare with a "Roses" duel – no matter how dull.

These games are not about scoring runs, getting wickets, snatching bonus points. They are matters of honour, pride and prestige, twice-yearly encounters where scores are settled.

Nobody outside these two Northern counties will ever understand what is at stake. Makepeace, the old Lancashire skipper, made a firm rule: "No fours before lunch against Yorkshire." And he meant it.

Sir Neville Cardus, the doyen of cricket writers, perhaps grasped the essence of the battle best with a story he told some years ago. Lancashire were 499 for nine wickets and their captain, Leonard Green, was at the wicket. He decided that, even if it killed him, he would score the 500th run.

Wilfred Rhodes bowled, Green pushed the ball gently on the off side and ran like a hare. There was a rapid throw to the bowler's crease. Green was safely home but the ball hit Rhodes on the arm. As the Lancashire captain was thanking his lucky stars he heard Rhodes muttering to himself: "There's somebody runnin' up and down this wicket. Ah don't know who it is, but there's somebody running up and down this wicket." As Cardus pointed out, the classic operative phrase was: "Ah don't know who it is."

So what more could Bramall Lane want as a farewell? It has seen a Test match, tourists by the score and county games that are listed as among the finest ever played. But Roses games have something special and today's is the last it will see.

Let us hope it is a fitting epitaph to a famous ground that will now see only football.

S. Africa Accept Non-Whites on Cricket Tour

27 *September* 1973; *Cape Town*, 26 *September*. The Government has approved the inclusion of two non-whites, John Shepherd, of the West Indies, and Younis Ahmed, of Pakistan, in Derrick Robins's cricket team which is to tour South Africa from October 20 to December 11. This announcement was made by the Sports Minister, Dr. Piet Koornhof, at The Cape Town University "Sportsman of the Year" dinner.

Cricketers Charged

15 *October* 1973. Cricketers who took part in a multiracial match in Pietermaritzburg yesterday are to be charged with contravening new Government proclamations, according to an official of the Group Areas Board.

Officials and detectives took the names of players and spectators at a private club during a match between a multiracial team and a white university side. The match was later continued.

British Author Knocked out at Test Match

FROM OUR CORRESPONDENT

7 *January* 1974; *Sydney*, 6 *January*. Laurie Lee, the British poet and author, was knocked unconscious today by a flying beer bottle on Sydney Cricket Ground's notorious "Hill". He was taken to hospital and had four stitches in his head. He was hit during the last 10 minutes of play after the Australian batting had collapsed to the New Zealand pace attack.

Mr. Lee, who is 59, said afterwards at his brother's home in Paddington, a Sydney suburb: "I enjoyed it, but if I go back again I will wear a tin hat." He is returning to England next Friday.

Jamaican High Court Judge Knows the Score

23 *February* 1974; *Kingston*, 22 *February*. There was a hush in Kingston High Court. The judge spoke in sombre tones. "I have to tell you, gentlemen, that Boyce is dismissed," he said.

"But m'lud", offered the defence counsel, "my client's name is Bryce."

"Ah, quite so," said his lordship, "but I thought you would like to know the latest Test score from Sabina Park."

The bank robbery trial was halted and everyone in court, including the accused, sat and listened as the judge read out details of the West Indies–England cricket match.

Occupational Complaint Strikes at Greig's Spinning Finger

FROM JOHN WOODCOCK, CRICKET CORRESPONDENT

29 *March* 1974; *Port of Spain*, 28 *March*. A spin bowler you can tell by his fingers, a wicketkeeper by his hands. Ask any old wicketkeeper to show you his hands and he will take you round them, bumps and all, saying where this bone was broken or how that one was cracked. I never had a better morning listening to a cricketer talk than when I asked George Duckworth to go round his hands.

It was on a boat to Australia and they were like one of those relief models of a golf course or a mountain range, all humps and crags and hollows. "That was Gubby at Perth", and there would follow a colourful account of how a knuckle had got knocked out of place, or whatever it was. In those days I doubt whether a wicketkeeper's gloves gave quite the protection they do now. Knott's hands have hardly a scar on them, which is a tribute to his skill as well, of course.

Today, on the flight from Georgetown to Port of Spain, the most interesting exhibit was Greig's spinning finger – the forefinger, that is, of the right hand. As a result of changing his bowling style, from medium pace seam to off cutters and off breaks, he is suffering from the spin bowlers' occupational complaint of a finger on which the skin has been broken, as a result of spinning the ball.

Laker's spinning finger is swollen and arthritic after years of service. Pocock's is generally quite raw during a season: Gibbs's too. In the Test match in Bridgetown Pocock had to leave the field to get his spinning finger treated, and now Greig is trying to grow the skin again on his before the last Test match starts here on Saturday.

Greig's new-found skill has answered the question that was worrying him before the tour began of how, at his usual medium pace, he could do much good. After failing in the first Test match to take a wicket he decided to slow down his pace and change his method. He bowls now more as Appleyard did with such success in Australia in 1954-55, or as Shepherd did for so many years for Glamorgan, using the crease for variation and changing his pace between slow and slow-medium.

His height is a virtue, occasionally giving him a bounce which others fail to get. As a direct result, in the last three Test matches he has been the most successful bowler on either side. England have taken 21 wickets in that time, Greig 11 of them.

This is bad news for Pocock, whose job Greig has taken over. Six weeks ago, had one written down a likely MCC side to go to Australia in October, Pocock would have been in it. Now Greig gets pencilled in as the "off spinner". With the new restrictions allowing only five fielders on the leg side applying in Australia by then and making things a lot harder for the off spin bowler, only one of their kind may go, and Pocock is not at the moment the first choice – or the second, for that matter. In Georgetown, Birkenshaw was preferred, as he probably will be again on Saturday if the balance of the attack stays the same.

It may not be until just before the match that England decide whether or not to bring back a third fast bowler. Meanwhile, Greig will be dipping his spinning finger into some sort of potion to try to toughen it and wondering whether or not to continue in England next season to bowl more slowly. Probably he will be one thing one day, and one another, according to the conditions, but it is in his slower vein that he is having such an impact on this series.

A Batting Machine they Called 'The Croucher'

BY ALAN GIBSON

"At one end stocky Jessop frowns,
The human catapult
Who wrecks the roofs of distant towns
When set in his assault"

18 *May* 1974. So wrote an American rhymester in 1897, when G. L. Jessop, a young man scarcely over the threshold of his career, was playing in Philadelphia. "The human catapult" was a fine hyperbole. The way Jessop sprang at the ball, the moment the bowler had realeased it, is what those who saw him most vividly remember.

English cricket has had bigger hitters than Jessop (he did not try for specially long hits; the boundary was good enough). English cricket has had batsmen who scored more runs with a higher average. But there has never been an English batsman who hit so hard, and scored so fast, and yet still scored runs so consistently. In his career, which lasted from 1894 to 1914, Jessop scored 26,698 runs, at an average of 32.63, and if one believes all one hears – those in Gloucestershire who remember him never tire of talking about him – hardly played a defensive stroke.

Shortly before Roy Webber died, he was talking to me about some statistical investigations he had been making to Jessop's career. Jessop scored 53 centuries in first-class cricket, with a highest score of 286, and so far as Roy had been able to discover, he had never batted for more than three hours. I don't know if Roy had time to confirm this, but it is an astonishing thought*. Take into account your different social climate, your changed over rate, your negative bowling tactics; take into account anything you like, but to score all those runs and all those centuries, and not to bat for more than three hours. . . .

In his early days Jessop was a successful fast bowler, twice taking 100 wickets in a season; and throughout his career he had a reputation for being one of the world's best cover fieldsmen. A. C. MacLaren, recalled to the England captaincy in 1909, demanded before the series began that Jessop should be picked for every Test, "because he will run Victor Trumper out for me". This plan did not work – rather the contrary, for Jessop strained his back while fielding in the third Test, and never played for England again – but it is a remarkable example of the value placed upon his fielding.

I felt I glimpsed a little of G. L. Jessop once, when I saw his son, the Rev.

---

* Gerald Brodribb's biography of Jessop, published a few months later and reviewed in *The Times* by Alan Gibson, revealed that Jessop took 200 minutes over his 240 for Gloucestershire against Sussex at Bristol in 1907.

G. L. O. Jessop, score a fast 80 or so for Dorset against Cornwall at Camborne. G. L. O. Jessop was then middle-aged himself, but a beautiful striker of the ball. He used the sweep a lot, as his father is said to have done, sometimes in the most daring circumstances, but he also had a splendid straight drive back over the bowler's head.

C. B. Fry always insisted that Jessop was not "a slogger", which used to be a pejorative term, but a true batsman who took risks, who stretched his technique to the limit, sometimes attempting more than he could achieve; but was nevertheless basically a sound player. That innings by G. L. O. Jessop, though he has never sought to compare his merits with those of his father, gave me a fairly clear idea of what Fry meant.

In Test cricket, it must be said, Jessop's record was disappointing. Although he was usually picked when he was available, over a period of ten years, he scored only 569 runs in 18 matches, at an average of 21.88.

Nevertheless, Jessop did win a Test, the famous one against Australia in 1902, when he redeemed a forlorn English cause in the last innings, scoring 104, his only Test century, in 75 minutes. The philosophy behind picking him must always have been, "Ah! But whatever his average, he's the kind of man who can swing a match", and that was an occasion when he did.

The number of times he did it for other sides, and particularly Gloucestershire, it would be a labour to count. He came to the Gloucestershire captaincy soon after the departure of W. G. Grace. Grace had left amid a large and loud rumpus, and Jessop's task was not an easy one. But although he was unable to lead the side to the championship, which was hardly surprising with the resources at his disposal, he kept up the gates and the spirit of Gloucestershire as much by his own marvellous example as anything else, and today his name is spoken of in the county in the same breath as those of Grace and of Hammond.

He was nicknamed "The Croucher". He bent low at the wicket, and sometimes would stoop down so far that his cap was on the level of the bails. He said that this helped him to judge the length of a ball early. It must have added considerably to the psychological and dramatic effects of his sudden spring, his pounce, his leap at the ball. But in later life, at least, he disliked the name.

About 1948, when I was a junior producer on the staff of the BBC, I was sent a capital script about Jessop, by Harold Gardiner, called "The Croucher". We put the programme into production, and billed it in the *Radio Times*. As a matter of courtesy, we sent a script to Jessop, though, as it was an almost entirely laudatory script, we hardly thought he would complain. But he did. He complained most sharply, particularly about the title: indeed, it took all the tact of Frank Gillard to calm him down, and the programme was postponed, to be broadcast at a later date under the less inflammatory title of "G. L. Jessop"

Well, most old men have cantankerous moments, but this incident has always baffled me. Did he resent the nickname because it was put upon him by the press? He did a good deal of journalism himself at one time and another. Did he resent it because the Gloucestershire public relished it? Amateurs in those days were inclined to disregard public esteem, but he must have been proud of the affection in which Gloucestershire held him (he was born and brought up at Cheltenham), and it is as "The Croucher" – the great cat about to jump – that he is still happily and proudly remembered.

Boycott Back in Swing

BY JOHN WOODCOCK

18 *June* 1974. Better after his bout of 'flu and keen to get back to the wicket, Geoffrey Boycott found a game in Bath yesterday – for the Lansdown Club against Selwyn College, Cambridge. He made 108 before retiring, with the same satisfaction, I imagine, as a crack shot killing low pheasants.

He was lucky to find a wonderfully good pitch. It was here that Vivian Richards, now playing for Somerset, re-wrote the local record book last season. The ground is beautifully kept and fast scoring, and had the sight of Selwyn's left arm opening bowler, operating from over the wicket in the style adopted so successfully by Solkar, unnerved the Yorkshire captain, there was a hospital behind the bowler's arm.

But all was well. In one of the early overs Boycott hit the second, third, fourth and fifth balls for four and took a single off the last. Soon afterwards he had the ball changed, not because it was out of shape or swinging too much but because of the red marks it was leaving on the blade of his bat.

Little can Selwyn have thought, as they left for their West Country tour, that they would be called upon as cannon fodder for England's most prolific batsman. As improbable, you might say, as a side of clerics finding that their opponents in the Diocesan Cup have a certain Prebendary Trueman opening their attack.

Two-match Suspension for Arnold

BY JOHN WOODCOCK, CRICKET CORRESPONDENT

8 *August* 1974. To Geoffrey Arnold, of Surrey, has fallen the unenviable distinction of becoming the first cricketer in modern times to be suspended from playing for his county for his behaviour on the field. Although available to play for England in the second Test match against Pakistan at Lord's today and also in the third Test in a fortnight's time, he will miss Surrey's championship match against Middlesex, starting on August 17, as well as their John Player League match against Northamptonshire on the following day.

While bowling for Surrey against Warwickshire in a Sunday match last month, Arnold bridled when Peter Wight, the umpire, signalled a wide. Mr. Wight and Arnold gave evidence at Lord's yesterday before the disciplinary subcommittee of the Test and County Cricket Board, as did David Evans, who was the other umpire, and John Edrich and Arthur McIntyre, Surrey's captain and coach respectively.

In the chair was David Clark, manager of MCC on their last tour to Australia when there was enough of this sort of thing on the field for the Cricket Council to issue a strong warning that they and the TCCB, through their disciplinary committee, would not hesitate "to use their wide powers, including the termination of the registration of a player" to put a stop to "incidents involving dissent from umpire's decisions whether by word or deed".

Arnold is a superb bowler in this country. Colin Cowdrey told me the other day that he considered him one of the best he had ever played. He might have added that on the field he was also one of the grumpiest. It will therefore come as no surprise to cricketers in West Indies, India and Pakistan, as well as in England, that Arnold has at last found an umpire who complained.

In South Africa and Australia, as well as in England, swearing on the field has recently caused concern. Swearing for the sake of it in everyday life is accepted as it never used to be in a less permissive, more gracious age. Swearing at an umpire is still, mercifully, a good enough reason for a cricketer to be censured, as it is even in football, which tolerates most of the more excessive forms of conduct but still cautions a player for firing four-letter words at a referee.

Llewellyn Suspended

9 *August* 1974. Glamorgan have suspended Michael Llewellyn, an all-rounder, who was sent off by the umpires during a second XI match at Pontypridd this week for allegedly refusing his captain's request to field at short leg.

Sobers Gives Notice of Retirement

BY JOHN WOODCOCK, CRICKET CORRESPONDENT

17 *August* 1974. Only for another three weeks will it be possible to watch Gary Sobers, arguably the greatest cricketer of all time, playing the game which has brought him such fame and which he has played so gracefully for over 20 years. He gave notice yesterday of his intention to retire at the end of the present season.

Nottinghamshire have eight matches left, three of them on Sundays, in which to take a last look at Sobers, and I advise those who can to do so. I say that for two reasons: first, because he will be really trying and secondly, because we shall seldom see his like again. Already this month he has made the fastest championship 100 of the year, in 83 minutes, for Nottinghamshire against Derbyshire.

Sobers is 38. He played his first first-class match, for Barbados against the Indians, in 1953. Chosen as a slow bowler, he sent down 89 overs in the match, at the age of 16. His first Test match was against England the next year, since when his all round record in Test cricket has surpassed anything ever achieved before. He has scored 8,032 runs in Test matches, including 26 hundreds, and taken 235 Test wickets and 110 Test catches. He played an innings of 254 at Melbourne which Don Bradman described as the best ever seen in Australia and one of the most perfect ever played. He could equally well have bowled an opening spell with the new ball to strike terror into the hearts of the best batsmen in the game.

It is this incredible versatility that has made Sobers pre-eminent in the game. I have heard famous and greatly gifted cricketers saying of him that it was simply not fair for one man to be so impossibly good at so many things. He has been as likely to win a Test match with a breathtaking catch in the leg trap as with a brilliant throw from cover point; as likely to turn another with a spell of orthodox, left arm spin, as he did only last February in Port of Spain, as with a dozen overs of chinamen and googlies or a couple of fast inswingers; as capable of a long defensive innings as an attacking tour de force.

As a captain, in Test and other cricket, he was never prepared sufficiently to involve himself with the whole running of a side, both on and off the field, to be particularly successful.

He saw his job, I think, as starting at 11.30, or whenever he led his side on to the field, and finishing when the day's play was done. Dedication was not in him. I suppose it never needed to be. Without trying, or without appearing to try, he was better than anyone else, and he has always considered that life is for the living. I have not often passed more than a few moments with Sobers without him laughing about something. He had the rare gift to go with his wonderful talent of being able to see that cricket is a game for the playing and not a war for the fighting.

At the end of MCC's tour to West Indies in 1967-68, Colin Cowdrey, who had led England through a hectic series to a narrow victory, said that if he had at that moment to choose one word to apply to Sobers it would not be his agility or his temperament or his eyesight or his footwork, or even his virtuosity, but his sportsmanship. In victory and defeat he was the same person, born in a humble Barbadian home, the son of a seaman, but with a remarkable way of getting the game in perspective. While others around were working themselves into a frenzy, Sobers was sharing a joke with the opposition, fortified by the thought that, win or lose, it was not going to be the end of the world.

There were times when his own players felt that he batted too low at No. 6, always his favourite place in the order. Often the effort was made to persuade him to go in higher, but even in his prime he rarely did. This suited England, of course. Deflating as it was, after taking the fourth wicket of an innings, to see Sobers walking out to bat, he would undoubtedly have made even more runs than he did had he batted higher up. Then, though, he would have had less time to study the racing form and that would never have done.

Away from cricket, Sobers has always been happiest either at the races or on the golf course. There was never a rest day last winter, during the Test series against West Indies, when he was not looking for 36 holes of golf. Out of the clubhouse window of the new Barbados Golf and Country Club, on the rest day at Bridgetown, I saw a file of golfers and caddies in the distance walking down a path from the 15th green to the 16th tee. Leading them was Sobers, with his unmistakable walk – sparing one leg because of the knee which has given him so much trouble but still extraordinarily feline and keen to get to the next hole, although it was his second round of the day.

He had played in the morning with David Marsh, a former British Walker Cup captain, who said of Sobers that he was a lovely hitter of the ball, long off the tee and with a good touch. In his retirement he will play a lot of golf and have a chance, he hopes, to put something back into cricket. Not that after such generous a career he is in its debt.

Life Jail for Man who Killed Cricketer

FROM OUR CORRESPONDENT

4 *October* 1974, *Bristol.* A promising young county cricketer was murdered by a man who had been planning a killing for two years and said he wanted to do it again, it was stated at Bristol Crown Court yesterday.

Simon Kerr, aged 20, a Rhodesian, who had paid his fare to England to join Gloucestershire County Cricket Club, died after being stabbed 10 times at a party.

Mr. John Hall, Q.C., for the prosecution, said that Desmond Carroll, aged 24, an engineer, who admitted murdering Mr. Kerr, had described the killing as "sheer ecstasy". Mr. Carroll, of North Road, St. Andrews, Bristol, was jailed for life.

Sir Neville Cardus

1 *March* 1975. Sir Neville Cardus, C.B.E., who died in a London hospital yesterday at the age of 85, began as a sickly child in a Manchester slum, and ended an octogenarian who had richly fulfilled his two-fold ambition, to make a name as a music critic and a writer on cricket. He had no formal training in either field. The start of cricket for him was bowling for hours at a bucket, shielded by a broad piece of wood. Music came to him naturally and gave him his first chance of getting into print. As a sporting writer, he ranks with the old masters of the art from Hazlitt to Bernard Darwin; his cricket books became classics in his lifetime.

A versatile all-round journalist, Cardus delighted in commenting on the contrasts he had known in the social scene over the years. He could talk as well as he wrote and he was as welcome in exalted music circles as among cricketers in a pub. No compliment pleased him more than that he had made many people wish they had actually been at a cricket match or actually attended a concert. He wrote on cricket as a cricketer; on music as a listener.

Born on April 2, 1899, Cardus was brought up in the home of his grandfather, a retired policeman. He never knew his father and the most he ever heard of him was that he had been one of the first violins in an orchestra.

In his *Autobiography* (1947) he wrote that his Aunt Beatrice, "a great and original girl", frankly, and his mother, more discreetly, joined "the oldest of professions".

A brief Board school education was interrupted by an illness which kept him in bed for nearly a year. Earning his first money as a pavement artist, he went on to scrape a living from a miscellany of odd jobs, selling papers in the street, delivering the washing for his mother and aunts, pushing a handcart for a builder, and serving as a junior clerk.

Learning to spin an off-break that whipped up viciously, he played as an occasional pro in club cricket, and answered an advertisement for an assistant to William Attewell, the old Nottinghamshire player and head coach at Shrewsbury School. He was taken on, and stayed for five seasons from 1912 to 1916. One day the headmaster, Alington (later headmaster of Eton and Dean of Durham), found him on the field reading Gilbert Murray's translation of the *Medea* of Euripides. This happy chance led to Alington making him his private secretary. Cardus always acknowledged his debt to Alington, who gave him the run of the library. But the clerical headmaster never shook his young assistant's faith in free thinking.

Having volunteered in August, 1914, for military service and been rejected, "Not to my surprise or dismay", owing to extreme short sight, he was placed in an awkward dilemma when Alington went to Eton. He became a casual labourer and sold policies covering funeral expenses among the poor for a burial society. Escape from this dreary task came when he wrote to C. P.

Scott asking for employment in the counting house of the *Manchester Guardian* and enclosing cuttings of what little he had written. Scott was impressed and took him on briefly as secretary, and, later, invited him to join his staff as a reporter at 30s a week, with 10s for expenses. This was in 1917, and for the next two years he did all sorts of work for the paper.

He became its cricket correspondent by chance. In March, 1919, he suffered a breakdown and, after he returned to the paper, the news editor, later editor, W. P. Crozier, suggested that he might convalesce by spending a few days at Old Trafford. His first cricket report appeared in June, 1919. Next year he began writing on cricket every day, covering the most important matches up and down the country and his salary was raised to £5 a week. Between 1920 and 1939 he wrote roughly eight thousand words a week on cricket every summer from mid-May to August, nearly 2,000,000 words in 20 years. He brought to this task an unusual combination of qualities. First, he was a player in his own right who knew from first-hand experience how professionals reacted, and, secondly, he had absorbed the passion for writing good prose which was the tradition of Scott's young men. He put everything that was in him into his reports, catching the atmosphere of a ground, the personalities of the men in the field, the excitement and the tedium of the day's play – all distilled through his literary and musical enthusiasms. For him, Macartney was the Figaro of cricket, MacLaren the Don Quixote with his stonewalling partner, Makepeace, as Sancho Panza, and J. W. Hearne the Dickensian Turveydrop of the crease. This often bewildered the players he was writing about, but they respected him for his technical knowledge of the game. He put his experiences as "Cricketer" into a number of books, including *A Cricketer's Book*; *Days in the Sun*; *The Summer Game*; *Cricket*; *Good Days*; *Cricket all the Year Round* and *Close of Play*.

Delighting in cricket, he never wavered in his regard for music as his first string. He had first got into print in 1910 with an article in *Musical Opinion* on "Bantock and style in music", which tempted him to throw up his job as a clerk and devote himself to freelance journalism. But a postal order for only 7s 6d in payment for this article made him prudent, and he stuck to his job. He wrote musical articles in his early days in the *Manchester Guardian*, acting as assistant to its great critic, Samuel Langford, who taught him much, and with whom he always maintained a disciple to master relationship. He succeeded Langford in 1927, and held the post up to 1940 when he went to Australia. After his return to England, he had a spell on the staff of *The Sunday Times* in 1948-49, and rejoined the *MG* as its London music critic in 1951. From 1941-47 he was with the *Sydney Morning Herald*, and, later, he again visited Australia to broadcast on music for one hour weekly.

Reflecting on the two themes which engaged him, he once confessed "I could say that the Hammerclavier Sonata was the last thing that Beethoven wrote, and I'd get a couple of dozen letters, perhaps, 75 per cent from foreigners. But, if I said that Hutton made 363 at the Oval in 1938, I'd get thousands from Yorkshire alone." He admitted, though, that "Cricket opened my door of escape; cricket brought me enough economic independence whereby to educate myself". His books on music, some of which were translated into German and Swedish, included *Ten Composers*; *Musical Criticisms of Samuel Langford*; *Kathleen Ferrier Memorial Book*; *Talking of Music*; *Sir Thomas Beecham, A Portrait*; *Gustav Mahler: His Mind and His Music* Vol I; and *The Delights of Music*.

He married in 1921, Edith Honorine King, who died in 1968. There were no children. He was made C.B.E. in 1964 and knighted in 1967.

7 *March* 1975. Mr. Yehudi Menuhin writes:

What made Neville Cardus unique and uniquely British was his love and loyalty to both music and cricket. As a small boy, when I was still alien to these shores, it came as a wonderful shock when after only a few bars Sir Edward Elgar left the responsibility of playing his Violin Concerto in my immature hands, to go to the races.

I was equally surprised to learn that the great critic, Neville Cardus, knew as much about a cricket bat as about a violin bow. These two memorable experiences convinced me ever since that sport and fresh air were in no way inimical to a profound knowledge of music.

Neville Cardus was indeed unique. No critic has interpreted music and performance to the public with greater insight and sensitivity. He always searched for and recognized the intention and the message of the performer as well as the character of the occasion. He was as alive to the public response, to the pulse of the audience, as he was to the specific performance and its ambience. His vision and integrity were such that he could preserve a balance between the diverse facets of his writing.

Above all he knew that music exists in time as an organism, not only as theory or law, above and independent of time. He lived the music and the occasion. He wrote not as a one-man dictionary, but with the combined reaction of heart and mind.

Danger Should be Crucial Word in the Laws

BY JOHN WOODCOCK

1 *March* 1975. No matter where one goes, or who one talks to, the conversation comes round to short-pitched bowling. So far as the Auckland incident is concerned, in which Ewan Chatfield so nearly lost his life, opinions vary widely: from that of the *Guardian*'s man at the match who wrote that "no one I have met in Auckland has held Lever in any way to blame for what happened", to my own that Lever's was a calculated act to take unreasonable advantage of a bowler's inability to bat.

In their efforts to keep such bowling within bounds, the authorities are thinking for the moment more in terms of persuasion than legislation. Any proposal for a change in the law would, in any case, have to await the next meeting of the International Cricket Conference, which is not to be held until the end of June. Pakistan have cabled Lord's asking for this meeting to be brought forward so that what is an urgent matter can be discussed before, rather than after, the World Cup.

The law as it stands ("The persistent bowling of fast short-pitched balls is unfair if in the opinion of the umpire at the bowler's end it constitutes a systematic attempt at intimidation") lends itself to too casual an interpretation. When, for example, does an "attempt at intimidation" become systematic? And when does "persistent" become persistent? For the sake of an easier definition, would it not be better to say simply, that "the bowling of fast short-pitched balls is unfair if in the opinion of either umpire it constitutes dangerous play"?

Specifying the number of bouncers to be bowled at each batsman according to his position and the order is altogether too cold-blooded. Neither, as we saw in Australia, is it practicable. How many, if you like, do you assign Walker, who, although he batted at number eight for Australia, and is primarily a bowler, averaged nearly 50 in the Test matches?

As for a line drawn across the pitch, who is going to watch it, unless (heaven forbid!) a kind of service-court judge is brought into the action? It would be asking too much of the bowler's umpire, with all he already has to do, to decide which side of the line each ball pitched. In the case of the square leg umpire, he is at too wide an angle and too far away to make a hairline judgment.

Baseball went a part of the way towards solving a related problem by making the wearing of helmets compulsory for the striker. It is also accepted as being morally wrong for a pitcher to aim at the striker. Although at baseball the ball is hurled at a faster speed than at cricket, and over a shorter distance, only one striker has ever been killed. Helmets, no doubt, have had something to do with this, though if they were to be worn for playing cricket, they would probably lead to more reckless bowling than there already is.

In seeking to make the game less hazardous, it is crucially important not to drive fast bowlers out of it. Some of the most thrilling innings ever played have been against bowlers bowling both fast and short. There are batsmen (but not bowlers) playing today who, with their eye in, would give a guinea a time for Lever's bouncers; just as there are thousands of people in England who are counting the days to the time when they can go and see for themselves just how fearsome Thomson and Lillee are. If, in the meantime, they were to hear that the bouncer had been banned, they might change their minds about going. "Have you got another Larwood, Bill?" asked the secretary of the Australian Board of Control of Bill Bowes, when he landed in Australia just after the war, "because if you have the grounds won't be large enough". This winter, on one or two occasions, they hardly were, because of Thomson and Lillee.

Should it be thought that we are getting soft in our old age, Mr. Bowes makes some relevant comparisons between the bodyline tour, on which he went as a player, and last winter's tour, snatches of which he watched on television. Although not liking to see the lack of mettle shown by some of England's present batsmen, he believes they had more to contend with than the Australians did in 1932-33 from Larwood, Voce and Allen. For one thing, the lbw law, as it applied then, made batting easier than it does now. You could only be out when the ball pitched between wicket and wicket, which meant that you needed to play nothing that was wide of the stumps. Today you can be leg before to a ball pitching outside the off stump.

More contentiously Mr. Bowes insists that Larwood never aimed to hit the Australian batsmen, which Lillee ("I bowl bouncers for one reason, and that is to hit the batsman and thus intimidate him") and Thomson both do, and which Lever ("I wanted to get him caught off the glove") did to someone whose highest first-class score was eight. This is what Mr. Bowes finds so horrifying: that there should be at large bowlers whose aim it is to hit the batsman. Some Australians, not surprisingly, would say that Larwood did. It was because of him, after all, that the word "intimidation" appeared in the laws. Now, because of Chatfield, the game's conscience is being troubled again – the conscience not least of the captains and the managers, for if the umpires are undecided what is fair, you can be sure the players are not.

Why Chinese Will Not Play Politics with Cricket

FROM RICHARD HUGHES

2 *April* 1975; *Hongkong*, 1 *April*. Harold Larwood, D. R. Jardine's incomparable bodyline Test bowler, will be specially invited to bowl a nostalgic over at the historic match which will finally draw stumps at the century-old Hongkong Cricket Club this year. Larwood, now an Australian businessman, who lives in Sydney but prefers to watch Tests from "the Hill" rather than the Sydney Cricket Club members' stand, has accepted an invitation to attend the requiem ceremonies at the colony's original cricket club.

Officially, he will be included in the "non-playing" guest-list, together with notable Australian Test veterans: Bert Oldfield, Lindsay Hassett, Bill O'Reilly and Bill Brown. But it is predicted that not only Larwood but also Oldfield, Hassett and O'Reilly will be asked to appear for a symbolic one-over appearance in their old roles as wicket-keeper, batsman and slow bowler.

The invited guests of the "playing" contingent of former Australian Test players will include: Neil Harvey, Bobby Simpson, Ian Craig, Alan Davidson, Jim Burke, Ron Archer, Ray Lindwall, Rod Marsh, Les Favell, Keith Stackpole, Ian Meckiff and Ian Johnson.

After this memorable final match, the old club will be moved from its honourable site in the congested heart of the colony to a cleared wasteland halfway up the Peak. On present plans, the old site will become a public park, topping one of the central underground stations on Hongkong's projected mass transit system. Sceptics are already suggesting however, that the land areas is too valuable to be preserved indefinitely as a park and that the site will inevitably become another skyscraper office complex, overshadowing both the adjacent Hongkong Club and the Communist People's Bank of China.

The ancient ground will certainly be crowded to standing accommodation to see the immortal Test veterans in action once more. There are unofficial hopes that one of the invited Australian batsmen may finally achieve the unique distinction of breaking a window of the towering People's Bank across the road with a six and thereby win the legendary but still unclaimed prize of a case of champagne.

One of the several urbane officials of the Communist bank who occasionally stroll into the cricket club to watch the curious foreign-devil game of cricket has said privately that no party protest would be made if a six did break a window of the bank. "Our ping pong balls have occasionally struck friendly foreigners watching our players in action abroad", he pointed out. "We well understand the rules and traditions of good sportsmanship,which have nothing to do with differing views on politics or ideology."

Pavilion Sale

3 *June* 1975. Lowdham Cricket Club, near Nottingham, has had to sell its pavilion because of a £36 rates demand. The building, which cost £225 seven years ago and had no services, fetched £25.

Sri Lanka Prospects Please until Thomson Injures Two Batsmen

BY ALAN GIBSON

12 *June* 1975. I was having a drink with this beautiful girl from Ceylon. It was rather a lot of years ago, perhaps it would be unchivalrous to say how many. She is now a famous broadcaster in her country. I had just begun as a cricket commentator. "One day", she said, "you will broadcast upon England against Ceylon at Lord's." We had another beer on the prospect. It was an evening when every prospect pleased, and the spicy breezes blew soft o'er

Ceylon's isle. "But", she went on to say, her golden eyes hardening, "when you do, you are to be kind to Ceylon."

Well, I have not yet seen Ceylon play England at Lord's, but I saw Sri Lanka – as they are now called – play Australia at the Oval yesterday, something which would have seemed even more improbable those years ago. As to being kind, there is no difficulty. They played extremely well, they batted better than they bowled, and their fielding varied between brilliance and wildness. Nevertheless, at one stage they had the mighty Australians worried, almost fumbling. Consider, Australia were 178 for no wicket in 34 overs at lunch, and went on to make 328 for five. All we expected of Sri Lanka was that they would do their best to bat it out and gain experience. But in the 32nd over they had scored 150, and lost only two wickets. Mendis and Wettimuny were going so well that anything seemed possible.

At this point Thomson laid Mendis out. It was not strictly a bouncer, but a short ball, aimed at the body. Thomson hit the batsman on several other occasions with similar balls. He was booed by the crowd, alike by those from the Indian subcontinent and those forthright souls from the Elephant and Castle. It will not, I am afraid, be a pleasant occasion when Australia meet West Indies.

Mendis was carried off, and in Thomson's next over so was Wettimuny, who had had several bangs on the legs and midriff. He limped most of the way, but had to be picked up before he reached the Pavilion. They were both taken to hospital for treatment. With two new batsmen needing to play themselves in, Sri Lanka could not keep up the scoring rate. Thus vanished their hopes, but not their bravery. They did not duck or dodge the fast bowling. They kept playing strokes: glances and cuts are what they do best. They will beat Australia one day.

Perhaps they were wrong to put Australia in, on a fast and true pitch. I suppose after their last experience they were afraid of an attack of early nerves, a sudden, irretrievable breakdown. They certainly played better as the day went on. They were not helped in the morning by an invasion of the field by some young supporters who were, I understand, protesting against the selection of their side.

Sri Lanka's 276 for four was the highest score made in the second innings of a Prudential Cup match: not that that breaks any long-standing records, but it was done against Australia and their dreaded attack. Although Australia dropped some catches, they were not fooling about. The man of the match, Laurie Fishlock decided, was Turner, whose innings we had almost forgotten in the flux of events. Not that he did not deserve it. The woman of the match was a golden-eyed girl from Ceylon who prophesied long ago.

AUSTRALIA 328 for 5 (60 overs) (A. Turner 101, K. D. Walters 59, G. S. Chappell 50)

SRI LANKA 276 for 4 (60 overs) (S. Wettimuny 63 ret hurt, M. H. Tissera 52, A. Tenekoon 48)

Australia won by 52 runs

The Great Day when London was Lloyd's

BY JOHN WOODCOCK, CRICKET CORRESPONDENT

23 *June* 1975. By the time the curtain calls had ended at Lord's on Saturday it was 9 o'clock. By the time the last of the speeches had been made, and the last of the lights put out, it was past midnight. As much as a cricket match, the final of the World Cup for the Prudential trophy, won by West Indies by 17 runs, had been a piece of theatre; of drama, tragedy, carnival and farce all rolled into one.

Already a great enterprise, the tournament ended as a great success. We shall know later this week where and when it is to be staged next. It went so well this time that it could even be in England again. As the most compact and cosmopolitan of the cricketing countries it makes in many ways the ideal setting, especially when the weather is as it has been for the past fortnight. Saturday was as beautiful a day as any there had been, and as eventful.

Worthy and colourful champions as the West Indians are, Australia will be kicking themselves for the blunders they made. Of these, perhaps the most expensive was the missing of Clive Lloyd when he was 26. Had Edwards, at short midwicket, held the low catch which Lloyd offered, as he would have done more often than not, West Indies would have been 83 for four with little chance of making as many as they did. There is no better Australian fielder than Edwards, either. Then, when Australia batted, needing 292 to win, they made a succession of irredeemable mistakes between the wickets. If either side was to be let down by errors of excitement I had thought it would be West Indies, not Australia.

Although Australia will be criticized for putting West Indies in I am not sure that that is fair. If at any time in the match the pitch held something for the bowlers it was during the morning, while there was still a little damp about; and the risk that Australia were taking of batting themselves in fading light was lessened by a cloudless forecast. In the event, as Thomson and Lillee showed in a last wicket partnership of 41, the ball could be picked up perfectly well, even at the end of the day.

But this is far enough to have gone without mentioning an innings of 102 by Clive Lloyd, which will always be talked about by those who watched it. To dwarf so many of the world's leading batsmen, as Lloyd did, was of itself the mark of greatness. Physically, and in terms of cricketing authority, he towered above the rest. He was larger than life. To have such gifts of height and power and timing is one thing; to use them at a time like this is another. Lloyd made the pitch and the stumps and the bowlers and the ground all seem much smaller than they were.

It was possible, because of the game that Lloyd played, for Kanhai to go from the twenty-third over of the West Indian innings to the thirty-fourth without scoring a run and yet do a service for his side. Kanhai cut loose eventually, when the crisis of 50 for three was safely passed. Boyce, turning three somersaults when he tripped over where one would have done, made a whirlwind 34, Julien a useful 26; and in the penultimate over even Murray hooked Lillee for six.

Yet Australia would have won, I think, had they not kept running themselves out. It was a supremely easy pitch by now, and a fast outfield, and when they reached 80 for one after 20 overs they had made just the start they needed. If the target was still far distant the ease with which Turner and his captain were batting, and with which others batted after them, showed what might have been, but for three fatal hesitations and the deadly aim of Vivian Richards. Turner and the Chappell brothers were all run out by Richards; each time when the single would have been safe, albeit narrowly, had the batsmen not wavered.

At 167 for three, with Ian Chappell and Walters together and 21 overs left and the West Indians worried, it remained an open match. At 233 for nine, after 53 overs, only Thomson and Lillee thought Australia still had a chance. With no pretence at style these two made us wonder whether the last twist of an enthralling game was to be the most dramatic. For 40 minutes the thousands of West Indians ringed the boundary, rocking, rolling, shouting, clanging, as they waited their victory to proclaim.

Standing on their balcony the Australians felt their hopes returning. Once, when Fredericks caught Lillee, off a no-ball, the floodgates burst, the crowd pouring across the grass as Fredericks's throw at the bowler's stumps, an attempt to run out Thomson, disappeared among them. By the time the field was cleared and the ball recovered, and the umpires had decided how many runs had been run there were three overs left and 21 were needed. When, at last, Murray ran out Thomson, bowling the ball at the stumps as Thomson, the striker, made a despairing dive for safety after being sent back by Lillee, we had had all that we could stand. Players, stewards, barmen and watchers had reached the end of their tether. So, too, had Thomson, when he emerged from an encircling horde of West Indians, without gloves and bat and sweater, perhaps, for all I know, without his box. As a seasoned surfer this was the worst dumping he can have had.

There it was then: West Indies were the champions, Australia the gallant losers, cricket the deserving winner. Whether, as the match went on, Prince Philip rang his home to ask for his supper to be put in the oven I wouldn't know, but it was not a match to leave. The cup and the award as Man of the Match he presented to Clive Lloyd, the hero of he day, the toast of every West Indian island from Camberwell to the Caribbean.

In 119 overs there had not been one of spin, which was more than sad; in all the excitement there had been several dropped catches. Of fast bowling which took the breath away there had been surprisingly little. Yet as a production to remember it was, as the sponsors themselves might put it, an "assured" success.

WEST INDIES 291 for 8 (60 overs) (C. H. Lloyd 102, R. B. Kanhai 55; G. J. Gilmour 5 for 48)
AUSTRALIA 274 (58.4 overs) (I. M. Chappell 62, A. Turner 40; K. D. Boyce 4 for 50)
West Indies won by 17 runs

Naked Runner is Fined £20

6 *August* 1975. Michael Angelow, who ran naked across Lord's cricket ground on Monday, was fined £20 when he appeared at Marylebone Magistrates' Court, yesterday.

Mr. Angelow, aged 24, a merchant seaman, of St. Albans, Hertfordshire, admitted insulting behaviour. When told that the escapade was for a £20 bet, Lieutenant-Colonel William Haswell, chairman of the bench, said: "The court will have that £20; please moderate your behaviour in future."

England Women Dispel Flippancy and the Australian Challenge

BY ALAN GIBSON

5 *August* 1976. The notices were still there on the pavilion doors: "The attention of all members of MCC, and Middlesex, their guests and visitors, is drawn to the conditions contained in regulation 3 (v) of the regulations of MCC which require them to wear a necktie and jacket whilst in the pavilion."

Regulation 3 (v) has never taken such a battering as it did yesterday. The doorkeepers turned their eyes away as the skirts whisked up to the dressing rooms. For this, as you will already know – it is not Rachael Flint's fault if you do not – was the first time the women had taken over Lord's. The editor of *The Cricketer* told me he had raced to the ground to be sure of seeing the first ball bowled. Not many others had. Only a few hundred were there at the start, and when Australia lost a wicket to the second ball, the noise was rather less than it will be if the same thing happens in the men's match next year. But, as a sunny afternoon drew on, more and more people came along until there was a larger crowd than Middlesex often get.

They saw Australia all out, for 161. When nine wickets were down for 127, it looked as if they would score less, but a last wicket stand gave them something to bowl at, and prolonged the innings to the sixtieth, and in any case last, over. Marie Lutschini batted very well in this stand, as Sharon Tredrea had done earlier. It cannot have been often that players of Italian and

Cornish extraction (as I presume these two to be) have made so big a contribution to an innings at Lord's.

I have never thought cricket a particularly suitable game for girls to play – I mean, I shall not grieve if my daughter Felicity does not take it up – but if they wish to, they should be encouraged by fellow-cricketers, not patronized or snubbed. I am glad Lord's has opened its door to them, in the jubilee year of the Women's Cricket Association.

In my student days, I played often against and with women's teams. Some of these matches were quite serious. Westfield College, for instance, were not a side you could take chances with. The batting of the women then was much better than their bowling. They could catch, and field smartly on the ground, but their throwing was poor, and I do not mean just through lack of physique.

Watching the cream of the game yesterday (I use the metaphor advisedly: they were playing for the St. Ivel Cream Jug) I thought that they still batted better than they bowled. They would score runs against a county, but it would take them a long time to get one out. The throwing, however, especially the Australian throwing, has improved vastly.

I dislike some of the W.C.A. publicity, those giggly bits about leg-glances, etc. I was disappointed at some of the antics at the fall of a wicket, like so many huge, hairy footballers (Australia were less emotional than England). They do not do themselves justice by these things. But I see their difficulties. They feel they must not spurn any chance of publicity.

Women's cricket, for all its well-established international pattern (England first toured Australia in 1934, and Australia returned the visit three years later) rests on a small numerical base. In 1970, Rowland Bowen estimated that one woman cricketer in a hundred plays for England, whereas the figure for men would be nearer one in a hundred thousand. Things have improved since then, but not by much.

Flippancy dropped away from the crowd, though, as England set out to get the runs. They were given a good start by two famous players, Enid Bakewell and Lynne Thomas. Thomas was caught at mid-on in the 38th over, Bakewell run out in the 41st. The score was then 93 for 2, with two new batswomen to play themselves in.

Chris Watmough, a Lancastrian, who now plays for Kent, and her captain, the pride of Wolverhampton, saw them through, amid genuine enthusiasm, with three overs to spare. Australia, however, took the St. Ivel Jug, because they had won at Canterbury on Sunday, and had a faster scoring rate over the two matches combined. So everyone had something to celebrate.

AUSTRALIA 161 (59.4 overs) (S. A. Tredrea 54)
ENGLAND 162 for 2 (56.2 overs) (C. Watmough 50 not out)
England won by 8 wickets

A Dish to Set before the Queen

FROM COLIN COWDREY

18 *March* 1977; *Melbourne*, 17 *March*. As the light began to fade after five gloriously sunny days of enthralling cricket, Knott was dismissed by Lillee, his fifth wicket and eleventh in the match, and Australia had won the centenary Test match by 45 runs.

By some coincidence, on March 17, 1877, a hundred years to the day, England were set a target of 154 and also lost by 45 runs. Today it was a stiffer task. In scoring 417, England achieved the highest total in the fourth innings of an Anglo-Australian Test match and in doing so have won all hearts.

The last day began with England left to score just 272 to win – 90 in each session, a task by no means beyond them on the slow, easy paced pitch. Provided that the early overs were negotiated safely only the clock might have presented a problem. As the ball becomes softer and the outfield is slow here a batting side can so easily get bogged down. So it was important that they did not lag behind and at lunchtime they were well in contention.

The first hour was fascinating, for Chappell had a problem. With Gilmour injured, Lillee was the trump card. He had to be thrown in to the fray to make the early break, if possible, but the new ball was available in 12 overs. O'Keeffe bowled tidily and took two vital wickets later on. Walker, faced with the prospect of some marathon spells later in the day, was discarded temporarily.

Needing just 13 for his first Test hundred, Randall was confronted with a burst from Lillee. If he was nervous he showed no trace of it. Brearley had provided the helpful word early in his innings and now he was fortunate to have the steadying influence of Amiss at the other end. In the event he played quite superbly, a deft sweep, a glorious late cut and he was soon on 99, facing Lillee. Next ball he tucked him away to fine leg for his first Test hundred and became the fourteenth batsman to score a hundred in his first Test match against Australia. The Yorkshireman, Willie Watson, was the last to do so in 1953.

I was delighted for him after his rigours in India where his previous best in a Test match had been 37, but he had made a huge contribution to the team's success by his enthusiasm. It would have been understandable if he had shown the odd lapse of concentration in the excitement of his achievement but he just played better and better as he went along. He is something of an irrepressible Jack-in-the-box both in batting and fielding but today he assumed a responsibility to fit the occasion. His timing never left him; only fatigue slowed him down and, in part, contributed to his downfall.

All the while Amiss looked a class player with plenty of time. He seems to have the broadest bat in English cricket today and Lillee did not unruffle him as much as I expected. His sudden dismissal by a ball that kept rather low was the turning point of the day. True, that while Greig and Randall were together we could still have won but somehow I had the feeling that we were beginning to live too dangerously.

When Randall made 161 he edged Greg Chappell low and wide where Marsh appeared to have scooped his glove under the catch. As he rolled over and over the umpire upheld the appeal and Randall departed a disconsolate figure. Without delay Marsh leapt to his feet and rushed down the wicket to tell his captain that the ball had bounced. The umpires conferred and Randall was recalled. It was indeed a chivalrous gesture at such a critical moment of the match.

Just before tea England were slowed down by some good bowling from Chappell himself and he elected to gamble with O'Keeffe. In his first over, Cosier dived full length to take a magnificent catch off bat and pad and Randall's historic innings had closed on 174. The whole ground rose to him.

Through the tears of joy he went out through the wrong gate, finding himself at the end of the path leading to the special box where the Queen and the Duke of Edinburgh were sitting. Within a few yards of them he discovered his mistake and stopped in his tracks and, much to the amusement of all, bowed before beating a hasty retreat across the public seats. It was a happy touch for the day had belonged to him.

It might be arguable that Lillee's great bowling could have earned him the prize of Man of the Match, but without doubt Randall was the man who had made the match complete. There were not four gladder hearts in Melbourne today than Larwood, Voce, Hardstaff and Simpson, giant names from Trent Bridge.

If the game tilted fairly sharply towards Australia after tea Knott made it clear that they were not going to have it all their own way. He played a series of astonishing shots, treating Lillee with utter contempt. He is a genius of improvisation.

But the day finished with Lillee summoning up energy and fire from I do not know where. He was bowling faster at the end than he was at the beginning and deservedly he was carried aloft, first by players and then by some of his ecstatic countrymen, while a dozen or more policemen surrounded him to keep him intact.

But alas, his medical advisers have determined that he is not quite intact although you could never have guessed it today. Sadly for the English pubic but to the relief of the English batsmen, he has withdrawn from the forthcoming tour of England.

We have had a remarkable week and life will be rather flat until we have had time to absorb it all. I do not know when I have enjoyed the last day of a Test match more than this one. It had everything, both captains playing their part in the challenge, both wicketkeepers making their mark, some wonderful fast bowling, good sustained spells of leg spin bowling, some fine fielding, a generous gesture and a large crowd. The result was open until near the end. When Randall and Greig were raking the embers just before tea there was still the prospect of an English victory. What a dish it was to set before the Queen.

AUSTRALIA 138 (G. S. Chappell 40) and 419 for 9 dec (R. W. Marsh 110 not out, I. C. Davis 68; C. M. Old 4 for 104)
ENGLAND 95 (D. K. Lillee 6 for 26, M. H. N. Walker 4 for 54) and 417 (D. W. Randall 174, D. L. Amiss 64, A. P. E. Knott 42, A. W. Greig 41; D. K. Lillee 5 for 139)
Australia won by 45 runs

---

11 *May* 1977, *Personal Column.* In affectionate remembrance of International Cricket which died at Hove, 9th May, 1977. Deeply lamented by a large circle of friends, and acquaintances. R.I.P.   N.B. The body will be cremated and The Ashes taken to Australia and scattered around the studio of TCN9 Sydney. NTJCBM.

Tony Greig Dismissed as England Captain

BY JOHN WOODCOCK, CRICKET CORRESPONDENT

14 *May* 1977. Tony Greig has been deprived of the England Test captaincy. Meeting at Lord's yesterday, the emergency committee of the Cricket Council announced that they would be instructing Alec Bedser, the chairman of the selectors that "Tony Greig is not to be considered for the position [captaincy of England] for the forthcoming series against Australia".

The committee said that, in reaching this decision, they had taken into consideration "the current England captain's clearly admitted involvement, unknown to the authorities, in recruitment of the players for an organization which has been set up in conflict with a scheduled series of Test matches. His action has inevitably impaired the trust which existed between the cricket authorities and the captain of the England side." The committee were referring to a projected series between Australia and a world eleven in Australia next winter, under a contract with Mr. Kerry Packer, a television proprietor.

Freddie Brown, chairman of the Cricket Council, added: "The captaincy of the England team involves liaison with the selectors in the management, selection and development of England players for the future, and clearly Tony Greig is unlikely to be able to do this as his stated intention is to be contracted elsewhere during the next three winters."

Yesterday's decision, besides being a great personal disappointment to Greig, is bound, to some extent, to be a setback to the recovery which the

England team launched with some success in India last winter. Disloyalty, though, such as that shown by Greig in involving himself and two more of England's leading players, Knott and Underwood, in a scheme which drastically reduces their availability for England, deserves what punishment it gets.

However plausibly Greig may claim that what he is doing is for the good of English cricket, however unselfish an act he may say it is, however truculently he may express the hope that the authorities at Lord's will be "sensible" in how they react to the Packer circus, no one is likely to be convinced that he has acted less than miserably as the reigning captain.

Like Knott and Underwood, Greig can play for England in the coming series – unless the International Cricket Conference, who may be convened within the next fortnight (their annual meeting is not due until July 26), should rule that any one who has already signed for Packer has, by doing so, excluded himself from official Test cricket. As the Packer party include most of the Australian team currently touring England and the Australian manager has said that no sanctions will be imposed on any of them for the duration of their tour, what action the ICC decide on is unlikely to take effect until the Australian tour is over.

There have been various occasions since he became an England cricketer when Greig has overplayed his hand. The most famous, or infamous, was at Port of Spain in 1975, when he ran out Kallicharran as he was making off to the pavilion after the last ball of a day's play. There was always this danger that, for some reason or other, his impulsiveness, or his commercialism, or the strangely insensitive streak which exists within a normally charming and considerate person might be his undoing.

What has to be remembered, of course, is that he is an Englishman not by birth or upbringing, but only by adoption. It is not the same thing as being English through and through. At the same time, I do believe that making the England team into a winning one has meant a great deal to him. There was a lot of truth in what he had to say after the Melbourne Test match about the strength of his team's team spirit.

For this reason, whoever is appointed to succeed Greig will have a difficult job. Within moments of being informed of the Cricket Council's decision, the England selectors met at the other end of the Lord's pavilion to decide where to go from here. The favourite for the captaincy must be Michael Brearley, of Middlesex, who was Greig's understudy in India. Like everyone else, he was rather dwarfed by Greig out there. But he is liked and respected by the players and he will almost certainly get into the England side on merit. Tactically, too, he is Greig's superior, which is not to say that he will make a better captain. Greig's aggressiveness and his fearless example on the field will be hard to replace.

There is no intention at present of asking Mr. Packer to come to England, or of requesting Mr. Bob Parish, chairman of the Australian Cricket Board, to see Mr. Packer before he himself flies over. One of the ironies of the whole affair is that it is with Mr. Packer's company that the Test and County Cricket Board signed a contract for £150,000 for the Australian television rights of this summer's fight for the Ashes. Mr. Packer's offer was preferred to the Australian Broadcasting Commission's which is the establishment of Australian broadcasting.

If, when they meet, the member countries of the ICC decide that no one shall be considered for his country while giving priority to the cause of Mr. Packer, Australia, West Indies and Pakistan, as well as England, are all going to have a lot of rebuilding to do. I hope yet that some compromise may be reached. It should be possible. It might even have happened already, and saved Greig his job, had his own part in a month of negotiations not smacked of concealment.

Referring to the payment which the England players will receive for playing in a Test match this summer, against Australia (£210), Mr. Peter Lush, speaking after yesterday's meeting, said that it was realized how inadequate it was. When the present pay restraints are lifted it will improve. As it is, the two sides this summer will be playing for prize money of approximately £20,000 – less than Mr. Packer would put at stake, but a great deal more than any one has ever before had the opportunity to win.

A Victory to Celebrate Jubilee Year

16 *August* 1977, *Leading Article*. Our new national obsession with the antics of the antipodean television tycoon can for a while, be laid aside for happier thoughts. England has won a mightily convincing and historic victory. What more fitting Jubilee event can there be than the recovery of the Ashes in this country for only the third time this century – the feat last being performed in 1953, the year of her Majesty's coronation, and before that in 1926? It was even longer ago, in 1886, that England last won three consecutive Test matches against the traditional foe in a home series, although they have done it several times in Australia.

It was little more than two years ago that the English side returned from their Australian tour, thoroughly beaten, dispirited and demoralized. A decade of Australian supremacy was predicted. That the tables have been so completely turned lies largely to the credit of Greig. He took over a side being compared with the very worst in England's cricketing history, made its members believe in their individual and collective abilities, and by his own flamboyant, perhaps over-aggressive example instilled confidence into a team that had become accustomed to losing. In particular, his insistence on the importance of good fielding has paid handsome dividends. The superb athleticism and sticky fingers of the English side contributed in large measure to its success.

It is not disparaging to the virtually flawless captaincy of Brearley to say that he inherited a side already filled with the enthusiasm and motivation to perform splendid feats. He took over, nevertheless, at an unsettled time in less than happy circumstances, and, with great tactical perception, went on to lead England's team to comprehensive victories in three matches. That makes him a very good captain indeed.

The dominant memory of the Test series will undoubtedly be of Boycott, returned like some banished prince to assume his birthright, bestriding the narrow crease like a Hutton, suspending belief in the possibility that his wicket, too, could fall like that of mere cricketers. But Boycott is already of a certain age. In the longer term, the youth of all but a few members of the team and the sudden embarrassment of talent among even younger players promise well for the future of English cricket.

There are those of little faith who say that the Australian team was the weakest ever sent to these shores, and that they were worried by the unmentionable commercial activities that have formed a backdrop to the season (why then did Greig, Knott and Underwood not suffer?). Why entertain such quibbles? England have achieved a magnificent victory. The Ashes are back. It is a time for every Englishman to feel proud.

America Wins its First Cricket Match

FROM MICHAEL LEAPMAN

5 *September* 1977; *New York, 4 September*. The Americans beat the West Indians yesterday on what the stadium announcer, with characteristic hyperbole, called the playing field of history. Yet you could not gainsay him, for according to the promoters it was the first professional cricket match ever staged in the United States.

It was played in a vast bowl-like arena, on artificial turf, under floodlights for the last 90 minutes and with an electronic scoreboard which provided instant replays and at the dramatic highlights of the game, would flash out phrases like: "Ouch!" "Did you see that", "Give 'em a hand, fans".

In spite of such blatant differences from Kennington Oval, it remained recognizably cricket. When Sir Gary Sobers was bouncing his cover drives off the bright blue boundary fence, it was cricket of a vintage kind.

The game attracted a crowd of 6,674, rather above the average for a weekend one-day county game in Britain. Nearly all were West Indians, and they had paid between $6 (£3.50) and $10 for their tickets. If you tell the organizers that this is a modest start for a sport they hope will sweep the country, they wag their fingers and say, "Yes, but what about soccer?"

The success of soccer is the big sports story in the United States just now. The New York Cosmos, champions of the season which has just finished (as, with a team that includes Pele and Beckenbauer, they should be), drew a capacity crowd of 76,500 for their last home game.

The local equivalent of the F.A. Cup was televised nationally. Soccer is being played at more and more schools and colleges. Yet only a few years ago it was hard to persuade anyone but a few homesick Europeans to watch. "Who would have thought," asked one of the backers of yesterday's cricket, "that 77,000 people would turn out to see guys in short pants bounce a ball off their heads."

The cricket match was played at the Cosmos home stadium, part of the new Meadowlands sports complex in New Jersey, just four miles from Manhattan. It is also the home of the New York Giants, who play American football. The wicket was marked out amid the numbered lines used in American football to calculate yardage gained. Because stumps cannot be poked into artificial turf, they were fixed to a wooden platform which was made fast to the surface. I could tell it was going to be a Caribbean crowd as soon as I stepped on to the bus at the Eighth Avenue terminal. My family and I were the only white people on it, apart from the driver. As we arrived at the stadium women were parading round the arena bearing placards with the names of the countries from which the players hailed. Each player was introduced individually to the spectators, waving as his name was announced.

The American side batted first, and the first ball bowled for money in America was a sensational one. Wes Hall, the formerly redoubtable but now balding fast bowler, delivered it to Peter Merritt, an Englishman who opens the batting for Staten Island, and of whom the programme note said that he "represented the United States in Bermuda with fair success". I thought this a rather uncertain recommendation and so it proved. Hall's first ball sent the bails flying and the electronic scoreboard went beserk. "Did you see that?" it asked. (In Merritt's case the answer was clearly "No".) "Give that man a hand"; and there appeared an animated picture of two hands clapping.

Yet the American side (itself composed mainly of West Indians) improved after that blow. Charlie Griffith, Hall's old partner, was ineffective, and Lance Gibbs was the only bowler who had consistently to be treated with respect. The ball bounced high on the artificial surface, but at no great pace.

As the innings progressed the Americans took advantage of the tiring and aging attack and at the end of their allotted 40 overs had scored 194 for eight.

The tea interval was unduly prolonged because the steel band due to perform in it took more than half an hour to set up their equipment. After an interval of an hour and a quarter the players and umpires had to take the field to persuade Lord Observer, the improvisation king of calypso, to leave it.

The Americans, a much younger side than the West Indians, bowled and fielded with enthusiasm and had soon sent back to the pavilion (or rather to the dugout below the stands) such eminent players from the past as Roy Fredericks, Lawrence Rowe and Seymour Nurse. They spent an embarrassingly short time "at bat", in the baseball parlance which the scoreboard was using to describe the action.

The scoreboard, and the commentator who was giving a ball-by-ball account of the game over the loudspeaker system for those unfamiliar with its mysteries, reserved their greatest enthusiasm for Sobers. "Sir Gary" was the message passed in electronic letters. "Fantastic" and "Attack" were flashed out as he stroked his fours and sixes.

It would have been a terrible anti-climax had he been out cheaply, but he was the highest scorer with 57, although limping badly. Apart from David Holford nobody else did much, and the West Indians were out for 170.

It was all very different from the county ground at Weston-super-Mare on a damp Tuesday.

On the debit side, there was nothing of cricket's bucolic tradition, unless you count the vaguely unpleasant smell drifting in from a sewage plant nearby.

The man behind the event was Bert Smith, a West Indian photographer, who managed to get the sponsorship of an airline, using the argument that if it had happened to soccer, why not to cricket?

But there were precious few genuine Americans there yesterday and whether it will catch on like soccer has I would not be so bold as to predict. It is, as they say in these parts, a whole new ball game.

Echoes of a Month-long Hearing in the High Court

9 *November* 1977.

The alacrity with which they [the players] joined was frightening – *Kerry Packer*

They want the penny and the bun – *Geoffrey Boycott*

I've heard the only way to get out of a Packer contract is by becoming pregnant – *Raymond Steele* (Australia)

Bob Taylor is one of the best wicketkeepers the world has ever seen – *Alan Knott*

Alan Knott is the best wicketkeeper in the world – *Boycott*

Cricketers [at the Cricketers' Association meeting] thought that if we got rid of a few more [overseas players] it would be nice – *Tony Greig*

We're not a philanthropic organization – *Packer*

The ban is a disservice to cricket – *Asif Iqbal*

The presence of Greig, Knott and Underwood would have been a great help to bring the crowds along – *Walter Hadlee* (New Zealand), referring to this winter's England tour

Mr. Packer waved a big stick – *Steele*

I don't think John Arlott is very knowledgeable on the game of cricket – *Jack Bailey*, ICC secretary

I'm always open to offers – *Boycott*

We were very anxious, indeed still are anxious, to avoid an horrific situation – *Douglas Insole*, TCCB chairman

The moment that one of my players is banned is the moment you have me for an enemy – *Packer*

There's a little bit of a whore in all of us – *Packer*

It's England first, last and all the time so far as I'm concerned – *Greig*, confirming an earlier newspaper interview.

The press get it right, the press get it wrong – *Greig*

It's degrading to have to virtually beg for benefits – *Michael Procter*

No one has to have a benefit – *Boycott*

We are the poor relations of world sport – *Greig*

". . . makes the language boggle" – *Robert Alexander, QC*

I'm a press man's dream – *Greig*

Gloucestershire want me to go on playing – *Procter*

I'm not a legal expert – *Derek Underwood*

I'm sure you [Underwood] are far better off being a cricketer – *Andrew Morritt, QC*

They thought they could have the best of both worlds – *Steele*

Pandora's chest – *Bailey*

A more severe ban is justified – *Boycott*

Tests are not built in a day – *Mutthian Chidambaram* (India)

We were prepared to fly our players home from Pakistan and fly them out to New Zealand six weeks later – *Insole*, discussing a possible compromise

I admire umpires – *Greig*

I've had nightmares about it – *John Snow*, on the prospect of becoming an umpire

I suggest they [the TCCB] are being dishonest – *Packer*

Unfortunately the Cricketers' Association is looked on as something of a joke – *Snow*

I would say the Cricketers' Association exists full stop – *Procter*, invited to say what the Cricketers' Association existed for

It [Test match revenue] goes to the counties, where it's to a large part wasted – *Snow*

I suppose I was a bit young and naive at the time and I let them [*Sunday Mirror* journalists] in – *Knott*

Australian players tend to pop out of holes in the ground when the opportunity's there – *Ross Edwards*, Australian cricketer

They [Australian cricketers] seem to come out in their thousands when they're knocking hell out of the Poms – *Boycott*

Thank heavens I don't have that prospect – *Edwards*, asked what happened if a batsman faced Dennis Lillee and got injured.

The next game could be your last. If you're playing against Lillee and he smashes your elbow you'll never play again – *Knott*

I didn't trust the Australian Cricket Board, and I don't trust them – *Packer*

They [the authorities] have undersold the game – *Greig*

I said there'd be a strike or something like this [the Packer series] – *Snow*

The tour [England to Pakistan this winter] is very doubtful because of the political situation – *Asif Iqbal*

World Series Cricket is essentially parasitic in its nature – *Michael Kempster, QC*

Test matches are vital to our survival financially – *Hadlee*

They [the TCCB] were trying to white-ant us – *Packer*, using an Australian expression derived from an insect that bores into wood and leaves the shell intact

Someone's white-anted my copy – *Mr Justice Slade*, examining a document in evidence

The establishment could benefit from a jolly good shake-up – *Greig*

The TCCB are not as dishonourable as the Australian Cricket Board – *Packer*

It's very depressing to go into a ground with 400 spectators – *Greig*, referring to county championship cricket

I'm not sure the British public would want four-day matches – *Boycott*

You have to play enough cricket to satisfy 13,000 members at 12 guineas – *Boycott*, arguing that the county championship should not be reduced to 16 matches a county

I would deny that absolutely – *Insole*, asked if the Australian Cricket Board were opposed to any compromise with Mr Packer

Ghulam Ahmed said "Soon there'd be 10 Mr Packers on the scene" – *Chidambaram*

Procter is one of the casualties of the battle – *Peter Short* (West Indies)

Being available to go to cocktail parties – *Greig*, explaining the work involved in earning the free use of a car

They [the Australian Cricket Board] were telling me untruths – *Packer*

"You're men of honour" – *Steele*, quoting Mr. Packer's reference to the ACB television negotiating sub-committee.

Give them the opportunity to draw back from the brink – *Insole*

I wish I'd never said "Draw back from the brink"; there are so many problems – *Insole*

Draw back from the drink, sorry, the brink – *Kempster*

Wars are not won by appeasement – *W. H. Webster*, ICC chairman

Chamberlain's Churchill – *Mr. Justice Slade*

We [the West Indies] had grave reservations as to the morality of a retroactive ban – *Short*

There was a deliberate attempt by the ICC to break down the negotiations – *Packer*

After that we had our toes insured – *Greig*, referring to an injury suffered by Fred Titmus in a swimming accident

They can play at Brighton in the water if they want – *Packer*, confirming his players' availability in the English summer

When we went into this we knew exactly what we were doing and it would probably get us banned from county cricket – *Snow*, confirming an earlier interview

When the donkey kicks you know which way it kicks – *Snow*

I did not expect they would blackball us altogether – *Greig*

You didn't have to be an Einstein to foresee the ban – *Packer*

Gloucestershire want me to go on playing – *Procter*

It's everyone for himself now and let

the devil take the hindmost – *Packer*

Nineteenth century lockout – *Alexander*

The changes in rules are no more stringent than are required to protect the conventional game – *Kempster*

Derek Randall [a big attraction] at Trent Bridge? I thought they were Yorkshiremen who'd come to watch me – *Boycott*

One should go to another county – *Knott*, referring to the competition between him and Paul Downton in the Kent team

Television of Mr Packer's series would have a very serious effect on official Tests. The public could sit at home and watch the circus match – *Steele*

The press, on behalf of the authorities have always tried to lampoon our games – *Packer*

We were in the gloaming if not in the dark – *Bailey*

We believed they [the players] were going to do irreparable damage – *Steele*

The players should be treated as outcasts – *Steele*

Mr Packer wanted exclusive television rights there and then – *Bailey*

The offer would have had to be quite a big one if I was to be banned from Yorkshire – *Boycott*

The word "grovel" followed me around – *Greig*

They [his cricketers] must be like Caesar's wife – *Packer*

David Brown [chairman of the Cricketers' Association] and I couldn't have changed anything

in a million years – *Greig*

I considered the Cricketers' Association vote [in favour of the ban] unfair and biased – *Underwood*

I would not have got a gun and shot Mr. Packer – *Steele*

We're not perfect – *Bailey*

He [Tony Greig] said "How the hell did you get involved in this" – *Boycott*

There is no fat at all – *Insole*, questioned about county clubs' finances

Our players had let us down because on their behalf we had negotiated a $350,000 team sponsorship and we'd taken on agreements to which they'd agreed – *Steele*

If there are no good guarantees, tours may have to be cancelled – *Short*

If overseas players are absent from a Sunday League match between Hampshire and Gloucestershire, the cricket ratings will go down and those of High Chaparral will go up – *Alexander*

Any believability in my word would be destroyed – *Packer*, if his series were cancelled

If Tests wane the game as a whole will languish – *Kempster*

The Australian Cricket Board would do anything, even to eating crow or humble pie, to prevent a holocaust – *Bailey*

. . . body and soul contract, more on his side than my side – *Boycott*

The series will be considerably better than first-class in the eyes of the public – *Packer*

I kissed them goodbye – *Steele*, referring to players who had already signed contracts

I was riveted – *Bailey*, by Mr Packer's appearance on David Frost's television programme

Kerry Packer picked my brains – *Boycott*

"Fabrication" is your word, not mine – *Boycott*, to Alexander

They found a very good living – *Insole*, referring to engagements in league cricket of Sobers, Lindwall, Ian Chappell and others

They'll fight . . . like Kilkenny cats – *Packer*, of the Australian Cricket Board

Since May 9 [the date of public knowledge of the Packer series] I think that's correct – *Steele*, asked if modern cricketers had become too commercial

They [the ICC] didn't want to compromise in any way, shape or form – *Packer*

We still hoped to prevent a hijacking situation – *Bailey*

We're all getting underpaid, except a few overseas stars who're getting all the money – *Boycott*

The county championship is the lynchpin of English cricket – *Insole*

The effect on the first-class game if the Test match profits diminish would be serious, very serious, or catastrophic – *Bailey*

The world cricket authorities are carrying the can for Australia – *Packer*

I don't know about that [Michael Brearley's double first] but he's certainly very brainy – *Boycott*

When a Yorkshireman shakes your hand that's all you need – *Boycott*

No, you should be expected to play as your form warrants – *Boycott*, asked if he thought Test cricketers should have more security

One can take only so much – *Greig*

Cricket Boards Face Huge Costs after Packer Victory

BY JOHN HENNESSY AND RICHARD STREETON

26 *November* 1977. Mr Kerry Packer and his group of cricketers gained a crushing victory in the High Court yesterday. In deciding between them on the one hand and the International Cricket Conference (ICC) and the Test and County Cricket Board (TCCB) on the other, Mr Justice Slade came down heavily on the Packer side.

He was giving reserved judgment after a hearing that had lasted 31 days. The judgment ran to more than 60,000 words and took five and a half hours to deliver.

The judge found, in particular, that the bans proposed by the TCCB and imposed by the ICC on Test and county cricketers were an "unreasonable restraint of trade" and thus void.

The Packer players are now free to reclaim their places in Test and county teams, should they be wanted. The judge also found for the Packer group in the lesser aspect of inducement to breach of contract.

The costs, amounting perhaps to £250,000, fall virtually on the cricket authorities in their entirety. The TCCB, which meets next Tuesday, will discuss the result of the case and decide whether to appeal.

The members of the ICC, who are spread around the world, will be consulted by telephone. The TCCB had withheld £10,000 from each county's share of this summer's profits in case of an unfavourable end to the case.

Mr Jack Bailey, the ICC's secretary, said of the judgment: "Of course we are disappointed. It is a blow; as the judge himself said, we acted in good faith and in the best interests of cricket but in law it was not enough." He thought that conventional Test cricket would still survive.

Mr Douglas Insole, the TCCB chairman, said the judgment would not make cricket administration any easier in the short term. "There is going to be no great joy in it either way for people who love the game."

He was asked if with hindsight he felt the authortities had acted too hastily. "On the basis of this judgment we were obviously wrong, but I would not say we were necessarily hasty at the time." He added: "The purpose of the ban was to try to draw a clear line. That was its only purpose."

In Australia Mr Packer said he believed the court's decision was a vindication of the players, according to Reuter. "I can say with some assurance that we are incredibly delighted at the decision."

Mr Packer forecast that the lifting of the bans improved the climate for a compromise with cricket authorities. "We can at last all get down to just playing cricket," he said.

"Now that the players are available for their country and counties the authorities have less to lose and maybe we can look at the good of the game rather than the interests of individual groups."

Mr Richard Rossiter, treasurer of the Gloucestershire county club, said that cricket's authorities should now sit down with Mr Packer and work towards a settlement, "something which should have been done four months ago."

The judge said yesterday that he had seen a number of people giving evidence on behalf of the authorities who were among the top administrators of cricket in one or other of the Test-playing countries. Without exception he had been "impressed by their obvious disinterested dedication and concern for the game.

"If they can be regarded as fairly representative of it, I am not surprised that cricket has traditionally been regarded by many as embodying some of the highest professional standards in sport.

"These witnesses all clearly regarded the official Test match structure as something which should represent the pinnacle of any cricketer's ambition.

"They thus find it difficult to understand how any cricketer could, even for good commercial reasons, bring himself to do anything which could be thought likely, directly or indirectly, to damage the structure of international cricket, of which Test matches at present form the all-important part."

The importance of Test cricket, however, was far from being based solely on sentimental or emotional grounds. They were extremely profitable.

"The Test matches played by the Australian touring team in England during the summer of 1977", the judge said, "are together likely to produce a net profit for United Kingdom cricket of not far short of £1m."

The very size of the profits that could be made from cricket matches involving star players must, for many years, have carried the risk that a private promoter would appear on the scene and seek to make money by promoting cricket.

"The risk might perhaps have been more limited", Mr Justice Slade said, "if the structure of official cricket in the Test-playing countries had been such as to offer the most talented a secure and remunerative career structure."

The decision for the court was whether the steps which the ICC and TCCB had taken to deal with the situation were justifiable in law. On July 26 the ICC passed a resolution changing its rules, the effect of which was that any player who, after October 1, should remain with Mr Packer would be disqualified from Test cricket.

Mr Justice Slade said he was not surprised that many of the plaintiffs' witnesses had expressed the view that their remuneration in county cricket was inadequate, or that similar views had been expressed about the level of Test match payments, "at least until the season immediately past".

The judge "totally rejected" suggestions that the authorities were careless of the difficulties and needs of people who played cricket for a living. But some of the officials who gave evidence for the defence gave the impression that, though dedicated lovers of the game, they found it hard fully to understand the feelings and aspirations of those who sought to make their living out of it.

The judge did not share the view that all the English players who had joined Mr Packer were in breach of any moral commitment.

He could see some criticism could be applied against Tony Greig, who had recruited others for Mr Packer when he was still generally regarded as the England captain. But it had to be borne in mind that neither the ICC nor the TCCB had entered into any commitment, legal or otherwise, ever to offer employment to Mr Greig or the other players.

It was straining the "concept of loyalty too far for authorities to expect players to enter into a self-denying ordinance not to play for a private promoter during the winter months."

There was no sufficient reason why the players, with the possible exception of Mr Greig, could justifiably be criticized on moral grounds for maintaining strict secrecy. "The subsequent actions of the defendants have made it abundantly clear that, had they been informed in advance of the World Series project, they would have done their utmost to prevent it from taking root."

Addressing himself to the nine questions he had earlier identified as requiring decision, the judge first dismissed the defence argument that the contracts were void. On the second question he ruled that there had been direct interference by the ICC with the contracts of World Series Cricket (a Packer organization).

The ban "contained a threat" and its publication in a press statement "was applying direct pressure, by means of an implicit threat, to the minds of all contracted cricketers". The TCCB ban, too, applied pressure or persuasion to the minds of the cricketers.

Holding that the proposed TCCB and ICC ban was "void as being an unreasonable restraint of trade", the judge said that to deprive, by a form of retrospective legislation, a professional cricketer of the opportunity of making his living in a very important field was both a serious and unjust step to take.

The last four questions related to the amended defence appeal under the Trade Union and Labour Relations Act, 1974. Mr Justice Slade gave judgment for the plaintiffs on all counts.

The judge accepted Mr Packer's evidence that, "contrary perhaps to some popular belief, he liked cricket". Discussing the collapse of a compromise meeting at Lord's in July, he thought Mr Packer had good reason for not thinking he would be fairly treated by the Australian Cricket Board of Control.

The Judge said the World Series venture had offered promise of greater rewards for star cricketers and regular remunerative employment during the English winter. It had stimulated new sponsors for traditional cricket. It had brought back to the game in Australia several talented players.

It had initiated a useful coaching scheme for young players in New South Wales. Finally, it had increased public interest in the game.

Mr. Herbert Sutcliffe

23 *January* 1978. Mr. Herbert Sutcliffe, one of the famous cricketers of his time, has died at the age of 83.

From Hirst, Rhodes and Jackson to Leyland and Hutton, Yorkshire has always provided England with cricketing backbone and at no time was the old saying, "When Yorkshire is strong, England is strong", so true as when Herbert Sutcliffe stood, in the words of his autobiography, ". . . For England and Yorkshire". His playing career spanned almost exactly the period between the two world wars and by any standard his figures were massive. In all, he scored over 50,000 runs, including 149 centuries. His England caps were 54, though he was seldom seen to wear one, and, of his 16 Test hundreds, half were taken off Australian bowling. In each of 21 home seasons and on three tours he made his thousand runs, a dozen times 2,000 and three times 3,000. Four times he scored two hundreds in a match and twice four successive hundreds. His records flowed opulently like the bequests of a generous millionaire.

He was born on November 24, 1894, in Pudsey, the West Riding home-town of his predecessor John Tunnicliffe, and his eminent successor, Sir Leonard Hutton. In his teens he caught the eye of the Yorkshire authorities and had already made an appearance or two for the county's second eleven when the First World War broke out. He enlisted in The Sherwood Foresters and later was commissioned. In the first post-war season Yorkshire called on him at once and after an attractive innings in the first game against M.C.C. at Lord's, he found himself in possession of his county's No. 1 batting position. By the end of the summer he had established himself so firmly that he was named as one of Wisden's Cricketers of the Year.

Each season saw him steadily advancing and his first 2,000 runs came in 1922. Two years later his selection for England against South Africa marked the beginning of his long association with Sir Jack Hobbs, the most impres-sive and prolific partnership that English batting has known. Their first stand produced 136 runs, the second 268 and the third 72, and this initial success brought Sutcliffe an invitation to tour Australia where, though the rubber was lost, his personal performance was magnificent, producing four successive hundreds and a Test average of over 80.

With that gayest of good companions, Percy Holmes, he broke virtually every Yorkshire batting record. Their century partnerships numbered 69 for Yorkshire (74 in all) and their highest was the record-breaking 555, scored at Leyton in 1932 at a rate of 74 runs an hour. This was Sutcliffe's richest season, bringing him 3,336 runs and keeping him at the head of the first class averages, a place he had held in 1928 and 1931. His three-figure partnerships with Hobbs totalled 26, of which 15 were against Australia. The understanding which inspired their almost uncanny running between wickets – daring, but safe – was foreshadowed in the days when Rhodes was Hobbs's prewar partner and was brought to perfection with Sutcliffe's in-telligent cooperation. Of their combined exploits two at least are outstanding. In the fifth Test of 1926, with the rubber still undecided, England began their second innings 22 runs behind. In poor evening light Hobbs and Sutcliffe scored 19, but a thunderstorm in the night made the morning's pitch at first dead-slow and then as the sun came out, vilely treacherous. If either Hobbs or Sutcliffe had succumbed, England could have been out for a hundred. As it was, the pair batted valorously, adding 112 by lunchtime and after Hobbs had been bowled for exactly 100, Sutcliffe stayed till the last over of the day. His share was 161 and sharply rising deliveries had bruised him all over. Connoisseurs of his batting speak with even greater awe of his innings for Chapman's side of 1928–29 on a Melbourne "sticky dog". In hideous conditions the two Englishmen fought their way to a total of 105, when Hobbs was out, and afterwards Sutcliffe went serenely on to take his individual score to 135, bringing England within sight of victory.

Sutcliffe's success sprang from his personal character, based on tenacious courage and unshakable concentration. In an age when bat dominated ball, he was among the giants; Hobbs, Hammond, Bradman and Woodfull at one end and Hutton, his own disciple, at the other. Though he fell short of the consummate artistry of Hobbs or the sheer brilliance of Hammond, he was a handsome batsman with an armoury of powerful on-side strokes and a defence that was a bowler's despair. He could score steadily or swiftly, as he judged the situation, and once, with Leyland, hit 102 off six overs against Essex.

As a mark of respect to his famous England first-wicket partner, Sutcliffe named his son, who was later to captain Yorkshire himself, William Herbert Hobbs. Sutcliffe's wife, Emily, died in 1974.

His appearance at the crease, from elegant buckskin boots to perfectly smoothed black hair, was as immaculate as his defence. His quiet voice masked a tremendous combativeness. Congratulated on his superb innings at the Oval in 1926, he replied softly: "Ah, Mr. Warner, I love a dog fight". And after his equally valiant effort at Melbourne Sir Jack Hobbs observed: "There was Herbert, black and blue, and not a hair out of place". Under the harshest of stresses, he was unruffled and unrufflable.

It was once said of Yorkshire's opening batsmen that, while Holmes looked as if he was off to the races, Sutcliffe had the air of an alderman about to lay a foundation stone. There was truth in the jest, for a characteristic innings by Sutcliffe formed the foundation of many a Yorkshire and England victory. Though he looked young all his playing life, he was England's "Old Imperturbable".

May Elegant not only in Style but in Manner

BY ALAN GIBSON

2 *January* 1980. Fifty years ago, on New Year's Eve, Peter May was born. Early in his life it became clear that he was going to be good at cricket. He was captain of Charterhouse in 1947, scored hundreds against both Eton and Harrow, and for the Public Schools against the Combined Services. He went on to Cambridge, after his national service (he made his first first-class appearance for Combined Services – and had played for Berkshire – he was born at Reading – in 1946).

For Cambridge he scored nearly 3,000 runs in three seasons, at an average of more than 60. In 1950 he played for Surrey, winning his county cap, and in a Test trial. In 1951 he played for England, against South Africa, and scored a century in his first Test innings. He played in all four Tests against India in 1952, and did well. There was something exceptional in the making.

In 1953 there was a mild setback. He played against Australia only in the first Test and the last. He failed in the first, in which he batted at No 6. He was always happier, even when young, with the responsibility of batting No 3 or 4. When he came back for the last Test, the decisive one, at No 3, he scored 39 and 37, both innings of much consequence in the context.

Thereafter, except for injury or illness (of which he had rather more than his share) he was always an England player. Before his early retirement in 1963, he had played in 66 Tests, in 41 of which he was captain. The number of captaincies is a record, although we should not make too much of it, because so many more Tests were being played. He averaged 47 in Tests, and 51 in first-class cricket – 27,500 runs, 85 centuries.

I put the figures in because they deserve it, but you may be thinking, especially those of you who did not see him, or only saw him when you were very young, "Yes, we know all that, we know he was one of the great English batsmen, but how would you describe his play?"

The word that occurs to me is *elegance*. "Elegant but not ostentatious", as Johnson said of Addison's prose. May, even if he was beaten, never looked uncouth. People who were there tell me that this was true even on the 1958–59 tour of Australia, when English batsmen were constantly reduced to inelegant attitudes by the "dubious actions" of the bowlers – rather as Australians had been, a quarter of a century earlier, on the "bodyline" tour.

May's style was the kind we call classical. The upright stance, the back-lift, the immediate judgment of length and adjustment of feet, the pounce to the overpitched spinner, the quick step back, almost to the stumps, for the cut: these were the things we had always associated with the Edwardians, the amateur batsmen of the golden age. May of Charterhouse made a fit companion for MacLaren and Jackson of Harrow, Fry of Repton, Foster of Malvern. At least he would have done, had he not been a couple of generations late.

You might say that, although not the least of the apostles, he was one born out of due time (you could say much the same of Cowdrey of Tonbridge, who came along a little later). Yet in another sense he was very much a man of his time. Only rarely, in Test cricket, did he display all his stroke-making gifts. Yet he had a mastery of concentration which none of the Edwardians had, except Jackson. He had greater patience than any of them but then he could afford it, since he did not have to face the challenge of three-day Tests.

He was often seen at his best for Surrey, when Surridge was captain. Surridge was a man who hated draws. As an England captain, and an England batsman, May crammed himself into the mould of his predecessor, Hutton, who was an even more beautiful batsman and an equally wise captain, but became increasingly cautious in both aspects. I have always thought that May was appointed to the England captaincy too soon. Another couple of years without the responsibility might have given him the confidence to be a little more adventurous. Also, we might not have lost him as early as we did.

May was elegant not only in style but in manner, not only in his cricket but his character. He came to the front at a time when pressures on top class cricketers were intensifying, although they were not so terrifying as those of today (of course the rewards were correspondingly less). A captain's lot was a particularly difficult one, with the press almost dictatorial in demands for constant attempts to pry into private life.

The more brash among them sometimes thought May remote, although he was always polite and tactful. When the 1958-9 side returned from Australia, he was immediately asked for his views on throwing. He replied that Englishmen should look forward to seeing Norman O'Neill, one of the best throwers (from the deep) that he had ever seen. His field manners were what we expected (rightly or wrongly) from the old-style amateur. There was one unfortunate mix-up about the use of a runner in the West Indies, when May was in the wrong, but it was no more than a misunderstanding, and May, although it was not generally known until he returned, prematurely, to England soon afterwards, was unwell.

Of his many great innings, the one that comes most readily to my mind was in the first Test against the West Indies in 1957. It was, in its earlier part, a defensive innings, but the circumstances demanded that. The West Indies bowled England out for 186, and scored 474. England had conferences and interviews, and lost three for 113 in the second innings, when May and Cowdrey came together. The next wicket, Cowdrey's fell at 524. He had made 154. May went on to 285 not out, until he declared at 583 for 4, E. W. Swanton wrote that "the concentration, the restraint, the technical excellence of these two innings could not be overpraised. Never have two young cricketers built such a monument to patience and determination". I did not see the match, but I would bet that they were, both of them, *elegant* innings.

May came in for some criticisms because he did not declare earlier, and certainly the weary West Indies' score at the end, 72 for seven, suggested that he might have done. But it was not unreasonable to feel that he had saved a match that looked hopelessly lost, and that would do for now. The West Indies were never the same side again that season.

I am afraid our sage and beloved Cricket Correspondent is not enjoying himself too much at present in Australia. I dare say, as he wilts beneath the barrage of ballyhoo (how inadequate a word that has become) he reflects on better days and better manners, and that his tours with May are often in his thoughts. And I dare say that May, from his ripe and rounded middle age (although remember that Woolley, Hobbs, and Rhodes, to take three, all played first-class cricket when they were older) feels relief to be well away from it, despite the monetary attractions. Of all leading English cricketers, at least since the first war, he would have looked the most incongruous in this setting. So perhaps he was not, after all, a man born out of due time.

French are Stumped by Lord's Taverners

FROM IAN MURRAY

23 *June* 1980; *Meudon, 22 June.* The French language and French credulity were strained this afternoon when a team of Lord's Taverners made merry with bat, ball and champagne on their first match in France.

Their opponents were the Standard Athletic Club, which boasts the only cricket pitch in regular use in France. For the occasion the club's gates in this Paris suburb were opened to as many of the local population as might be tempted to learn about the game of cricket.

The onlookers were not all that numerous. One of the girls, who had put together the publicity hand-out, frankly confessed: "The French are not that crazy, you see." The only celebrity on the Taverners' side who meant anything here was John Taylor, who not so long ago was a familiar scourge of the French rugby fifteen when he donned the red shirt of Wales. Names like Nicholas Parsons and Colin Milburn meant nothing.

And then the game itself was so strange. During the tea break, while a recorded brass band played "Abide with Me", small knots of puzzled men gathered round the *guichet* and stared in silence at the footmarks made by the *lanceur* as he hurled the ball at *batman*. They inquired of any English present which of the players was the "maiden".

The predominantly British crowd did their best to help explain what was going on.

For the benefit of a perplexed television crew, Mr. Willie Rushton tried to explain, in an accent that would even encourage Mr. Edward Heath to speak more French, the importance to the game of a cup of tea. A fellow Taverner wearing a donkey's head mask nuzzled his shoulder, "*Poussez-off Euroâne*", roared Mr. Rushton as the producer snatched back his microphone. "*Poussez-off*, or it's French cricket at Lourdes for you next week."

Despite their overall incomprehension the French onlookers came away, perhaps, with a better idea of why Britain is so difficult to beat at EEC negotiations and why the word "fair play" is untranslatable in French.

The afternoon produced a profit for French and British charities.

Language of the Terraces Comes to Lord's

BY RICHARD FORD

1 *September* 1980. Has civilization as we know it ended with the disgraceful scenes in the Members Enclosure at Lord's before the start of the third day of play in the Cornhill Centenary Test?

Even the august and dignified members of the world famous MCC would appear to have among their number an element who are not averse to using a rather coarser sort of language than one expects on the cricket field.

The abusive language and jostling that took place as the two captains and umpires returned to the Long Room is the kind of behaviour we have come to expect on the football terraces but not from the gentlemen of the Pavilion at Lord's.

It just is not cricket and today the MCC will start an inquiry into this most unsporting behaviour.

Many might prefer a dignified veil of silence to be drawn across the unseemly incidents on Saturday in which Ian Botham, the England captain, was hit on the head and David Constant, an umpire, grabbed by the tie and jostled. But they have received so much publicity that an investigation will begin with Botham and Greg Chappell, the Australian captain, being seen by Mr. Jack Bailey, secretary of the MCC.

He had heard a complaint from Chappell that intimidatory and abusive language was being used and that one of the umpires had been jostled as they returned from making a fourth inspection of the pitch, where 22,000 spectators were waiting for play to start. Mr. Bailey investigated this and spoke to two members pointed out by Chappell but said he thought, from what they had told him, that they had not been behaving unreasonably.

Mr. Bailey said: "I spoke to the men and felt they were innocent, but of course it could have been a case of mistaken identity. There is no question about it, the members were not pleased at having to wait and made their feelings known, but I thought they were doing it in the reasonable English way and that it would not go beyond this."

From the hotel where he is staying in London, Botham described the incidents as "the behaviour one expects from football hooligans." He added, "I was walking out to make the final inspection with Chappell and the two umpires when I was hit on the back of the head by a hand.

"I did nothing about it but as we were all walking in a man in his twenties grabbed the umpire David Constant by the tie and shoved and jostled him. Greg Chappell and I moved in to break it up."

He said the man thought he was being clever and added that the abusive language being shouted in the Pavilion had disgusted him. "It was a disgrace especially as it involved the captain of an opposing team. I feel very sorry and embarrassed about people who to my mind are a disgrace to the game."

So the language and behaviour of the football hooligan has at last invaded the home of English cricket. W. G. Grace would turn in his grave at the thought.

The Voice of Cricket Declares

BY ALAN GIBSON

3 *September* 1980. When the centenary Test match came to its end yesterday, there also came to an end, at least as far as Test matches were concerned, the most famous of cricketing voices.

Broadcast cricket commentary began soon after broadcasting itself, but for a long time it was rather amateurishly done. The usual practice was to find some distinguished old cricketer, such as Pelham Warner, prop a microphone in front of him, and leave him to get on with it.

In the 1930s, Howard Marshall appeared, and after him E. W. Swanton (and we must not forget Arthur Wrigley, who founded the technique of modern scoring).

But it was only after the war that we heard the voice of them all, John Arlott.

He came from Basingstoke, and his Hampshire accent was in those days sharp. The Hampshire accent is not naturally a mellow one, such as that of Dorset, which helped to make Ralph Wightman such a broadcasting success.

It took a year or two for the public, brought up on Marshall and Swanton, to grow accustomed to Arlott. He did not sound like a member of MCC. But by 1948 he was established, and ever since has remained, for every Test in England, a necessary part of the scene.

He did that because he was a cricketer and a poet. He was never, I think, expected to be an outstanding cricketer, though he had a passion for the game, and when he abandoned his first-class ambitions he was determined to stay in touch with it somehow.

He became very knowledgeable, partly because he pestered cricketers for information: not the dressing-room gossip, but technical stuff. "What does he *do*? What's his dangerous ball?" he would demand if a new bowler appeared.

"We all loved and admired John in the Hampshire dressing-room", said his old friend, Desmond Eagar, then the Hampshire captain, "but we did sometimes wish he would stop asking questions".

The greatest honour that he feels he has been paid is to have been invited to be chairman of the Cricketers' Association, a post he will retain in retirement. Not that he really retired: he is going to live in his beloved Alderney, but he will speak and write as long as he lives. He has immense industry, a constant urge to work, more than any man I have known.

But he would not have become so famous had he not been a poet. He was considered one of the most promising post-war poets. He gave that up too ("The words don't come any more"), but his adventures in poetry gave him a command of words, a gift of phrase such as no other cricket commentator has possessed.

He also had an unforced sense of humour. When he used phrases such as "the fieldsmen are scattered in the wilderness like missionaries", people used to think he had thought them up beforehand. Sometimes, I suppose, he may have done, but he never needed too.

I remember one Test morning at Trent Bridge when I was in the commentary box with him and Trevor Bailey. Trevor began, as usual, with his introduction about the state of the game, finishing with "and now come the umpires in their new-style short coats, looking like dentists. Over to John Arlott".

John immediately said: "It occurs to me, Trevor, that it is rather suitable for the umpires to look like dentists, since one of their duties is to draw stumps".

Everything but the Real Thing at Bristol

BY ALAN GIBSON

18 *September* 1980. England played the Rest of the World at a game purporting to be cricket last night, on the Bristol City ground at Ashton Gate. I had been warned that I would find it a repellant spectacle, but the half had not been told me. I felt bitterly towards our cricket correspondent who had been unavoidably prevented from attending by a previous sporting engagement (boating on the Thames with Brian Johnston). Not since I played for Yorkshire against the Rest of the World on a rough common outside Smolyensk have I seen a more gross caricature of the game, but the competitors at Smolyensk were a coach party of tourists, and at Ashton Gate they were some of the best cricketers in the world. In this was the tragedy.

No doubt floodlit cricket has a future, for this is the age of the sporting stunt, and it is only fuddy-duddies who remember that it was once the meadow game with the beautiful name. I did meet one or two regular cricket followers among the crowd – about 9,000 it was estimated – and they muttered shamefacedly things like "a bit of fun" and "does no harm".

I suppose the harm has already been irredeemably done. But how any cricketer with any feeling for the game at all can regard the sight of the best players in the world bashing monotonously into the stands on a narrow football field as fun passes my comprehension. Never mind. In 10 year's time, mark my words, we shall have the pylons up at Lord's and the riots to go with them. They have had a promising trial run for rioting already.

The emetic-yellow pads, the umpires dressed in red nightgowns like Chinese mandarins, the white ball, the black sight screens, the indiscriminately yelling crowd (I imagine the things they like most about soccer are sudden death penalties) the artificial pitch, combined to make it all a hideous nightmare.

England were sent in to bat, and lost four wickets for 31, but Boycott and

Botham put a stop to these brief hopes of an early finish. It was just the game for Botham, able to mis-hit as much as he liked, and still score sixes. Boycott, whose inner soul must have shrunk from what was going on around him, could not resist the temptation to play a proper cricketing stroke now and then. Doshi showed that even in such conditions bowling a length could bring a reward. The fielding was of high quality, even in the difficult period when daylight gave way to floodlight. These are the only polite things I can think of to say.

The English innings ended for 214 in the 38th over. The Rest of the World scored 220 for two. The players, and Bristol City both made some money, and Bristol City, at any rate, need it. But the end does not always justify the means, and I would have thought it much better to see Bristol City in the third division than survive by such tales told by an idiot, full of sound and fury, signifying nothing.

ENGLAND 214 (I. T. Botham 84, G. Boycott 68; D. R. Doshi 6 for 48)
REST OF THE WORLD 220 for 2 (S. M. Gavaskar 67, Sadiq Mohammad 64)
Rest of the World won by eight wickets

It Was an Exceptional Summer for Batting

BY ALAN GIBSON

26 *November* 1980. Most county cricket championships have been won by bowling. The one great exception was the victory of Middlesex in 1947. It was a summer of sunshine, the golden season of Compton and Edrich; Compton scored 3,816 runs, Edrich 3,539, still the two highest aggregates, and unlikely ever to be bettered, certainly not while the present pattern of an English season lasts (the next highest are Hayward in 1906, Hutton in 1949, and Woolley in 1928, the year he was dropped for the Australian tour). But that was not all for Middlesex in 1947; Robertson and Brown, the openers, scored more than 2,000 each. These four scored their runs at such a pace, something like 80 runs to the hour, that they gave Middlesex the time to bowl the other sides out.

And they did need plenty of time, for they were short of bowlers. Jack Young, a slow-medium left-arm spinner, had made a big advance since the war. He was 35, but, with an economical action, could still bowl a long and accurate spell; he was chosen for England once that season and seven times more in the next couple of years, though he performed without much success (17 wickets at 44). He was a sound county bowler, rarely more. Jim Sims, a tall and genial leg-spinner, who had played for England four times before the war (11 wickets at 43) was nine years older than Young; he was a cunning old warrior, of whom Robertson-Glasgow had written only a few years earlier that he could "unbuckle about the most difficult googly in the game today" (I presume he was not including Australians).

So the Middlesex spin bowling was at least adequate, but there was not much in the way of pace. Gray, who was 32, had lost his best years to the war, a more severe imposition in the case of a fast bowler than a spinner. The edge of his speed had gone. Edrich could bowl fast for a few overs – some said he was then the fastest in England, not a large claim to make. He had some bowling successes, and so did Compton, who was beginning to develop his back-of-the-hand left-arm spin. Robins, the captain, had been a leg-spinner of high class before the war, but he was 41 and did not bowl much. With three other spinners turning the ball from the leg, he could not give himself many opportunities. It was an uneven attack, not at all that of a champion side, yet it proved sufficient because of the flood of runs.

Middlesex played 26 matches that season, won 19, lost 5, and drew 2. The last figure was the most significant. Robins was a captain in the style of Sam Woods, half a century earlier, who believed that draws were only any use for bathing in. Two instances illustrate the Middlesex approach. At the Oval they scored 537 for two on the first day (the only occasion in the season when Robins allowed his side to bat through after he had won the toss). Brown scored 98, Robertson 127, Edrich and Compton (both not out) 157 and 137. So Middlesex had two days to bowl out Surrey twice – and managed it.

The other match was at Leicester. Middlesex had difficulty in getting Leicestershire out in the third innings and it seemed as if the match was saved when the last wicket fell: Middlesex had to score 66 in 20 minutes. Robins was not playing that day and Edrich was captain. As Middlesex walked from the field, he came alongside Compton, and said: "We'll go in first, Denis, and get these runs." So they did, with a minute to spare. I remember someone in Common Room saying next morning, "Aren't Middlesex marvellous?" and there was not a dissenting voice, though we were, mostly, a North Country college.

I remember feeling that nothing was going to stop them. Yorkshire, to whom Middlesex had been second in 1937, 1938, 1939 and 1946, were out of it halfway down the table (hardly believable to a Yorkshireman in those days); but Middlesex did have a challenge, from Gloucestershire, whom they played at Cheltenham in August. The Cheltenham pitch was then known as Tom's Delight, because Tom Goddard, though 47 years old, had had many triumphs there and was still about the best off-spinner in the country (Laker was some years from his peak). It was a very good idea, at Chelten-ham, to win the toss; Gloucestershire lost it, and the match. Tom did his stuff with 15 wickets, but Middlesex won by 68 runs. They were without Compton and Robertson, both playing in the Test against South Africa; however, they did have Edrich, who would also have been playing for England but for a strain. He had told the selectors that he could manage to bat, but not bowl or throw. Middlesex chose him simply as a batsman and he made 50 in the first innings, the highest score of the match.

When it began, Middlesex were four points ahead of Gloucestershire, each side having played 21 matches. Gloucestershire fielded three seamers, which seemed silly when Goddard and Cook had Cranfield, another useful spinner in reserve. The Gloucestershire seamers wasted some overs, especially during Edrich's innings. Middlesex brought in Harry Sharp, a middle order batsman and off-spinner, nearly 30 years old (what a match it was for the not-so-young!) who had learnt his trade on the ground staff before the war without winning a place. It was only his second championship match, but he made the Middlesex attack more balanced and suitable for the occasion. In the last innings he took the wickets of Neale, Emmett and Wilson, after scoring 46 going in as nightwatchman. Young took nine wickets and Sims eight, but you could say that Sharp did as much to win that match as anybody. He took those three wickets in seven balls after Gloucestershire, 67 for two in their second innings, were still in with a good chance.

This shows the strength that Middlesex had in reserve; so did the performances of some of their amateurs, the two Manns (J. P. and F. G.). Fairbairn and Bedford. It also shows the shrewdness of their captain. Robins resigned at the end of the season, and though he returned as nominal captain in 1950, he did not play much more. He was a remarkable and, so most found, an agreeable man, and nothing in his cricketing life can have given him so much pleasure as to lead Middlesex, in the evening of his career, to their first championship (and the first championship of any southern county) in 26 years.

It was a victory compatible with Warner's in 1921, in several ways; but it was the batting that did it: the first four batsmen all having the season of their lives at the same time. Brown never played for England; Robertson did, 11 times (average 46) but only twice at home, and never against Australia. But when you remember that nine times in 1947 they put on more than 100 for the first wicket, you can see how much they helped to polish the golden path. Imagine the feelings of a bowler on a hot day: second wicket just fallen, 150 or so, momentary relief, long time to tea. And now who had he got? Compton and Edrich, thank you, both gently settling in. The only thing to do was to bowl for run-outs, in which Compton would sometimes cooperate.

I must add that in those days the match, Champion County v. Rest of England, was played over four days, and taken seriously (I am sorry it was ever abandoned; the shivering spring match, M.C.C. v. the previous champions, is no sort of substitute). Only Yorkshire had ever beaten the Rest of England before; Middlesex now did so, against a strong side which was trying hard, by nine wickets. Bedser had Brown and Robertson quickly caught at the wicket when Middlesex batted first. Edrich and Compton then made 426 between them. Compton hit Goddard for four to mid-wicket while falling flat on his face; it was that sort of season for him.

But there was a worrying sign. His knee was in bandages, and for all he thereafter did, it was never to be quite that sort of season again; nor, indeed, for Edrich, nor, for a long time, for Middlesex. They shared the championship with Yorkshire in 1949, but they have returned to the lead only in the past few years. By then it had become a different game in a different world – though Brearley has some things in common with Robins.

When Dark Blues Radiated a Certain Light

BY DAVID GREEN

20 *January* 1981. Many reasons can be advanced for the current low standard of Oxford and Cambridge University cricket. Two particularly valid ones are the increased emphasis placed by examiners on academic ability, and the ending of National Service which effectively lowered the average age of sides by two years from 1960 onwards. It is interesting to reflect that, even when unemcumbered by such handicaps, the universities had their problems.

In the five seasons from 1954 to 1958, of 85 matches played by Cambridge only 13 were won against 35 losses: of the wins, only seven were against counties, and this during a period when they included players of the quality of C. S. Smith, Barber, Dexter, McLachlan, Pretlove, Wheatley and Goonesena. Oxford's record over the same period is even more dismal: they lost 42 of their 76 games, and could manage only three wins against county sides, though they could call on players like Cowdrey, Mike Smith, Chris Walton, J. A. Bailey and Esmond Kentish.

Against this grim background the achievements of the Oxford sides of 1959 and 1960 glow with a certain radiance. In those two seasons 10 out of 31 first class matches were won, and only eight lost: against counties, of 24 matches played seven were won and 10 drawn. Much of the credit for this change of fortune must go to A. C. Smith who was captain and wicketkeeper in both years. It could be argued that he inherited seven Blues from the previous year, but I have it on good authority that the morale of the 1958 side was so low that it spent much of its time with its collective eye on the roof of Keble College, for when clouds came from that quarter, play for the day was normally washed out.

Sinister cloud banks were referred to as "good weather coming up" and were seen as the only means of avoiding defeat. A.C.'s inspiration was mainly responsible for a complete change in attitude. He told us that if we got our minds right we would certainly field better than our opponents, and that we should not assume that counties would necessarily bat or bowl better than us.

Though 1959 was a glorious summer, April was wet, and I remember finding batting in the nets extremely difficult. I looked around to see if anyone appeared to be a worse player than me. I was relieved to see a small Indian trying to get a big bat on the ball, with notable lack of success. He was alleged to have played first class cricket for Hyderabad, which was manifest fantasy, and I wrote him off as competition for a batting place. It is adequate commentary on my judgment of a player to state that this was Abbas Baig, who was to score 1,149 runs for Oxford that year at an average of 46, make a century for India at Old Trafford in his first Test, and in all play 10 times for his country.

Abbas was Oxford's leading batsman in 1959, and he got reasonably solid support, but their greatest strength was in their bowling. The spearhead was David Sayer who, in an era when England were not short of fast bowling (e.g., Trueman, Statham, Harold Rhodes, Flavell, Jackson, Loader, "Butch" White), was considered to be among the more hostile performers. He was tall and very strongly built, with a rhythmic and powerful approach followed by a very full body turn before delivery. He possessed a spiteful bouncer, with which he was fairly liberal, and very occasionally, when the body-turn got slightly mistimed, let fly a truly terrifying beamer; he was known as "The Slayer".

Andrew Corran, his partner with the new ball, was tall and angular, possessed of boundless stamina, and moved the ball around in the air and off the wicket at fast medium pace. He had firm opinions on a wide variety of subjects: the freedom and frequency with which he expressed them caused him to be known as "Oracle".

The off spinner was the slim, red-haired Dan Piachaud, from Ceylon. Though he bowled fairly quickly, he had a peculiar looping flight and a skilful change of pace, so that he was effective on flat wickets, as well as when the ball turned. In three seasons Sayer took 146 wickets at 21 each, Piachaud 138 at 23, and Corran 108 at 19. John Raybould, a chunky Yorkshireman, bowled leg spin which on good days could trouble the best.

Abbas's chief support came from Javed Burki, a strong, stocky man, who captained Pakistan in 1962 and scored a century at Lord's. Alan Smith and I usually opened the innings, and the batting line-up was completed by Charles Fry, Mike Eagar and Richard Jowett. Fry had to operate under the considerable handicap of being "grandson of the great C.B.". He made himself into a useful performer, and was a most brilliant fielder at cover. Eagar, a fine hockey player, was also a high-class fielder and a good batsman, though prone to excessive theorising. At one stage he worked out that the only safe attacking shot was the sweep, or "lap", as he called it. This obsession, which was the cause of some strange-looking innings, was fortunately dominant only for a few weeks.

In 1960, Alan Duff replaced Raybould as the leg-spinner; Colin Drybrough, an all-rounder later to captain Middlesex, replaced Jowett and the Nawab of Pataudi came in instead of Eagar. I am not alone in believing that, but for the loss of an eye, Pataudi would have been numbered among the greatest. Though small, he could drive powerfully and was strong off his legs, but his chief glories were his cutting and his hooking.

He was normally addressed as "Noob", which apparently had been the practice at Winchester, but this seemed an unsatisfactory arrangement to one young man, who insisted that A. C. Smith told him what the Nawab's Christian name was. A.C., wondering how a Muslim could have such a thing anyway, regarded his interlocutor in perplexed silence. The question was repeated and, after some deliberation, A.C. replied "Sidney". This amused the Nawab greatly, and thereafter he was more often than not addressed as "Sid" by his team colleagues.

The object of any Oxford side is to defeat Cambridge. This was achieved in 1959 by 80 runs: Oxford batted disappointingly, but "Slayer" and "Oracle" bore all before them, taking 15 wickets between them in the match. The 1960 match would almost certainly have been won but for the loss of two and a half hours on the last morning. Cambridge finished 90 ahead in their second innings with one wicket standing, the Nawab, in his first University Match, having made a beautiful 131. Cambridge's second innings resistance depended entirely on an elegant and resolute 95 from Tony Lewis. In this game "Oracle", in 76 overs, took 12 for 118.

The side was happy, played some excellent cricket, and had an enormous amount of fun. I do not suppose that Alan Smith would wish for any other summary of his teams' achievements.

Chappell: Skipper whose Ship Died of Shame

FROM DILIP RAO

3 *February* 1981; *Sydney*, 2 *February*. There could not be a lonelier man in the cricket world today than Greg Chappell, Australia's captain, who yesterday took the unorthodox and unethical measure of having his younger brother, Trevor Chappell, deliver underarm the final ball of the third match in the best-of-five final against New Zealand in the Benson and Hedges World Series Cup one-day competition at the Melbourne Cricket Ground. He has been assailed by angry words from all directions, Ian Chappell, another brother, not excluded.

The tactic, which Chappell now regrets having employed, was designed to prevent Brian McKechnie, of New Zealand, hitting a six and levelling the scores. It succeeded and Australia advanced to a 2–1 lead in the series. The remaining legs will be played at the Sydney Cricket Ground tomorrow and on Wednesday, although an additional match may be played on Thursday if either is washed out or tied.

As is their practice in an emergency, the Australian Cricket Board "met" today by telephone hook-up and decided that if New Zealand agreed, the playing conditions of the competition would be amended "to prohibit the use of underarm bowling in the remaining matches". But they also decided that as no existing rule had been infringed, the Melbourne result must stand.

But Philip Ridings, chairman of the board, said after the meeting: "The board deplores Greg Chappell's action and has advised him of the board's strong feelings on this matter and of his responsibility as Australia's captain to uphold the spirit of the game at all times. "We acknowledge that his action was within the laws of the game, but that it was totally contrary to the spirit in which cricket has been, and should be, played".

Chappell, after being rebuked by the board, said: "While I took a decision which was within the rules, I recognize in the cool light of day that it conflicted with its spirit. I made my decision in the heat of the moment, when I was under pressure. But I regret it now. It is something I would not do again".

The board's censure would have hurt Chappell less than the outburst in *The Sun* this afternoon from Ian Chappell, never known to be a great upholder of cricketing traditions. Several former Australian captains waxed eloquently on the issue and not one of them with any sympathy or support for Greg.

Ian, forthright as ever, wrote: "Fair dinkum, Greg, how much pride do you sacrifice to win $35,000?" Another rebel of his time, Keith Miller, said: "Yesterday one-day cricket died and Greg Chappell should be buried with it."

This plea from Miller did not fall on deaf ears for, it is widely said here, some of the members who "attended' the telephonic board meeting wanted Chappell relieved of captaincy but were dissuaded by the prospects of a bitter feud over his succession.

Premiers react: The Prime Ministers of Australia, and New Zealand Malcolm Fraser and Robert Muldoon, respectively, joined the fierce controversy over Greg Chappell's action. In Wellington, Mr. Muldoon said the underarm delivery was an act of cowardice" and it was appropriate that the Australian team were wearing yellow.

In Canberra, Mr. Fraser said that he would not respond to Mr. Muldoon's comment, but he said that Greg Chappell had made a serious mistake, ontrary to the traditions of the game.

Chappell's action has engendered such hostility that the good cricketing relationship between Australia and New Zealand has probably been irreparably damaged and Chappell's own international reputation as a sportsman severely impaired.

A Sydney radio station said that several callers had urged that Australia's ambassador be recalled as an expression of national shame.

AUSTRALIA 233 for 4 (50 overs) (G. S. Chappell 90, G. M. Wood 72)
NEW ZEALAND 229 for 8 (50 overs) (B. A. Edgar 102 not out, J. G. Wright 42)
Australia won by 4 runs

It Is for the Selectors to Select

27 *February* 1981, *Leading Article*. The failure of the Guyana authorities to respect the right of the English selectors to include Robin Jackman in the side for the Test to be played there, and their insulting demand that he be removed from the territory, left the Cricket Council with no choice but to cancel the fixture and take the players elsewhere.

The council will now have to ascertain whether the same attitude prevails where the remaining Tests are to be played. If it does (and Jamaica indeed seems to have done something to urge upon Guyana the need to make an example of Mr. Jackman on account of his South African connexions) that is the end of the tour. Guyana's decision is a serious blow to the future of Test cricket and may mar Commonwealth harmony.

The British position has been stated before and it was right for Mr. Hector Monro to restate it yesterday, for it needs to be understood by West Indians and Africans who oppose it from feelings which must be respected. The Commonwealth Gleneagles agreement on sport and apartheid does not abridge the freedom of the selectors who choose any team of sportsmen to represent Britain in international events: of this basic principle cricket is only a particular case. At Gleneagles in 1977 the governments committed themselves to discourage their nationals and sporting bodies from playing South African teams as long as apartheid in sport is practised there. But it was recognized that such commitments would be differently interpreted under different systems of law. Countries with all-powerful governments can (and do) make it illegal for their sportsmen to have contacts with South Africa. This is not possible for countries where individual liberty is prized as the first article of democracy: neither British public opinion nor Parliament would tolerate a Bill making it illegal for British citizens to participate in sport in South Africa, Russia or any other country. That is a fact – more easily understood in the West Indies indeed than in Africa.

The British government has repeatedly sought to discourage British sports bodies from playing in South Africa, and not without success at times. But what eventually brought about the cessation of Test cricket with South Africa was the rejection of Basil d'Oliveira as a member of the English side by Mr. Vorster in 1969. The (then) MCC wobbled, but eventually set the rule that it would not be interfered with. Those events have a direct bearing now, and they should, if read correctly, enable President Burnham to reject, not emulate, the Vorster line.

Many British sportsmen, after consulting their consciences, do decide that it is licit for them to participate in South African games. Several of the England side now in Guyana have exercised their rights as British citizens to ignore their government's advice and play in South Africa. Guyana accepted them. It is for the West Indian authorities to explain how one degree of contact with South African sport is more or less heinous than another. They need to remember that Britain is a very heterogenous country nowadays: it is multiracial, but also every part and strand of the "old empire" is represented in the composition of its nationals, South Africa included. We are not ready to have anyone discriminated against – anyone.

If British principles cannot be reconciled with West Indian priorities on this issue then, on occasion, international cricket will not be possible. Everyone will have to accept such casualties as the product of politics becoming so entangled with sport. On the issue of personal liberty Britain cannot give way, even if cricket suffers.

The Players who Came in from the Icy Cold

BY RICHARD STREETON

25 *April* 1981. What was believed to be the unique occurrence of a first class cricket match being halted because of the cold took place at Fenner's yesterday. The umpires took the players off the field to give them some relief from the wintry weather. A biting, gusty south-easterly wind made the near-freezing temperature almost unbearable. The bowlers were unable to grip the ball properly and Pringle, the Cambridge batsman, who wears contact lenses, was troubled by his eyes streaming and could not see.

At first the scorers assumed the match had been stopped for bad light, but the umpires sent them a message to say that "extreme conditions" should be recorded as the reason. Don Oslear, the senior umpire standing in the game, said that after seeking the captains' agreement, the umpires had invoked the law which – under the new 1980 code – allowed them to suspend play when conditions were so bad that it would be unreasonable or dangerous to continue.

Both factors applied, Mr. Oslear said. (It is not inappropriate at this point to note that Mr. Oslear, a former footballer with Grimsby, Hull and Oldham, is also the only championship umpire who used to play professional ice hockey.) It was a little after noon when the umpires stopped the match after what had been a miserable 70 minutes for everyone. An early lunch was taken and a further 35 minutes lost before play resumed.

The match was finally abandoned an hour later when it rained.

The reference books closest to hand show no instance of the cold stopping a first class game before, though it will probably have influenced bad light decisions on occasion. Before overseas cricketers claims about the English weather finally being acknowledged even by the English as being too cold for cricket, it should be noted that England also provides the only known case of a match being halted because it was too hot. This happened between

Surrey and Lancashire at The Oval in July, 1868 when the heat brought an hour's postponement after lunch.

Gerald Brodribb's *Next Man In* (Putnam & Co.) is always the main source of this sort of information. Mr. Brodribb also lists instances where cricket had been interrupted by an earthquake at Lahore in 1937-38; by a deranged monkey (Poona 1951-52); and a runaway horse (Scarborough 1892). Perhaps we were fortunate at Cambridge merely to flirt with pneumonia.

Cambridge, resuming at 82 for 4, soon lost Goldie, the night watchman, but both Pringle and Russom played some good strokes as they added exactly 100 runs in the same number of minutes against bowlers and fieldsmen who showed stoic perseverance. Lever, who missed the morning's play because of a funeral, and Foster had just taken the new ball and Pringle had edged a slip catch, when the rain brought a welcome end for everyone.

One other piece of history must also be recorded. Cambridge's three-day match against Hampshire starting today includes Sunday play for the first time at Fenner's against a county. The University officials have secured the agreement of Hampshire, and that of the TCCB that play should start at 11.30 tomorrow. Cambridge do not charge admission at Fenner's so the statutory 1.30 Sunday start can be waived.

> CAMBRIDGE UNIVERSITY 146 (S. Turner 4 for 20) and 204 for 6 (D. R. Pringle 66, N. Russom 47 not out, J. P. C. Mills 43)
> ESSEX 244 (M. S. A. McEvoy 54, K. W. R. Fletcher 46; D. R. Pringle 4 for 56)
> *Match drawn*

Model Cricketers Make a Bishop Very Happy

BY GERALDINE NORMAN, SALE ROOM CORRESPONDENT

18 *July* 1981. Cricket brought good fortune to the Assistant Bishop of Hereford, the Right Rev. W. A. Partridge, at an Andrew Grant sale in Droitwich on Thursday. He had consigned for sale 15 biscuitware models of Victorian cricketers of a type sold as cake decoration for a few pence in the late nineteenth century. They comprised two umpires, two batsmen and 11 fielders, rather a large team, and he had been told to expect about £5 a figure.

In the event the collection was sold for £210, almost three times that estimate. They were bought by Mr. A. Berg, a Warwickshire dealer, on behalf of a friend who is a cricketing enthusiast. Mr. Berg told the auctioneers afterwards that his friend had been prepared to bid up to £800.

England Awake to a New Jerusalem

John Woodcock Reports on a Famous Victory

22 *July* 1981. England's victory in the third Test match, sponsored by Corn-hill, at Headingley yesterday was greeted by the kind of scenes reserved for great sporting occasions. After Australia, needing only 130 to win, had been bowled out for 111, the crowd massed in front of the pavilion, cheering their heroes and waving the Union Jacks they were saving for the Royal wedding.

While at one end of the balcony Brearley and his victorious team were being serenaded, at the other Allan Border, who had not long before been out for nought, was to be seen with his head buried in his hands. It was a moment of disaster as well as triumph.

Kim Hughes, even so, was gracious in defeat, giving credit where it was due and saying that, whereas from tea-time on Monday the luck had gone mostly England's way, before that the Australians had had the greater share of it.

If Botham's unforgettable innings made the recovery possible, it was Willis who crowned it with a marvellous piece of bowling after Australia had got to within only 74 runs of their target with nine wickets standing. When play started yesterday morning the chances seemed to be that Willis was playing in his last Test match. He had bowled below his best in England's first innings and it was not until his second spell now, after he had changed ends, that he caught the wind.

That was where Brearley came in. His return to the England side has not only released Botham to play his game unhampered by the burden of captaincy; it meant that England, with so few runs to play with, were under the command of a supreme tactician. To everyone on the ground, except those who wanted Australia to win, it was a great reassurance to see Brearley handling the situation with calm and understanding.

After England's last wicket had added only another five runs at the start of the day, Brearley opened the bowling with Botham and Dilley, England's third different new ball partnership of the match. His reason for this was partly psychological: Botham and Dilley having shared such a decisive partnership with the bat, it was worth seeing whether they could repeat it with the ball.

In the event Dilley, though he was to hold a great catch later in the innings, was taken off after two unimpressive overs. Although in his second over Botham had Wood caught at the wicket he looked hardly in the mood to move another mountain.

That Willis was the man to do this, at the age of 32, and with knees that have often had to be supported by sticks, was a mark of rare courage. He had started with five rather laboured overs from the Football Stand End. At

48 for one, half an hour before lunch, Brearley gave him the breeze, the decision which launched him on his devastating spell.

It was noticeable even in his first over from the Kirkstall Lane End that Willis was bowling faster than in his earlier spell; not only that, he was making the ball lift as well. At 56, he got one to rear almost geometrically at Chappell, who cocked it up for Taylor, running forward, to take the catch. At 58, in the last over before lunch, Hughes and Yallop both went without scoring, Hughes beautifully caught at second slip by Botham, diving to his left, and Yallop also out to a very good catch. Gatting, standing his ground at short leg and reacting quickly to Yallop's desperate attempt to keep down another kicking delivery, threw himself forward for the ball.

Whereas at the start of the day the skies were clear, by now the clouds were rolling in, causing the ball to move about rather more, even to bounce more steeply. To keep his hands warm for the slip catch that could have gone his way, Brearley was constantly blowing into them.

With Yallop's departure, off the fifth ball of an over, lunch was taken. I harboured a fear that during the interval Willis might stiffen up; but not a bit of it. Brearley had him on again straight away afterwards, bowling as furiously and well as I have ever seen him. When in making a superhuman effort he was occasionally no-balled, Brearley told him not to bother: bowl your fastest, he said, and keep digging it in.

After Old had knocked out Border's leg stump, a vital contribution, Willis did the rest. At 68 he had Dyson caught at the wicket, hooking, as important a wicket as any in view of the skill and resolution with which Dyson had played.

At 74 Marsh, a dangerous customer, hooked Willis to long leg where Dilley, only a yard in front of the crowd, judged to perfection a high and horrible catch. At 75 Lawson gave Taylor his 1,271st first class catch, a new wicket-keeping record, though in all the excitement few knew it.

There followed a partnership between Bright and Lillee which rekindled Australia's fading hopes. Taking their lives in their hands, they added 35 in four overs before another fine catch, this time by Gatting, accounted for Lillee. Running in from mid-on, Gatting dived forward for a mis-timed hook. The ball was a long time in the air and Gatting had a lot of ground to cover.

With only 20 needed and Lillee and Bright going as well as they were, Lillee's wicket was a vast relief. There was only Alderman to be dealt with now and to finish things off Brearley brought back Botham in place of Old. Botham would have done it, too, had Old, at third slip, not dropped Alderman twice in the over. As it was, in the next over Willis yorked Bright and the match was won.

It was not a good Test pitch. Nor it was at Trent Bridge for the first Test of the series. At Edgbaston next week it should be different. In trying to produce something fast and true, the groundsman at Headingley made one that was unpredictable and patchy. But at least he tried.

England's choice of four fast bowlers proved, after all, the right one. Had Australia followed suit Lillee, Alderman and Lawson would not have been as tired as they were on Monday evening when Botham played his marvellous innings.

But what does that matter? They shared in a match that was a victory for cricket. To hear them singing Jerusalem down below you would think that it had revived a nation, too.

"Ian Botham, they call him Jessop in the paper today. It was the most remarkable innings I've ever seen". That was Brearley on his young lion. Botham's 149 not out, as Hughes has said, must be one of the finest innings of all time. Very few could have played it, not only among contemporary cricketers, partly because of his enormous strength. He weighs 16 stone, all of which went into the marvellous drives that made up the majority of his 28 boundaries.

> AUSTRALIA 401 for 9 dec (J. Dyson 102, K. J. Hughes 89, G. N. Yallop 58; I. T. Botham 6 for 95) and 111 (R. G. D. Willis 8 for 43)
> ENGLAND 174 (I. T. Botham 50; D. K. Lillee 4 for 49) and 356 (I. T. Botham 149 not out, G. R. Dilley 56, G. Boycott 46; T. M. Alderman 6 for 135)
> *England won by 18 runs*

Where Cricket is 20-a-side and Rich in Laughter

BY GEOFFREY WATKINS

28 *July* 1981. Samoan cricket has to be seen to be believed. It is rich in laughter, has elements of farce, echoes of tribal warfare, a touch of the Glee Club, gives a nod or two in the direction of MCC laws and is played in noisy enthusiasm against exotic backgrounds of blue lagoons, waving palms, rubber trees and the beautiful feathery tamalingi with its red flowers.

It is a game that is played with pleasure by men and women equally. In Apia, the capital of Western Samoa, it is played on an area of land recovered from the sea called the Eleelefou. The concrete wicket is slightly longer than ours and four feet wide. It is raised about three inches off the ground so this makes no-balling virtually impossible. The bats are three-sided and 44 inches long, tapering to a rounded handle bound in coconut cord. Individual marks in bright colours are painted on the base part.

Some people are reminded of baseball when they first see the bats, but I see tham as tribal clubs, smashing the hard rubber ball which the players make themselves from strips of raw rubber off the trees, as they used to crack the skulls of their Tongan or Fijian enemies. There are no bails as the strong sea breezes would keep shipping them off.

The teams are 20-a-side and it is a picturesque sight when they take the field in their colourful lavalavas (cotton wraparound skirts worn by both sexes), wearing T shirts and bare-footed. Each side brings its own umpire. In the harbour tall-masted yachts gently swayed at anchor, and overlooking the town and the pitch is the thickly wooded Mount Vaea where Robert Louis Stevenson lies in his simple tomb on the summit in the paradise he made his own.

The batting side does not repair to the pavilion when the game begins as there is no such place. Instead the other 18 players sit in a semicircle in the position of the slips. Most of the fielders being on the leg-side as the game proceeds – runs are called points – the seated batting side will break into song: sad traditional melodies or war chants accompanied by handclapping. Leading the musical entertainment is "the teacher", a chorus master-cum-cheer leader of charisma, and whatever he does the rest of the team dutifully follows. He also has a whistle which he blows from time to time and he will go into rhythmical gyrations as if on a dance floor, followed by his team.

Now it might be thought that this was done to encourage the batsmen at the wicket or to put the bowlers out of their stride. Not a bit. It was just done out of Polynesian *joie de vivre*. But the fielding side had their secret weapon also.

The "teacher" would blow his whistle, leap in the air with whoops, twisting and turning in impromptu dance and grimacing like a gargoyle. He would end by jumping up and clapping his hands above his head with his team emulating him. This, too, was an expression of unhibited joy and had nothing to do with intimidation.

When a wicket fell, however, the performance was intensified with leaping and shouting and laughter and with the more athletic doing cartwheels and somersaults. It made me think that Derek Randall might have visited this pearl of the Pacific; he would be in his element in this game.

The batsmen have two stances. Some will rest the bat over their shoulder as if waiting to brain some creature emerging from the swamps, while others point it to the ground like a golfer lining up for a prodigious drive; and both men and women, perhaps a little inelegantly, thrust the folds of their lavalavas between their muscular thighs before taking guard.

All the bowlers are fast and they only take three or four paces before hurling the ball down. Women bowl underarm. The ball is always well pitched up, usually middle and leg, and rises sharply. Sometimes the batsmen were hit in the tenderest of places. As they scorn such sissy aids as helmets, boxes, gloves and pads, I winced for them. But they seemed unaffected and just laughed when they were hit.

In fact, whatever the players did they laughed in doing it: dropping a catch, being out first ball, missing a run-out or whatever were causes for loud laughter, and they laughed just as loudly when making a mighty hit into the sun or into the long grass in the outfield where fielders were up to their waist in couch grass.

The ball is bowled from whichever end it lands – there are no overs – and the bowlers are also the wicketkeepers. Although most of the batting reminded me of the village blacksmith having a bash after a skinful of scrumpy, the other aspects of the game were more skilful. Men and women throw straight and hard – learned from their childhood when they threw stones at tins and other objects – and they all seemed to have a flair for wicket-keeping, going through the motions of whipping off the imaginary bails like a Rodney Marsh.

Batsmen always go for the big hit as it is too tiring to run for singles in the heat. When it was time for a break – the lunch or tea interval – both teams sat on the grass drinking soft drinks and eating biscuits and chatting.

One of the happy sights in Apia between 4 p.m. and 6.15 p.m. is to see a few hundred women of all ages and shapes and in a variety of costumes, playing cricket on the Eleelefou. The scene is a happy blend of colour, noise and enthusiasm and when it comes to the histrionics of the game the men pale beside the women.

The woman "teacher" will grimace grotesquely, thrusting her arms to her side and waggling her fingers. Then she will bend her knees, roll her buttocks, kick out in puppet-like movements, straighten up and jump up and down as if demented, all the time blowing her whistle. Then she will kick her left leg as if getting rid of a persistent admirer and leap into the air with both arms extended. She was followed in all her actions by the rest of the team.

On occasions the performance would end with the women facing the men and lifting up their lavalavas for what could have been a full frontal if they had not been wearing a kind of cut-down cotton long johns. It must have frightened the living daylights out of their enemies in the old days.

The men's cricket season has now ended and I saw the last game between the town area and the village of Ifilele Aasa. The town team had 15 Mormon bishops playing for it and one of the umpires was Bishop Afamasaga Laulu, who is also the tribal chief of Fasitootai. He was a splendidly dignified figure in his creamy jacket, ecclesiastical purple lavalava and his clipboard.

As each side had won a game they played a decider – but only 15 players each this time to shorten the proceedings – and the game was won by the visitors.

Last Saturday saw the start of the women's cricket season with a game between Vineula ladies, of Apia, and Miliemo. The home team scored 60 points, the visitors 24. So it was a comfortable win of 36 points for the locals, ranging from slimlegged, doe-eyed schoolgirls to muscular, big-busted and broad-beamed ladies.

Although Samoan cricket is fun from beginning to end it once had a tragic sequel. In a match not far from Apia a visiting batsman was given out when the ball was caught by a young spectator. The batsman protested, but the home umpire, proud of his young brother who had made the catch, stuck to his decision. The batsman killed him with one savage swipe of his bat.

But things like that do not happen today. Samoan cricket seems to make many of its rules as it goes along. But who cares? It has a logic of its own, and so long as it is an occasion for so much laughter and pleasure long may these Polynesian "flannelled fools" in their cotton lavalavas make a spectacle of themselves and make an entertainment for us.

Was Botham's Innings the Greatest Ever?

BY JOHN WOODCOCK, CRICKET CORRESPONDENT

17 *August* 1981 (*front page*). Ian Botham's innings of the fifth Test Match at Old Trafford on Saturday was, of its kind, perhaps the greatest ever played. It began just before half past two, when England, in their second innings, were 104 for five after starting the day at 70 for one. With a relentless display of tight fielding and accurate bowling, Australia had recovered from an apparently hopeless position to one from which they could well win.

In 34 overs, Boycott, Gower, Gatting and Brearley had fallen to Alderman and Lillee, while a mere 34 runs were being scored. Although still in, and batting with the utmost resolution, Tavaré, England's No. 3, had made only nine in the two hours of the morning, and another two in the first 20 minutes of the afternoon. The light was grey, the pitch not unhelpful to the faster bowlers.

When Botham walked out to bat he left an England dressing room in which few could bring themselves to watch the play. There is nothing worse than to see a hard won advantage against Australia being gradually whittled away. Contrasting with England's abject surrender was Australia's unconcealed joy.

The cheers which greeted Botham were of desperate encouragement, the position being scarcely less fraught than at Headingley where he made his historic 149 not out. His 118 on Saturday was an even finer innings. It was more calculated for one thing, and less chancy.

At Headingley, he played a wonderful, unforgettable slog, but it was also a lucky one. On Saturday, with a full sense of responsibility, he played himself in. If Brearley said anything to him as they passed on the pavilion steps, other than the customary "Good luck", it might simply have been: "Now, take your time" – and to the Australians it must have been increasingly worrying the way he did so.

Off his first 32 balls Botham scored five runs. With a new ball available in only 17 overs from the time he took guard, Bright was bowling at one end and Whitney at the other. When Alderman did take the new ball, immediately it was due, Botham had made 28 from 53 balls. At the other end,

Tavaré was taking good care of himself, not scoring much but relieving Botham of the anxiety of seeing a partner in distress. Of the 149 they added together, Tavaré's share was 28.

Botham had been in for 65 minutes when the new ball was taken. At 150 for five, one or two of the England side were to be seen watching the cricket again. Tavaré, wrapped in his cocoon, had completed the slowest half century ever made in a Test match in England. Then, suddenly, the floodgates opened.

Rather than finishing off the England innings, as they were expected to do, Lillee and Alderman took a dreadful hammering. Lillee had already bowled 14 overs in the day and Alderman 16. If they had lost their edge, it would not have mattered had it not been for Botham.

When, 13 overs later, Botham was caught at the wicket, he had made another 90 runs in 49 balls. Off Alderman's first over with the new ball he took seven; off Lillee's, 19. In the remaining nine overs in which he received a ball he made six and 10 off Alderman, five, six and 13 off Lillee, eight and seven off Bright and one and eight off Whitney. I refuse to believe that a cricket ball has ever been hit with greater power and splendour.

Where England's earlier batsmen, apart from Tavaré, had found survival impossible, Botham made the boundaries seem far too short and the wicket far too good. When Lillee bowled bouncers to him he hooked them off his eyebrows for six. When Alderman tried one it was pulled to mid-wicket for six. The crowd became a mass of dancing people and waving flags. Never before in Anglo-Australian Tests has anyone hit six sixes in an innings. Having reached his hundred with one, a sweep off Bright, Botham drove Bright over the sightscreen for another. He also hit 13 fours.

The fastest hundred in Test cricket, in terms of balls received, was by the West Indian, Roy Fredericks, at Perth in 1975. It took him 71 balls. In 1902 the mighty Jessop scored 102 against Australia at the Oval in 75 balls. On Saturday, with the Ashes in the balance, Botham's hundred took 86 balls (one fewer than at Headingley), though he went from five to 118 in 70 balls.

It was an innings that could have been played in the first place only by a man of astonishing power. Botham's attack on the new ball was a mixture of crude strength and classical orthodoxy.

At Trent Bridge in 1938, while Stan McCabe was scoring 232, Bradman called from the balcony to those in the dressing room: "Come out here, you may never see the like of this again."

So it was on Saturday. Botham, as McCabe occasionally did, is able to scale heights beyond the reach of ordinary men.

Till Cricket Us Do Part

26 *August* 1981. Mrs. Mildred Rowley, a nursing sister, of Helming Drive, Wolverhampton, was granted a decree nisi yesterday on the grounds of her husband's unreasonable behaviour. She had complained that he was "cricket mad".

After the hearing at Wolverhampton Divorce Court, Mrs. Rowley said: "Cricket was not just a hobby – it was a total obsession. I had just had enough of it." Her husband, Mr. Michael Rowley, was not in court because he is on tour in the West Country with Stourbridge Cricket Club.

He was in Torquay yesterday with his team playing under their touring name of the Worcestershire Marauders battling it out against Torquay Cricket Club.

When asked to comment on his divorce he said: "Really there is nothing more that I can say. I cannot stop . . we have got to get on with the game."

An Open Letter to the Yorkshire Chairman

17 *September* 1981. *At a series of emergency meetings at Headingley today, attempts will be made to resolve the latest crisis within the Yorkshire club arising from last week's suspension of Geoffrey Boycott by the Yorkshire manager and former England captain, Ray Illingworth. Remarks made by Boycott on radio and television, in which he said he was not being given a fair deal by the county, brought the trouble to a head.*

Here we publish an open letter from our cricket correspondent, JOHN WOODCOCK, *to the chairman of the Yorkshire club, Mr. M. G. Crawford, whose day begins at 10.30 this morning when he meets members of the Yorkshire Reform Group, who are calling for Illingworth's dismissal. At 2 p.m. the cricket committee will meet to discuss the position and consider what proposals to present to the full committee convened for 5.30.*

Dear Michael,

Poor you, having to give up a golfing holiday in Scotland to knock two such illustrious heads together! If it is any comfort to you, you have a fine reputation within the Yorkshire club for fair dealing. "No one better than Michael", they say, "to sort things out."

As soon as Ray's appointment as your manager was announced there were those who saw as inevitable a clash between him and Geoff. It seems that they have come to resent one another in a way that was never evident in Australia when Ray was regaining the Ashes. There, they both wanted their own way and got it. Geoff was allowed to do as he pleased because Ray needed his runs. When Geoff threw his bat on the ground at Adelaide, in disgust at being given out, it suited Ray to have as small a part as possible in censuring him.

Now that you have discovered what happens when an implacable nature meets an iron will, we are all agog to see what you do about it. I suppose you will feel beholden to Ray because of the free rein you have given him. It is too late now to realize that it never does to reengage someone you have sacked, let alone to make him foreman.

It seems to me that the role of team manager in cricket, certainly when you have a captain who is worth his salt, can be so difficult to define as to be hardly worth the bother. The idea of a supremo running English cricket alarms me almost as much as a Reform Group running Yorkshire's.

What troubles you do have up there! Bill Bowes says it never used to be so, but I am not so sure about that. I always think there is nothing to compare, for pure vitriol, with one Yorkshireman talking about another if he doesn't care for him, or for rabid loyalty, when the same two people may be moved to defend each other.

Those of us looking in from outside are getting a good deal more amusement from Benn v. Healey than from Boycott v. Illingworth. When Yorkshire tear themselves apart it is bad news for English cricket.

It is true to say, I think, that Yorkshire have more support among the cricketing public now than they have ever had before. This, of course, is because of your admirable resolve to make do with your own kith and kin. I hope the present dispute won't change that. What we are hoping to see is a rapprochement between the two protagonists, but to achieve it you will need to be at your most cogently persuasive.

Both, clearly, are very angry. Neither, as you well know, likes to be run out. Both have an eye for the main chance. Both have their futures to consider. Both have powerful support, though some of those who, up to now, have thought that Boycott could do no wrong, must be beginning to wonder about that when he falls out with Illingworth. Not all of them can be aware of how difficult both can be – as David* found out in Australia.

I suppose England can more afford to lose Boycott today than they could Johnny Wardle when Yorkshire suspended him in 1958 and he was withdrawn from our side to Australia. Johnny was a bad loss to the first-class game. But I hope it won't come to that this time.

My sympathies are inclined to be with Geoff, my money on Ray, and my hopes are for seeing the two of them forgetting their differences and doing what is best for Yorkshire cricket – which they profess to have so much at heart.

With best wishes for a quick end to the turmoil and a happy return to the links.

Yours, John.

*David Clark was manager of the M.C.C. side to Australia in 1970-71, captained by Ray Illingworth.

Moreover . . . Miles Kington

24 *September* 1981. DITHERING HEIGHTS – a rip-roaring novel of passion and searing emotion.

"There's trouble up at t'crease!" The dread cry went up and was taken round the little Yorkshire town of Hutton-on-t'-Moor. A beautiful little town it was, although the grimy and dreary moorland was only 10 minutes' walk away, and its one industry was cricket. Generations of Hutton men had gone to work on the county ground, patiently hewing runs out of the resistant pitch. It was man's work in which women took no part, yet when a disaster was reported it was the womenfolk who crowded round the pavilion doors, weeping and waiting for the worst.

This was one of those days. The flag had gone up over the pavilion, meaning that men were trapped inside in a sudden and violent committee meeting. They could be there for days, and nobody knew who would come out alive. The crowd was silent.

"They do say as 'ow big Geoff Boycott has bought it", said an old man whose crouching stance showed him to be an ex-middle of the order batsman.

"But there have always been Boycotts at the ground!" exclaimed a woman.

"It only seems that way, lass", said the old man. "It's always been Geoff, the greatest cricketer Yorkshire ever produced."

"Any news of Ray Illingworth?" someone asked. Ray Illingworth! The greatest player Yorkshire had ever produced. The man who had gone down south to seek his fortune and had come back again to Hutton-on-t'-Moor as they all did with the possible exception of Mighty Brian Close, the greatest cricketer ever to come from those parts.

Suddenly the crowd pressed forward as the doors opened, then fell back slightly as two stretchers were carried out. The women gasped and the men went pale as the two recumbent forms proved to be those of Boycott and Illingworth.

"Are they dead?" asked the old man. No one answered him. In true gritty, direct Yorkshire style he went up to Boycott and bent over him. "Art tha dead, lad?"

There was no reply. The women moaned. Then a microphone was thrust in his face and a soft voice said: "BBC here, Mr. Boycott. Have you any comment to make in the light of today's disaster?"

The words had a magical effect. The eyelids fluttered, the lips opened and with a great effort the wounded man said: "I am fighting fit and raring to play for Yorkshire every day of my life and I demand to see my solicitor". The roar that went up from the crowd awoke the other man, and Ray Illingworth suddenly sat up from his coma.

"I am the manager!" he cried. "What I say goes! I think, therefore I am! Consider the spinners of the field! Tha shalt have no other manager!"

Exhausted, both men fell back and were carried off. Before the crowd could look grief-stricken again, the doors opened once more and out strode a spruce figure carrying a suitcase. It was the greatest cricketer Yorkshire had ever produced – John Hampshire.

"'Appen you'll not see me round 'tton again, lads!" he cried. "I'm off to bonny Derbyshire. If you need a new manager or captain, give me a ring!'"

"I always doubted he were a true Yorkshire lad", growled the old man. "There's got to be summat wrong wi' a man who names hisself after a southern county."

As Hampshire pushed his way through the crowd, a young man came the other way with all his worldly goods in a small bag. "I have come to play for Yorkshire, good folk", he said loudly. "Tell me to whom I should apply."

They looked at him. They noticed that he was jet black. They smiled. Even the women laughed. "Th'art a gradely lad", said the old man to him, "but no one not Yorkshire born can ever dig for runs on 'utton pitch."

"Know then, old man", said the black youth, "that I was born and bred in Bradford and proud of it." There was a short, stunned silence. "Lord be praised!" shouted the old man. "We've got our own West Indian at last!"

And that is how Heathcliff, the greatest cricketer Yorkshire ever gave birth to, came to play at Hutton-on-t'-Moor.

No Ball

2 *March* 1982, *Leading Article*. "I think it will be treated as one of total deception", said the Minister for Sport, Mr. Neil Macfarlane, yesterday, referring to the action of a dozen English cricketers in touring South Africa. He was right: what is at issue is not a question of judgment but a matter of trust. There are certainly two points of view about the merits of resuming sporting contacts with South Africa at this time. It can be argued that there is no longer a case for continuing to ban South Africa from international competition in those sports where outside pressure has led to people of different races playing with and against each other, that to maintain a boycott in such circumstances is not to protest against apartheid in sport but to use sport as a political instrument against the wider evil of apartheid in society. It may also be argued, less controversially, that it would be an infringement of personal rights for any government or sporting authority to forbid anyone, as an individual, to play wherever he wishes.

But neither of these arguments can be deployed to justify this tour. These cricketers are not going as a bunch of carefree, if irresponsible, individuals in search of some enjoyable play in a pleasing climate. They are being paid large sums of money to compete against a representative South African team, who will receive international caps for their endeavours. That is in direct contravention of the policy of the Test and County Cricket Board, which wrote to every first-class player in England towards the end of last summer warning them that if they played in any international or representative match in South Africa they would jeopardize their chances of being selected for England.

If that policy is mistaken it should be changed: if it is changed it should be done so openly. The worst way for it to be challenged is for players to slip out of England secretively, "playing it very close to their chests", as the TCCB spokesman put it with sour restraint.

The impression of deception is all the greater because of the assurances that were given before this winter's tour of India was allowed to proceed. The Indian Government was wrong in the first instance to raise objections to Geoffrey Boycott and Geoffrey Cook as members of the English team because they had played or coached in South Africa. But to allay Indian suspicions the TCCB emphasized its disapproval of representative tours of South Africa and the two players publicly expressed their opposition to "the principle and system of apartheid".

Boycott's words have now been made to appear as no more than a gesture of convenience; and there will inevitably be doubts over the sincerity of the TCCB's assurance, even though the board has in fact acted impeccably throughout. This is the most serious aspect because the thoughtless or selfish attitude of this touring party will put in jeopardy the future structure of Test cricket. There could all too easily be a division between the white and non-white cricketing nations, which would be tragic for the development of the game and a denial of its spirit.

The correct course now would be for the TCCB to live up to the spirit of its earlier warning and ban these players from selection for England. However, to go further, as some would like, and bar them from county cricket would be wrong. But to do less would almost certainly lead to the cancellation of this summer's tours by India and Pakistan, and quite possibly to the end of Test cricket as we have known it.

The players were banned from Test cricket for three years.

A Restrained Innings against Pace Attack

FRANK JOHNSON IN THE COMMONS

3 *March* 1982. "Maggie Fury at South Africa Cricket Tour" said a headline in *The Sun*. Other morning newspapers had variously described the Prime Minister as dismayed, and concerned and angry.

Some of us went into Prime Minister's question time, then, with foreboding, being dismayed and concerned at her anger. For that is not what we regard her as being for. We like her fury to be directed at the great liberal causes.

But it turned out that all was well. Throughout the exchanges she bore the rebellious cricketers' action with marked composure. She preferred to dwell on the importance of allowing citizens of a free country to travel where they liked. This, for a minority of us, is the true issue. So the Maggie Fury at the South Africa tour was presumably that day's page three girl, a descendant perhaps of the pop artiste of old, Billy Fury. ("Maggie's ambition is to travel. She will be in South Africa for the cricket tour".)

It was an historic question time. Mrs. Thatcher presumably entered *Wisden* by becoming the first Prime Minister to bat steadily through an entire Commons uproar without once supporting the Government.

The pedantic may object that she is the Government. Well, not always. All the evidence suggests that she regards the Government as a vast force with a life of its own. It is entirely made up of such uncontrollable phenomena as Sports Ministers who have no alternative but to denounce cricket tours of South Africa, and various spokesmen who have to put it about that she is "concerned" about such visits to forbidden lands.

For these purposes, she tends to include the official Opposition, much of the press, and the BBC, as part of the Government; certainly the SDP is included, indeed she probably sees it as the permanent government.

But, like Mao Tse Tung, every now and then she generates cultural revolution against the regime over which she nominally presides. Such an occasion was yesterday. The right winger Mr. Nicholas Winterton (Macclesfield, Con) rose. He is a co-author of a Commons motion congratulating the errant cricketers. He has a loud voice, as befits a man who bullies for England. He demanded that Mrs. Thatcher defend the principle that "any law-abiding citizen of this country has the right to travel where he wants to".

Some of us more delicate souls might have preferred that our cause be championed by a more *verlichte* figure than Mr. Winterton, but one cannot always choose one's allies. Matters were not helped by the fact that Mr. Winterton is burly, blond, and has a military background.

Mrs. Thatcher replied that all citizens were free to travel and no restrictions would be placed upon them. With that she sat down. There was no condemnation of the tour. It was in this not entirely subtle way that she revealed her lack of fury. One assailed oneself for ever having doubted her.

The Labour benches were enraged. Actually, they were delighted. What one means is that they made out they were enraged. Mr. Foot rose. He denounced Mr. Winterton's motion as "deeply humiliating to the House of Commons". He urged her to condemn it. She rose again and repeated that citizens were free to travel. If they were restricted, we would no longer be a free country".

Mr. Foot got up again and condemned the Tory motion. Mrs. Thatcher returned to her theme about freedom. Some Labour Members shouted at her to condemn the tour. "Say it, say it", said others, taking up the cry. She did not. Mr. Foot and Mrs. Thatcher continued their exchange on the same lines as before. Two Tory wets, Mr. Hector Munro, the former Minister for Sport, and Mr. Peter Bottomley, did condemn the tour. This intensified the Prime Minister's lack of fury.

The other *Wisden*-type fact to be recorded is who was the first Labour Backbencher to shout "racialist!" and after how long into the question time. (Mr. Martin Flannery: five minutes.)

The Unmasking of a Dashing Oriental Star

BY ALAN GIBSON

19 *May* 1982. Fifty years ago I saw the Indians play at Leyton. I can tell you the date: it was May 28, my ninth birthday – no, I tell a lie, because there was no play on the Saturday, but I had a chance of watching them on the Monday and Tuesday.

Our house overlooked the Leyton ground and on the Saturday, as a birthday treat, I had been allowed to go in, paying sixpence, to watch from closer quarters. It was a disappointment that there was no play, after numerous consultations, but I can remember several things about the rest of the match, though by then I was only surveying it from the balcony at home.

I had bought a scorecard (twopence, a stiff price we thought) and conned it eagerly. No. 1 in the Indian side was described as H. H. Porbandar, with an asterisk to show he was captain. When India went in, after bowling Essex out for 169, their No. 1 played some handsome strokes.

We had some romantic ideas about Indian cricket at that time, because of Duleepsinhji, and the Nawab of Pataudi, and vague folk memories of Duleep's uncle, Ranji. So, although neither Duleep nor the Nawab were available for the Indian party, we expected magic. When the Indian No. 1 was so dashing, I thought that this Porbandar was going to be another oriental star.

"Cor, old Porbs looked good", I said to my friends. I wondered what the H.H. stood for. 'Arry? my friends suggested, or 'Erbert? I cannot swear to this, but I do believe I suggested 'Orace, because I knew he was something foreign.

Alas! I discovered later that though Porbandar had played in that match, he had not batted, and that the No. 1 who had played the strokes was Naoomal Jeeoomal – or words to that effect (even *Wisden* was uncertain in its transliteration of Indian names in those days). Naoomal played three times against England and averaged 27, so he cannot have been too bad. He made 1,300 runs in that 1932 season, 1,500 in all matches. So I had seen a pretty good innings; but it was a disappointment that he had not been Porbandar.

H.H., I also discovered, stood for "His Highness', and the full title was "The Maharajah of Porbandar". *Wisden* of 1933 described his appointment as captain of the Indian side (there had been touring sides from India before, but this was the first to be granted a Test match) in these terms:

"Some little difficulty was experienced with regard to the captaincy, and after one or two disappointments the choice fell upon the Maharajah of Porbandar . . . For reasons apart from cricket, the necessity existed of having a person of distinction and importance in India at the head of affairs, and it was almost entirely because of this that Porbandar led the team."

(Did anyone murmur anything about sport and politics?).

Wisden continues: "No injustice is being done to him, therefore, by saying that admirably fitted as he was in many respects for the task, his abilities as a cricketer were not commensurate with the position he occupied."

I checked Porbandar's figures for the tour:

At Pelsham, v. Mr. T. Gilbert Scott's XI (not first-class): b R. S. G. Scott 0; b Owen-Smith 2.
At Hove, v. Sussex: b Tate 0.
At Maidenhead, v. Mr. H. M. Martineau's XI (not first-class): b Lowndes 2.
At Cardiff, v. Glamorgan: b Jones 2.
At Cambridge, v. the University: c Titley, b Rought-Rought 0.

He did not play again after the Cambridge match in the second week of June: at least, I can find no trace of it in *Wisden*, which nevertheless attributes 8 runs to him in all matches (average 1.14). Where are the missing runs? I can agree with their verdict on first-class matches (2 runs, average 0.66), but there is a problem here which I feel the Society of Cricket Statisticians should immediately investigate. There is no record of his bowling or taking a catch.

That is not all there is to say about the Maharajah. The tour was difficult, experimental, and it passed off happily. India ("All-India" as the team was then called) did well and though they lost the only Test match, it was not before they had given England a shock or two. E. W. Swanton wrote that Porbandar "made a creditable success of keeping his men a happy and united party". It was also graceful, if inevitable, for him to step out of the side.

That it was not so easy to captain an Indian side in England was shown on the next tour, in 1936, when the amiable Vizianagram ("call me Vizzy", he used to say in the commentary box) struck trouble, and Amarnath, the best all-rounder, was sent home. In a later book Swanton refers, rather unkindly, to Porbandar's "fleet of white Rolls-Royces", but also states that he had made only two runs on the tour – "from a leg-glance at Cardiff, I seem to recall".

Fifty years later, with cricket between England and India still going on, I think we owe a salute to him. Porbandar – the state – produces limestone, which, according to the *Encyclopaedia Britannica*, "is used for buildings in Porbandar without mortar, and is said to coalesce into a solid block under the influence of moisture". Well, the limestone still holds, and he applied his touches of moisture in those early days.

8 *June* 1982. It was a pleasure at Edgbaston to meet Robert Brooke, the editor of *The Cricket Statistician*, who has solved the Porbandar mystery, of which I wrote in these columns some weeks ago, and which has perplexed a number of correspondents. Brooke has confounded *Wisden* and demonstrated that the Maharajah did make two more runs, equalling his highest score, in a match, twelve a side, against Blackheath in 1932. This confirms his tour average, for all matches at 1.14. He still holds the record for a touring captain.

Turner: Man of Principle and a Perfectionist

BY JOHN WOODCOCK

2 *June* 1982. Of the 19 cricketers to have scored 100 first class hundreds none can have been more of a perfectionist than Glenn Turner, or have reached the landmark in a more spectacular way than when he scored 311 not out in one day against Warwickshire last Saturday.

He has no time for the slovenly, whether in his own game or anyone else's. As a young man he dedicated himself to developing a technique based on the teachings of the text book, realizing that was the surest way of achieving consistency. A career average of 50, as near as makes no matter, shows how successful he has been.

To be such a very good player and yet find it necessary to score 239 not out against a weak Oxford University attack, as he did in his first innings this season, tells, as well as anything could, of Turner's single-mindedness. Some of Worcestershire's later batsmen were hoping for an early-season knock. Yet by doing things his way Turner wins more matches for them in a season than even Vivian Richards does for Somerset. That this is so is an indication of how over the years he has widened the scope of his game.

In his time he has twice carried his bat through a Test innings, with infinite patience and in vastly different conditions, and yet so dominated an attack in a county championship match (Worcestershire v. Glamorgan at Swansea in 1977) as to score 141 not out out of a total of 169, a record in percentage terms. In most recent seasons he has made a habit of scoring at least one hundred before lunch.

Only Walter Hammond has ever scored a hundred in each innings of a match more often than Turner. Hammond did it seven times to Turner's six. Turner's 10 hundreds in a season (1970) for Worcestershire constitute a record for the county.

In 1973 he became the seventh and last batsman and the only one since the last war to score 1,000 runs before the end of May. In the West Indies in 1971-72, playing for New Zealand, he scored 672 runs in the Test series at an average of 96. In successive innings in Georgetown, against Guyana and then in the fourth Test match, he scored 259, and batted altogether for nearly 22 hours. So one could go on.

Turner was born in Dunedin, in the South Island of New Zealand, in 1947. He was 35 on May 26, and now that he has put his 100th hundred in the bag he will probably retire at the end of the season. Once Billy Ibadulla, then coaching in New Zealand, had persuaded him to try his luck in England soon after leaving school, Turner's course was set. Besides being fastidiously correct, for a long time he was tediously slow. Yet today, of all the batsmen playing first class cricket, he makes as good a model as any for youngsters to study.

If he has not been a great success as a captain it may be because of the permissiveness of the age: he sets higher standards both on and off the field than many today find acceptable. He made no secret of his distaste for the way some of the Australians played the game in New Zealand when they were there in 1974, or for the antics of the West Indians, also in New Zealand, in 1980.

It was unlike him when, to show the West Indians what he had thought of them then, he refused to bat properly while playing for Worcestershire against them soon afterwards. It would have been in character had he kept them in the field for a couple of days with an immaculate display of manners and batting method.

In New Zealand there are those who feel, not altogether surprisingly, that he should have made himself available to play for them more often. His last Test match was in 1976 when he was only 29. He has preferred in recent years to spend his time out there in the commentary box rather than at the wicket, watching far less good players trying to cope. Because of this he has never proved himself at the highest level against the fiercest pace. Some say he never could, though I disagree with that.

His record entitles him to be ranked as the foremost right-handed batsman New Zealand has produced (Martin Donnelly and Bert Sutcliffe, both great players, stood the other way round) and with such character, determination and technique he could, I am sure, have made a hundred against Holding at one end and Roberts at the other. The last batsmen to reach 100 hundreds were Geoff Boycott and John Edrich in 1977; the next will almost certainly by Zaheer Abbas who needs only nine more.

Match that Needs a New Home

BY ALAN GIBSON

28 *June* 1982. On Saturday Oxford won the toss, batted and six overs were bowled, enough to see several handsome strokes from their captain, Ellis. But nobody was deeply interested, for obviously the rain would soon blot

things out, which it did so comprehensively that play was abandoned for the day at half past two.

This was sad, sadder than usual when a day's cricket is washed away, because we had some hopes of this match, hopes that it might do something to restore the quality of the occasion. Both sides had played presentably against the counties, Cambridge actually beating Lancashire.

They have plenty of good batsmen, though, as usual with university sides, the bowling has been weak or at least inexperienced. They should have done better in the Benson and Hedges Cup, though they did well enough against the Indians. I felt the bowling lacked an aged, prayerful character like Wingfield-Digby, but I suppose even theologians have to end their courses sometime or another.

What we expected, given the weather, was a high scoring match, with admirable batting, a cautious declaration by whoever was batting on the third morning, and a draw. You could expect a draw anyway. Since 1960, of the 21 matches played, 17 have been drawn. In the first 100 years of the fixture, which began in 1827 (though irregular in the early years) nine were drawn.

The object then was to win at all costs. The object now is to avoid defeat at all costs. This is why this historic game has lost public interest: even if it had been fine on Saturday, few more people would have been there to watch.

The only man who might have stirred some interest, because he was the only bowler with the talent to get the other side out, and had an air of class about him, was Pringle, who preferred to play for England, although he was the Cambridge captain. A previous Cambridge captain, Majid, chose his university before Pakistan, although he had played for Pakistan twice that season. It clashed, he felt, with the duties he had accepted when he accepted the captaincy.

Pringle's decision, and I see the force of the argument that a young man needs money and must not risk his place in the England side, reduced the status of the university match to a second class fixture. That his colleagues should be reported as being "delighted" with his decision reduced it even more.

I wrote some years ago that the match would be better played at Bletchley, or possibly Scarborough, or Torquay. I was confirmed in my view by a letter from the Bletchley Cricket Club, an old established club enjoying a boom since it is adjacent to Milton Keynes, saying they would be delighted to house it and could guarantee a good gate. All the authority, grit and dignity of the occasion at Lord's has been lost. And I do not say this just because of Saturday's rain. The sooner the fixture is moved, the better.

OXFORD 249 for 5 dec (R. G. P. Ellis 86) and 136 for 6 dec (R. J. Boyd-Moss 4 for 42)
CAMBRIDGE 114 for 2 dec (R. J. Boyd-Moss 41 not out) and 272 for 3 (R. J. Boyd-Moss 100, S. P. Henderson 50, N. E. J. Barrington 48 not out)
Score after first day: Oxford 23 for 0
Cambridge won by 7 wickets

Window on the World of Lord's

Gubby Allen at 80

BY JOHN WOODCOCK

31 *July* 1982. Eighty today, G. O. Allen has become as intrinsically a part of Lord's as Father Time or the Grace Gates. Whatever the match in progress, he is to be seen framed in the window of the Committee Room, dispensing the wisdom of his long experience.

The years have not so much wearied as mellowed him. Although it is still sometimes said that this or that decision is "one for Gubby's Lawn", the term is used by way of definition, not of resentment. He is more a father figure now than a high priest, more the Emeritus Fellow than the Secretary of State.

Lord's, almost literally, is his own back garden. Only the pavilion prevents him from seeing "the green circle" as he lies in bed. On August 9 he is being honoured with a dinner in the Long Room. The only other dinner to have been held there was for Sir Pelham Warner in 1953, also to mark his 80th birthday. It is a little like giving a dance on the Centre Court at Wimbledon.

As one of three Trustees of MCC, Gubby Allen is still the holder of an important office at Lord's. At some time or other he has been both president and treasurer of the club, captain of England, chairman of the Test selectors, a constant guardian of the welfare of the game and a tireless worker for youth. For most of this century no important decisions have been taken at Lord's without first having been through the hands of Plum Warner or Gubby Allen.

When at his best as a cricketer, Mr. Allen was busy enough in the City never to be able to play anything like a full season for Middlesex. Twice, though, he went to Australia – as one of Douglas Jardine's formidable array of fast bowlers in 1932-33 (Allen never bowled bodyline himself) and again as captain in 1936-37, when he suffered the agonies of losing the last three Test matches after having won the first two.

After the war, at the age of 45, he took MCC away again, this time to West Indies. On his 50th birthday Mr. Allen made a hundred, playing for the Arabs against Sir William Worsley's XI at Hovingham Hall in Yorkshire. At 80, with a notable collection of hip operations to be incorporated in his swing, he still plays golf, a game with whose theory, like that of cricket, he has had a long and romantic attachment.

In Adelaide earlier this year, Sir Donald Bradman, his erstwhile adversary, commenting on a piece of Mr. Allen's in the 1981 *Wisden* entitled "Fifty Years On", said: "To have been more critical would have been much easier but much less helpful." There was in the article a strong note of understanding, the contentment of twilight.

Peerless Percy George

BY RICHARD STREETON

21 *August* 1982. The world's senior Test match cricketer, P. G. H. Fender, is 90 tomorrow, the last famous survivor from the golden age of English cricket before 1914 when his early contemporaries were such legendary figures as Ranjitsinhji, Sydney Barnes and Jessop.

The First World War delayed Fender's Test debut until the 1920-21 MCC tour to Australia, J. C. W. MacBryan (Somerset) is a month older than Fender, but he did not win his solitary England cap until 1924. "Stork" Hendry, Australia's longest surviving senior, played his first Test a few months after Fender and is a mere 87.

Fender's last games for Surrey were in 1935. Senior citizens down Kennington way can still be found who claim that nobody at the Oval since "Percy George" has been such fun to watch; whether as a ferocious hitter, guileful spinner or controversial captain. Fender in his elongated sweater – immortalized in Tom Webster cartoons – has remained a vivid memory for them.

These days Fender is recalled most often as the scorer of first-class cricket's fastest 100 in history and also for the failure by England to choose him as captain.

It was at Northampton in 1920 that Fender reached three figures in 35 minutes, having faced between 40 and 46 balls. The precise number cannot be deduced from the only surviving scorebook.

It remains uncertain why Fender never led England. He was regarded as the shrewdest cricketing brain in the country and he worked near miracles in the early 1920s with Surrey's limited bowling attack on unhelpful Oval wickets. In his thinking and behaviour, though, Fender was frequently ahead of his time. Several minor skirmishes with authorities probably did little for his cause.

Fender, now blind, celebrates tomorrow with a family luncheon party in Horsham, Sussex, where he lives with his son. He still deals with telephone inquiries on behalf of the family firm, the London Wine Exchange, but the 1980 Lord's centenary Test was his last major outing. He cannot see the screen and follows cricket by listening to the television. In a typically succinct Fender remark, made without malice, he says: "Can't get on with those radio chaps, but Benaud is worth listening to."

Plans to make a film about the bodyline series have aroused his interest. "I shall write and protest if anyone blackens Jardine's name. I still maintain he was blameless."

Dissent by players and other bad behaviour appals him. He was delighted when Peter May – an occasional visitor – became chairman of the selectors this summer. As Fender recently said: "You know, Streeton, I was always considered a bit of a rogue but I would never have done, or allowed to be done, half of what goes on these days . . . I do hope those in charge of the game can get it back on the right rails."

Twist Again

Qadir Brings Back the Leg Spin

BY DONALD WOODS

26 *August* 1982. Many old gentlemen of England will have a smile in their hearts today because of the revival of an art they had thought lost forever.

For years they had lamented the passing of leg spin bowling. Where were the successors to Bosanquet, Mailey, Grimmett, Tich Freeman, Peebles, Faulkner – or even that young feller Benaud? Gone and forgotten, it seemed, was the wristy, back-of-the-hand delivery so hard to control that it was too expensive in this era of limited-over cricket.

Now the lament is no longer necessary, thanks to Abdul Qadir, of Pakistan, who proves with the essence of the risky art of leg spin that he can weave spells around England's best batsmen without squandering runs to buy victims. But never mind the figures. It is the way in which he does his devious work that makes Qadir the embodiment of all the composite characteristics of classical leg spin.

It is, after all, the most subtle and sinister of all the cricketing arts, and it is not for your open-hearted extrovert. To go to the unnatural trouble of screwing the ball out of the back of the hand over a cocked wrist requires a nature both complicated and contrary, as well as a readiness to wrench the shoulder, elbow and other parts of the body into unconventional positions.

Action pictures of the great leg spinners give some idea of the sheer inconvenience of this method of delivery. Douglas Wright's action was once described as a cross between the barn dance and the swallow-dive. Roly Jenkins, by all accounts, did a sort of hornpipe. "Tiger" O'Reilly grimaced as if in agony, and perhaps he was.

But it gets to you. Dabble in the dark arts of leg spin and your whole approach to life is affected. I knew a schoolmaster so addicted that he seemed unable to walk an ordinary pavement very far without going compulsively into the tangential foot-shufflings and shoulder-shruggings apparently inseparable from preparation to bowl a leg-break.

Yet the real leg spinners are the true princes of cricket, and if they have to do a sort of Mephistophelean deal to reach the top orders of the mystical rite they certainly pay the price.

It seems that Qadir could not be other than a leg spinner. He even walks like one between deliveries, with his feet apparently magnetized to the turf for preparatory purchase (remember Colin McCool?) and he has the right face, too, one of calculation and conspiracy.

The eyes narrow ominously and the fringe of dark beard hints at brigandage and plunder, not at all like the straightforward yeoman growth of Gatting.

You could imagine that face emerging from the mystic gloom of a Karachi bazaar to whisper dread tidings of deceit in high places and intrigue in the back streets, and the name Abdul is somehow appropriate, hinting at the mystery and magic that is about to be worked on some poor plodding Englishman at the crease.

As is fully to be expected, Qadir goes into a most complicated set of movements to begin his bowling action. He holds his left hand high as if in final salute to the doomed batsman, while his right hand twirls the ball urgently to appraise it of future rotational requirements, then squirts the ball into the upraised left hand while his feet begin a ritual dance on the spot.

The left hand brandishes the ball momentarily, then transfers it back into the right, which is already beginning a series of small circular sweeps as he bounds and gambols into his curving (of course) approach run.

In all this activity his entire body is the mere servant of the cocked right wrist as it sweeps over out of a flurry of wheeling arms to float the buzzing ball at his victim, and so complete is all bodily involvement that even after releasing the ball Qadir twirls after it up the pitch as if urging it on to work its own wickedness, and his bowling arm repeats an echo motion of the delivery to quench itself of every last vestige of spinfulness.

What the ball then does is variously astonishing. Taking on a life of its own it loops and dips, pitching to spin vastly to left or right or to spear straight on with topspin, and if it raps the batsman's pads Qadir has a range of appeals for lbw – one supplicatory, one accusatory, one challenging and one slyly inquisitive, then the major one, the total and ultimate appeal.

With this one he dances an angry tattoo upon the turf, jumping up and down and uttering fierce cries of the sort that surely terrified whole generations of marauders clear out of the Khyber Pass. At such times Qadir makes John McEnroe seem like a calm exponent of reasoned remonstration.

But ultimately it is his superb art that one remembers, and it is a fitting irony that the torments of the googly which he now inflicts on innocent Anglo-Saxon lads had their origin not in the mystical regions of the East but on the playing fields of England.

Bosanquet knew not what he was visiting upon later generations of his countrymen, but Abdul Qadir certainly does, and as a worthy custodian of the rescued art of legspin he will surely continue to delight millions with his magic.

A Master of the Mind Game Steps Down for a Back-bench Role

BY JOHN WOODCOCK, CRICKET CORRESPONDENT

14 *September* 1982. Garlanded with honours, the latest of them the county championship of 1982, Mike Brearley retires today from first-class cricket. His next career will be as a psycho-analyst; his first was as a university lecturer. Such is his knowledge of the game and those who play it, as well as the goodwill which attaches to him, that his recent election to the cricket committee of the Test and County Cricket Board is much to be welcomed.

It is 21 years ago that a Cambridge undergraduate, a little under medium height and a scholar to St. John's from the City of London School, began to be talked about as a batsman of unusual promise. When the 1961 Australians came to Fenner's, three weeks after Brearley had played his first first-class match there, he made 73 and 89, batting at No. 8 in the first innings and going in first in the second. Jack Fingleton commented that he had seen a great batsman in the making.

In the event that was something Brearley never became. His record during his four years at Cambridge was so outstandingly good, and he has scored so consistently for Middlesex in the years that he has played regularly for them, that it has to be one of the disappointments of his career to have no better a batting average in Test matches than 22.88 and in 66 innings for England never to have made a hundred.

Despite that, he was a winner of Test matches, more so than many a great batsman, and a veritable thorn in Australia's side, because of his qualities as a captain.

Some captains are Olympian, some genial, some bluff, some autocratic, some are confused, some fussy, some anonymous. Brearley was brilliantly analytical. He has worked out the modern game better than anyone else except perhaps for Ray Illingworth. Few have had more to do with the most recent stages of cricket's evolution on the field or more strongly influenced trends off it.

He looked more objectively than most at the Packer intrusion, his aim, right from the start, being that some good should come out of it. He has been ruthless in his pursuit of success for Middlesex, whether that has meant going against the wishes of many of the county's members by importing fast bowlers from South Africa, West Indies and Australia, or preferring, as he did last week, a young Oxford Blue, Richard Ellis, to such a trusty servant as Clive Radley.

Owing, though, to Brearley's reputation for clear thinking, his decisions, although they may not always have brought agreement, have inevitably been respected. Rodney Hogg, the Australian fast bowler, once said of him that whatever other degrees he may have, he certainly has one in "people". When it has come to getting the best out of his players he has had few failures.

Having, some years ago, been a sort of cricketing Wedgwood Benn, he retires from active service more as a Joe Gormley, prepared, as it were, to take a seat in the House of Lords so long as that did not mean having to wear a tie. If he were, in fact, the next cricketing knight, it would be no surprise.

His fellow players will miss his counsel, the game his prestige, the reading public his fascinating books on the Ashes. He has scored 44 first-class hundreds and over 25,000 first-class runs. He led England to 11 victories over Australia (as against four defeats), the most gratifying of them coming last year when he returned and pulled together, so dramatically, a dejected and disjointed team.

Under Brearley's captaincy, Middlesex have won four county championships and two Gillette Cups, and if, at some time in the future, they find themselves in desperate straits, and he has no patients for a day or two and has been playing a little, he would help them out. As someone who likes to be fully stretched he probably will.

Causing a Stir

20 *September* 1982, *Diary*. The metal bat with which Dennis Lillee gained headlines almost three years ago has proved a failure as a soup stirrer. Six of the aluminium bats were tested by the West Australian Department of Mental Health, which hoped they would prove more durable than big wooden spatulas used to stir huge vats of soup being prepared for patients. The bats have been declared out by the catering staff, who find them hard to clean.

Lillee, who hurled his bat towards the dressing room when told he could not continue using it in the Perth Test of December 1979, said: "It should have been an ideal soup stirrer – bacteria free and virtually indestructible." He and his partner, Graeme Monaghan, are still seeking alternative uses for the redundant hit-wear.

Kortright – the Quick and the Dread

BY ALAN GIBSON

11 *December* 1982. While in chase of some quite different information recently, I noticed that C. J. Kortright died on December 12, 1952, only 30 years ago. I say "only" because we think of him as one of the great fast bowlers of the 1890s. He died, however, just short of his 82nd birthday.

Arguments about the relative speeds of fast bowlers of different generations are often entertaining but inevitably fruitless, although I suppose in future the electronic eye may give us some rough guide. Up to 1914 it was commonly accepted among English cricketers that Kortright was the fastest. Australians were inclined to prefer the claim of their own Ernest Jones. Englishmen agreed that Jones was fast, although suspecting he was a chucker. It was Jones who was said to have bowled a ball through W. G. Grace's beard (there are various versions of the story, all improbable).

As late as 1942, E. H. D. Sewell described Kortright as "the fastest bowler, right or left, ever". Sewell's judgment was marred because he could never bring himself to believe that much good cricket was played after the First World War; but he had played and reported cricket for more than half a century when he wrote those words, and fielded in the gully for Essex when Kortright was bowling. So he had some experience on which to base his assertion.

He quotes, in partial support, J. T. Hearne, who said that the fastest bowlers were Kotze (South Africa), Knox (Surrey), and Kortright. Sewell adds that Hearne "did not specify the fast ones in that order, but if he places them in the order in which he wrote them, I am surprised. I have held catches in the slips off Kotze and Kortright and managed to get a hundred with Knox doing his full share of the bowling, and, on those experiences, I put Kotze third and Kortright always head, shoulders, arms, legs and brain, easily first."

Well, we might minimize the importance of Sewell's tribute, but it was not unsupported. Altham wrote that in 1895 Kortright "was probably as fast as anyone who has ever lived"; and confirms it in a different part of his *History* (written in 1926) by saying that Kortright was "by fairly common consent the fastest of all bowlers within living memory". H. D. G. Leveson-Gower, writing in 1953, says that "the fastest of them all was C. J. Kortright."

P. F. Warner, in 1911, wrote that "I think Kortright at his best was just a shade faster than anyone else. Tall, loosely built, and very strong in the back, Kortright, with his long, springy run up to the wicket, was at times almost terrifying. One had to shut one's teeth very tight, and to remember that for honour's sake one could not run away, to face him on a rough wicket. Some of the professionals, in particular, feared him with a mortal fear!" In a footnote to a later edition of the book in 1943, Warner adds that "Larwood is probably as fast as anyone in the history of the game".

There is, however, substantial evidence from these comments that Kortright was PDQ. But he never played for England. He probably would have done in 1899, but for an injury. He played often for the Gentlemen. He began at Brentwood, then Tonbridge in 1887, played for Essex, not regularly, from 1889 to 1907 (captain in 1903), and took 489 first-class wickets at an average of 21. He also had a batting average of nearly 18, with a couple of centuries. A lot of his time he spent playing country house cricket. He was very much the amateur and used to boast that he had never done a day's work in his life.

I must pinch John Arlott's account of a conversation, from his introduction to David Frith's *The Fast Men*. Kortright was asked: "What did you *do*, Charles?"

"What do you mean, *do*?"

"Well, you know, for a living?"

"Didn't have to earn a living, father left enough for me and my sister."

"Well, what did you do except bowl fast?"

"Bowled leg-breaks and played golf."

In the 1948 *Wisden* Kortright said he had always wanted to "project things further and faster than anyone else". He recalled the time he once bowled six byes in a club match at Wallingford. He was a temperamental character, and had a famous row with W.G., amicably settled when they shared a last-wicket partnership in a tight finish against the Players.

It is sad, as Frith says, that we have no action photographs of Kortright; it is sad, too, that a man who could take seven for 73 against the Players was never pitted against Australia. Sad for us, that is. I doubt if it ever occurred to him to care tuppence about such details.

Pavilioned in Splendour

BY RUPERT MORRIS

27 *April* 1983. Today's cricket match at Lord's between MCC and Middle-sex, the county champions, is not only the traditional opening fixture of the season, when Test match hopefuls aim to impress the selectors. It is also the cricket follower's annual opportunity to cast off the leaden cares of winter and imbibe the sight, sounds and smells that are an irreplaceable part of an English summer. More than that, it enables him to escape into a time-warp.

The ground, which opened in 1814 as the home of MCC, is universally regarded as the Mecca of cricket. Despite many structural changes to the international game it remains the administrative headquarters; the President and Secretary of MCC still automatically occupy the same positions within the International Cricket Conference, cricket's supreme body, and MCC still makes the laws of the game.

Hardly surprising, perhaps, that Lord's today should remain cocooned in traditions that comfort those who belong there and warn strangers to mind their manners.

Unless you have a match ticket, a membership card or a specific appoint-ment you will have trouble passing through the huge wrought-iron Grace Gate. Middlesex players arriving for practice in a car they have used all the previous season have been known to find difficulty getting in.

Bill Leonard, at 81 the most venerable of those who mind the gate, arrived at Lord's in 1922. He became a gateman in 1965; six years ago, when his wife died, he was told he could stay in the job as long as he liked. The club's generosity is the reward for his instinctive loyalty, and epitomizes the benevolent feudalism fundamental to Lord's and the Marylebone Cricket Club – a well-defined hierarchy which perpetuates, in subtle ways, the old cricketing distinction between "gentlemen" (amateurs) and "players" (professionals).

The home of the gentlemen of Lord's is, of course, the members' pavilion, a magnificent late Victorian three-tier stone building, a bastion of male privilege, where women and children are admitted only at specially ordained times.

Downstairs, the members take their ease, strolling among the cricketing memorabilia in the famous Long Room, or in the reading room and bars, while on the first floor Jack Bailey, the Secretary, and his three assistant secretaries run the show.

Mr. Bailey cut short a holiday in Majorca last week to return for another in a seemingly endless round of committee meetings. At the back of his mind is the special meeting later this summer when the members will decide whether or not to send an MCC team to South Africa, an issue that threatens to throw the cricketing world into a turmoil with repercussions as far-reaching as those of the D'Oliveira Affair. This morning, however, his main concern will be the weather.

That, too, will be the chief preoccupation of Lieutenant-Colonel John Stephenson, assistant secretary in charge of cricket, who will have bicycled in from Swiss Cottage shortly before 9 a.m., and will soon be on the telephone to RAF Northolt for the latest forecast.

Known to everyone as "Colonel" ("It's not quite pally-pally, but it's not too formal", he says), his is the unmistakably military figure that strides out to the wicket during weather-induced stoppages in matches to talk to the umpires and discuss the prospects for resumption of play with Jim Fairbrother, the groundsman. His arrival – as impressive in its way as the famous walk to the wicket of "Lord Ted" Dexter, or that of the arm-swinging superman Ian Botham – invariably prompts a cheer.

In his office, with its fine view of the pitch, the Colonel was explaining last week how the MCC organizes its 260 annual away fixtures and its foreign tours.

The average MCC club side is rather stronger these days than it used to be. Probationary playing members, of whom there are between two and three hundred, are given five matches in which to prove their worth under the eye of the match manager, before their applications are considered in August. Half are rejected.

Match managers' reports and records of every player's performances are kept in the Cricket Office, at the corner of the pavilion, where they are constantly updated by the manager, Steven Lynch, assisted by a clerk and a typist. In the files lie such fascinating details as the performance of I. T. Botham in his first MCC match in 1972 against the Universities Athletic Union. He made nought and took no wicket for 23 runs.

Botham was once an MCC Young Cricketer, a group of 20 school leavers taken on by Lord's for up to three seasons. It is their chance to learn the game (28 of them have gone on to be current county players), with the benefit of daily coaching, but they have to earn their keep by doing odd jobs, bowling at members, and occasionally being drafted into MCC sides at short notice.

They arrived fresh faced on Monday to be given a pep talk by the Colonel. Today they will sell scorecards, man the scoreboards and be ready to help Jim Fairbrother with the covers.

The chief coach is Don Wilson, a genial 45-year-old Yorkshireman who played for England just before the sudden explosion in cricketers' pay in the 1970s, and who keeps a fatherly eye on the Young Cricketers, the schoolboys who come to Easter coaching classes, and even some seasoned professionals.

Few games encourage such eccentricity and give so much time for contemplation as cricket; it is no coincidence, for example, that many cricketers love music.

One day recently the indoor school was brought to a halt by a sudden burst of beautiful choral singing. Those familiar with Don Wilson's eccentricities may have carried on playing, but others dropped their bats and listened. He had been coaching the boys of the Westminster Abbey choir school, and at the end of their net, he asked them to sing. He always does.

Another music-lover is Christopher "Gus" Farley, a small, rotund, Pickwickian figure who is the ground superintendent, responsible for policing, general upkeep, and hiring winos. Winos? Surely they'd never get through the gate?

"Without them this place wouldn't be open", he replies. "They know there's casual work here, so they come from the arches at Charing Cross to paint the seats and clean. We give them a meal and pay them in cash.

"Mind you", he adds, "you have to look closely at their eyes before you take them on. And if there's one propped up between two others, you have to make sure he can stand up."

Two of the regular winos are, curiously enough, trained opera singers. Sometimes, after dark, when the cleaning is done, their fine voices echo across the deserted square.

In lyrical mood Mr. Farley describes the peculiar atmosphere of Lord's: how it livens up on the Monday when the Young Cricketers arrive, how on the morning of a match the ground "opens out like a flower", and how the life drains out of it at the end of the day as the last spectators leave.

Elsewhere in the pavilion Roy Harrington, the 62-year-old dressing-room attendant, prepares to bring the players their 10 a.m. tea, attend to any repairs to equipment, then bring lunch, towels, tea, and clean up the showers and baths afterwards.

This summer there will be no Geoffrey Boycott, always grabbing one of the two dressing-tables with a looking-glass. And Roy regrets the departure of characters like Denis Compton, who would often arrive late and rush out to smite centuries with a borrowed bat.

Behind the scenes, undoubtedly the most important figure is Jim Fairbrother, the groundsman. Foreign visitors, anxious to learn from the man who, as curator of the Lord's pitch, is the most distinguished practitioner of his art in the world, assume that he earns at least £20,000 a year, and drives a Mercedes. He does not.

To the cricket watcher, the square over which he presides is just a flattish patch of grass, albeit carefully trimmed. To Jim Fairbrother, it is 18 numbered pitches. The Test match pitch is No. 10, bang in the middle; no one else will play on it all year. He and the Colonel will have decided yesterday whether pitch No. 12, on the Tavern side of the centre, has dried out sufficiently to be used for today's game, or whether to switch to Pitch No. 3, higher up on the square. (There is a notorious "hill" at Lord's which runs down towards the Tavern.)

By the end of a season, the earth on the whole square has tightened as hard as a pavement. It has to be softened up by sprinkling over two days; then it must be raked with a scarifier, brushed with a besom, hollow-tined by machine, treated with a sorrel at the batting ends, grass seed inserted to a special formula, holes filled in with a top-dressing of soil with a high clay content, then covered with more soil and levelled with a lute. Jim illustrates this highly sophisticated procedure with an artist's hand gestures.

He had been thinking of taking a holiday last week, but the weather put paid to that. With rain about, it is all a matter of hairline decisions: which roller to use, how low to cut the grass, when to allow the Middlesex players to have nets or use the practice ground.

Under the Grand Stand work the Lord's printers, a team of three long-serving men, updating scorecards during matches, printing annual reports, invitations and notices for the club's 18,000 members.

"It's not like working in a factory", says 62-year-old Charles Reason. "They are not unreasonable people here. Also you've got the atmosphere of the match, with people coming in and out wanting scorecards. You get caught up in it. I used to belong to a union, but you don't need it here."

A similar attitude prevails elsewhere round the ground. The Clerk of Works, Ted Collins, has an office next to the Grand Stand. His deputy, Dave Norman, is also the Lord's electrician – happy to work round the clock if necessary to get the place ready for a big game. Like many others, he often works seven days during peak cricketing periods.

The staff canteen, a homely place with cricket pictures on the walls, is run by Sharon Clarke, the 22-year-old manageress, and her mother, Anne. They provide special lunches at Christmas and at the end of the season when the nursery ground comes into its own for the use of the Cross Arrows, the club for permanent members of MCC staff. Finally there is the annual staff fixture between two fairly ramshackle teams, one captained by Colonel

Stephenson, the other by Wing Commander Lawrence, the chief accountant. The result doesn't matter, of course. The game's the thing.

Art of Cricket

BY JOHN RUSSELL TAYLOR

3 *August* 1983, *Galleries.* The British Museum's current *Sporting Life* exhibition seems to open up an infinitude of possibilities. Why range so widely – would there not be more than enough material in just one sport? Why be so narrow – how about including paintings and sculptures as well as prints? As though in answer to both these questions, John Player has sponsored a sizable exhibition, and a substantial book to go with it, devoted exclusively to that most English of games, cricket. *Art of Cricket*, at the Fine Art Society until August 13, begins at the beginning, in the approved manner, and goes on, if not until the end (for who would dare to predict that?), at least up to Ruskin Spear's lively Pop-Arty portrait of Fred Trueman.

Inevitably in such a show, the balance between art-interest and subject-interest is at times a little precarious. Funnily enough, this is not much of a problem with the earliest works, perhaps because for any artwork to survive for more than two centuries it is likely to have some sort of artistic quality, while any scrap of evidence about the origins of the game is bound to have its own historical significance. The cricket enthusiast can observe the gradually changing forms of the bat in the long series of cricketing portraits (almost a genre of its own in portraits of boys and young men during the second half of the eighteenth century), while those whose interest is mainly artistic will appreciate rather the variety of character painters like Francis Hayman or Joseph Wright of Derby were able to get into what might be strictly stereotyped works.

Cricket even managed to get into family groups and conversation pieces like Thomas Hudson's *Mrs. Matthew Michell and her Children* or Thomas Beach's *The Tindall Family*. It crops up in Victorian times in the occasional rustic genre piece, such as the Tate's charming *A Country Cricket Match, Sussex* by John Robertson Reid (now when, I wonder, did the Tate itself last find wallspace for that?), and we have probably forgotten that before he made himself into a Victorian sage Watts earned an honest penny in 1837 by making five lithographs to illustrate the finer points of batsmanship. We may also forget that Camille Pissarro was sufficiently charmed by the atmosphere, if not the technicalities, of the game to paint it a couple of times on his visits to England. Its impact seems to have been less on twentieth-century painters – you have to look quite hard to determine why Carel Weight's *The First Cricket Match of Spring* is actually so called. But there is still plenty of material left undisturbed: Sir Gerald Kelly, for example, painted some of his most evocative small panels at the Oval facing towards the gasworks during cricket matches, but none of them is included. So the way is open for further explorations – not to mention *Art of Football* and all the rest of the sports in turn.

West Indies' Finest Batsman Bore his Burdens Lithely

BY ALAN GIBSON

14 *December* 1983. I once took part in a television programme with Lord Constantine and Harold Pinter. We were asked to play the old game of choosing an all-time cricket XI. An odd selection committee, you will agree, but we enjoyed ourselves, whatever the viewers thought. We settled on Hobbs and Trumper for the opening pair, and then considered batsmen to follow.

"Headley", said Learie, at once. "Bradman?" suggested someone. "Yes," agreed Learie, "we will have Bradman as well, because after all, he was the white Headley." This was a reference to the constant description of Headley by English and Australian journalists as "the black Bradman", a description which did not altogether please Headley or his fellow West Indians.

George Headley, whose recent death we mourn, was not perhaps quite so good as Bradman, but had to bear heavier burdens. He was probably the best West Indian batsman there had ever been, despite the magnificence of Worrell, Weekes, Walcott, Sobers and Richards. None of the others was so unsupported as Headley.

When he began, shortly after West Indies Test cricket began, it was usually a case of "Headley out, all out". He had no comparatively easy Tests to boost his figures: his opponents were England and Australia. Nevertheless, he scored 10 centuries in 40 innings in 22 Tests. His Test average was 60.83: in all first-class matches, from 1927 to 1954, it was 69.86.

He played his first Test in 1930, when he was 20. England sent a side to the West Indies. It was not a full Test side (another "England" team was playing in New Zealand at the same time), but a strong one, including Hendren, Ames, Wyatt, Sandham, Voce, Gunn (aged 49) and Rhodes (aged 52). Rhodes took Headley's wicket in the second innings of the first Test, but only when he had scored 176, one of four centuries in the four-match series. Rhodes played his first Test in 1899, Headley his last in 1954; it must have been an interesting confrontation.

In 1930-31 West Indies made their first tour of Australia. Headley was then almost entirely an off-side player and the Australians tied him down for a while, as they did Hammond, by attacking his leg stump. He realized an extra dimension was needed, with the result that Grimmett, who had been causing him problems, later said that he was the greatest master of on-side play whom he had met.

Headley toured England twice and was particularly effective on wet pitches. His record in such conditions was, as C. L. R. James points out in his remarkable book, *Beyond a Boundary*, much better than Bradman's. He had a successful series at home in 1934-35, ending with 270 not out in a Test which West Indies won by an innings. After the war he was not quite the same force again. He mostly lived in England. He was the first black man to captain West Indies, when England toured in 1947-48, but had to retire after the first Test because of a back injury. In 1953 the Jamaican public subscribed to bring him home for the next England series, but he played only in the first Test and Lock got him twice, for 16 and 1.

I saw Headley bat before the war. I have quite a clear recollection of his innings at the Oval in 1939. He scored 65 and a century seemed sure, when he was run out. The culprit was Victor Stollmeyer, and it must have been a horrifying moment for him in his first and, as it proved, only Test, although he made amends with a brave 96. What impressed me about Headley was his lightness of foot, his litheness. You would have to say that he was primarily a back-foot player, as Bradman was, but he always seemed to be dancing.

I saw him again after the war, indeed I saw what I think must have been his last first class match, in 1954, when he played in the Torquay Festival, batted beautifully for an hour or so for 64, and capered happily around the field. He seemed as nimble, as lithe, as ever. The circumstances were not, of course, testing, but I remember I was sitting next to Jack Walsh, one of the best Australian leg spinners of the day, and Jack said: "I'd love to be bowling to that blighter, just for the pleasure of watching him carve me about."

Dismissal of Franks Sets off a Collapse

BY ALAN GIBSON

24 *April* 1984. Our sports editor, generous man, in sending me a note about plans for the season, said: "I will do all in my power to keep you away from Didcot." He then sent me to Oxford, and it is very difficult to get to Oxford from the south except via Didcot. However, I examined the timetable, and found that by leaving Bath at 1.26 a.m., and changing at Bristol, Cheltenham, and Worcester, with peaceful halts at Moreton-in-Marsh and Ascott-under-Wychwood, I could arrive at Oxford at 1.02 p.m., If I cheated a bit and left early, catching the 7.03, I would arrive back at Bath at 6.40 a.m.

Still, we respect our sports editors: but unfortunately I had not noticed that the initial 1.26 from Bath was marked MX-Monday excepted. So it had to be Didcot after all, and though there were some trifling difficulties, I reached the Parks well before lunch.

The Oxford innings fell into three phases: a collapse, a brave recovery, and another collapse. The fifth wicket fell at 47. Then there was a stout stand of 76 between Carr and Franks. Carr we already know to be a good one. Franks, a St. Edmund Hall man, was new to me but looked just the kind of solid character a university needs in the middle of the order. . .

16 *August* 1984, *Announcements*.

IN MEMORIAM
ENGLISH CRICKET
which finally passed away at The
Oval, 14th August 1984, will be
sadly missed.
R.S.V.P.
T.I.S.

England has just been beaten 5-0 by West Indies.

Gower's Side Fight for their Pride

BY JOHN WOODCOCK, CRICKET CORRESPONDENT

27 *August* 1984. England's cricketers are being paid £1,500 each for playing in the current Test match against Sri Lanka, sponsored by Cornhill, and by Saturday evening I was feeling that most of them deserve to have the money withheld. Their batting, following an exhibition of supreme mediocrity in the field, was of unprecedented indifference. In reply to Sri Lanka's 491 for seven declared, they made 139 for two in four hours 20 minutes, the last 107 of them in 56 overs.

If, from lunchtime onwards on Saturday, they had set out to be seen in a worse light, they could hardly have managed it. No self-respecting club side would have been content with the way England batted. In two hours and a quarter Tavaré made 14, four of those off the edge. The longer Broad lasted, the less convincing he became. He was dropped twice while on his way to 69 not out. As for Gower, he even slunk off at the end, having scored 16 in 70 minutes before the clock showed six.

There must be hundreds of batsmen in England – yes, hundreds – who could have played better than Tavaré, Gower and Broad did now against the bowling as it was. That England had bowled so poorly on Thursday and Friday was partly because Sri Lanka had batted so unexpectedly well; but for England's batsmen there was no such excuse. By playing as they did they not only let themselves down but the whole body of English cricket.

Instead of making 500, as they easily could have, Sri Lanka decided to give England 20 minutes' batting before lunch on Saturday. This was a nice, positive move. Yet one felt that if England were to play anything like properly, they could run the Sri Lankan bowlers off their feet and still win the game. I doubt whether Sri Lanka, when they took the field, had banished from their minds all thoughts of defeat. Three hundred by close of play, a not unreasonable target for England, would have opened up the game.

Lamb, it is true, was unfit to bat, having done something highly improbable like pulling a muscle while drawing his bedroom curtain, but it was the sort of day and pitch on which Botham could have made 150 in an hour and a half, with the Sri Lankan bowlers, several of them carrying injuries, powerless to stop him. Instead, Tavaré played like a frightened rabbit, Broad like a man terrified of not making a hundred and Gower like a captain who had lost all urge to lead.

Countless sides would have been disappointed not to score at five runs an over on Saturday evening. Instead, de Silva, though handicapped by a badly sprained ankle, was allowed to bowl 10 overs of gentle leg-breaks for 18 runs, and play ended with Broad treating Madugalle's even gentler off-breaks with laughable respect. The Sri Lankans must have suspected some unfamiliar, unfathomable joke.

Why, then, do I think that good will come to England from the match? For several reasons. It has shown that Agnew is hardly ready yet for an overseas tour and that to take Tavaré to India (a week ago he was the odds-on favourite to be Gower's vice-captain) would be to settle in advance for stalemate. Broad's limitations are better known than they were at the end of the West Indian series, and the need for a constructive influence behind Gower, to prevent the winter expedition from getting bogged down, is clearer than it was.

Perhaps, too, the team will come to realize how much they need help. Cricketers tend these days to spurn the advice even of the old masters. Yet to bat at No. 3 for England as Tavaré did on Saturday, in the footsteps of some of the greatest batsmen of all time, seems heretical to me. It was because Fletcher condoned such cricket, as well as a truly shocking over-rate, that he lost the England captaincy. It smacked then, and still does, of funk.

So today England really are on trial. If on a public holiday not many turn up to watch them, that will be not least because of the way they batted on Saturday. Unless they set out to erase the memory of that, this will be remembered as the England side who had no pride, and they surely cannot want that.

One last stricture. On Saturday morning, when he persuaded Mendis to slog him to deep mid-wicket, where Fowler held a good boundary catch, Pocock leapt and danced and raced across the field like a child on his way to the Christmas tree. Come on England, be your age and play the game.

SRI LANKA 491 for 7 dec (S. Wettimuny 190, L. R. D. Mendis 111,
A. Ranatunga 84) and 294 for 7 dec (S. A. R. Silva 102 not out, L. R. D.
Mendis 94; I. T. Botham 6 for 90)
ENGLAND 370 (A. J. Lamb 107, B. C. Broad 86, D. I. Gower 55, R. M.
Ellison 41; V. B. John 4 for 98, A. L. F. de Mel 4 for 110)
Score after third day: Sri Lanka 491 for 7 dec, England 139 for 2
Match drawn

Record Breakers still not Home

FROM JOHN WOODCOCK, CRICKET CORRESPONDENT

16 *January* 1985, *Madras*. There seemed not to be many batting records left
by the close of play in the fourth Test match here yesterday, and who should
have spent the day breaking them but England's much maligned batsmen?
In reply to India's first innings total of 272 they have so far made 611 for five.
Fowler scored 201 and Gatting 207.

England made 318 runs yesterday against mainly protective fields, fielding
that was an appreciable improvement on Monday's and bowling that was
never unarguably ragged. It is, I need hardly say, a mercilessly easy pitch.
There is little pace left in it, and the ball is hardly turning. It is this that may
yet prevent England from winning. They can be expected to declare some
time tomorrow morning (today is the rest day) and if India get anything of a
start they could take a lot of bowling out, even in a day and three-quarters.

On Monday Fowler batted through the day, yesterday Gatting almost did.
Never before, in over 600 Test matches, have two Englishmen scored double
hundreds in the same Test innings. Bradman, first with Ponsford and then
with Barnes, did it for Australia, as did Simpson and Lawry. Mudassar and
Miandad have done it for Pakistan, and Hunte and Sobers for West Indies.
But not even Compton and Edrich in 1947, did it for England. England's
total is not yet their highest against India – that still stands at 633, made at
Edgbaston in 1979. But they have never before had such a total on the board
(563) at the fall of their third wicket.

Until Gatting beat it, Fowler's was the highest score by an Englishman in a
Test match in India. So far as I saw, Gatting gave only one chance, a low and
barely catchable one to Siva off his own bowling. More than once, on Monday and again yesterday, he must half have expected to be given out leg-
before; but this was a triumph after many disappointments.

One of the first to congratulate Gatting was Peter May, chairman of the
England selectors, who at one stage in England last summer had grave
doubts as to whether it was worth persevering with him. The best analogy
could yet be Bobby Simpson, who, once he had scored his first Test hundred
in his 52nd innings for Australia, never looked back. Yesterday's was
Gatting's 58th innings for England, his first Test hundred, at Bombay,

having come in his 54th. His dynamic game is just what England need. He is as strong as an ox, has a good feeling for cricket and his best years lie ahead.

Monday's play had ended with Pocock padded up for the second evening running, to act as nightwatchman should it have been necessary. Yesterday a refreshed Fowler and a much more confident Gatting made 39 in the first hour and 36 in the second. Gatting was the first to find his form. Right from the start he played very well. For half an hour or so Fowler, by comparison, looked insecure. To make it harder for the batsmen to assume total command, Gavaskar slowed the tempo of the game right down.

Watching him do so, it was easy enough to see how, at times, India bowled only 10 overs an hour when England were here last. Under the quite excellent regulation which requires a minimum number of overs to be bowled in a day, India were obliged now to tot up 80 – and there was no chance that the light would go yesterday before they had done so. There is a good hour's more daylight in Madras than in Calcutta. Even so, they took over six hours about it, this despite the spinners bowling a majority of them.

India, in fact, bowled consistently better than they had on Monday. Kapil Dev began with an admirable spell, with a ball that was still fairly new, and Siva was never to be treated lightly. The batsmen, therefore, had to work for their runs. The crowd, numbering some 25,000, were wonderfully generous, welcoming each landmark almost as though it was India who had passed it. The first of these came when Fowler reached 180. Until then Amiss's 179 at Delhi in 1976-77 had been the highest individual score by an Englishman in India. Before lunch the nearest thing to a chance was when Fowler, then 160, edged a ball from Siva past Kirmani's chest.

Early in the afternoon Fowler pulled and then on drove Yadav for two towering sixes in the same over. Next, Gatting went to his hundred; and soon their partnership had broken the record for England's second wicket against India, held previously by Amiss and Edrich with 221 in the Lord's Test of 1974.

Until a breeze blew up off the sea the day was very hot. But India, to their credit, showed few signs of wilting, and 55 minutes after lunch they had the consolation of the wicket of Fowler, caught behind off a ball from Kapil Dev which left him off the pitch. Fowler had batted for nine hours 25 minutes (an hour longer than Amiss for his 179), faced 411 balls and hit three sixes, 21 fours and one five. He and Gatting had added 241 in 72.3 overs.

By now India were under the command of Amarnath, Gavaskar being off the field from lunchtime onwards with an allergy which was soon being known as "Fowlergy". As Gatting had been on Monday, Lamb was some time getting off the mark. By the time he was bowled, though, taking a great heave at Amarnath, he had scored 62 of a third-wicket partnership of 144. Ten over were left and it was disappointing that Gower thought it right to send in first Edmonds, when Lamb was out, and then Foster, when eventually Gatting was out, even if their intention was to attack. In the end, when

Foster was out, Gower appeared himself.

It was nice for India that they took a late trick or two. They deserved to. Having just reached his double hundred and passed Fowler's score with the same stroke, Gatting was caught on the long-on boundary. He had gone from 192 to 198 with two of those awful reverse sweeps. His innings had lasted for 506 minutes and included 20 fours and three sixes. He faced 308 balls and was cheered in all the way, wet through but very happy. So was I.

INDIA 272 (M. Amarnath 78, Kapil Dev 53, M. Azharuddin 48; N. A. Foster 6 for 104) and 412 (M. Azharuddin 105, M. Amarnath 95, S. M. H. Kirmani 75, Kapil Dev 49; N. A. Foster 5 for 59)
ENGLAND 652 for 7 dec (M. W. Gatting 207, G. Fowler 201, R. T. Robinson 74, A. J. Lamb 62) and 35 for 1
England won by 9 wickets

Wet Times

24 *June* 1985. Heavy rain which persisted throughout the day at Broadhalfpenny Down, Hambledon, on Saturday, caused the abandonment of *The Times* Bicentenary match arranged to launch the book *Double Century: 200 years of Cricket in The Times*. Mike Brearley, the former England captain, scored 50 not out in *The Times* total of 128 for 3 declared to which the Collins Authors and Publishers XI replied with 66 for 2.

THE TIMES 128 for 3 dec (J. M. Brearley 50 not out, D. M. Green 28 not out)
COLLINS XI 66 for 2 (D. E. J. Frith 22 not out, R. G. D. Willis 16 not out)

Mistress of Passionless Gavotte

BY SIMON BARNES

15 *July* 1985. When you read the words, "Scorer: Wendy Wimbush", on the television screen at the end of a day's cricket, you know there are only two possibilities. The first is that this is the alliterating nickname for a mechanical device, reminiscent of the way that flyers call the automatic pilot "George". The second is that Wendy Wimbush is the daughter of a Kentish clergyman.

It is the second possibility that is the true one, though at 6.30 of a Test match evening, the lady feels that the first one is becoming truer to the ball. "It is like going to an exam every day," she said, but the game, and the whole trick of recording the game in figures, charts and coloured pens, is an incurable fascination for her.

The innumerate outsider can only gawp: "Across the page the symbols moved in grave morrice, in the mummery of their letters, wearing quaint caps of squares and cubes. Give hands, traverse, bow to partner: so imps of fancy of the Moors." So James Joyce wrote about a maths lesson: such is cricket for Miss Wimbush.

"It is so satisfying when two lots of figures balance. I love working with figures. If I hadn't become a scorer, I would have been an accountant. But I started scoring when I was 14, for my father's team. An elderly gentleman, who was scoring for the opposition, told me what to do. And I was hooked."

She is now a full-time cricket scorer for television: she goes to Australia every winter to carry on, presumably because she is so good she can do the job standing on her head. She lives most of her life from suitcases, one crammed with coloured felt tips. One of the great joys of life is stationery: Miss Wimbush is a wonder with the lovely stuff, turning her corner of the commentary box into a viziers' kitchen of carefully cut-up cards, charts, tables and records, three ticking clocks and a calculator to hand, and, inscrutable as cuneiform script, the crisp, clean page of the ball by ball record.

She uses the system that all top scorers use, and have done for 40 years or so, and it makes the classic greenbook of club cricket look like a Stone Age implement. Miss Wimbush can tell you at a glance who has done what how many times to whom, when they last did it, and how many times the same thing has been done by an England captain at Trent Bridge against the Australians.

She also compiles those fascinating starburst charts of each batsman's innings, on which the direction of every stroke is recorded. (She gives them to centurions.) Different colours for each bowler: a pink line (Emburey), and the neat little figure of 100 as Wood makes it. "Murder with a splinter at each end," she said, whizzing through all the charts and grids at maximum speed, telling commentators how many balls Wood has faced, and how many boundaries he has hit.

For each player, she makes·out a kind of National Health card of vital information. She also has a list of "milestones" – she would have let us know that Wessels had scored 1,500 runs in Test cricket if he had not been out before making 41. She did let us know that Gower's century was in fact the fourth by an England captain against Australia at Trent Bridge and, when he passed 149, the highest.

People go to cricket and find beauty in many things: the church spire. Holding's unholy run up, the rhododendrons. Gower's timing. Sobers's chinaman. There is a beauty, too, in the figures and it is Miss Wimbush who is the past mistress of this, the passionless gavotte of cricketing statistics.

Owzat for a Last Knock?

24 August 1985, *Sporting Diary (Simon Barnes)*. The hooliganism problem raised its ugly head again with a pitch invasion in Scotland last week. A cricket match was held up for five minutes as a result. The incident happened at a Strathmore Union League match between Dundee High and Brechin, and was triggered by a rising ball from Rajiv Kulkarni, the Brechin professional and Indian Test hopeful. The delivery struck a Dundee High batsman, John Mitchell, on the cheek and provoked an instant response from the crowd.

Lesley Mitchell, wife of the stricken batsman, marched on to the pitch, grabbed Kulkarni, demanding an apology, and refused to leave until one was made. Kulkarni was heard to mutter, "I didn't mean to hit him." Eventually, Mrs Mitchell retreated to the boundary, to watch the rest of the game. The match had already been announced as John Mitchell's official farewell.

Inconvenient

24 August 1985, *Sporting Diary (Simon Barnes)*. This season I have hunted far and wide for examples of batsmen who have been dismissed "timed-out" in cricket matches. I have unearthed a batsman slumbering behind the sightscreen, a county side trapped in a traffic jam, and a fictitious rajah batting from a sedan chair. Now I learn that last weekend saw the first ever timed-out dismissal in a Minor Counties match. While Dorset were replying to Oxfordshire's 181, they lost three wickets in four balls. Next batsman in was Ian Saunders – but when the wickets started to tumble, he was marooned in the gents. The Dorset captain, realizing that time was ticking away, yelled in vain for someone to come out without pads to face the bowling. Saunders eventually appeared only for the umpire to dismiss him on appeal under the two-minute ruling – Law 31, to be exact. Dorset's 12th man, Russell Jamieson, said that once the follow-on had been averted, his captain saw the funny side of it.

Knott Decides to Hang up his Golden Gloves

BY IVO TENNANT

18 *September* 1985. Alan Knott, one of the greatest wicketkeepers ever to play cricket, announced his retirement yesterday. Still at the peak of his profession – no one disputes that he is the best in the country – he is going partly because of concern over his fitness and partly to concentrate on his

sports shop and gymnasium business. No retirement will be more widely regretted.

Quite apart from Knott's ability as wicketkeeper and batsman – Downton, once his understudy at Kent, described him yesterday as a genius – there were other reasons why he was so admired. His unselfishness and sense of fun were transmitted to beyond the boundary. The twinkle in his eye was there from when he first played for Kent in 1964. He looked like Mr Punch, or at least as pleased as him. The peak of his cap competed for prominence with the point of his chin, and he threw himself around, happy as a sandboy.

Here, clearly, was an England cricketer. His friend and partner Derek Underwood remembers that when they played together for Kent Schools he was out of the ordinary at the age of 13. They followed each other all the way up the ladder. Heaven knows how many Tests and victims they would have accumulated had they not strayed to World Series and Johannesburg's streets of gold.

But then Knott's decisions were born out of financial insecurity. He comes from Belvedere, hardly the most flush part of Kent, and he was on the dole one winter when England had no tour. A committed Christian, he always put his wife and family before his career.

He was quirky, faddy, conscientious, courteous, generous, as introverted off the field as he was extroverted on it. He played for the team and always tried. Kent and England do not know how lucky they were. Others had their peers, but above Knott was only the sky.

Cricket: from Bible to Bunyan

28 *December* 1985, *Sporting Diary (Simon Barnes).* Shakespeare was by far the finest cricket writer of them all. When I solicited hidden references to cricket in the literature of the ages, the response was startling. So many great writers have touched on cricket – even the Bible is filled with allusions, right from the moment when the Great Umpire started play and "saw light, that it was good". But Shakespeare is tops.

Many readers offered me that reference to the days when close catchers were slimmer than Botham and Gatting: "I see you stand like greyhounds in the slips" (*Henry V, III i*). Even more offered me a biblical example of poor spelling: "And Peter went out with the eleven, and was bold," which they all claimed was *Acts 2:14*. It isn't, in fact, not in the Authorised or the Revised Standard, but has achieved extraordinarily wide currency.

There is, however, a genuine Shakespearean precedent for Peter May's speaking out against the reverse sweep: "This is the bloodiest shame, the wildest savagery, the vilest stroke" (*King John, IV iii*). And the bouncer is obviously no modern thing, but was in use centuries ago: "You have broken his pate with your bowl" *(Cymbeline, I iv)*.

Nor is the turmoil that affects one of the northern counties a thing of recent years only: "Alas, poor York, I should lament thy miserable state" *(Henry VI part 3, I iv)*. However, southern traditions of gentility have long given rise to hostility from outsiders – hence the reference to "the filth and scum of Kent" *(Henry VI part 2, IV ii)*.

A Midsummer Night's Dream contains a clear reference to the last Ashes series, a remark doubtless uttered by an Australian perplexed with the wiles of Edmonds and Emburey: "Hence, ye long-legged spinners, hence." Interesting too, to note that the googly was known in Roman times: "He put it by with the back of his hand, thus" *(Julius Caesar, I ii)*.

Antony and Cleopatra contains a nicely written – almost worthy of Cardus – description of Lillee appealing for leg-before. "His legs bestrid the ocean, his rear'd arm crested the world, his voice was propertied as all the tuned spheres, and that to friends; but when he meant to quail and shake the orb, he was as rattling thunder" *(V ii)*.

It is hardly surprising to find the rumoured excesses of the England team in the dressing room in New Zealand echoed in the Old Testament. "Ben-hadad was drinking himself drunk in the pavilion" *(I Samuel 2:9)*. Evidence, too, that all cricket is morally reprehensible. "He that touches the pitch shall be defiled by it" *(Ecclesiasticus 13:1)*.

Weather played as big a part in cricket matches in biblical times as it does now: there is a reference in the Psalms to a couple of boundary fielders exhorting each other to get back to the pavilion: "Deep called to deep at the noise of the water spouts" *(69:15)*. Yet as every cricketer knows, rain can be – a godsend: "Thou, O God, sentest a gracious rain" *(Psalms 68:1)*.

Then there is a mysterious reference to the sacred symbol of Anglo-Australian conflict: "The priest shall put on his linen garment . . . and take up the ashes . . . and he shall put them beside the altar. And he shall put off his garments, and put on other garments, and carry forth the ashes without the camp unto a clean place" *(Leviticus 6: 10-11)*. The clean place the Lord's pavilion.

Dr Johnson was clearly a cricketer in Bothamesque mould: "I never think I have hit it hard, unless it rebounds." Elizabeth Barrett Browning, surprisingly, had a penchant for treating her copies of *Wisden* in a rather playful spirit: "Do you see this square old yellow book? I toss i' the air and catch again."

Bunyan knew a thing or two about cricket, and writes allegorically about the game: "Then said Evangelist, pointing with his finger over a very wide field. Do you see yonder wicket? . . . So I saw in my dream that the man began to run."

A number of writers show an uncanny knack of predicting recent events. Shakespeare has it in *Pericles* that "from ashes ancient Gower is come";

perhaps the man is older than he looks. In *Henry V* we have the undentable, though unspectacularly expressed notion that "Gower is a good captain, and in good knowledge", while Chaucer, writes: "O moral Gower! This book I direct at thee."

The moral problems of the game have fascinated writers for several millennia. Omar Khayyam, in *The Rubaiyat*, tells us:

> *"The ball no question makes of ayes or noes,*
> *But right or left as strikes, the player goes;*
> *And he that toss'd thee down into the field,*
> *He knows about it all – he knows, he knows!"*

Boundless Zest of Bill Edrich

BY JOHN WOODCOCK, CRICKET CORRESPONDENT

25 *April* 1986. When a friend of Rocky Marciano was told that the great boxing champion had died, he replied: "If you stand over him and start to count to 10, I think you'll find he will come round." Bill Edrich, who died on Wednesday night at the age of 70, had the same reputation for indestructibility.

It was this which caused the people of England to take him to their hearts after the last war. Having won the DFC against the Germans as a bomber pilot, he became a symbol of defiance against Lindwall and Miller.

Short in height, Edrich had the heart of a lion and an enormous enthusiasm for cricket. Rather than playing the odd game for the Forty Club or on the occasional Sunday for the Whitbread Wanderers when his career with Middlesex came to a natural end, he went back to his native Norfolk, where, until he was 55, he inspired them with his guts and zest and fighting spirit. On the field and off it he never spared himself, and he was intensely loyal.

Coming into the England side for the first time when he was just 22, against Australia in 1938, he had a staunch supporter in Walter Hammond. It was Hammond's advocacy more than the runs which Edrich made which kept him in the England side until he finally became an established member of it, which he had done by the outbreak of war.

In 1947, Edrich and Denis Compton, his Middlesex and England partner, broke all batting records; it was a truly golden year, for us as well as them. Compton spoke yesterday of a friendship with Edrich which knew no cross words. Any disagreements they may have had were between the wickets. Edrich had none of Compton's genius. He achieved what he did by being fearless and wholehearted. For a year or two after the war he could bowl the fastest overs of any Englishman.

As for Edrich's popularity, it was based on his being the same to all people, young and old, an irrepressible enthusiast and incurable romantic.

Botham Banned Until End of July

BY JOHN GOODBODY

30 *May* 1986. Ian Botham was banned yesterday from playing all first-class and international cricket until July 31 by the Test and County Cricket Board in a surprisingly light ruling by its disciplinary committee.

Botham's two month suspension for bringing the game into disrepute after admitting smoking cannabis means he will miss all three Tests against India, two one-day Texaco internationals, one Test against New Zealand, and fixtures for his county Somerset.

The England all-rounder was found "guilty" on four charges by the nine-man disciplinary committee chaired by Mr Peter Bromage, a Birmingham lawyer, after a seven-hour hearing at Lord's.

The charges were that he used cannabis, admitted to having used cannabis, denying in the past that he had used drugs and making public pronouncements without clearance of his county.

The hearing was called after a signed article by Botham in *The Mail on Sunday* on May 18 contained an admission that he had smoked marijuana in his younger days. The board reacted to the article by barring Botham from last weekend's two Texaco internationals against India while it conducted the inquiry.

Mr Alan Herd, a solicitor who represented the England and Somerset all-rounder at the hearing, said afterwards: "We are obviously very disappointed. We will be considering an appeal to the Cricket Council over the weekend."

The Cricket Council is responsible for the overall control and welfare of the game.

Botham left the hearing with an action full of the enterprise he displays on the field. John Emburey, his England team-mate, had his car running at the back door of the pavilion and with most of the 50 members of the media watching other doors, he sped through the Grace Gates.

Botham was fined £100 in Scunthorpe last February for possessing 2.19 grammes of cannabis. Earlier this month detectives questioned him about allegations that he took drugs during his charity walk from John O'Groats to Lands End which raised £714,000 for leukaemia research.

In March 1984 *The Mail On Sunday* alleged that Botham had smoked "pot" during England's cricket tour of New Zealand. Botham instigated a libel action against the newspaper, but in his signed article on May 18 he said he was withdrawing the action.

Botham has scored 4,577 runs for England and is two wickets short of Dennis Lillee's world record of 355 Test wickets.

Stumped

25 *September* 1986, *Leading Article.* If our society has seemed a divided one for the last quarter of a century, the fault must lie with Yorkshire County Cricket Club and its most celebrated player. It has not been an issue of the Red Rose versus the White, the haves and the have-nots, or the North against the South. It has been a case of whether every decent Englishman (or woman) has been for Geoffrey Boycott or against him.

Bear that in mind and his dismissal this week by the county he has always been proud to call his own should cultivate a wistful tear or two. Whatever the rights and wrongs of it, summers will never seem quite the same again.

That he is at least partly to blame for the controversy which has always clouded his illustrious career is beyond question. He has in his time refused to play for England – apparently piqued at not being appointed captain – has disqualified himself less directly by playing a winter's cricket in South Africa and, on one notorious occasion in India, has walked away from a match pleading sickness, only to be subsequently discovered quietly playing golf. It has not been the kind of conduct to endear him to the England selectors.

But Boycott has been still less popular with his fellow players. He has been accused of dullness at the crease and dourness away from it, of playing for himself rather than for his team, of a selfish dedication to his cricketing career, and of being unacceptably professional.

At 45 years of age, however, he remains a rare cricketer. To be sacked by his county after topping its batting averages again (he averaged over 50 this season) seems a curious way to go. Is he really that unplayable? Industry, politics, finance are worlds peopled (if not entirely) by extremely "professional" persons, whose contributions to the nation's well-being go unquestioned. Moreover, to dismiss Boycott on the grounds that he is blocking the path of advancement for younger promising players is an explanation which makes little sense outside Yorkshire. Nor is it easy to understand why he should be penalized for making runs slowly, when at least he makes plenty of them.

This nation's cricket grounds have surely not seen the last of Geoffrey Boycott, which must mean that we have not heard the last of him either. This is a happy thought on which to end. Whatever one may have thought of this enigmatic cricketer, the last 24 years would have been the poorer without him. To be stumped by his own county side must make him feel rather hard done by.

Rebellion Bowled Out in Two Minutes

BY DAVID MILLER, CHIEF SPORTS CORRESPONDENT

10 *November* 1986. Any doubt about the future of Viv Richards and Joel Garner with Somerset disappeared at 3.55 on Saturday. After an hour and a half of rambling and often irrelevant debate among more than 3,000 county members at the Bath and West Showground at Shepton Mallet, Nigel Popplewell, the young former player, spoke from the floor and in his allocated two minutes unequivocally pulled the rug from under the West Indians and their rebel supporters.

From that moment the argument was over, the rebels knew it, and one might as well have voted and left. Many did.

In an informal, unemotional voice, and even more informal frayed pullover, Popplewell said that halfway through the 1985 season, at the end of which he left to continue his career in law, the dressing-room atmosphere was dreadful and he was miserable because the two players' commitment to county cricket was different from everyone else's; that Richards and Garner contributed only when it suited them but expected 110 per cent from the rest; and that in 1984 there had been a team in every sense of the word with Martin Crowe.

It was an unanswerable charge and a critically timed intervention on behalf of the committee whose defence of a sound position had lacked presence and impact. The truth is that had Richards and Garner, and come to that Botham, been subjected to the ruthless logic of Anfield's boot-room, they would unquestionably have been on their way.

The maintenance of a real team has no place for sentiment, however great the player, and the management's responsibility is to determine the need before it is apparent, or even acceptable, to the public.

Whatever the glories of Richards's batting in the past, most notably in one-day matches, that was not necessarily going to keep the club harmonious and successful in the future. Garner has possibly only one more season left in him. As for Botham, and his continuing threat to leave in sympathy, he should reflect on showing the same loyalty which the county have exhibited towards him. Roebuck, the captain, Australia-bound yesterday, is going to talk with him about it.

The rebels thought they were fighting for the county when in fact they were fighting only for the short-term interests of Richards and Garner and their personal entertainment. It is not being a male chauvinist to say that Bridget Langdon, their moral leader, would not understand the nuances of a dressing-room.

Popplewell's evidence had been cogently supported by Philip Squire, the club medical officer and replacement for David Challacombe, whose support of the rebels weakly centred on his antagonism towards Roebuck.

Though the committee sorely needed the aid of Roebuck's articulacy, it was wise that, as a focal point of recent hostilities, he did not speak.

Popplewell said afterwards: "I had been reluctant to speak and it was only a couple of weeks ago that I decided to. I believe in the sanctuary of the dressing-room and its affairs but it reached the point where I was forced by my feelings for the youngsters."

Countless members later quietly thanked him. He had been on the verge of adding that Davis and Marks had taken more wickets in one harmonious season in 1984 than Garner in three seasons.

It is said that neither side on Saturday could be victorious, such was the acrimony that had been generated, yet the occasion was a testimony to traditional British democracy as the huge crowd packed into the hall, quietly opening their sandwich tins and Thermos flasks and remaining civilized and orderly throughout. Apart, that is, from the opening comment for the rebels by John Foley, a barrister, who said there should be no spitefulness and proceeded to liken the committee to Gadaffi.

If the rest of Foley's opening speech was authoritative, his summing up was wholly misjudged and probably cost the rebels any chance of narrowing a more than two-to-one majority. Over-emotional, he talked down to the audience as though they were a jury and not people well familiar with the facts. You could sense the rustle of resentment.

Among the five nominated speakers for each side, Roy Kerslake cut a poor figure as the man the rebels wished to reintroduce as secretary while Graham Burgess was unconvincing in suggesting that the split in the dressing-room was caused by the committee.

Peter Denning brought a laugh when saying that it had taken him 14 seasons to equal Richards's nine, allegedly unsatisfactory, centuries in one season but he had not the impact of Jimmy James, another former player, who put the finger on player power. This echoed the earlier comments of Herbert Hoskin, for 29 years a committee member, who told how he had warned Brian Close and then Tony Brown, the present secretary, "not to let the tail wag the dog".

The afternoon was a total vindication of Roebuck, who has always stressed that the argument was about cricket and not about him. He now has to be vindicated by events. He says that Somerset have no cause for defeatism and can immediately challenge for honours with Crowe and the addition of one or two bowlers.

The meeting demonstrated that the committee have handled a legitimate decision often without efficiency or tact. The logic of their case survived their incompetence, their honesty remaining visible. The rebels deserved to lose on the main principle but established the fact of incompetence.

Yet the moral of the Somerset story is a lesson to every modern sport: that the game must always be bigger than the individual or the game itself cannot survive. How do we explain that to Botham?

Bye and Bye

10 *January* 1987, *Sporting Diary (Simon Barnes)*. To hit a six is glorious, but to concede six byes in one ball is almost unique. The famous occasion when Charles Kortright bowled a ball that bounced in front of the batsman, took wing and cleared the boundary, thus prompting the umpire to signal six byes, was mentioned in a recent piece on the sports pages, and prompted a letter from Lawrence Pearse, chairman of Cheltenham Civil Service Cricket Club. In the glorious drought summer of '76, one of his own bowlers managed the same feat. But the umpire only signalled four byes. Being the wicketkeeper, Pearse was upset. He wanted six byes signalled – so that all those who saw the score book would understand that it could not *possibly* have been the wicketkeeper's fault. I have been to Lord's for a ruling and have to tell Mr Pearse and wicketkeepers everywhere that Kortright's umpire was wrong. You cannot have six byes, not even if you bowled a beamer straight to the sightscreen. The crucial point is in Law 19.2: ". . . and six runs for all *hits* pitching over and clear of the boundary . . .".

MCC Secretary and Treasurer Both Depart

BY RICHARD STREETON

23 *January* 1987. An unprecedented rift in the MCC Committee has led to the departures of both secretary and treasurer in the past five weeks and could mar the club's bicentennial this season.

Following the surprising announcement earlier this week that Jack Bailey, the MCC secretary, was taking early retirement, with immediate effect, it has now emerged that David Clark relinquished his post as treasurer last month.

Clark's on-the-spot resignation occurred at a committee meeting on December 17 and went unannounced at the time. This in itself was surprising, as the MCC treasurership has always been considered next in importance to that of the club's presidency. Though reticent about his detailed reasons, Clark confirmed to *The Times* that his action was partially linked with Bailey's leaving.

The MCC committee now has to prepare a background report on the walk-out by the two men for its 18,000 members. This will be included in the annual report and accounts sent to members before the annual meeting in May, when, presumably, the committee will face numerous questions. The inevitable brouhaha will distress many older members. They have never come completely to terms, in the well-worn phrase, that MCC, though a private club, has a public function.

For MCC to lose two top officials in circumstances which reek of discontent will send the same sort of shock waves through the world of cricket as the City has experienced recently over share deals.

MCC will mark its bicentenary with a number of social occasions this year, plus a five-day match between MCC and the Rest of the World at Lord's in August. There is the added complication that the MCC secretaryship carries with it the same role in the International Cricket Conference (ICC). It stages the game's fourth World Cup next October in India and Pakistan.

Precisely what has gone wrong must largely be speculation. It has been common knowledge, though, for some months that Bailey, MCC's senior paid executive, and the club commitee have found it increasingly hard to remain in sympathy with each other. The formula under which he is now leaving was carefully worked out. It has the time-honoured euphemistic ring common in this sort of situation; but is probably mutually satisfying to both parties.

It can only be surmised that Clark was a dissenting voice to some of the arrangements made for Bailey's unexpected retirement. The two men have been close friends and fellow administrators for many years. In particular, they worked ceaselessly on the establishment's behalf when the Packer dispute began in 1977, during Clark's term as MCC president.

Clark declined to answer specific questions about Bailey when contacted by *The Times*. He admitted to being unhappy about several matters at recent committee meetings, which take place monthly. "There were issues on which I felt I could no longer support the majority decision. One was the method of financing the new Mound Stand, though I would not have resigned for that alone.

"There did come a time, however, when I felt decisions were being taken which were unwise in the interests of the club as a whole. It was not easy for me. There is no honour in resigning from anything. There is, however, one's own conscience. After a connection of more than 20 years working for MCC, it hurt deeply to go and was a big decision. I only hope this whole business brings no permanent damage to the club."

Clark added: "I am not going into details. But what you can say is that I certainly told the committee that it did not make sense for the secretary to go at the beginning of our bicentennial programme. Jack Bailey is an extremely efficient man. He might not be everyone's cup of tea in some aspects, but then who is?"

Bailey, who is 56, is only the eleventh MCC secretary since 1822. There have been 13 treasurers in virtually the same period. Clark, who is 68 next week, still had four years of his second five-year term of office to run.

There is unlikely to be any public comment from Bailey, who is in Australia. He can be said, though, I feel, to be a casualty of English cricket's domestic politics. More flak from this flies around Lord's than is generally known.

Bailey succeeded Billy Griffith in 1974, six years after the English game's administrative structure was completely remodelled.

The Cricket Council was established and MCC in effect lost much of its unwritten but traditional power and status. The Test and County Cricket Board (TCCB) came into being to administer the first-class game; MCC joined it and other bodies as members of the Council. MCC retained responsibilities for the laws and it also continued, of course, to own Lord's, where all the main cricket organizations have their offices.

In recent years the TCCB, conscious that it brings the most revenue into the game, has strengthened its influence. Bailey, to outsiders, seemed to see it as his task to battle hard constantly for his members' rights as MCC's authority was eroded more and more. An obvious area for potential friction were Test matches and other important occasions at Lord's, where dual control of such events has seldom proved easy.

Conflicting interests and personality clashes between officials have been inevitable. A close friend of Bailey's told me: "Jack can be abrasive and unsympathetic as he fights whole-heartedly for what he thinks is right. An awful lot of his friends enjoy his company on a golf course and elsewhere but you can find him unaccommodating in some areas."

As a cricketer Bailey was a new-ball bowler for Oxford University, where he was captain in 1958, and later he played for Essex. He went to Lord's in 1967 as an MCC assistant secretary with special responsibility for public relations and promotions. A significant achievement, early on, was to secure the John Player sponsorship for cricket.

During his period as secretary several notable rebuilding programmes have been carried through at Lord's; with the ICC he has dealt diplomatically with the increasing political strife in world cricket.

The bicentennial programme is already drawn up and MCC will probably not be in a hurry to find Bailey's successor. Lt-Col John Stephenson, the assistant secretary for cricket, is to be acting secretary and an efficient administrative organization is already in existence.

MCC will probably advertise the secretary's job in due course. With Alan Smith, the TCCB's new chief executive, having started his duties on January 1, both MCC and the Board this time next year will have a new helmsman on the bridge. In some ways it could be seen as a second chance for English cricket as the game continues to try to adjust to modern day realities.

Ashes Claim Down in Flames

BY MARCUS WILLIAMS

10 *March* 1987. MCC's bicentenary year started inauspiciously with the departure of the secretary and treasurer. However, the threat of further embarrassment for the club – concerning, probably, their most famous possession, the Ashes – was allayed yesterday by an Australian professor.

A report at the weekend from Australia had claimed that the Ashes urn – the object of cricketing contention between England and Australia since 1882-83 – contained not, as is widely accepted, the charred fragments of a ball, but the remains of King Cole, an Aboriginal cricketer. King Cole was a member of the very first Australian side to visit England, in 1868, and he sadly died of tuberculosis at Guy's Hospital during the tour.

In the article, which was published in a Melbourne popular newspaper, the *Sunday Press*, Robbie Thorpe, an Aborigine spokesman, called for the opening of the urn and scientific testing of the ashes, leading to the ultimate return of King Cole to his native land and a proper burial.

Lord's, in the person of MCC's acting secretary, Lieutenant-Colonel John Stephenson, expressed polite interest in the story and said that, subject to a committee decision, they might consider taking the top off the Ashes urn to establish the facts.

Yesterday, however, Professor John Mulvaney, the authority on early aboriginal cricket and a leading student of aboriginal history, blew the lid off the King Cole argument by describing it as "absolute nonsense" and "chronologically impossible".

Professor Mulvaney, Emeritus Professor of Prehistory at the Australian National University and author of *Cricket Walkabout: The Australian Aboriginal Cricketers on Tour 1867-68*, told *The Times* that, though King Cole did indeed die in Guy's Hospital on June 24, 1868, "he was buried in England in a cemetery near the Oval. He was not cremated, so there could be no ashes."

There was, anyway, he said, "no earthly reason" why the remains of an aboriginal cricketer should end up some 15 years later in an urn presented, as the accepted version goes, by a group of Melbourne women to the Hon. Ivo Bligh, captain of the England side who had just defeated Australia to avenge an unprecedented home defeat at the Oval the previous August.

It was that victory by Australia that prompted the now-famous obituary notice in the following weekend's *Sporting Times*: "In affectionate remembrance of English cricket, which died at the Oval, August 29, 1882. Deeply lamented by a large circle of sorrowing friends, and acquaintances, R.I.P. N.B. The body will be cremated and the Ashes taken to Australia."

After the death of Bligh (later Lord Darnley) in 1927 his widow presented the urn to MCC, in whose possession it has remained irrespective of who wins an England v Australia series.

Professor Mulvaney is a firm advocate of the cause of aboriginal cricket and, in 1980, *The Times* published a letter from him, pointing out that the Centenary Test match in England that year was celebrating the wrong centenary – the first Australian touring side, the Aborigines, had come 112 years earlier. He suggested that the King Cole argument was "a straight political statement".

At all events, relief pervaded the corridors of Lord's yesterday. King Cole – and his touring colleagues, Mullagh, Dick-a-Dick, Twopenny, Red Cap, Mosquito, Peter, Cuzens, Tiger, Jim Crow, Bullocky, Dumas and Sundown – should, meanwhile, not be forgotten as the pioneers of Australian cricket.

Laying Down Ground Rules

BY JACK BAILEY

28 *May* 1987. Scenes at Edgbaston during the Texaco Trophy match between England and Pakistan have sent shock waves around the country, and rightly so. Ground invasion and fighting in the stands are no part of cricket.

It is always easy to be wise after the event and the further away you are the easier it is to promote instant remedies. Politicians, at this sensitive time, have been predictably quick to call for reports.

The banning of alcohol and a larger police presence have already been put forward as possible governmental measures. There has been discussion about fencing in the crowd, *à la* football grounds here and cricket grounds in Pakistan and elsewhere overseas.

Speaking from my own experience as secretary of MCC during some pretty hair-raising moments over the years, I am convinced that while the strongest possible police presence (though not necessarily an overt one) should always be welcomed by clubs, other snap remedies are to my mind neither desirable nor necessary.

Because of the particularly volatile circumstances involved at Edgbaston, it was, of all the big matches of 1987, likely to be the most combustible.

The deciding match in the one-day series, the particularly strong Pakistan element in the Midlands, the inherent need for a voluble and vociferous minority to express themselves and if possible to be identified with a winning team, the undoubted annoyance felt by other spectators at having their day ruined: these factors formed a mix which, with the one-day series at an end, is virtually certain not to be repeated.

Some of the problems will remain potential dangers, however, both for the Test matches and for the domestic finals at Lord's. Matches at Lord's will have been the subject of discussion between MCC and the police before the start of the season.

The ground rules established and built on during the past decade will apply:

1. Flags, banners or similar objects, capable of being waved or wielded, will be confiscated before the match. Any that slip through will be gently but firmly removed during the game.

2. "Musical" instruments such as big bass drums or bugles will likewise be put into pound until the match is over.

3. Provision will be made for a limitation on alcoholic consumption before and during the hours of play, a voluntary move made by MCC at Lord's for several years now, affecting both public and membership, and not always popular, but with a noticeably beneficial effect and causing no great hardship to the reasonable imbiber.

4. No excessive quantities of alcohol will be allowed to be imported into the ground.

5. Ground stewards will be employed in large enough numbers to ring the boundary. The police, rightly, see themselves as the back-up authority to the club staging the match, for it is the club and nobody else who is legally responsible for what occurs.

6. An efficient and instant means of communications between the club executive and the police will be installed and used frequently for constant monitoring, consultation and agreed courses of action.

These examples and other standard measures should apply on all Test match grounds. The degree to which they are used and the need to build in further safeguards are subject to the individual requirements of the ground and a detailed, up-to-date analysis of the particular needs of that particular match.

The Safety of Sports Grounds Act and the Popplewell Report set out requirements and guidelines. Cricket grounds working within the some-times contradictory requirements of these constraints and those of local government authorities have a tough row to hoe.

Weather Cannot Mask MCC's Success Story

BY JOHN WOODCOCK, CRICKET CORRESPONDENT

26 *August* 1987. The prospects of a fitting finish to the bicentenary match between MCC and Rest of the World at Lord's were washed out yesterday by heavy and persistent rain. By the time the umpires abandoned all hope, soon after noon, the ground was already awash.

This was, of course, a great disappointment, and to some extent an anti-climax. But in such a wet and dismal summer, perhaps we should be grateful to have had four days with few interruptions and full of good things. The occasion turned out so successfully that the absence of three such outstanding cricketers as Ian Botham, Martin Crowe and Vivian Richards was soon forgotten.

MCC decided that those who played had done well enough for the money they shared for drawing the match to be raised from £25,000 to £30,000. Allan Border said he "wouldn't have missed the game for anything". It had been played, he thought, in just the right spirit. "Personal pride came into it," Border said. "The players had their own reputations to protect. All the ingredients were there for a serious confrontation." In saying that it had been a "real pleasure to play", Mike Gatting, Border's opposite number, sounded equally convincing.

The individual award for bowling, with Sir George Allen making the choice, went to Malcolm Marshall. He showed in several spells how good and formidably fast the modern West Indian fast bowler is; and he did it on the easiest of pitches, without resorting to more than the occasional bouncer. Denis Compton's choice as the batsman of the match was no less straight-forward: Sunil Gavaskar's 188 in the first innings made a perfect end to his first-class career.

For the fielding prize, the winner jointly chosen by Sir "Gubby" and Mr Compton, there were two obvious candidates – Clive Rice for holding two splendid catches, and Roger Harper, whose running-out of Gooch off his own bowling, in MCC's first innings, had to be seen to be believed. Rice was the winner. He, Gavaskar and Marshall were awarded £2,000 each.

Off the field, all was warmth and nostalgia. It is no good expecting Test matches to be played as open-handedly as this game was. They never were. At the same time, some of the grievances that have arisen over the years between the Test-playing countries have been resolved over the period of the jamboree. The new Mound Stand won admirers among those seeing it and sitting in it for the first time; I fancy they outnumbered its detractors. Nor should the groundsman and his staff be forgotten. A poor pitch could have spoilt the party, and this was the last thing it was.

If these anniversary matches are to continue to take place every 50 years, no one who is to play in the next one is likely to be born until at least 10 years from now. By then Lord's will have changed as much as it has in the last 50 years. There will be a new stand at the Nursery End and the Grand Stand will have been rebuilt. Although it is the intention not to turn the ground into a stadium, the capacity may have been increased to 30,000. But the atmosphere, I am sure, will be the same.

So far as changes in the game itself are concerned, nothing is more important than that the spinners should be cared for. Fifty years ago, every county side and every Test side depended heavily on them. In 1937, for example, the Middlesex spinners took nearly 250 wickets between them.

This season they will be lucky to take 100. Something must be done to halt this decline. Otherwise in 2037 the game, if not the occasion, could have lost an essential part of its charm.

> MCC 455 for 5 dec (M. W. Gatting 179, G. A. Gooch 117, C. E. B. Rice 59 not out) and 318 for 6 dec (C. G. Greenidge 122, G. A. Gooch 70, D. I. Gower 40)
> REST OF THE WORLD 421 for 7 dec (S. M. Gavaskar 188, Imran Khan 82) and 13 for 1
> *Match drawn*

The Show Must Go on No Longer

FROM JOHN WOODCOCK, CRICKET CORRESPONDENT

9 *December* 1987; *Faisalabad*. There was another thoroughly regrettable and undignified scene here yesterday, this time just as play was ending in the second Test match between England and Pakistan. It developed into a direct and heated confrontation between Mike Gatting, the England captain, and Shakoor Rana, Pakistan's most experienced, despotic and contentious umpire.

Relations on the field have become so strained that England are reminded at the start of each day not to become involved in controversy and conflict, whatever the provocation. But now, as in Lahore, they allowed their emotions to get the better of them: first when Athey was spoken to by Shakoor for exchanging words with Ijaz, whom he thought should have been given out, and then, much more seriously, when Gatting lost his temper.

Hemmings was bowling what was to be either the last or the penultimate over of the day. The timing is important because it was in his keenness to get in another over that Gatting, fielding at backward short leg, informed Salim Malik, verbally and hurriedly, that he was bringing Capel in from long leg. Malik was the striker and Hemmings had already started his run-up when Gatting signalled to Capel that he had come far enough, whereupon Shakoor called for play to stop and accused Gatting of cheating.

There is certainly a case for saying that Shakoor was exceeding his authority, for there is nothing in the laws (as distinct from the spirit) of the game to stop Gatting from moving the field when he likes, so long as there is no distraction upon the batsman. Most captains – and obviously Javed Miandad is up to all the tricks – occasionally shift a fielder a little this way or that as a bowler is running in. Should the move be of some significance, the non-striker usually takes it upon himself to inform his partner. I have never before seen an umpire intervene as Shakoor did now, and Gatting insists that he had notified Malik of what was afoot.

I have little time for Shakoor. At best he is a bad umpire. He has had rows with one touring side after another. At Karachi, for example, in 1984-85 Jeremy Coney, the New Zealand captain, threatened to take his side off the field because of Shakoor's umpiring. Shakoor is not one to avoid a quarrel if he can help it. Already on this tour he has had one with Gatting, when England refused Pakistan's request for a specialist wicketkeeper to replace the injured Salim Yousuf during a one-day international.

For all that, unless the umpires are allowed to run the game as they see best, it becomes a shambles, and it was because Gatting argued the toss with Shakoor yesterday, not mildly but in a rage, that England were in the wrong. Shakoor said afterwards that Gatting had used abusive language and told him to go back to his place and get on with his job.

The whole thing has become so thoroughly distasteful that I am inclined to think that the best way to bring everyone to his senses would be to call the tour off. There is no rapport whatever between the England management and the Board of Control for Cricket in Pakistan, whose announcement of Test umpires, without due reference to the England party, is undoubtedly a sequel to the TCCB's insistence on appointing David Constant in England last summer against the wishes of the Pakistanis.

England, too, are convinced that they are not going to get a square deal; that the umpires are not controlling the game "with absolute impartiality as required by the laws". It is all very bad for cricket.

Peter Lush and Micky Stewart describe it as being "very sad". Stewart said: "Everyone is expecting another incident; we're on a knife-edge." Gatting said, "I've nothing to apologize for." Lush said: "I shall be taking no disciplinary action." Not a word of contrition. There is a closing of the ranks, and I have much sympathy for Gatting; but Test captains, most of all England captains, just cannot behave as Gatting did yesterday, however mortified they may be. I can say no worse than it is the sort of thing one expects of Miandad or McEnroe.

England, too, had bowled themselves into a strong position in the match. After losing their last six first innings wickets before lunch for only 38 runs, they reduced Pakistan to 106 for five, still with three days left for play and on a pitch on which a lead of 150 should prove decisive. With the ball turning appreciably, Emburey has already taken three for 25 in 15 overs.

England's first innings was finished off yesterday morning by Iqbal Qasim after Qadir had made short work of Capel and Tauseef had taken care of Broad. Qasim's figures for the morning were four for 17 in 12.2 overs; Qadir's, after three England innings, are 115-34-200-17. But the way the ball had turned could only be of encouragement to England.

Foster and Capel bowled well enough when Pakistan went in for Gatting to wait until the sixteenth over of their innings before introducing a spinner. In his third over Foster had Mudassar caught low down at the wicket off a ball that left him and in his fifth he had Ramiz caught at second slip, thrashing at a ball of full length. Sandwiched between these two wickets, Miandad, when he was four, was missed at first slip by Gatting – the sort of chance which Gatting normally swallows. This would have been Capel's first Test wicket.

Miandad was in a noticeably grumpy mood, which led in the end to his giving Emburey the charge and being bowled. From then on England were tightening their grip. At tea Pakistan were 70 for three. For most of the 90 minutes afterwards Emburey was bowling with four men round the bat – Gatting at backward short leg, Robinson at square short leg, Athey very close at silly point and Gooch at slip.

England thought they had to get Ijaz out twice, caught each time at short leg off Emburey. When, first time, Shakoor turned down the appeal, an exchange of words between Athey and the batsman soon brought Shakoor down the pitch to remind Gatting who was in charge of the game. In Emburey's next over Ijaz was not so lucky. Pushing forward again, he turned an off break low to the right of Robinson, who held a good catch.

The next ball, an off break that must have turned the best part of a foot, bowled Shoaib. Playing neither forward nor back, he had no possible chance against it. Sixty-five minutes remained and Aamir Malik came in on a hat-trick to play his first Test innings. Having saved that, he revealed a solid forward defence.

Although still only 24, Salim Malik played like an old pro, even sharing the odd joke with the fielders and pulling and square-cutting for four a couple of loose balls that came his way. Night had almost closed in when eyes began to flash and tempers to flare – and once again the cricket itself was forgotten. As all are agreed, it cannot go on.

ENGLAND 292 (B. C. Broad 116, M. W. Gatting 79; Iqbal Qasim 5 for 83, Abdul Qadir 4 for 105) and 137 for 6 dec (G. A. Gooch 65)
PAKISTAN 191 (Salim Malik 60; N. A. Foster 4 for 42) and 51 for 1
Score after second day: England 292; Pakistan 106 for 5
Match drawn

Test Starts and Stops in a Bad Light

FROM JOHN WOODCOCK, CRICKET CORRESPONDENT

12 *December* 1987; *Faisalabad*. Bitterly as he resented being made to do so, Mike Gatting yesterday gave Shakoor Rana a brief but unconditional apology for having lost his temper with him on Tuesday and the second Test match against Pakistan restarted. He handed the unlovable umpire a note which read, simply: "Dear Shakoor Rana, I apologize for the bad language used during the 2nd day of the Test match at Fisalabad (*sic*) – Mike Gatting." Whereupon they shook hands.

But even then, with play restricted to just under two hours by bad light, the main interest of the day centred on an unprecedented statement from the England dressing-room, issued with the knowledge, though not the authority, of Peter Lush, the manager, in which the players state categorically that Shakoor was the first to use "foul and abusive language" in his row with Gatting.

This, of course, put the events of the previous two days into a different light. While not excusing Gatting's own outburst, it went some way towards explaining it and also towards accounting for England's prolonged reluctance to take all the blame. In the end they felt they had been sold down the river by the Test and County Cricket Board who, having said at one moment that it was very difficult for them "to make decisions on matters happening many thousands of miles away", were soon afterwards ordering their manager to "take whatever steps necessary" to get the players back on the field.

As darkness fell last night Pakistan's last chance of making a goodwill gesture was spurned when they rejected England's request, made more in hope than expectation, for an extra day to make up for the one already lost. This means the match will almost certainly be drawn. With only today's play to come, England will start their second innings this morning with a lead of 101.

At the best they will be able to give themselves 50 overs in which to bowl Pakistan out a second time on a pitch on which Qadir and Qasim were able to add 52 in 55 minutes for Pakistan's ninth wicket yesterday; at the worst they could hardly be bowled out themselves in half a day.

It was 8 a.m., an hour and a half before play was due to begin, before Gatting decided that on balance he had best accept the TCCB's directive. Even then, play started 35 minutes late, one last abortive attempt having been made to get Shakoor to do the decent thing; and no sooner had it done so than the umpires upheld an appeal against the light. With Foster bowling at the time, fast and aggressively, this was a fair decision. But between then and 3 p.m., when the sun at last came out, there were long periods when it seemed ridiculous not to be playing.

However, the delay gave the England players time to work on their deposition, released eventually by their vice-captain, Emburey, after close of play. Their manager, knowing what he did, had been left by the TCCB with what amounted to an unplayable lie; their captain felt, as they did, that he had been required to sacrifice his own integrity "to protect an umpire who has been causing shock waves for the last 10 years".

In issuing their statement, they took into account that they might well be fined for indiscipline. The senior members warned the younger ones of this but the decision to go ahead was unanimous and in the event it may have helped to save Gatting his job.

The captain admits that he was wrong to be drawn into a slanging match with Shakoor. Once it had happened, I still think the least harm would have been done by trying at the first opportunity to patch things up. I am not sure that Gatting agrees with that. No one likes being wronged and as he had said to me in Lahore after the first Test match: "There comes a time when one can take no more." No more provocation was what he meant.

I suppose no England captain has ever had two months of the type of pressure which the World Cup and now this tour have imposed. If an international panel of umpires and an objective review by the TCCB of England's touring schedule comes out of a wretched business, that will be something.

"A storm in a cup of tea" was how Haseeb Ahsan described it. I am afraid the Pakistan Board are marvellously unsusceptible when it suits them and also extraordinarily elusive. There could be no better example of this than that, when the crisis was worsening last Wednesday afternoon, the secretary of the Pakistan Board left for Lahore, the best part of 100 miles from here, without informing the England manager or leaving anyone in a position to act as his proxy. Mr Lush had to go after him.

It is the view of the England players that at all times Pakistan "completely ignored the wider interests of the game". That, I think, is sanctimonious of a side who have been known to ignore them themselves; but they could be right.

When there was a sudden change of tone from Lord's, speculation followed as to whether or not a higher authority than the TCCB had been at work. The Foreign and Commonwealth Office had been in touch with Lord's and the British Ambassador to Pakistan was known to be keen for England to make all the necessary running in settling the issue. Whether, had they not done so, Pakistan would have made a last-minute move of their own we shall never know.

"Cricket will go from bad to worse unless we do something to change that now," Ahsan said as Pakistan waited until after play yesterday before deciding whether or not they were in a strong enough position to offer England an extra day. If that sounds cynical, it is not easy at the moment to be anything else.

By the time the chairman and chief executive of the TCCB arrive in Karachi in time for next week's last Test, Gatting will have had the chance to collect his thoughts, though anything like an attractive game of cricket is probably too much to hope for. There was something unreal about yesterday's play, not only because it was as cold a day as I can remember in these parts, watched by another very small crowd. It seemed to be taking place in a vacuum.

How the French View the Affair

FROM PHILIP JACOBSON

15 *December* 1987; *Paris*. Now I have seen everything. A whole page in one of France's leading daily newspapers devoted to "*la guerre des umpires*" raging on the cricket fields of Pakistan. And yesterday's edition of *Libération*, the best of the leftish Press, did a remarkably good job of explaining to the French why this *affaire* has so convulsed the Commonwealth that it knocked the Washington summit off some of our pages.

Mind you, *Libé* had fun doing so. "*Le cricket est un sport de gen-tle-men*," its headline announced solemnly before observing that "*le capitaine de XI Anglais*" had apparently given Shakoor Rana what the French describe as "*un grand merde*".

Wisely avoiding any attempt to explain the laws of the game (which it assured readers are complicated beyond belief), *Libération* devoted considerable space to examining the supreme importance of fair play in this most Anglo-Saxon of sports. The perceptive analysis of cricket's role in cementing British rule in the old Empire and holding together today's Commonwealth could have come straight from MCC. "For more than a century London has been exporting a certain image of itself: tolerance, good manners, fairness." But most important, observed the writer, Pierre Grundmann, the British exported one quality respected above all others – restraining oneself no matter how trying the circumstances (in other words, the stiff upper lip). A quotation from an editorial in *The Times* followed, every bit as sonorous in French as in the original version.

True to its leanings, *Libération* also took the opportunity to examine the larger sociological aspects of the row. Gatting's conduct, it maintained, had drawn such stern criticism partly because his origins are modest and he is just a vulgar professional "player". Even in Mrs Thatcher's meritocracy, the article seemed to be arguing, there were limits to a young fellow's prospects of self-advancement.

By now, one imagines, French readers who had stuck with the story were hooked and there was plenty more to keep them happy. Enter Imran Khan, "*l'idole de 75 millions de Pakistanais*". As *Libération* viewed it, conceivably correctly, a Pakistan-India World Cup final in Bombay would have amounted to "the revenge of the old subjects of the Raj against their former masters". In the event, although the paper's geography strays somewhat, the English were still able to give "King Imran a cricket lesson in his own kingdom".

Any number of similarly delectable phrases could be encountered in *Libération's* enterprising coverage. This affair is no *"tempête dans une tasse de thé"*, the French were assured: for the English, cricket, "like war", is a continuation of politics by other means.

In the circumstances, what were readers to make of the information that, despite the game's superficial lack of urgency, a cricket ball travels at 150 kilometres an hour towards a batsman only 20.12 metres away?

For the further cricketing education of the French, the article made the point that most umpires are *"des gentlemen très âgés"* who had to stand up for six hours, sometimes under *"un soleil brûlant"*, and it must surely be the only international sport, *Libération* surmised, in which those in charge of the game come from the home country.

According to my Parisian colleagues, this is by no means the first time *Libération* has manifested a reasonable knowledge of, and an evident admiration for, the ancient enemy's national obsession.

One shudders to think what this might be doing to the newspaper's none-too-healthy circulation but it deserves to be saluted for sheer courage. When I tell you that yesterday's issue also contained not one but two pages of philosophical exchanges about the inner symbolism of football between the great Michel Platini and the immensely distinguished French writer, Marguerite Duras, you will surely share this admiration.

Insider's View of Haseeb on Tour

BY ANTHONY SMITH

24 *December* 1987. Listening to England's captain saying his visit to Pakistan and his recent experience with one of their most infamous umpires was something he would very much like to forget and that he would certainly not be touring the country again, my sympathies go out to him, especially after my own treatment during the summer.

As baggage-master to the visiting Pakistan touring team, no one in England had more day-to-day personal contact with both the players and the management than myself, and I can honestly say that having had 16 years of looking after nearly every international team to tour here, I had never experienced anything quite like it before.

The captain, Imran Khan, and his highly-talented and very successful team excelled themselves, and it was a great privilege for me to be associated with Pakistan winning their first Test series in this country, but it was their controversial manager who left a lot to be desired, and who, in my opinion, has been largely responsible for our lovely game of cricket being dragged through the mire.

As was stated in *The Times* on August 14, Mr Haseeb Ahsan tried to order me about like a "hired servant", often ranting and raving in front of other people, so much so that I had embarrassed players apologizing for his out-of-order antics.

Then there were several instances of being told, *not* asked, as is usually the case, to make extra, unreasonably long journeys by road, way outside the normal terms of my contract.

On top of this, we had the whole trip during the tour seemingly being run on a shoestring, with no official scorer or physiotherapist accompanying the team. The manager laid a trail of controversy which culminated, in the final Test at the Oval, with the abuse of umpire David Constant, whom he called a "disgraceful person".

There is little doubt in my mind that Mr Ahsan came to these shores this year determined to be as big a mischief-maker as was possible, and that this unfortunate atmosphere and general ill-feeling will continue in Pakistan cricket while this erratic man is allowed to remain at the helm of their affairs. He came here with a chip on his shoulder which he acquired in 1962 when he was sent home because of a suspect bowling action.

After having to endure the tantrums of Haseeb for 15 weeks, you can imagine my utter relief and joy in joining up with Clive Lloyd and Allan Border, respectively the manager and captain of the Rest of the World team, for three of the most happy and exciting weeks of my cricketing experience, something that will remain with me for the rest of my life.

My advice to the Pakistan Board of Control is to get rid of their present so-called supremo as soon as possible and to appoint someone like Imran Khan, if available, on a long-term contract as team manager, before more irreparable damage is done to this most beautiful game of ours.

Botham Bowls into Turin
to Complete £6m Trek

FROM ALAN FRANKS

20 *April* 1988; *Turin*. Ian Botham, elephants and all, finally arrived at the gates of Turin yesterday afternoon to the kind of civic reception which would have alarmed even the much-travelled Hannibal.

Thousands of Italians, including a hard core of cricket fans, thronged the city centre to greet the England and former Queensland player 21 days and nearly 500 miles after the start of his epic charity march from Perpignan in the South of France.

After welcoming Botham and his party in the Piazza Castello, the Mayoress of Turin, Signora Maria Magnani Noya, said: "Whereas Hannibal, 2,000 years ago, came to this country to bring war, you have come to bring with you messages of hope."

Botham displayed his characteristic distaste for the British media's handling of his activities. "Right from the start they have painted an inaccurate picture of what has been going on, and of what we are trying to achieve. Now that we have got to Turin I think it's one in the eye for all the critics who said that it could not be done."

Asked what he was considering for his next project, Botham said that he was planning a walk from Aberdeen to Ipswich, possibly this autumn.

For almost the entire length of yesterday's final stretch from Bussoleno to Turin passing motorists sounded their horns in the national manner, and with the regularity of falling governments. Even the two elephants, on loan from the Italian National Circus Medrano, made it home. Contrary to rumours, only one of their number had failed to complete the journey through injury.

Yesterday Botham became one of only seven out of the 23 starters at Perpignan to complete each of the 21 legs. This was his 65th day of walking during the past three years to raise money for the Leukaemia Research Fund; proceeds from the trans-Alpine hike are expected to exceed £6 million.

Now, having missed the pre-season training session for his new county, Worcestershire, Botham flies home today to join his team-mates for the opening fixture of the season. The team's medical consultant, Dr Steve Carroll, said Botham would be "probably the fittest cricketer in England".

One of the warmest greetings for Botham came from Signor Simone Gambino, president of the Italian Cricket Association, which has a league of 20 clubs. "We take our cricket very seriously in Italy," he said, "and it is a great honour for us to entertain a player of such ability as Signor Botham. One day perhaps he will come and play in our country."

Perhaps, but first there is the small matter of the English county season, and the struggle to regain his place in the Test side. Botham also says he would like to make a sponsored walk from Paris to Moscow in aid of leukaemia research. He is being urged to walk the 600 miles from Sydney to Brisbane, the very city which three weeks ago closed its doors to him as firmly as Turin has just opened them.

Hick is the Man of the Century

BY RICHARD STREETON

7 *May* 1988. Graeme Hick scored a prodigious 405 not out, the second-highest score ever made in England, as Worcestershire amassed 628 for seven wickets against Somerset on the second day of their four-day championship match at Taunton yesterday. Hick, who is 21 and Zimbabwean by birth, is the seventh man in history to make 400.

He batted for nine-and-a-quarter hours and hit 11 sixes and 35 fours during an innings marked by immense concentration and stamina. For most of his stay he had to combat defensive fields, with five or six men round the boundary, and a slow outfield.

It was not until Hick reached 300 with two sixes in the same over by the medium-paced Rose that he cut loose and attacked the bowling. His final 105 runs came in 71 minutes from 58 balls, with eight more sixes and six fours. Hick was 392 when the seamer, Dredge, began the last over before·tea and he knew that Worcestershire intended to declare at the interval.

Hick straight-drove Dredge's first ball for six and then cut a single to reach 399. Illingworth, his partner, took a single before Hick pulled the fifth ball for six over mid-wicket with another great blow and walked off the field. This was cricket's eighth score of 400, Bill Ponsford, the Australian, achieving the feat twice.

The only higher score in English cricket was the 424 Archie MacLaren made for Lancashire against Somerset on this same ground in 1895. Neale, the Worcestershire captain, and Hick said afterwards that they were unaware of MacLaren's score. Neale was unapologetic about closing the innings. "Whenever you declare people say there are records pending. Graeme was quite happy to come off. He knew our intention. We have got to bowl out Somerset twice."

Hick, who qualifies to play for England in 1991, concurred and said: "It has not all sunk in yet but I suppose it will tomorrow when I wake up and think about it. I gave a few chances early on and I think I batted better today than I did on the first day. I got tired at the end of each session. I had a bit of luck but took things as they came."

Hick also said that he felt his 212 at Old Trafford a fortnight ago on a turning pitch was the better innings.

Botham said: "This was probably the greatest innings I have ever seen and I have been involved in and have seen a few. I cannot imagine you will see a greater innings by anyone."

The most remarkable facet of Hick's batting in some ways was the manner in which he monopolized the scoring. Hick made his 405 out of 550 added while he was in. MacLaren also batted under 10 hours and scored his 424 out of 792. The nearest approach to Hick's statistical domination came when Bert Sutcliffe, the New Zealand left-hander, made 385 out of 500 scored for Otago against Canterbury at Christchurch in 1952-53.

Hick resumed yesterday at 179 and for long periods was almost metronomic as he drove and pushed runs to the deep fieldsmen. He claimed 197 out of 265 added for the sixth wicket with Rhodes and 137 out of 177 for the eighth wicket with Illingworth, both stands being county records. By the end Hick had brought his tally from six innings this season to 815, and has possibly six more innings to reach 1,000 runs by the end of this month.

Hick gave two hard chances on Thursday but his only serious mistake yesterday came at 391 when he skied a big hit against Roebuck, and Dredge, running backwards at cover, was unable to hold the ball with his right hand as he twisted round. Only about 1,200 watched Hick's innings in hot sunshine, but no one present will forget it.

Hick faced 460 balls and in addition to his 11 sixes and 35 fours his score was made up by seven threes, 40 twos and 98 singles. He was still running his own and his partner's singles at the end as vigorously as when he first arrived. Drives, cuts and sweeps predominated as he made 78 before lunch and 148 in the afternoon. Most of his sixes were perfectly timed straight drives which sent the ball soaring to enormous heights.

Somerset were left needing 479 to avoid the follow-on. Hick joined the attack with off breaks at 61 and by the close had figures of 8-3-18-2, with Felton caught low at short extra cover and Harden leg before. The relevant *Wisden* is not to hand but even MacLaren almost certainly did not match that.

> WORCESTERSHIRE 628 for 7 dec (G. A. Hick 405 not out, S. J. Rhodes 56, G. J. Lord 49)
> SOMERSET 222 (V. J. Marks 42; P. J. Newport 4 for 59, N. A. Radford 4 for 77) and 192 (M. D. Crowe 53; P. J. Newport 6 for 50)
> Score after second day: Worcestershire 628 for 7 dec; Somerset 103 for 4
> *Worcestershire won by an innings and 214 runs*

Richards Remaking Team in Own Image

BY JOHN WOODCOCK

11 *May* 1988. Although he is established, securely and incontestably, as a great batsman, no one will be more keyed up than Vivian Richards when the one-day internationals, and, more especially, the Test matches, take place in England this summer. What accounts for that is his fierce determination to become respected for his captaincy as well as for his batting. I use the word fierce advisedly, such, I suspect, is Richards's susceptibility.

It comes of having taken over from Clive Lloyd, whose successor was bound to have to suffer comparisons. By the time Richards was given the job, it had long since been forgotten how unconvincing Lloyd himself was in his early days as the West Indies captain. He was linked instead only with as formidable and successful a side as has ever taken the field, one which toured the world bringing joy and harmony to the Caribbean.

If, by virtue of his wonderful batting, Richards was owed much of the credit for this, he was, nevertheless, neither the easiest nor most tolerant member of Lloyd's family. Extraordinarily dashing, Richards has been as much the centre of attraction as Denis Compton was in his heyday. But the longer Lloyd went on and the more fatherly he became, the harder it was going to be for whoever followed him.

It must have been a blow, too, to Richards's pride when Lloyd was persuaded by the West Indian board to defer his retirement, bringing into the open, as it did, the doubts that existed concerning Richards's suitability for the job. Richards was appointed eventually in 1985, everyone's idea of the perfect West Indian cricketer, but with patience to acquire.

For a while victory continued to come almost as a matter of course to the machine, some would say the battering-ram, which Lloyd had created. Not until a few fast-bowling bones began to creak did the team show signs of faltering. Since October 1986, though, West Indies have played four Test series without winning one, and surrendered their supremacy in the one-day game.

In Australia in 1986-87 they were a palpably unhappy side. Last winter in India and Pakistan they failed even to reach the last four of the World Cup. After they had lost there, first to England and then to Pakistan, in two desperately close finishes, they were visibly distraught.

But the worse things got, the more intense became Richards's determination to rebuild in his own image a side to be the equal of Lloyd's. It is an honourable enough ambition, and something happened in the West Indies recently, purely by chance, which did his cause much good.

He was unable, through illness, to play in the first Test match against Pakistan at the start of last month and Gordon Greenidge took over. Disaster struck, West Indies receiving their first home defeat for 10 years and Richards being badly missed, not least as captain.

In his own island of Antigua (appreciably smaller than the smallest English county), Richards is king. The little wooden house where he was born in the capital, St John's, is a kind of shrine. American tourists go there off their cruise ships, hoping to track down "this Babe Ruth guy". For the moment, Antigua has superseded Barbados as the prime source of precocious cricketing talent.

But even there Richards is looked upon as a phenomenon. Danny Livingstone, who caught the catch that won the match that won the county championship for Hampshire in 1961 and now coaches in his native Antigua, says: "We've got a lot that could be very good. It just comes naturally to them. But it'll be only every 50 years that one comes along like Viv."

But he is a combustible fellow, our Viv. As a boy, playing cricket and football for Antigua (before they achieved first-class cricketing status), he was already being idolized. In 1969, having disputed an umpiring decision, which led to a riot in the crowd and a break in play, he was given a two-year suspension. He still has it in him to argue the toss with an umpire, not gently but with a short temper. In Calcutta last December, when he did so there, the umpires were on the point of walking off.

As the years have passed he has become racially more sensitive, sometimes defiantly so. When his cricket has taken him to Jamaica he has been drawn towards the Rastafarian community, whose colours he has worn on his sweatband. The "Calypso Cricketer", carefree of approach, is to be found now more in the lower echelons of the West Indian game.

Richards was 36 in March. Being so highly competitive helps him to stay in good shape. No one in his side subjects himself more rigorously to the exercises with which these days cricketers prepare for battle. Younger players hold him in awe for the way he keeps himself fit. Woe betide anyone who loafs around when he should be wincing from the pain of the morning's callisthenics. It is all a part of the single-mindedness which moves Richards towards his personal goal.

If I am right and he does feel unfulfilled, it is a dangerous sign for England. Many sportsmen, their fame established, their popularity immeasurable, are driven to seek further honours, not in the least because of money but as a challenge. Tom Watson, already a golfing legend, would probably put a fistful of his titles up for auction to win just one more "major". Boxers, already obscenely rich, climb back into the ring, seemingly with much beyond a single fight to lose.

In Richards's case it is different in that he is barely, if at all, past his prime. No one has ever batted more stunningly or given more pleasure or looked more the part or been a much greater attraction. He has a great record and wants nothing more than to lead West Indies through their present transition.

Having matured effortlessly as a batsman, he still has the art of captaincy to accomplish. Watching him in the World Cup, congratulating the winners and consoling his own side, made me think that by staying cool he can do it and retire a contented man.

Gatting Sacked in Disgrace by England

BY ALAN LEE, CRICKET CORRESPONDENT

10 *June* 1988. Mike Gatting last night paid the ultimate price for "irresponsible behaviour". He was sacked as England cricket captain after a day of emotional meetings at Lord's, and he immediately told the selectors he did not wish to be considered as a player for the second Test next week.

Gatting was interviewed at lunchtime yesterday following newspaper allegations of late-night drinking, sex parties and drink-driving. He denied the stories and the selectors accepted his version of events, yet still they felt he had let down the team and the image of the game.

Peter May, the chairman of selectors, was clearly upset as he told a packed press conference that the invitation previously issued to Gatting to captain the team next week had been withdrawn. He is, in effect, fired in disgrace, rare if not unique among England cricket captains.

A new captain will be appointed today, although, somewhat obtusely, the selectors insisted that it would be on a one-match basis. May also refused to rule out the possibility of Gatting leading the team again, a fanciful prospect in all the circumstances.

Gatting said that his solicitors would be issuing writs for libel against the newspapers which had carried the stories earlier this week. He apparently admitted, however, that he had invited a girl back to his hotel room for a late-night drink on two occasions, and this was sufficient to persuade the selectors that he must go.

Investigations are continuing into the alleged behaviour of other players during the Trent Bridge Test. Paul Jarvis, Phillip DeFreitas, Allan Lamb and Paul Downton have all been summoned to Lord's this morning to give their version of the story. Micky Stewart, the England team manager, said: "They will be seen separately to clear the whole thing up. If they deny any involvement, then we will believe them."

A statement explained: "Warnings had previously been issued to all England players concerning the standard of behaviour expected of them at all times, both on and off the field, and these had been ignored."

Gatting, said to be a sad and remorseful man last night, will go back to leading Middlesex, a position which will not be threatened by the events of this week.

Stewart, who linked up with Gatting on the all-conquering Australian tour two winters ago, inevitably felt dismayed by conduct which reflected badly on his own management. But he said: "I feel sadder still for the game. Cricket has been let down by this. The fact that Gatting laid himself open to all that has appeared in the papers has damaged the image of the game and the England team.

"No player must put himself in a position where the image of English cricket is at risk. It has been spelt out to them all very clearly."

A new and tougher code of conduct for England players, possibly including the imposition of curfew times, could be imposed before the Lord's Test next week.

May, who appointed Gatting exactly two years ago, would not say whether his withdrawal saved the selectors having to drop him. He simply added: "Gatting has lost the highest honour in cricket – the captaincy of England."

Another Milestone Passed by Bradman

BY RICHIE BENAUD

26 *August* 1988. Sir Donald Bradman is 80 years old tomorrow! Yet it seems no time at all since I first saw him. It was at a distance on the Sydney Cricket Ground, captaining South Australia against New South Wales before a crowd of 30,400, still the record attendance for a single day in a Sheffield Shield match.

It was my initial experience of first-class cricket and I came away enthralled, not by him or the NSW batting, which was dominated by Stan McCabe and Mort Cohen, but by the little man who, wearing a cap, bowled leg spinners and took six wickets, dismissing both Sid Barnes and Arthur Chipperfield without scoring, with what I later learned was the "flipper".

Six years after that day, during the school holidays, I saw my first Test match on the same ground and watched Bradman make 234, as did Barnes; then, in 1947-48, I raced with other members of the NSW Colts' squad to the gap between the M.A. Noble and Old Members' stands to see him score the single off Kischenchand to bring up his 100th first-class century. It can fairly be said I was one of the many on whom "The Don" had a vast influence in those early days.

I never had the challenge of bowling against him because he retired from first-class cricket the year I began and, from then, until 1958, we met only as chairman of selectors and member of the team losing regularly against England.

The good fortune for me came with the fact that I was the surprise choice by the Board of Control as captain of the Australian team in 1958-59, after Ian Craig had been forced out of the reckoning when he contracted hepatitis; Sir Donald was chairman of selectors. He had the sharpest mind for the job of anyone I have known in the game and it was easy to understand why he was rated such a good captain.

His instant ability to assess the skill and weakness of the opposition, as well as of the Australian players, set him apart from others. He remains far and away the best selector with whom I have had contact either as a player, captain or commentator.

There will forever be arguments about who was, or is, the greatest batsman, but when I ask of an alternative nomination, "well, what made him a better batsman than Bradman?" the answers tend to ramble. The talk turns to "sticky" pitches, prettier style and other cosmetic matters, but it is difficult to deflect the runs Bradman made, the speed at which he made them, the acknowledged mastery over the bowlers and rating of him by the bowlers against whom he batted.

When I once told Keith Miller I was sad I had never bowled against him, he laughed. "Don't be too sad about it," he said, "you only missed a caning!"

I cannot see how anyone could have been a greater batsman than Bradman, and a minor and parochial confirmation of this might be that in Australia, people only talk of having found "another Bradman". No other name, even today, ever hits the headlines concerning the new batting hope of the country. And he has been retired 40 years!

He was, and still is, a very private person but, in the time I was a young player in the team and before I was captain, he always seemed helpful to the younger cricketers.

One thing I found very quickly, though, was that under no circumstances would he offer any advice which might be construed as changing a young player's natural style. It gave him a reputation in the team of being sparing with advice, but you could guarantee if he told you something it was well worth going to the nets to have a long, hard look at.

Bear in mind that cricketers of any era are suspicious of dressing-room visitors and the advice they might tender, no matter with what degree of success they played. I have always contended that cricketers of the past should keep out of players' rooms unless specifically invited; on a personal note, I have been in an Australian dressing-room only three times since I retired in 1964; twice at the invitation of Ian Chappell and once, at the Melbourne Cricket Ground, when I delivered a magnum of champagne to Dennis Lillee the day he passed my tally of Test wickets.

I know from talking with him over the years that Bradman had the same reluctance to interfere in any way with the workings of the team, unless specifically invited.

He did, though, once ask my permission to come to an Australian team meeting, on the eve of the 1960 Test against the West Indies in Brisbane. The theme he stressed was along the lines that the selectors would stick with the players and the captain providing we played in entertaining fashion and continued to look as though we were enjoying ourselves.

He told us it was of vital importance to cricket in Australia that this should be a good series which would delight the cricketing public, and the selectors were hoping for attacking cricket which would bring victories rather than dull draws.

That tied first match was a fluke, but it was no fluke that brought him from the executive room at the "Gabba" during the tea interval that last afternoon.

I was outside the dressing-room, ready to resume batting again with Alan Davidson, when Bradman sat down; Australia had only four wickets in hand and what seemed a mountain of runs to make.

The conversation went: "Are you going for a win or a draw?"

"We're going to try to win it."

"Good."

No history-making repartee there, but then, given the prelude of the team meeting, a long boring speech seemed rather superfluous!

When, in Adelaide last year, we had dinner with our wives and two friends from Chapel-en-le-Frith, his vision for the game and his incisive thinking on the future of it in the modern era was as clear as always. Nor had he lost sight of the fact that he would be 80 in 1988. But I suspect today, when he has time to escape the well-wishing, he will be practising his putting.

After all, reaching four score has given him another challenge: to play to his age over 18 holes of golf!

Umpires Duck Issue as Bouncers Fly

FROM JOHN WOODCOCK

28 *December* 1988; *Melbourne*. The third Test match became a game of thuggery here yesterday as the West Indian fast bowlers, with the exception of Marshall, bombarded the Australian batsmen with salvo upon salvo of short-pitched balls. Yet the ugliness of it seemed entirely lost upon the umpires. Not once, that I saw, did they demur, as West Indies were gaining a first innings lead of 38. Between cool scuds of evening rain, West Indies, batting again, made 69 for one wicket.

On such a day it was ironic that the worst casualty should have been Logie, who had his nose broken while fielding close at short leg. It is a position in which he has become an important accomplice to the fast bowlers, using his cat-like agility to pounce on anything fended off in the least uppishly. Knowing to expect something short from Ambrose, Hughes slammed it straight at Logie, whose visor buckled under the impact.

The West Indians seemed to become bleak and implacable after a couple of decisions had gone against them in the first hour. From then on they bowled indiscriminately short. The umpiring might just as well have been done by robots or a couple of traffic wardens, except that the latter like to enforce the law.

Richards's mood, the psychological pressure he put on the umpires, after first Waugh, then Wood, had been given in, both to appeals for catches at the wicket, meant that the "corrector", awarded to level things up, was sure to come. When it did the victim was Healy, leg-before to something that must have been passing well over the stumps.

It is no sort of a game played like this, as we have seen before in Jamaica on England's last tour of the Caribbean, for example, and on an infamous occasion at Old Trafford in 1976, and sometimes when West Indies have not been bowling. When, yesterday, an Australian batsman was hit, there was not the slightest sign of concern or regret from Richards and his side. I found it thoroughly unedifying, and no one will ever produce the heavy equipment to pursue such tactics as relentlessly and effectively and consistently as the West Indians. Others try, but even when Thomson and Lillee were in their prime, Mallett would bowl 20 or 30 overs of off breaks in a match.

On one of the old-time Melbourne pitches, bowling as West Indies did yesterday would have been a waste of effort. But much has been done to quicken it up, and it is now harder, with more bounce and grass, than anything seen here before. The Australians are known not to have been best pleased when they first sighted it, simply because it would encourage the West Indians to bowl as they did yesterday.

Just how thankless a business batting was can be seen from what Wood, an attacking player by choice, had to show from 130 minutes at the crease. When he drove Patterson low to cover point – one of the few balls which Patterson pitched up – he had hit 12 singles and collected as many bruises.

Taylor ricked his back when ducking, which he spent much of the 50 minutes of his innings doing, and Waugh's fingers cannot have been a pretty sight by the time he slashed the second ball after lunch to second slip, where Greenidge caught him brilliantly. The batsmen spent very little time protecting their stumps; it was their ribs and above at which the bowlers aimed. There is simply no orthodox counter to it on a pitch such as this; it not only maims batsmen, it paralyses batsmanship.

Waugh's last four innings in the series have been 90, 91, 26 and 42. As Australia's best player at the moment, he managed two or three strokes off the back foot, past extra cover, that had the stamp of greatness. Australia's biggest partnership yesterday was one of 44 between McDermott and Hughes for the ninth wicket. They had a slog and the best crowd (32,845) of the three days enjoyed it, and, although the short bowling continued, McDermott's left hand was the only target to be hit.

Much the best of the day's proper bowling came from Alderman at the start of West Indies' second innings. Pitching the new ball up and swinging it around, he had four good shouts for leg-before turned down. Marshall, than whom no one has inflicted more injury and pain in his time, had once again looked a shadow of himself. When he did have Waugh caught at short leg, it was off a no-ball. His best balls were missed, and if the batsmen skied him the ball fell just wide of the field. Marshall has been trying now for 222 balls for his 300th Test wicket. I doubt whether any of the 299 he has taken can have proved quite so elusive.

> WEST INDIES 280 (C. G. Greenidge 49, C. E. L. Ambrose 44; T. M.
> Alderman 4 for 68) and 361 for 9 dec (R. B. Richardson 122, I. V. A.
> Richards 63, P. J. L. Dujon 46; S. R. Waugh 5 for 92)
> AUSTRALIA 242 (S. R. Waugh 42; B. P. Patterson 4 for 49, C. E. L.
> Ambrose 4 for 60) and 114 (B. P. Patterson 5 for 39)
> Score after third day: West Indies 280 and 69 for 1; Australia 242
> *West Indies won by 285 runs*

TCCB Wins Vital Concessions

BY ALAN LEE, CRICKET CORRESPONDENT

25 *January* 1989. Three months of tireless negotiating by the England cricket officials last night brought the best available outcome on the South African crisis. The special meeting of the International Cricket Conference (ICC) at Lord's, threatened throughout by legal and political sabotage, reached a unanimous verdict on the issue which has divided the game for decades.

As from April 1 this year, any cricketer who visits South Africa in a playing, coaching or administrative capacity will receive an automatic suspension from Test cricket. The length of the ban will be three years for players aged over 16 and under 19; four years for those aged 19 and over; and five years for any who take part in an organized tour. A second or subsequent offence could increase the maximum ban by two years. A register of inelegible players will be kept by the ICC secretariat. The right of any country to call off a tour if an eligible player is refused entry has been reinforced.

Two vital points were won by the Test and County Cricket Board's delegates, Raman Subba Row and Doug Insole. The sanctions will not be retrospective, which theoretically clears all the England players with present South African links to continue their Test career, and the ban is not open-ended unless a player's home authority wishes to extend it.

The resolution, proposed by the West Indies and the subject of many amendments during the conference, was voted upon at 2.35pm yesterday. It was carried by 32 votes to nil, whereupon all the other tabled resolutions on the issue were withdrawn. It had taken the meeting nine hours of official debate to reach that verdict but this is nothing compared to the untold hours of private bargaining which made it possible.

The South Africa delegates were not admitted to the conference to put their case and it is believed that a provisional attempt, by England, to acknowledge the steps they have taken towards non-racial cricket, was later withdrawn.

Last night, there was an air of quiet triumph in the committee room of the TCCB as Subba Row said: "Last week's Board meeting gave us a mandate to accept sanctions within a certain limit. I am pleased we have managed to stay within that limit.

"We didn't want to take this course. We would have preferred there to be no ban at all. But we have had to be realistic to preserve international cricket and to protect our own domestic game."

The decision was announced in a packed Long Room, by the ICC chairman, Field Marshal Lord Bramall. He said it had been reached "after careful, constructive and purposeful discussions". Then he said: "We are confident that this will clear up the current uncertainty and disarray affecting international cricket.

"Nobody has surrendered to anything. Things were not working well and we have taken a realistic stand to maintain the unity and continuity of the game."

The retired soldier smiled when asked how he had coped under fire these past two days. "It was quite tough," he said, "and before the meeting I don't suppose there were many who would have swapped places with me. But the atmosphere was amazingly cordial and I did not get a particularly rough ride."

Although the verdict has now been reached, approximating to general expectation, actually implementing it remains fraught with potential opposition from governments, the law and even the English players' union.

Nobody was being glib about the prospects of every government accepting an essentially cricketing ruling, but Lord Bramall voiced optimism. "Most of the delegates have consulted their own government. I am quite certain we will have their support, which is vital. If we have a hypothetical case of a government refusing to admit a player who was not disqualified by us, we would be back to square one."

Subba Row admitted that this remained the most worrying aspect of the matter, one which will be put to an early test when England tour the West Indies next winter. He said: "It would be very disappointing after all this effort if any government turned round and said they would not accept it. We can only say we have done everything possible to ensure that they will and I know that the West Indies, in particular, have done a great deal of work among their politicians."

The legal threat, as still posed by the Freedom Association, may not be formidable. Lord Bramall confirmed that the ICC had taken the best legal advice available on whether its resolution was sound in law. He also pledged: "If it is contested, I can assure you we will fight it all the way and agreement has already been reached to set aside financial resources."

The final barrier, the response of the English players whose movements are now limited if they have international ambitions, will not be known until the Cricketers' Association has a full meeting, probably early next week. Their reluctant acquiescence, however, is expected. The Association chairman, Geoff Cook, has been kept in close touch with the TCCB moves and he said of the decision: "It goes against what we have stood for and fought for but over the past few weeks there has been a quiet acceptance that there would be some sort of ban."

Insole, whose efforts alongside Subba Row were a triumph of negotiation, agreed: "If we have one specific regret it is that we have had to put a curb on our own players, something we have always resisted and we would still rather not do." Insole knows, however, that the alternatives were very much bleaker – several member countries were keen to press for a lifetime ban.

Subba Row, whose energy and commitment to an acceptable solution have been staggering, confessed there were many times when he and his colleagues feared the odds were insuperable. "The worst moment came some weeks ago when one country was insisting that any resolution had to be retrospective or the deal was off. We could never have embarked on anything under those terms."

Now the English negotiators, along with everyone else in the game, are hoping that we can return to cricketing normality. It may be an improbable ambition but yesterday's apparent unity is a success few could have anticipated until very recently.

Woeful England Plumb the Depths

BY ALAN LEE, CRICKET CORRESPONDENT

15 *August* 1989; *Trent Bridge.* The depths to which England's Test fortunes have descended can best be illustrated by the fact that it was difficult to locate anyone here yesterday who was remotely surprised that this fifth Cornhill Test barely survived two sessions of the penultimate day.

England's second innings, optimistically billed as their latest battle for pride, was over in four hours and three minutes. The margin of defeat was England's biggest ever in a home Test against Australia and, within an hour of the bitterly predictable surrender, rain was falling in mocking torrents.

Finding the words to describe the gulf between these two sides is increasingly fraught. Nothing does the situation justice.

Sorrow has replaced anger among those who have observed the entire, one-sided summer, but the mood could turn nasty again unless our reactionary selectors come up with something more imaginative when they choose the side for the final game at the Oval.

That meeting is pencilled in for either Friday or Saturday. David Gower, his humour just about intact, suggested: "It might actually take both days." Ted Dexter, chairman of the committee, confirmed that "a good opportunity remains for us to look to the future."

Whether this opportunity will be taken remains to be seen. For now, the unpalatable inquest on yet another overwhelming defeat ought first to pay handsome tribute to Allan Border's team. "Australia have grown and grown in confidence and stature as the series has gone on," Gower said enviously.

The most visual evidence of this comes at the outset of every England innings. Alderman and Lawson came, early in the series, to expect the quick breakthrough; England's batsmen now expect it too, with the sinking certainty of slavish puppets.

It was to be anticipated that England would be following on in a matter of minutes yesterday, and despite a defiant six from Malcolm, so it proved.

Then came the first surprise of the day as Gower marched out to open the innings with Curtis. Various explanations were offered but the most compelling was Gower's commendable desire to take a close interest in such vital proceedings. "It was meant to be a positive move but it did not quite work out," he explained.

Gower did drive Alderman's first ball through mid-off for four, but in the next over he misjudged the line of an inswinger from Lawson, offered no shot, and had his off stump extracted.

For Michael Atherton, the one consolation was that he again had no time for nerves to gnaw. In the two innings of his debut, England's openers had protected him for an aggregate of 13 balls. This time, however, he was immediately off the mark and proceeded to play the one convincing innings of the day.

Atherton batted $2\frac{1}{2}$ hours for 47 before driving a low, return catch to Trevor Hohns. Four partners had deserted him by then, but his technique and temperament had stood up to this rigorous examination. Most of his runs accrued through firm off-side blows marked by showing the full face of the bat to the ball.

The same could not be said for Curtis, leg-before to Alderman for the second time in the match; nor for Moxon, once more failing to get forward and finding himself in no position to counter the low bounce.

Atherton and Smith had added 54 in 14 invigorating overs. Here unquestionably were two players batting together for England as they will be many more times over the next 10 years if nothing occurs to sap their flair and commitment.

Once Smith had failed to pick the length of a good yorker from Hughes, the odds were always on a four-day finish.

Botham was in no state to bat, the damage to his finger now being regarded as almost certain to discount him from the final Test, and it is neither fair nor realistic to go on demanding salvation from Russell.

He failed this time, turned awkwardly square on by Lawson who then believed he had struck again as Hemmings edged him low to third slip. Waugh scooped up the ball and claimed the catch. Hemmings declined to walk. The umpires, when brought into the argument, decreed that the ball had not carried, a verdict which found no favour at all with Lawson and the close fielders.

Sadly, words and gestures were exchanged between Hemmings and Lawson as the players left the field for tea. The crowd booed and Border, rightly anxious to protect his team's reputation, later reported that he had reprimanded his players for over-reacting. "I told them I would not tolerate that sort of behaviour," he said.

Healy suffered a facial wound soon after tea as a ball from Hohns lifted out of the rough. Taylor, later to be named man of the match, took over the gloves. It was no more than a minor diversion for the Australians.

> AUSTRALIA 602 for 6 dec (M. A. Taylor 219, G. R. Marsh 138, D. C. Boon 75, A. R. Border 65 not out)
> ENGLAND 255 (R. A. Smith 101; T. M. Alderman 5 for 69) and 167 (M. A. Atherton 47)
> *Australia won by an innings and 180 runs*

Two at a Time

28 *October* 1989; *Diary (Simon Barnes).* Has any reader ever played in two cricket matches simultaneously? I have received a charming letter from Robert Aguile, who tells me that back in 1937 or '38 he did just that. He supports his claim with a cutting from *The Hinckley Times* – which described him as "the Earl Shilton speed merchant" – and wonders if anyone else has done the same.

Having double-booked himself, he played for both the *Hinckley Times* team and for his own office side, hopping from one match to another – fortunately on adjacent pitches. He took five for 12 for *The Hinckley Times* and then went across to field for his office. His memory of his performance after that is hazy. He remembers batting at least once – being out for a duck for the *Hinckley Times* – but apart from that can only say that all ended well.

Much More to Mervyn than Meets the Eye

FROM SIMON BARNES

20 *January* 1990; *Adelaide*. To go to Australia and not see Merv Hughes would be like going to London and not seeing Trafalgar Square. Perhaps I mean not seeing the Queen: not seeing a person in whom so great a part of the national identity is invested.

He is a ludicrous figure, an Australian of popular imagination, an Australian of parody. You expect him to speak solely in the quaint locutions of the Bazza Mackenzie cartoon strip: "Ah, fair suck of the pineapple, mate."

Hughes also happens to be a very useful cricketer. Last summer, he was a central part of the team that destroyed England with such relish.

But his role in the side clearly goes beyond mere cricket: he combines a silly haircut with the most absurd moustache, a caricature of Australian masculinity, a moustache of baroque intricacy. The beer adverts that featured the Australian team last summer centred on Hughes: centred, more accurately, on Hughes's moustache.

He has attracted the kind of gleeful attention that goes with such buffoonery. He is invariably portrayed as the wild man of cricket. Someone described his run-up as being like "a wardrobe going downhill", which is a delightful phrase but a little inaccurate. He rather minces to the wicket, as it happens.

He is not really a wild man, not an out-and-out speed merchant. He tends to come on as first change and is quiet and modest about his abilities, keen to tell you how marvellous the opening bowlers are.

Peter Roebuck, one of the smarter observers of the game, believes that Hughes is the man who is, more than any other, responsible for Australia's change of fortune: from wooden-spooners to a position in which they have just beaten Pakistan, the best side in the world after the West Indies.

Last Australian summer, Lawson had his jaw broken by Ambrose, leaving Hughes with the responsibility for carrying the attack. Australia lost, but Hughes took 13 wickets in the game, bowling over after over of unreduced effortfulness. "You do that to me mates, you see what you get."

Australia is the country of mateship, and Hughes demonstrated the favourite national virtue at full throttle. And at long last, his team had something to cheer itself up with.

One of cricket's points is that it is a team game and an individual game at the same time. You can balance these aspects according to your temperament: Boycott understood the individual side of the game better than anyone; Edmonds can still be heard to say that he should have been a golfer. But Hughes thrives on team spirit: it is a drug to him, it is his greatest inspiration. One of the great disincentives for catching a ball is, if you are an Australian, the very real possibility that Hughes will kiss you. If you win, he is likely to want to pour beer over you for at least an hour and a half.

He has not the arrogance of the great strike bowlers like Lillee or Hadlee, bowlers who win matches on their own. He speaks quietly, modestly, happy to go through the motions without really wanting to talk about himself at all. "Oh no, I don't think I'm an established player in the side yet. I'm working towards it. I work hard, I train pretty hard. And you need a pretty good cricket brain to get this far."

His batting began as another Australian joke, but it has become a very useful little bonus. To score 72 against the West Indies is something many batsmen would envy. It came as support for a Dean Jones double-hundred while Australia made 515. Richie Benaud has even suggested that he should now be considered an all-rounder. "When I make runs, it's a combination of two things: luck, and even more luck." But of course, he also nets with great seriousness and concentration.

Looking back, it seems that the Ashes win was forged in that series against the West Indies, with Hughes at the very heart of it. He is unlikely to become a cricketer of the first rank, but he has had the incalculable effect of raising morale and changing the nature of his side. He simply gives everything: because everything is what you give for your mates: right?

He is not the spearhead of the side, but is, perhaps, the heart and soul of the team. He is a totem of mateship: he loves a tight spot because it gives him the chance to give his all for his mates once again. "I s'pose I love a challenge. The last 12 months have been great – everyone likes to see everyone succeed. Yeah, it's nice to know they're all behind you when you're out there."

It must be. But now it was time for Hughes to get back to the team room. Thanks, Merv. "No worries."

Pretoria the Ultimate Umpire on a Hapless Tour

FROM RICHARD STREETON

29 *January* 1990; *Kimberley*. Any possible abandonment of the tour by Mike Gatting's team – and it is a thought never far from the mind every hour – seems more likely to come from the South African government in Pretoria than the cricket administrators. The first significant anti-apartheid demonstration in South African sporting history passed with only minor

incident at the ground here on Saturday. There were, however, clashes with police as the protesters headed for home to the townships and violence there when they arrived.

Cricket remains irrelevant after 10 days of what has emerged as an ill-timed and hapless tour. With other civil disturbances about issues reported elsewhere in the country, the English team's visit is only one of several problems with which the government must be grappling. To the outsider, it is extraordinary in many ways that they even permitted the tour to start.

Even some senior South African Cricket Union officials initially were not convinced that the tour was apposite at this juncture as South Africa braces itself for further law relaxations when President F. W. de Klerk opens parliament next week. Coupled with the expected release shortly of Nelson Mandela and other political prisoners, they wondered if a cricket tour would "rock the boat" and to date they have not been far wrong.

SACU finally convinced itself that the tour would become a tour proper once the protesters had the wind taken out of their sails by these larger, more important events. What SACU originally never bargained for has been the ongoing, well-organized protests being mounted.

Until two years ago such happenings were not possible in this complicated country. SACU, of course, conceived the right for peaceful protests and the one on Saturday only took place when Dr Ali Bacher, its top official, ironically secured the necessary permit for the demonstrators.

There is, though, as this weekend has shown, always the danger of a potential knock-on effect. The government has not yet deviated from its view that the tour is a matter for cricket officials. It is awful to contemplate but presumably it would have to intervene should the team's visit indirectly bring fatalities in its wake.

For mere sport to be allowed to continue against a background in which this dreadful possibility could happen must be regarded as a terrible indictment of everyone concerned.

In terms of numbers, the demonstration at the ground was far from the size expected, with a hard core of around 500 always present and roughly 1,500 at its peak. Problems connected with finding buses and leaving the townships were alleged to be the reason, though a police spokesman denied that the force had anything to do with these factors.

Demonstrators stood outside the two barbed wire perimeter fences for nearly four hours, 35 yards from the boundary edge, and chanted slogans, danced and waved their banners. Police with dogs were stationed between the two fences. There was a brief attempt to force open a gate, quickly foiled before the worst incident followed the throwing of a bottle by a white spectator from inside the ground. It brought retaliatory stone-throwing from the protesters and other white spectators "returned" these stones. Nobody was hurt but it could easily have been a flashpoint.

For many in the cricket crowd it was obviously their first sight of a racial demonstration. Family groups were among those who watched with curiosity while the atmosphere deteriorated with jeering as Afrikans speaking men hurled abuse.

When the protesters left, they were prevented by police from entering Kimberley, where property and cars were damaged on Friday. Police fired low-velocity rubber bullets into the ground to force the demonstrators to return home by other routes in minibuses they themselves provided.

Later in the evening there were reports of tear gas being fired as a black policeman's home in a township was burned down. Gatting is bearing up well, though clearly out of his depth. He said after yesterday's match: "As far as I was concerned it was just a few people singing and dancing and that was it. I do not know about anything else that happened. I am more concerned with playing cricket than anything else."

The team remained well protected from the realities of South African life. Black staff have refused to serve them at their hotel but extra white help has been drafted in. On Saturday evening they were gratified to find a small black demonstration outside, favouring the tour, the first they have seen.

Later at a civic reception, the mayor of Kimberley presented each cricketer with a tiny diamond worth, Graveney understands, about £20. Gatting himself has become almost a cult figure to white South Africans, helped by widespread coverage with pictures of an incident in a restaurant when black staff left as he walked in.

Gatting donned a chef's hat and helped cook steaks and pizzas and also acted as head waiter for one couple who did not know who he was. It brought a fleeting moment of comedy to a tour which is going to find that an increasingly scarce commodity.

INDEX

THE PAVILION LIBRARY

New Titles

Cricket Cauldron
Alex Bannister

Masters of Cricket
Jack Fingleton

Backlist

Cricket All His Life
E. V. Lucas

The Cricket Captains of England
Alan Gibson

Farewell to Cricket
Don Bradman

Jack Hobbs
Ronald Mason

In Celebration of Cricket
Kenneth Gregory

The Best Loved Game
Geoffrey Moorhouse

Bowler's Turn
Ian Peebles

Lord's 1787-1945
Sir Pelham Warner

Lord's 1946-1970
Diana Rait Kerr and Ian Peebles

Through the Caribbean
Alan Ross

Two Summers at the Tests
John Arlott

Double Century Vol II
Marcus Williams (ed.)

In Search of Cricket
J. M. Kilburn

Double Century Vol I
Marcus Williams (ed.)

Sort of a Cricket Person
E. W. Swanton

End of an Innings
Denis Compton

Ranji
Alan Ross

Batter's Castle
Ian Peebles

The Ashes Crown the Year
Jack Fingleton

Life Worth Living
C. B. Fry

Cricket Crisis
Jack Fingleton

P. G. H. Fender
Richard Streeton

Hirst and Rhodes
A. A. Thomson

Crusoe on Cricket
R. C. Robertson-Glasgow